WHO'S
WHO IN
CHURCH
HISTORY

D0708683

WILLIAM P. BARKER

WHO'S
WHO IN
CHURCH
HISTORY

Baker Book House
Grand Rapids, Michigan

Copyright 1969 by
Fleming H. Revell Company

Paperback edition issued 1977 by
Baker Book House Company
with permission of copyright owner

ISBN: 0-8010-0705-4

Library of Congress Catalog Card Number: 74-85306

PHOTOLITHOPRINTED BY CUSHING - MALLOY, INC.
ANN ARBOR, MICHIGAN, UNITED STATES OF AMERICA
1 9 7 7

To
Joanne
and
Fred Rogers

PREFACE

What was the basis of determining which names to include in this "Who's Who in Church History"?

After careful thought, it was decided to include only names which met three requirements:

1. They were persons who consciously thought of themselves as part of the Christian community.
2. They were persons who had some effect on the ministry of the Church.
3. They were persons no longer living.

This means that those of other faiths were not included, even though in many cases these were involved in the history of the Church.

These requirements also mean that the names of millions of valiant Christians who lived obscure lives are omitted. This does an injustice to countless unsung heroines and heroes of the faith who have quietly but responsibly carried out Christ's ministry through His Church. Someone really should write a "Who's Who" about the old Joe Joneses and plain Susie Smiths in Sioux Falls—Christians whose names never made the headlines but which are recorded in the Book of Life.

Not all of those mentioned in *Who's Who in Church History* were conventional or orthodox churchmen; nor were all the characters mentioned in this book ones who furthered Christ's ministry. Nonetheless, they qualified for inclusion in these pages by fulfilling the three requirements mentioned above.

Of the many who helped make this book possible, several must be mentioned by name for a special "thank you." Mrs. Ellis G. Cashdollar and Mrs. D. Wayne Fraker typed and proofread the manuscript. Ford L. Battles, Dikran Y. Hadidian and Robert S. Paul, colleagues at Pittsburgh Theological Seminary, gave helpful suggestions. Finally, Jean, Ellen and Jock provided their usual encouragement.

WILLIAM P. BARKER
Pittsburgh, Pa.

WHO'S
WHO IN
CHURCH
HISTORY

A

ABBON of Fleury (945[?]–1004) A French theologian who served as Abbot of Fleury, Abbon made two trips to Rome for his king, Robert II, to ward off papal interdicts.

ABBOT, Ezra (1819–1884) An American Biblical scholar, Ezra Abbot was active in the American New Testament Revision Committee in the 1880's.

ABBOT, Francis Ellingwood (1836–1903) A well-known 19th century Unitarian leader, Francis E. Abbot founded the influential magazine, *Index.*

ABBOT, George (1562–1633) An unpopular and narrow-minded Archbishop of Canterbury, Abbot is remembered primarily as the English prelate whose unsympathetic treatment of the Puritans and Separatists caused a small congregation from Scrooby, England, to emigrate first to Holland and later to Plymouth in New England.

ABBOTT, Benjamin (1732–1796) An American Methodist who experienced a startling and dramatic conversion experience at thirty-three, Abbott became a spellbinding frontier revivalist preacher who drew great crowds.

ABBOTT, Edward (1841–1908) Beginning as a Congregationalist, Abbott switched to Episcopalianism. He became an Episcopal priest in 1878 after a successful career as a Congregational minister, and subsequently was well-known as an editor and writer in the American religious press.

ABBOTT, Lyman (1835–1922) An American Congregationalist pastor and writer, Abbott succeeded Henry Ward Beecher at Plymouth Church, Brooklyn, and won a following as the editor of *The Outlook.* Abbott was one of the first churchmen in the 19th century to champion the Theory of Evolution.

ABÉLARD, Peter (1079–1142) A famous French scholastic, thinker, teacher and philosopher, Abélard's brilliant lectures at Paris gave him fame and a promising future. At that point Abélard was asked to tutor the lovely and studious young woman, Héloise, whose uncle was Fulbert, the canon of Notre Dame. Abélard and Héloise quickly developed a deep romantic attachment and were secretly married.

Héloise denied being married to Abélard, however, to avoid impeding his chances for advancement in the Church. Héloise's uncle, Fulbert, forced her to take refuge in a convent and led a crew of toughs who attacked Abélard one night and castrated him.

Forbidden to be a priest as a mutilated man, Abélard retired to a monastery in disgrace. He continued to lecture, however, and achieved new popularity. His rational discourses had a deep note of piety but enemies in the Church sniffed heresy and had him condemned.

Throughout these years Abélard and Héloise continued to correspond. (Her *Letters* are some of the most moving expressions of love ever written.) Although remembered principally because of his affair with Héloise, Abélard was one of the first and ablest to try to express church doctrine in formal, rational ways, and paved the way for the ascendancy of the Greek philosopher, Aristotle, in the thinking of the Middle Ages.

Héloise outlived Abélard by twenty-two years. Today, they are buried together in the Paris cemetery of Père-la-Chaise.

ABSALON (or Axel) (1128–1201) A great Danish hero, Absalon was a bishop, soldier and statesman. He functioned as an esteemed adviser to King Valdemar I and served many years as Bishop of Roskilde. His many exploits include building a fort on the site which became Copenhagen, eliminating piracy from the Baltic Sea, and destroying the Pomeranian enemy fleet. In 1178, he became Archbishop of Lund.

ACACIUS, Patriarch of Constantinople (A.D. 5th c.) In the political-religious squabbles in the Church between Rome and Constantinople after the Council of Chalcedon (A.D. 451), Acacius tried to modify some of the western church emphasis in the Chalcedonian creed to make it more palatable to eastern believers. He urged Emperor Zeno to publish a conciliatory statement, the *Henoticon*. Acacius was accused of opening the way for rejection of the Chalcedonian creed and was excommunicated by Pope Felix III, touching off a rift between eastern and western Christians.

ACCOLTI, Bennedetto the Younger (1497–1549) From a great Florentine family, Accolti was presented a Cardinal's hat by his uncle, Pope Clement VII, but was later jailed by Pope Paul III for gross mismanagement of Church affairs.

ACUNA, Cristobal d' (1597–1676) A great Spanish missionary to South America, Acuna explored vast stretches of the Amazon, Chile and Peru. His writings, reflecting a keen scientific observer's eye, were widely read.

ADALBERT (937[?]–997) The "Apostle of the Prussians," Adalbert engaged in fruitless efforts to convert the Bohemians while serving as Bishop of Prague before accompanying Emperor Otto III to Germany. He met with great success in Prussia, Poland and Hungary, where he baptized Stephen, later King of Hungary and remembered as "Saint" Stephen. Adalbert became Archbishop of Gnesen, Poland, but was killed by an angry pagan priest. He later was made a saint by the Roman Church.

ADALBERT (1000[?]–1072) A tyrannical and powerful Archbishop of Hamburg and Bremen, this prelate, by controlling King Henry IV of Germany, in effect, ruled much of northern Europe for a time.

ADALDAG, Archbishop (937–988) An energetic and persuasive Scandinavian missionary, Adaldag influenced King Harold Bluetooth of Denmark to be baptized as a Christian. Denmark became Christian and bishoprics were established under Adaldag's leadership.

ADALWOLD See **AETHELWOLD.**

ADAM of St. Victor ([?]–1192) The most famous Medieval hymnologist, Adam of St. Victor, wrote more and better hymns than any other person in Medieval times, many of which are still sung. No details of his personal life have been preserved.

ADAMNAN (624[?]–704) A relative of the great Irish monk, Columba, Adamnan was part of the great group of Irish monastics who carried Celtic Christianity to distant places. Adamnan became abbot of Iona Abbey, off the coast of Scotland, in 679. He was one of the first Celtic churchmen to be won over to the Roman way of setting the date for Easter. At the Synod of Tara, Adamnan arranged to have the rules of warfare changed so that women and children would no longer be taken prisoner.

ADDAMS, Jane (1860–1935) A famous American social worker, Jane Addams in 1889 bought a house in Chicago's seamy west side which became renowned as Hull House, a prototype for settlement-house social service. A devout Christian, Jane Addams spent the rest of her life working for the poor, immigrants and minority groups in her neighborhood. She was one of the first to set up health clinics and playgrounds for slum dwellers and won the Nobel Peace Prize in 1931 for her efforts for world peace.

ADELWOLD See AETHELWOLD.

ADEMAR, Bishop of Puy ([?]–1098[?]) Appointed legate by Pope Urban II, Ademar designated Constantinople as the gathering place for the Crusaders' three great armies.

ADEOTATUS (372–389) Son of the illustrious Augustine of Hippo, Adeotatus was deeply loved by his father. The boy showed early sign of brilliance, but died tragically young at Tagaste two years after he and his father were baptized.

ADHEMAR of Puy See ADEMAR, Bishop of Puy.

ADRIAN I, Pope (also Hadrian) ([?]–795) Elected pope with the backing of Charlemagne (who crushed the Lombard States in 774 to protect Adrian),

Adrian I laid the foundation for the Papal States and the growth of the papacy's temporal powers.

ADRIAN II, Pope (792–872) Pope from 867 to 872, Adrian II called the Eighth Ecumenical Council at Constantinople in 869, which condemned the schismatic Photius, Patriarch of Constantinople.

ADRIAN III, Pope ([?]–885) Pope from 884 to 885, Adrian III was later canonized.

ADRIAN IV, Pope (1100[?]–1159) Born in England and named Nicholas Breakspeare, Adrian, the only Englishman to become pope, was a boy servant in a French monastery who rose through Church orders to become pope in 1154. His high-handed tactics against the citizens of Rome made him so unpopular that he was once even forced to flee for his life. He devoted most of his energies to enlarging the papal sphere in the stormy politics of the Middle Ages.

ADRIAN VI (1459–1523 Elevated as pope in 1522 when the Roman Catholic Church was weak and the Reformation was making headway in Germany, Adrian VI tried to correct abuses in the Church while opposing Martin Luther's teachings. His career was cut short after a year, however, before he could put any of his reforms into effect.

ADRIAN of Castello (1460[?]–1521) A conspiratorial Italian cardinal who served as secretary for a time to the infamous Borgia Pope Alexander VI (who is believed to have died when his plot to poison Adrian backfired), Adrian was involved in the notorious plot to poison Pope Leo X.

AEGELBRIGHT See AETHELBERHT.

AELRED See AETHELRED.

AETHELBERHT ([?]–794) A king of East Anglia in ancient England, Aethelberht lived a saintly life and was later canonized. Over twenty Anglican Churches are dedicated to him. He should not be confused with another, better known king by the same name.

AETHELRED (1109[?]–1166 An abbot in England who was renowned as a historian, Aethelred wrote many works, including a biography of Edward the Confessor.

AETHELTHRYTH (630–679) An East Anglian princess in ancient England who persuaded her husband to permit her to become a nun by refusing to consummate the marriage, Aethelthryth founded a convent at Ely, where she became well-known as the abbess. She was later canonized for her works. Also known as St. Audrey, she is the source for our word "tawdry," referring to the cheap goods shown at local fairs on her feast day, St. Audrey's Day, June 23.

AETHELWOLD (908[?]–984) A reform-minded English monastic, Aethelwold in 963 became Bishop of Winchester, and began building the famous cathedral.

AETIUS of Antioch ([?]–367) A Syrian theologian known as "the atheist" for rejecting Christ as "begotten by God," Aetius founded a sect known as the Aetians. Aetius was banished by the Emperor Constantius II in 359.

AFFRE, Denis (1793–1848) The Archbishop of Paris during the June, 1848, French Insurrection, Affre was shot and killed while climbing one of the street barricades to get to a Church.

AGAPETUS I, Pope ([?]–536) Pope from 535 to 536, Agapetus I (later canonized) was a firm disciplinarian who upheld the Council of Carthage's strictures against Arianism.

AGAPETUS II, Pope ([?]–955) Pope during the period of deepest humiliation for the papacy, from 946–955, Agapetus had the misfortune to serve during the reign of the tyrannical Emperor Alberic of Rome.

AGATHA ([?]–251) The patron saint of Malta, Agatha was a beautiful Sicilian who, inspite of hideous tortures by the Roman governor of Sicily, remained true to the Christian faith, finally dying in prison.

AGATHO ([?]–681) Pope from 678 to 681, Agatho is remembered chiefly as the first pope to refuse to pay tribute to the new Roman emperor in Constantinople. The Sixth Ecumenical Council was held during his pontificate, in 679. He was later canonized.

AGLIARDI, Antonio (1832–1915) A Roman Catholic cardinal who rose to become Vice Chancellor of the Roman Church, Agliardi was active in many papal missions to various governments in the late 19th and early 20th centuries.

AGLIPAY, y Labayan Gregorio (1864–1940) The founder of the Independent Catholic Church of the Philippines in 1902, after he was excommunicated because of his involvement in the insurrection against the Spanish, Aglipay was originally a Roman priest in the Philippines. He was made Vicar General (head of the Independent Catholic Church of the Philippines) by the Philippine patriot, Aguinaldo. In 1935, Aglipay was an unsuccessful candidate for President of the Philippines.

AGNES (292[?]–304) The much-adored saint in the Roman Catholic

Church in Medieval lore who refused to renounce her Christian faith to marry the son of the prefect of Rome, Agnes died as a young girl of twelve or thirteen in Diocletian's terrible persecution. According to tradition, when the flames failed to kill Agnes, she was taken out and beheaded.

AGRICOLA, Johannes (1494–1566) A German reformer who supported Luther from the earliest days at Wittenberg, Agricola was one of the signers of the Augusburg Confession.

AIDAN ([?]–651) Part of the intrepid band of Irish monks who spread the Celtic Church from the Isle of Iona, Aidan came at the request of King Oswald to the Isle of Lindisfarne, off the northeast coast of England and re-introduced Christianity to that part of Britain.

AILLY, Pierre d' (1350–1420) A famous French theologian, d'Ailly strove to end the shameful papal schism in which two rival popes claimed exclusive power over the Church. His scholastic writings on nominalistic philosophy were widely read and influenced Martin Luther.

AILRED See AETHELRED.

AINSWORTH, Henry (1571–1622) An English Congregationalist, Ainsworth's non-conformist views and adherence to conviction forced him to flee to Amsterdam where he acted as teacher to a congregation of fellow exiled Englishmen.

ALACOQUE, Marguerite (1647–1690) A French nun to whom visions were attributed, she urged devotion to the Sacred Heart of Jesus, popularizing an old office in the Roman Catholic Church. St. Marguerite Alacoque was

canonized in 1920. She is also known as St. Margaret Mary.

ALBERT, St. See AETHELBERHT.

ALBERTUS MAGNUS (1206[?]–1280) A German theologian, philosopher, and scientist, Albertus Magnus was dubbed "Doctor Universalis" because of his great learning. One of his pupils was Thomas Aquinas. Albertus Magnus wrote widely, including many books on Aristotle, philosophy, chemistry or alchemy, botany, zoology, astronomy and geography, and made important contributions to science. He was the greatest Dominican Schoolman.

ALCUIN (735–804) A famous churchman, scholar and teacher, Alcuin worked with Charlemagne in introducing Latin language and culture to the rough Franks. Alcuin was influential in Charlemagne's reign and in the life of the Church in the Empire.

ALDHELM (640[?]–709) An early English churchman and scholar who became Bishop of Sherborne, Aldhelm founded many monasteries and churches in ancient England.

ALEANDER or ALEANDRO, Girolamo (1480–1542) Luther's opponent at the Diet of Worms, Aleander was a fiery extremist who served as papal nuncio. He harshly denounced Luther and later ordered the burning of two monks at Antwerp, the first two martyrs in the Reformation.

ALENIO (1582–1649) One of the first Jesuit missionaries to China, Alenio was an Italian who painfully learned and published Chinese texts, dying in Fuchow after many years in the Orient.

ALESIUS, Alexander (1500–1565) A Scottish Lutheran theologian who, after imprisonment in Scotland for his reformation sympathies, fled to Germany in 1532. There he had a distinguished academic career as a professor in the universities of Leipzig and Frankfurt and signed the Augsburg Confession.

ALEXANDER, Bishop of Alexandria ([?]–326) Opponent of the heretic Arius, who insisted that Jesus Christ was neither fully God nor fully man, Bishop Alexander in 321 called a synod in Alexandria, Egypt, which ignited the bitter Arian controversy. Later, in 325, at the Council of Nicea, Bishop Alexander led a faction known as the Alexandrian School.

ALEXANDER of Hales ([?]–1245) An English Franciscan Schoolman, Alexander of Hales taught in Paris and helped foster the rise of Scholasticism in the Middle Ages. He and Albertus Magnus broadened learning and popularized Aristotle, whose writings Aquinas later used to develop the basis of his philosophical system.

ALEXANDER NEVSKI (1220–1263) One of best known Russian heroes and saints, Alexander Nevski defeated the Swedes at the decisive battle on the site of present day Leningrad, on the Neva River (the origin of the name Nevski) in 1240, and later, in 1246, repulsed the Teutonic knights. He was appointed Grand Duke of Kiev, and kept the Mongols in check by astute diplomacy. A loyal churchman, he was deeply venerated in traditional Russian Orthodox Church lore.

ALEXANDER I, Pope ([?]–115) One of the earliest popes, ruling as Bishop of Rome from 105 to 115, Alexander introduced the use of holy water for blessing various objects, and promoted changes in the ancient service of eucharist which moved the ceremony

toward the Roman Mass. He died a martyr, and was canonized.

ALEXANDER II, Pope ([?]–1073) The first pope to be elected under new rules (1061) permitting a pope to come from anywhere in the Church, to be elected outside of Rome if necessary, to take office immediately upon election, and to be elected by the cardinals, Alexander II was resented by traditionalists in Rome and by the Imperial court of Germany which had previously managed papal elections. The hostile parties teamed up and nominated a rival pope, who for many years jeopardized Alexander II's position.

ALEXANDER III, Pope ([?]–1181) Another who faced dissension and a rival pope for some years, Alexander III is remembered principally for calling the Third Lateran Synod or Eleventh Ecumenical Council, which helped put the Church in order, introducing rules requiring, for example, a two-thirds vote by the Cardinals before a man can be elected pope. Alexander III bumblingly tried to halt the spread of the Waldensians in Italy. He was more effective in checkmating Frederick Barbarossa of Germany and humbling King Henry II of England for his part in the murder of Thomas à Becket.

ALEXANDER IV, Pope ([?]–1261) Served as pope from 1254 to 1261.

ALEXANDER V, Pope (1349[?]–1410) Pope for less than a year, Alexander V tried unsuccessfully to suppress the ideas of Wycliffe and Hus, two of those who paved the way for the Reformation. Many of his energies were spent battling the claims of two rival popes.

ALEXANDER VI, Pope (1431–1503) The most famous of the eight popes bearing the name Alexander, Alexander

VI strengthened the power of the papacy through skillful administration. He also advanced education, patronized the arts, beautified Rome and showed kindness to the Jews. Unfortunately, he was most renowned for his corruption and immorality. Alexander VI cunningly advanced two of his illegitimate offspring, Lucrezia Borgia and the murderous Cesare Borgia, to positions of power, where their intrigues and cruelties set a new low in Italian politics. When Savonarola preached against Alexander VI's evil acts, Alexander VI excommunicated the great Florentine preacher and mercilessly hounded him until Florence tortured and executed Savonarola in 1498. A thorough-going secularist, Alexander VI patronized the Renaissance while encouraging greed and scandal in the Church.

ALEXANDER ([?]–250) Known as the "charcoal burner" because of his preference for menial assignments, this St. Alexander was forced to accept the post of Bishop of Comana in Pontus. He was martyred during Decius' persecution in 250 and eventually declared a Saint.

ALEXANDER ([?]–251) Also martyred during Decius' persecution, this St. Alexander was the Bishop of Cappadocia (in what is now Turkey) and the gatherer of an excellent library.

ALEXANDER SEVERUS, Emperor (208–235) One of the few Roman Emperors to show leniency to Christians before Constantine, Alexander Severus was a syncretist who even placed a bust of Christ in his private chapel.

ALIGHIERI See DANTE.

ALLARMET See BROGNI.

ALLEINE, Joseph (1634–1668) A brilliant Oxford scholar who became a Puritan preacher, Alleine suffered imprisonment repeatedly for refusing to stop preaching after the 1662 Act of Conformity (directed against non-conformist preachers). He was the author of the best-seller, *Alarm to the Unconverted.*

ALLEN, William (1532–1594) An able and conscientious English Catholic who was forced to take refuge in France during the anti-Catholic feeling in the Elizabethan period, Allen organized a seminary at Douai in 1568 to train English priests in exile. He took part in the intrigue in which Spain tried to invade England. This stirred the anti-Catholics in England to take stern reprisals. Although made a cardinal, his influence waned after the defeat of the Spanish Armada, 1588.

AMALARIUS of Metz ([?]–850[?]) A noted writer on liturgy in the 9th century, Amalarius influenced the formation of Roman worship forms in western Europe. He studied under Alcuin, served as bishop of Treves, and acted as envoy to Constantinople for a time.

AMALRICH of Bena ([?]–1204) A radical pantheist-mystic in the Middle Ages, Amalrich of Bena taught in Paris that God is all, is incarnate in the believer as in Christ, that a believer cannot sin, and that all previous Christianity is abrogated by the coming of the Holy Spirit. Although forced to recant by Pope Innocent III, Amalrich's influence lingered among some extremist mystics.

AMBROSE, Archbishop of Moscow (1708–1771) The practical-minded but misunderstood head prelate of the Russian Orthodox Church from 1761 until his unfortunate death, Ambrose energetically helped the poor and established monasteries. During the severe plague of 1771 in Moscow, Ambrose, noting the crowds gathered around the statue of the Virgin, removed the statue to disperse the crowds in order to reduce the spread of disease. The superstitious crowds, angry at the loss of a favorite shrine, mobbed Ambrose's palace and killed him.

AMBROSE, Bishop (340[?]–397) One of the most distinguished 4th century Church fathers, Ambrose was a talented Roman civil servant serving as governor at Milan when he, although not baptized, was elected Bishop of Milan by popular acclamation. He was quickly baptized, turned over his wealth to the Church, studied theology, and devoted his administrative skills to managing the affairs of the Church. His persuasive writings, eloquent preaching and ascetic living made him deeply respected. He rigidly resisted any Arian trends in the Church, and won the accolade "Doctor" (or authoritative teacher) in the Roman Church.

His most famous moment came when he stood up to Emperor Theodosius, calling on Theodosius to repent publicly for ordering a massacre of the people of Thessalonica in 390 in reprisal for the murder of an official. Theodosius did publicly repent.

Ambrose's preaching so deeply influenced the then-pagan Augustine that Augustine sought baptism and began his career as a Christian leader. Many of our loveliest hymns came from Ambrose's pen.

AMMANN, Jakob (1644[?]–1711[?]) Stern and censorious Swiss schismatic Anabaptist-Mennonite elder, Ammann brought about the split within the German-speaking Anabaptist-Mennonites between 1693 and 1697 which resulted in the formation of the Old Order Amish. Ammann, the contentious and ultra-conservative "bishop" of the Erlenbach congregation, canton of Bern, tried to force his views on all other congregations, demanding that they shun all non-believers and ostracize lapsed members. The others balked; Ammann stirred dissension, excommunicating recalcitrants. Ammann's sect was forced to adopt his rigid rules regarding uniformity of dress, untrimmed beards and foot washing as a practice in worship. After experiencing severe persecution, particularly in Germany, the Amish emigrated to William Penn's colony, settling on the rich farmland near Lancaster, Pennsylvania, where they carefully preserve the Swiss-Alsatian-Palatine-Mennonite practices of 1700.

AMSDORF, Nicolaus von (1483–1565) A lesser-known German Protestant reformer, von Amsdorf was one of Martin Luther's earliest supporters and associates at Wittenberg. Von Amsdorf, a keen thinker, attended the Diet of Worms with Luther and took a lively part in the disputes within Lutheranism. He often differed from the gentle Melanchthon, but influenced Lutheran thought during its early, formative stages. Concerned about education, von Amsdorf helped found the University of Jena.

AMYRAUT, Moïse (1596–1664) A deeply-respected French Calvinist theologian in high circles in France, Amyraut courteously but clearly pointed out to the French king how the Edict of Nantes (protecting Protestants from persecution in France) was being widely disregarded. Previously, Amyraut had attended the Synod of Charenton, where his integrity and ability impressed even the imperious Cardinal Richelieu. Amyraut made numerous brave but futile attempts to try to start talks between Protestants and Catholics in France, hoping to bring about eventual reunion.

ANASTASIA ([?]–68[?]) A Christian woman who studied the faith under the Apostles Paul and Peter, this Anastasia died a martyr during Emperor Nero's persecution. She was later canonized.

ANASTASIA ([?]–304[?]) A martyr during the horrors decreed by Emperor Diocletian, this brave woman was the wife of a pagan named Publius, who betrayed her to the authorities. She was declared a saint by the Roman Church.

ANASTASIA (6th c.) A Greek woman who lived at Constantinople, this Anastasia fled to Alexandria, Egypt, to avoid being dragged into Emperor Justinian's harem. She lived disguised as a monk for twenty-eight years in Egypt.

ANASTASIUS I, Pope ([?]–401) Anastasius I, pope from 399 to 401, condemned the heresies of the Donatists and Origen. He was renowned for his charity as well as his orthodoxy, and was declared a saint.

ANASTASIUS II, Pope ([?]–498) Anastasius II condemned Acacius, Patriarch of Constantinople, but agreed that the Patriarch's sacramental acts were valid. This pope ruled from 496 to 498.

ANASTASIUS III, Pope ([?]–913) Pontiff from 911 to 913, Anastasius III determined the ecclesiastical divisions of Germany.

ANASTASIUS IV, Pope ([?]–1154) Pope Anastasius IV held Peter's Chair from 1153 to 1154, and was remembered as the pope who restored the Pantheon and extended privileges to the Knights Templars.

ANASTASIUS ([?]–251) A tribune in Emperor Decius' army, Anastasius was assigned to the execution-squad to put Christians to death. He was so impressed with the courage and conviction of those he was killing that he became a Christian himself. He was beheaded, along with his family, and was later canonized.

ANASTASIUS ([?]–304) A fuller from near Venice who moved to Dalmatia, this staunch Christian refused to conceal his faith but painted a cross on his door. He was put to death by drowning, and later declared a saint.

ANASTASIUS, Antipope (810[?]–880) A rascally politician, Anastasius fled Rome in 848, was excommunicated in 850, but got himself elected pontiff by the faction supporting Emperor Louis II. Anastasius seized the Lateran palace and jailed Pope Benedict III briefly before being expelled from Rome.

ANCHIETA (1533–97) A fearless Portuguese Jesuit missionary to Brazil in 1553, Anchieta established the first institutions in Brazil for converting the natives.

ANCILLON, Charles (1659–1715) A French Protestant attorney, Ancillon directed the colony of Huguenot exiles residing in Berlin. He is remembered in academic circles as being a co-founder with the great Leibnitz of the Academy of Berlin.

ANDERRSON, Lars (1482–1552) A leader in the Reformation in Sweden, Anderrson was originally a Roman Catholic archdeacon but was convinced of Luther's doctrines by the persuasive preaching of Lars and Olaf Peterson. Anderrson became chancellor under King Gustav and encouraged the Crown to appropriate Roman Catholic Church lands in Sweden. He is also known as Laurentius Andreae.

ANDERSON, John (1748–1830) Scottish-born Associate Reformed Church pastor, Anderson answered the plea for ministers from the American colonies in 1783. He gathered an 800-volume library from Scotland, and emigrated to the frontier of western Pennsylvania, where he opened Service Seminary, the oldest and first Presbyterian Seminary, today called Pittsburgh Theological Seminary. Anderson trained pioneer pastors and circuit riders for many years in his log seminary in what is now Beaver County, Pennsylvania.

ANDREAE, Jacob (1528–1590) A German Lutheran theologian, Andreae participated in the disputes within Lutheranism and taught at Tubingen. In 1577, he helped draw up the last great Lutheran creed, *The Formula of Concord.*

ANDREW of Crete (660[?]–732) Born at Damascus, Andrew took up the monastic life at Jerusalem and was sent to the Sixth General Council at Constantinople in 680 as the deputy of the Patriarch of Jerusalem. Andrew was raised to be Archbishop of Crete, but fell away for a time with the Monothelites. Acknowledging his error, he returned to orthodox Christianity before his death on the Isle of Hierissus in 732. Many of his hymns are still sung in the Greek Church.

ANDREWES, Lancelot (1555–1626) A beloved and saintly Anglican whose name is first on the list of those appointed to make the authorized (King James) translation of the Bible, Lancelot Andrewes was a prominent churchman and Bishop of Chichester. He helped at the coronation of James I, took part in the Synod of Dort and

served as a counsellor to three monarchs. He was best remembered for his genuine humility and concern for others.

ANDREWS, Charles Freer (1871–1940) English-born Anglican missionary to India for thirty-five years, Andrews identified himself closely with Indian causes and leaders, becoming the trusted friend of such notables as Gandhi and Tagore. Andrews was one of the first to seek meaningful forms to express the Christian faith to Indian people, urging that hymns, architecture and art of India be used to present the Gospel to those in India.

ANDREWS, Lorrin (1795–1868) A Congregational missionary from New England to the Hawaiian Islands from 1828 until his death, Andrews founded some of the Islands' first schools. He started the first newspaper (1834 and made the first translation of the Bible into Hawaiian. Andrews later served as a judge in Hawaii.

ANICETUS, Bishop ([?]–167) Bishop of the Church at Rome in its early days, Anicetus argued with Polycarp and leaders of the Church in the East on the time at which Easter should be observed. Anicetus and those at Rome held Easter services on Sunday; Polycarp and the Easterners, on the evening of the 14th of Nisan, regardless of what day it fell, like the Jewish Passover. Polycarp visited Anicetus at Rome but the two could not agree on the date, although they parted amicably.

ANSELM, Archbishop of Canterbury (1033[?]–1109) "Father of the Schoolmen" and influential thinker-theologian, Anselm introduced a new theory of the atonement—the "satisfaction" theory— in his *Cur Deus-homo.* Previously, theologians had taught Christ's death was a ransom paid to the devil. Anselm said that man's sin is a debt to God, not the devil, and that Christ's death alone has satisfied God's offended sense of honor. As the first scholastic philosopher, Anselm tried to make the content of Christian faith clear to human reason, yet insisted that faith must precede reason. His critics, however, claim that he carried his rational explanations to the point where human intelligence unassisted by faith could penetrate even the deepest mysteries of the Christian faith. Anselm's proofs for the existence of God, his rational defenses of the doctrines of creation and the Trinity and his treatises were never systematic theology, but he has intrigued thinkers ever since. Although Archbishop of Canterbury, his years in that position were unhappy, due to almost constant struggles with the English kings.

ANSELM of Laon ([?]–1117) A student under the illustrious Anselm of Canterbury, Anselm of Laon taught at Paris (where one of his pupils was the great Abélard) and made the first interlinear gloss of the Latin Bible, a widely-used aid to Bible study for many centuries in Europe.

ANSGAR (801[?]–865) A fearless and tireless missionary to Scandinavia, Ansgar was a monk from Corbie who eventually became Archbishop of Hamburg. He patiently suffered a series of rebuffs in his valiant efforts to organize the Church in Denmark and Sweden in the 9th century, and died without accomplishing his goals.

ANTHONY (250[?]–356[?]) The first Christian monk, Anthony retired to the Egyptian desert as a hermit to live a more Christian life. He practiced severe self-torment, but suffered extreme fleshly temptations. Unintentionally attracting crowds of imitators who took up residence near him and tried to practice his ascetic living, Anthony finally organized them into monastic communities. Later, he sought complete solitude once more and lived to an incredibly old age, fasting and worshipping alone. He was canonized by the Catholic Church.

ANTHONY, Sister (1815–1897) Born in Ireland and baptized Mary O'Connell, Sister Anthony became a nun in the United States in 1835 after emigrating with her family from Ireland. She joined the Order of the Sisters of Charity, and won the accolade-title, "The Angel of the Battlefield," after the bloody battle of Pittsburg Landing in the Civil War when she nursed the wounded and brought scores of invalided soldiers on a boat to her convent at Cincinnati, Ohio.

APOLLINARIS ([?]–390[?]) Bishop of Laodicea of Syria, Apollinaris was a fervent opponent of Arianism and a persuasive theologian who lived at the time when the Church was hammering out a normative viewpoint on the nature of Jesus Christ. Apollinaris attempted to answer the question of how Jesus could be both God and man by proposing that Jesus had the body and animal soul of a man, but that the reasoning spirit in Him was God. The Church struggled for years on this and other "explanations" of who Jesus was, and rejected Apollinaris' theory because it actually denied Christ's real humanity. The Council of Constantinople (the Second Ecumenical Council) in 381 condemned Apollinaris' viewpoint.

AQUINAS, Thomas (1227[?]–1274[?]) Dominican monk-turned-teacher, Aquinas was the author of the monumental *Summa Theologica*, the summary of the theological system of the Roman Catholic Church. Aquinas' profound learning and deep piety won him the sobriquet from his students, "angelic doctor."

Scholasticism reached its pinnacle in Aquinas' writings. Combining the greatest thinking of the ancient Greek philosophers, particularly Aristotle, with Christian thought, Aquinas built a theological system which has been accepted as the basis for all Roman Catholic theological instruction today. Aquinas the Dominican was challenged by Duns Scotus, the Franciscan, and theological rivalry between the "Thomists" and the "Scotists" continued in the Church until the Reformation. No other theologian except Augustine has more profoundly influenced the language and thinking of the Western Church. Aquinas' two sources of knowledge, reason and revelation, have also deeply affected all philosophical thought in the western world. In spite of his voluminous writing, Aquinas found time to be active as a teacher and as a consultant on many important civil and church matters.

ARC, Joan of See JOAN OF ARC.

ARISTIDES (2nd c.) A Christian philosopher who lived in Athens about 140, Aristides wrote a stirring appeal to the Roman Emperor Antoninus Pius about the Christian faith. Aristides pointed out the helplessness of ancient cults to meet human aspirations and impressively stated the meaning of Gospel. His writing falls into the category of what is called an "Apology," and Aristides is classified as one of the early Christian apologists.

ARIUS ([?]–336) A presbyter in charge of a large congregation at Alexandria, Arius was a faithful, industrious pastor and a loquacious, persuasive speaker. When Arius was an old man, his views on the doctrine of Christ gave rise to a movement in the Church known as Arianism, and triggered an intense controversy.

Basically, in spite of his deep piety and personal devotion to the person of Jesus, Arius tried to emphasize the unity and simplicity of the eternal Creator-God by downgrading Christ to a demigod position in which Christ was not quite God nor quite man. Even though Jesus Christ was greater than all other beings, according to Arius, He was in no way one with the Father in essence or eternity.

Arius insisted on promoting his viewpoint so strongly that he brought on a showdown with Alexander, Bishop of Alexandria. Arius was condemned by a synod at Alexandria and fled to Nicodemia where his friend Eusebius was bishop. Arius quickly drew Eusebius to his side and stirred further controversy.

When Emperor Constantine got news of the theological squabble in the Church, he summoned Arius and all the other disputants to the first Ecumenical Council, known as the Council of Nicea in 325 to work out an agreement. The Council decided against Arius. Constantine resolved to stand behind the decision and banished Arius who had already been excommunicated. Five years later, however, Constantine relented enough to invite Arius to come home.

Arianism, meanwhile, had not died in the Eastern Church and the old squabble still continued. Constantine tried to ameliorate the feelings of the angry Arians by demanding that the bishop of Alexandria receive Arius back into the Church, but Arius died suddenly in 366 before being readmitted to the Church.

ARMINIUS, Jacobus (1560–1609) A progressive Protestant Dutch theologian, Arminius was the author of the brand of reformed theology known as Arminianism as a reaction against the sternness of Calvinism. Arminius discarded the idea of unconditional predestination and taught that man had freedom to choose or reject salvation. Arminius was one of the first to urge that the State tolerate all religions and emphasized the more practical aspects of faith instead of the creedal. Although mild-mannered, his liberal views soon embroiled him in controversy. Rigorous Calvinists castigated Arminius and his position. Continuous debate for many years caused him gradually to emphasize more strongly man's freedom. Years of tense and disputing persecution wore out this gentle and irenic, progressive and sensitive thinker. The Remonstrant Church in Holland is his monument.

ARNAUD, Henri (1641–1721) A persistent and fearless Waldensian soldier-preacher, Arnaud organized the hapless Waldensians (members of a pre-Reformation group of Reformed Christians in northern Italy's mountains) who had been driven from their Piedmont homes into exile in Switzerland. Arnaud and his fellow-exiles made repeated heroic (but futile) attempts to return to their home territory, suffering harsh reprisals and bloody defeats.

ARNDT, Johann (1555–1621) A German Lutheran ascetic mystic, Arndt was the author of *True Christianity*, a treatise on a personal mystical piety emphasizing a vital, inward relationship between the believer and God. Arndt and many other early pietists were tired of the sterile creedalism in much of organized Christianity in the late 16th century, and asserted the importance of feelings in one's Christian experience. Philipp Spener, founder of German Pietism, was deeply influenced by Arndt.

ARNOBIUS ([?]–300) Once a violent opponent to Christianity, Arnobius, af-

ter a dramatic conversion, wrote seven outstanding books refuting the accusations of critics of the Church. Arnobius was one of the earliest "apologists," or defenders of the faith in writing.

ARNOLD of Brescia ([?]–1155) A stern ascetic who taught that every clergyman should renounce all property and power, Arnold of Brescia touched a sensitive area in the 12th century when many church leaders were money-grabbing political schemers. His radical views on "apostolic poverty" as the only form of Christian discipleship won him a large following among the poor in Brescia but the bitter enmity of the Establishment at Rome. He was excommunicated and banished, restored and allowed to return. He organized a power bloc, however, that forced Pope Eugene III (the pope who had lifted the excommunication against him) to flee. Later, newly-elected Pope Hadrian IV expelled Arnold and engineered his execution.

ARNOLD, Thomas (1795–1842) The beloved headmaster of Rugby School, England, Thomas Arnold was a broad church leader and a man of deep personal piety. Thomas Arnold's tact and kindness toward his pupils, most of whom became famous leaders in England in the 19th century, steered many into a close affiliation with the Church and a profound sense of Christian duty.

ARSENIUS, Autorianus ([?]–1273) A brave Patriarch of Constantinople, Arsenius excommunicated his emperor, Michael, for cruelty in 1261, but was deposed and exiled shortly afterward by the vindictive emperor. Arsenius' irate supporters organized themselves into a schismatic group in 1264 which lingered until 1315.

ARTEMON (230[?]–270) A prominent teacher and theologian at Rome in the 3rd century, Artemon held views that because God was one, Jesus was the Son of God by adoption. Despite Artemon's insistence that all the earlier bishops of Rome had held the same viewpoint, he was excommunicated by Bishop Zephyrnus.

ARUNDEL, Thomas (1353–1414) The politically-minded Archbishop of Canterbury, Arundel crowned Henry IV as King of England and continually involved himself in intrigues. Arundel, fanatically opposed to dissent, secured papal permission to begin burning heretics in England.

ASBURY, Francis (1745–1816) The organizing genius of the Methodist Church in the American colonies, Francis Asbury was an English lay preacher who was converted when sixteen by Wesley's preaching. Although he had little formal education, he was such a fluent, direct speaker that he was appointed an itinerant preacher and later, missionary to the colonies. When he landed at Philadelphia in 1771, there were only 300 converts to Methodism in all the colonies. Asbury energetically organized scores of new congregations. When the Revolutionary War broke out, Methodists were suspected of loyalist views and often persecuted. Many fled; Asbury stayed. In 1784, John Wesley, disregarding the authority of the established church, appointed Thomas Coke and Francis Asbury as superintendents, or "bishops," of the Church in the new nation, ordaining Coke in England and instructing Coke, in turn, to ordain and consecrate Asbury. Asbury refused to accept the office, however, until the decision was ratified by the American conference. The Methodist Church in the United States officially came into being at that same conference, and Asbury can be called the "Father of American

Methodism." He covered thousands of miles on horseback while supervising his growing denomination. By the time Asbury died, Methodism had grown from 300 to more than 214,000.

ASCLEPIODORUS (2nd c.) An early teacher of heretical views of Jesus, Asclepiodorus hailed from the East and lived at Rome. He taught the doctrine propounded by Theodotus, his teacher, that Jesus was merely a man on whom the Holy Spirit had descended at baptism and should not be given title "divine." Asclepiodorus tried unsuccessfully to found a rival group to the community of Christians at Rome.

ASKEW, Anne (also Ascue) (1521–1546) A faithful Protestant English woman who was denounced by her husband for her Protestant views, Anne Askew was arrested and tortured on the rack. She refused to recant in spite of horrendous tortures, and died in the flames as a martyr.

ASSER ([?]–909) A Welsh monk, saint and Bishop of Sherborne, Asser was a noted churchman in Medieval England, and the tutor-companion of the esteemed English King, Alfred the Great.

ASTRUC, Jean (1684–1766) The Royal Professor of Medicine at Paris, Astruc is remembered not so much because of his notable career as a physician as for his work as a Biblical critic. He was one of the first (1731) to point out that there are two main sources which can be traced in the book of Genesis. Later, Old Testament form criticism built on Atruc's beginnings.

ATHANASIUS (293[?]–373) The great defender of the Nicene faith, Athanasius was bishop of Alexandria through the tumult in the Church over the question of who Jesus Christ was. For Athanasius, it meant living in constant tension and attack and experiencing banishment five times from Alexandria. Athanasius refused to curry favor with anyone, (unlike most others of his time) and so persistently clung to the Nicene faith as normative for the Church's Christology, that it is due entirely to him that Nicene Christianity triumphed.

Athanasius' protagonists were Arius and Eusebius of Nicomedia. Arius, whose theory of Christology was known as Arianism, taught that Christ was not quite God and not quite man, but something in between. Athanasius insisted that salvation came only because the full and real Godhead came into union with full and real manhood in Jesus Christ, and that Arianism was basically pagan.

A long, bitter dispute between the Arians and the Alexandrians had erupted during the reign of Athanasius' predecessor, Bishop Alexander of Alexandria. Politics, as well as theology, had played a part and Emperor Constantine had been drawn into the fray. Constantine called the Council of Nicea in 325 to resolve the matter once and for all and had decided in favor of the Alexandrians. Although Athanasius was not permitted to participate in the official proceedings at Nicea, he exercised considerable influence behind the scenes.

In spite of the decision at Nicea, Eusebius of Nicomedia and Arius cleverly attacked Athanasius, attempting to discredit him in the eyes of Constantine, and trying to get Arius restored to his old position. A long, wearying period of charges and counter-charges, banishments and recall followed. Although no original thinker nor systematic theologian, Athanasius almost single-handedly kept alive the Nicene faith during this turbulent period.

ATHENAGORUS (2nd c.) A writer who defended the Christian faith about A.D. 177, Athenagorus is known as one of the "apologists" who attempted to refute charges made against Christians and to soften the hostility of the Roman government.

ATTERBURY, Francis (1662–1732) An English high churchman and eloquent preacher whose hot temper and relish for politics got him into many entanglements, Atterbury became involved with the plots to restore the Stewarts to the English throne and was banished to France.

AUDREY, Saint See **AETHEL-THRYTH.**

AUGUSTINE, Missionary to England ([?]–613[?]) First Archbishop of Canterbury, this famous Augustine, not to be confused with Augustine, Bishop of Hippo (see below), was sent by his friend Pope Gregory the Great from a comfortable monastery at Rome to near-pagan southern England to organize the Church. Augustine was well received by King Aethelberht, who, although a non-believer at the time, was friendly toward the Church because he had married a devout Christian Frankish princess, Bertha. Augustine was presented a site at Canterbury for his Church. Augustine soon baptized Aethelberht, but had slow progress in winning obedience from British bishops and in making great numbers of converts. Augustine was given authority over the Celtic Church group in northern Britain, as well as bishops consecrated in south-central England. Augustine was unable to meld the two factions into one, however, particularly when he called a conference to force the Celtic Church to accept the Roman Church date for Easter.

AUGUSTINE, Bishop of Hippo (354–430)

One of the greatest and most influential leaders of the western Church, Augustine lived during the turbulent days of the disintegration of the Roman Empire.

Although he had a devoted and saintly Christian mother, Monica, Augustine as a young man was a sensuous, pleasure-loving intellectual, deeply skeptical of Christianity. He lived with a mistress, fathered a son, studied assiduously, dabbled in Manichaean philosophy. Moving to Milan, Augustine was swayed by the preaching of the great bishop, Ambrose. Although he left the Manichaean sect, Augustine still did not renounce his immoral ways, especially with women. Ambrose's preaching, however, had brought about a profound sense of dissatisfaction within Augustine. His dramatic conversion experience is vividly described in his *Confessions*.

Following this crisis, Augustine experienced a change of character. He was baptized and began to write and speak with deep insight on the meaning of sin and grace. Leaving Milan for his native North Africa, he went through the sorrowful experience of losing, within a year of each other, both his mother and his son, to whom he had been very close. In 391 he was ordained a priest and four years later was elevated as Bishop of Hippo.

At Hippo, Augustine opened the first monastery in North Africa and embarked on a writing career. At that time, the Church was ripped by controversies and the Empire was under siege by half-civilized tribes. Augustine's unshakable faith during his tempestuous lifetime was reflected in his writings (especially in his classic line, "Thou hast formed us for Thyself, and our hearts are restless 'til they find their rest in Thee").

Shortly after his conversion he devastatingly attacked the Manichaean position (a blend of Zorastrianism, astrology and Christian gnosticism or secret wisdom). Following his arrival in North Africa, he was embroiled in controversy with the Donatists—a schismatic group claiming itself to be the only true church with a clergy free from "deadly sins" and with valid sacraments. Augustine's writings against the Donatists covered the subjects of the nature and authority of the Church, and deeply affected the stance and image of the Medieval Roman Catholic Church.

The Pelagian controversy, however, brought out the best and most distinctive of Augustine's theology. Pelagianism, briefly, is the notion that man is not so much a sinner that he cannot by his own efforts save himself. Augustine wrote fifteen treatises through the long battle with proponents of this heresy, and through these fifteen treatises permanently affected the direction of all Christian thought. Augustine's own personal experience of sin and grace lent a touch of intensity and realism to these writings, so that readers even one thousand years later (such as Luther) were stirred.

Augustine's most elaborate writing, *The City of God,* written as the Empire was crumbling, portrayed the Church as a new civic order in the midst of the ruins of the Roman Empire. Augustine died while the Vandals were besieging the very gates of Hippo, A.D. 430.

AUGUSTINUS TRIUMPHUS (1243–1328)

An Italian Augustinian monk, he vigorously defended the claims of the pope at the time when criticisms were beginning to appear against the papacy's powers and claims. Augustinus Triumphus wrote *Summa de Potestate Ecclesiastica* in which he put the pope above all temporal rulers, maintaining that the pope was empowered to abrogate any civil law and remove any civil authority or prince.

AUSTIN, Saint See AUGUSTINE.

AVILA, Juan d' (1500–1569) An effective Spanish Roman Catholic preacher who was called the "Apostle of Andalusia," Avila wrote the widely-read *Spiritual Letters.*

B

BABCOCK, Maltbie Davenport (1858 –1901) Vigorous American Presbyterian pastor who enjoyed sports, music and the outdoors, Babcock served pastorates in Baltimore, Maryland, and New York City, and wrote pantheistic poetry sometimes set to music, including "This Is My Father's World" and "When the Great Sun Sinks to His Rest."

BACH, Johann Sebastian (1685–1750) The composer known as the "master of masters" because his works inspired so many subsequent composers, Bach lived in relative obscurity. Although he composed magnificent chorales week after week as organist of St. Thomas Church, Leipzig, Germany, Bach during his lifetime was noted primarily as an organist. His music was almost overlooked until 1829 when Mendelssohn conducted a performance of Bach's *St. Matthew's Passion,* and "discovered" Bach. Since then, Bach's choral and organ pieces have enriched Christian worship everywhere.

BACKUS, Isaac (1724–1806) A onetime Separatist who turned Baptist in New England, Backus was leader and organizer of the Baptist revival during the Great Awakening in the mid-1740's. Later, in 1788, when Massachusetts called a Convention to debate the new United States Constitution, Backus spoke vigorously against those proposing to limit office holders to those passing a religious test, and led the fight for religious liberty in New England in the last part of the 18th century.

BACON, Francis (1561–1626) The English philosopher who developed the inductive method of reasoning, Francis Bacon is said to have contributed more to scientific progress than any other man since the Greek philosophers. His thinking has influenced all subsequent thought, both in the theological and the scientific community.

BACON, Roger (1214–1294) English friar and thinker, Roger Bacon possessed an inquiring mind and demanded rational proofs for theories then in vogue. Obviously far ahead of his time, he was accused by his fellow Franciscans of dealing with the devil in the "black art." Bacon was put in prison for ten years without books or instruments, then released and imprisoned a second time. He made notable discoveries in optics, chemistry, physics, and astronomy, and is regarded as one of the fathers of the scientific method of investigation.

BAILLIE, John (1886–1960) Scottish theologian, John Baillie was one of the first to popularize the writings of Søren Kierkegaard and, later, Karl Barth. Baillie played an active, if unobtrusive part, in the World Council of Churches.

BAILLIE, Robert (1599–1662) One of the five Scots sent to the Westminster Assembly in 1643 which drew up the Westminster Confession, Baillie was a distinguished Scottish divine and educator. He participated in the Glasgow Assembly of 1638, and was one of the commissioners sent to Holland in 1661 to invite Charles II to Scotland.

BALDWIN I ([?]–1118) An impetuous adventurer and warrior in the First Crusade, Baldwin I became the first king of the Latin Kingdom of Jerusalem.

BALDWIN II ([?]–1131) Nephew of Baldwin I, Baldwin stretched the Kingdom of Jerusalem to its largest size.

BALL, John ([?]–1381) A follower of the early English reformer, Wycliffe, John Ball, a priest, was frequently imprisoned and twice excommunicated for his extreme political and religious views. He ultimately was hung for his complicity in the Wat Tyler insurrection.

BALLOU, Hosea (1771–1852) An influential pastor at Boston for many years, Ballou was an Arian or Unitarian who spearheaded the early Universalist movement.

BALTIMORE, Lord George Calvert (1580[?]–1632) A convert to Roman Catholicism while serving as secretary of state to King James I of England, Baltimore resigned to organize a colony in the New World where fellow Catholics could find a haven from persecution. After an unsuccessful effort in Newfoundland, Baltimore secured the charter to establish a colony called Maryland. Although Baltimore died before he could found his Maryland colony, his ideas of religious liberty and toleration were carried out, first in Maryland, and later in the United States.

BALTZER, Johann Baptista (1803–1871) A German Roman Catholic theologian, he refused to subscribe to the doctrine of papal infallibility when it was announced. Baltzer was sus-

pended from the Roman Church in 1862, and became active in the group of disaffected Roman Catholics which organized themselves into the Old Catholic Church.

BANCROFT, Richard (1544–1610) An outspoken defender of episcopalianism during the struggles in England between the Puritans and the Anglicans, Bancroft became Archbishop of Canterbury. He not only denounced Puritanism but insisted that Anglicanism existed by divine right. Bancroft's views encouraged royal and civil authorities to repress Separatists and Puritans.

BARBARA (3rd or 4th c. [?]) The patron saint of stonemasons, architects, and builders, and the protector of miners and artillerymen, Barbara secretly became a Christian but gave herself away when she designed her bathhouse with three windows (to remind her of the Trinity) instead of the usual two. She was ordered beheaded by her irate pagan father. Immediately after Barbara's death, however, lightning struck and killed the father.

BARBAROSSA, Frederick See FREDERICK THE GREAT.

BARBON See BAREBONES.

BARCLAY, Alexander (1475[?]–1552) A Scots-born priest with gifts as a satirist, Barclay wrote the stinging *The Shyp of Folys of the World* (*Ship of Fools*), which indicted most of his society, including the Church in the 16th century.

BARCLAY, John (1734–1798) An eccentric Church of Scotland minister who was dismissed from his congregation because of his peculiar traits and interpretations of Scripture, John Barclay founded a sect known as "Bereans" (from Acts 17:2) or, more popularly, "Barclayites," which flourished for a time at Edinburgh and London.

BARCLAY, Robert (1648–1690) An educated Scot who was won to the Society of Friends (Quakers) by George Fox, Robert Barclay was the earliest defender of Quakerism in writing. His literate treatise, *Apology for the Quakers* presenting fifteen propositions which were widely debated in the late 17th century Britain, won Barclay the reputation of "the Quaker theologian." Barclay was an associate of William Penn and, like Penn, served as a governor of a colony in the New World (East New Jersey). His gentle ways and deep integrity won him respect, even from King James II.

BAREBONES, Praisegod (1596[?]–1679) A Fleet Street leather peddler and Baptist preacher, Praisegod Barebones achieved immortality by lending his unusual name to Oliver Cromwell's short-lived "Little" Parliament of 1653. Barebones, although a member of that Parliament, never spoke or made any contribution to it. His staunchly Puritan parents gave one brother the name Christ-Came-Into-The-World-To-Save Barebones. Another brother was baptized with the name, If-Christ-Had-Not-Died-Thou-Hadst-Been-Damned Barebones (nicknamed, "Damned" Barebones!). Praisegod Barebones, a Fifth Monarchy man, offered his house as a secret rallying point and once barely escaped being lynched by an angry mob.

BARNES, Albert (1798–1870) An American Presbyterian pastor and writer who was tried for heresy but acquitted for his belief in an unlimited atonement, Barnes was the cause of the trial which was the cause of an ultimate split of American Presbyterians into the Old School and New School Presbyterians in 1837.

BARNES, Robert (1495–1540) An English Augustinian monk who was converted to Luther's views in 1526, Barnes was forced to stand trial before the formidable Cardinal Wolsey, threatened with death, and made to recant his Lutheranism under duress and torture. Barnes escaped to Germany and, before he lost favor with Henry VIII, served for a time as Henry's emissary to Germany. He was burned at the stake in 1540 for heresy.

BARNETT, Samuel Augustus (1844–1913) A well-known pioneer in slum work in England during the latter part of the 19th century, Barnett, a Church of England priest, opened the first "University Settlement," bringing university students to live in the inner city. In 1884, he opened the renowned Toynbee Hall, and served as its first Director.

BARROWE, Henry (1550–1593) A courageous English attorney who tenaciously clung to his Congregationalist ideas, Barrowe and the Rev. John Greenwood were imprisoned for holding meetings of Separatists in London. They smuggled writings from their cell to Holland to be printed and secretly circulated in England. Their writings roasted both Anglicans and Puritans and carefully explained the Congregationalist position. Barrowe's strictures against bishops and the established Church of England as being polluted with the remnants of Roman Catholicism finally caused him to be hanged in 1593.

BARTH, Karl (1886–1968) Peerless giant among twentieth century theologians, Swiss Protestant Barth dropped his blockbuster *Commentary on the Epistle to the Romans* in 1918, shattering forever the blithe liberalism of western Protestantism and launching a muscular system of Biblically-based thinking.

Barth, serving a country pastorate at Safenwil in Aargau Canton, Switzerland, heard the distant thunder of the guns of World War I, became acutely aware of sin as man's desire to be independent of God and ruthlessly questioned the idealism of religious individualism of the 19th century. Out of this experience came Barth's commentary on the Epistle to the Romans. Two years later, he accepted a chair at Göttingen, Germany. In 1925, he moved to the University of Munster; in 1930, he was called to Bonn, Germany, where he taught until he was forced to leave for refusing to take the oath demanded by Hitler. Barth then accepted a professorship in his home city of Basel, Switzerland, where he taught the rest of his life.

Barth, deliberately provoking a crisis in Christian thinking by stabbing at the subjectivism of Protestant theology which confused man with God, demanded that God be allowed to be God, and that man learn again to be man. Barth penetratingly analyzed man's sin as man's continual attempt to twist truth even in religion to suit his own private ends. Barth's purpose was to force man into a confrontation by the holy, transcendent God of the Bible. Barth's theology came to be called dialectical because his questions led to profound and disturbing contrasts between Holy God and sinful man, Creator and creature, grace and judgment, God's *Yes* and *No.*

Barth relentlessly insisted that it is not important what man thinks about God, but what God thinks about man. This led Barth to a renewed emphasis on the Christ who addresses men out of the Bible. Barth's theology became increasingly a theology of the Word. De-

termined to state a consistent and complete Biblical theology, Barth began writing *Church Dogmatics,* publishing the first volume in 1932. Barth's *Dogmatics* placed him in a category with the great of the "greats" who contributed to the development of theology and greater understanding among Christians, including Augustine, Anselm, Aquinas, Luther and Calvin.

Barth personally was beloved as a warm, witty human who never lost his country parson's simplicity. For years, the world-famous theologian preached regularly to the inmates of the Basel jail.

BARTHOLOMEW ([?]–1333) The "Apostle of Armenia" (present-day Turkey), Bartholomew was a Dominican who became Archbishop of Nakschiwan in Armenia. He translated the Missal, the Psalter and other liturgical books into Armenian.

BARTON, Elizabeth (1506[?]–1534) Known as "the Maid of Kent" or "Holy Maid of Kent," Elizabeth Barton was an emotionally-disturbed woman whose ravings against King Henry VIII were exploited as "prophecies" by certain churchmen to stir up opposition to Henry VIII's divorce from his first wife and his plans to break with the Church of Rome. The unfortunate Elizabeth Barton was tried and executed for treason.

BASCOM, Henry Bidleman (1796–1850) The most eloquent American Methodist preacher of his day, Bascom, who sided with the Southerners when the Methodist Episcopal Church split in 1844 over the slavery question, became a famous bishop.

BASIL, The Great, Bishop (330[?]–379) A leading Churchman in the 4th century and a vigorous defender of Nicene Christianity, Basil served as bishop of one of the largest and most influential sees in the East, Caesarea of Cappadocia. In spite of a personal preference for the ascetic, monastic life (he popularized monasticism in Asia Minor), Basil was a gifted administrator who used his position to promote in the Eastern Church the orthodox Christology of the Nicene Council in the struggle with Arianism (the viewpoint that Christ was not quite God or man). Theology was intertwined with politics in the East at the time, and Basil skillfully, if imperiously, maneuvered the Church through troublesome waters. He worked tirelessly to strengthen the delicate ties between leaders of the western Church and his anti-Arian men in the East. A humanitarian, Basil also has the distinction of being the first to open a shelter to care for stranded strangers. His outstanding career was cut short by an early death.

BAUR, Ferdinand Christian (1792–1860) A German Biblical scholar and professor at Tubingen, F. C. Baur was one of the first to employ historical criticism in studying the New Testament. Using the philosopher Hegel's idea that every thesis has its antithesis, Baur taught that the Apostles' belief (thesis) was followed by Paul's Christianity (antithesis), and used this idea to detect which New Testament books were, in his opinion, written by Paul and which were not. Baur stirred up furious debate. Although Baur's theory is not taken seriously today, his work was a pioneer effort in Biblical studies and helped open the way for careful research on the Bible.

BAXTER, Richard (1615–1691) A saintly Presbyterian minister during the fierce struggle between Royalists and Puritans in England during the 1600's, Baxter was one of the few who would put his commitment to Christ ahead of commitment to a denomination.

Baxter served his parish at Kidderminster for nineteen years, and was a model of what a parish minister should be. (His book, *The Reformed Pastor*, is still a classic on the responsibilities of clergymen.) He even managed to organize his fellow pastors in the area into an association for mutual encouragement and edification, regardless of their denominational differences—a real feat in those days.

After the Act of Uniformity of 1662 was passed, Baxter was urged to become an Anglican to escape persecution, even being offered the bishopric of Rochester. He refused, and eked out a poor livelihood the rest of his days, harassed as a Non-conformist by the authorities. Although he was fined numerous times and jailed frequently, once for eighteen months when he was past seventy, Baxter continued to preach faithfully and write voluminously.

BEA, Augustin, Cardinal (1881–1968) Brilliant German Jesuit Biblical scholar and founder of the Vatican's Secretariat for Promoting Christian Unity, Bea shaped efforts by the Roman Catholic Church in the 1960's to advance ecumenism, to retract ancient slanders against the Jews, to improve relations with the non-Christian world, and to encourage previously forbidden scientific study of the Bible. Made a cardinal by Pope John XXIII in 1959, Bea was assigned the task of designing plans to bring about Pope John's dreams of the Ecumenical Council and closer unity among Christians. Bea produced two major documents bearing on Rome's relations with non-Catholics: the decree on ecumenism, and the decree on religious liberty.

BEATON, David (1494[?]–1546)
The autocratic pro-French cardinal of
Scotland who had no patience with the
stirrings of Reformed thinking or Scottish nationalism in Scotland, Beaton
callously burned a succession of Scottish reformer-patriots.

In revenge for Beaton's killing an
outstanding preacher, George Wishart,
and in anger at Beaton's pro-French
policies, a band of Scots attacked St.
Andrews castle, murdered Cardinal
Beaton and rallied supporters for the
Reformation and independence. Among
those who joined the group after Beaton's murder was young John Knox.

BEATON, James ([?]–1539) Arch-
bishop of St. Andrews and uncle of
Cardinal David Beaton, murdered by
Scottish reformer-nationalist partisans,
James Beaton tried to steer Scotland
away from Protestant tendencies by
strengthening the political alliance with
France. Beaton condoned the burning of
the first Scottish Protestant martyr,
Patrick Hamilton, 1528, and urged
repressive measures on any preaching
Protestant doctrine.

**BEAUVAIS, Jean Baptiste Charles
Marie de** (1731–1790) The French
bishop and preacher to the Court of
France who boldly criticized King Louis
XV yet was invited to preach the King's
funeral oration, Beauvais uttered the
famous phrase, "The silence of the peoples is a lesson for kings." In 1789,
Beauvais was elected by the Paris clergy
as deputy to the States General.

BECKET, Thomas à (1118[?]–1170)
Ex-crony of King Henry II of England
who, as the dedicated Archbishop of
Canterbury defied Henry, Becket was
murdered on the king's orders.

Thomas à Becket, prior to his appointment as archbishop, was an able
civil servant, serving Henry in many

offices, including chancellor. His love of
luxury and entertainment made him a
boon companion to the King. King
Henry put Becket in office as archbishop, expecting him to continue to
be a compliant friend. Instead, Becket
quickly showed that his main allegiance
was to God and the Church. He abandoned his expensive habits, championed
the rights of the people and defied
Henry's authority. A long, bitter conflict between Becket and Henry II ensued. Although Becket fled once to
France, he returned, tried to patch
things up with Henry but again found
himself opposed to royal authority.

Henry's anger at Becket served as an
order for four knights to cut down
Becket while at vespers at the altar of
Canterbury Cathedral.

BEDE (673[?]–735) Known as "The
Venerable" (not because he lived to
such an unusually old age, but as a
title given to learned priests in his time),
Bede lived from the age of seven to his
death in the northern England monastery of Wearmouth and Jarrow. Bede
(or Beda or Baeda) was one of the
earliest historians and theologians in the
Church in England and is called the
Father of English History. An outstanding intellectual who combined missionary zeal, unaffected piety and a
passion for learning, Bede also wrote
ably on scientific subjects, nature, grammar, chronology and the calendar. His
chief place in history's hall of fame,
however, is earned by his epochal
*Ecclesiastical History of the English
People.*

BEECHER, Henry Ward (1813–1887)
Son of Lyman Beecher (see below),
Henry Beecher was a dramatic, witty
preacher at the Plymouth Congregational Church, Brooklyn, where his
comments on current topics were widely
quoted and respected.

BEECHER, Lyman (1775–1863) American Presbyterian clergyman, Lyman Beecher, father of Henry Ward Beecher (see above) and novelist Harriet Beecher Stowe, was a magnetic and controversial figure in the church storms of the first half of the 19th century. Lyman Beecher served for some years as president of Lane Seminary, Cincinnati, Ohio, where he vigorously opposed the inroads of Unitarianism on Protestant thought. At the same time, he was suspected of heresy by the ultra-orthodox faction of Presbyterians, but was cleared of charges of being a "moderate Calvinist" in 1836. As early as 1813, his sermons against drunkenness were influencing the formation of the American Temperance Movement.

BEISSEL, Johann Conrad (1690–1768) Founder of the Seventh Day Baptists, Beissel was a mystic and pietist who was born in Germany but emigrated to America in 1720. In 1724, he was baptized as a Dunker. He broke with the Dunkers because of his rigid belief in celibacy and observing Saturday as the Sabbath. He attracted a group of followers in 1728 which called themselves Seventh Day Baptists. Moving to Ephrata, Pennsylvania, in 1732, Beissel established a settlement which observed strict celibacy and communal living. Known as "Solitary Brethren," this community for a time numbered several hundred.

BELLAMY, Joseph (1719–1790) Pupil of the great American theologian Jonathan Edwards, Joseph Bellamy was a Congregationalist parish pastor who wrote the famous theological treatise, *True Religion Delineated,* in 1750. Next to Jonathan Edwards, Bellamy was the most influential churchman in colonial times. For years he conducted classes for clergymen in his home, expounding his "system of divinity." He participated in the Great Awakening of the 1740's, and supported the American War of Independence.

BELLARMINE, Robert Francis Romulus (1542–1621) Italian Jesuit who vigorously defended Roman Catholic doctrine during the Protestant-Catholic controversies of the last quarter of the 16th century, Bellarmine was selected by successive popes to answer Protestant charges. He was later canonized.

BELLARMINO See **BELLARMINE**.

BENEDICT of Aniane (750[?]–821) Founder of a monastery at Aniane in southern France, Benedict was a strict ascetic who brought monasticism back to its original purposes of worship, contemplation and self-denial. Benedict of Aniane was disinterested in monks' involvement in educational or cultural activities, although he personally served as Emperor Louis the Pious' chief monastic advisor.

BENEDICT of Nursia (480[?]–543[?]) The great reformer and organizer of monasticism in the western Chruch, Benedict wrote the *Rule,* which institutionalized the life of all monks in the west down to and including the present. Shocked at the undisciplined and dissolute living of fellow monks, austere Benedict organized a new monastic community at Monte Cassino in 529, and instituted order and purpose in his model monastery through the *Rule.* The *Rule* reflects Benedict's organizational genius, his insights into human nature, his practicality, and his balance between the contemplative and the active. Benedict's *Rule* placed each monk in a monastery under an abbot, prescribed the daily schedule (allowing for worship, work and study) and outlined the responsibilities of each member of the monastic community. Benedict was both a reflective activist and an active reflectionist. His Monte Cassino on a high pinnacle between Rome and Naples (destroyed during World War II and later rebuilt) was the main center for spiritual life for centuries in western Europe.

BENEDICT BISCOP (or Benet) (628[?]–690) English Benedictine scholar and church builder, Benedict Biscop made five trips to Rome from England, bringing back treasures, relics and the arts of stained-glass window making and stone-masonry for erecting lovely buildings. He built the monasteries of Jarrow and Wearmouth in England.

BENEDICT I, Pope ([?]–578[?]) The first of fifteen Roman Catholic prelates to carry the name, this Pope Benedict served during the terrible days of the Lombard invasions and the famines and plagues which followed.

BENEDICT II, Pope ([?]–685) Pope from 684 to 685.

BENEDICT III, Pope ([?]–858) Popularly chosen by clergy and laymen at Rome in 855, Benedict's installation was long delayed because Emperor Louis II had picked Anastasius the antipope.

BENEDICT IV, Pope ([?]–903) Pope from 900 to 903.

BENEDICT V, Pope ([?]–965[?]) A hapless prelate who was caught in the political maneuvering between Emperor Otto I (Otho) and his resentful Italian vassal states, Benedict V was elected by the Romans but not approved by the Emperor. Otto carried Benedict off to Hamburg to exile (where Benedict V died) and re-installed compliant Leo VIII as pope.

BENEDICT VI, Pope ([?]–974) Hand-picked choice of Emperor Otto I, Benedict was installed with great splendor. When Otto died two years later, however, the restless citizens of Rome revolted. Benedict VI was strangled and replaced as pope by a complaint deacon who took the name Boniface VII.

BENEDICT VII, Pope ([?]–983) Pope from 974 to 983.

BENEDICT VIII ([?]–1024) A not-so-spiritual opportunist, Benedict VIII shrewdly recognized that he and the Emperor, Henry II of Saxony, could better advance personal interests by each supporting the other. Benedict VIII's most memorable ruling prohibited clergy marriage.

BENEDICT IX, Pope (1025–1056[?]) One of the worst characters ever to serve as pope, Benedict IX was first installed as pope at the age of twelve through influential family connections. His conduct was so disgusting that he was deposed and re-installed three different times (the only reason why he was able to secure re-appointment was because of political rivalries among various Italian states). At one time during his office, Benedict IX was one of four competing popes, each insisting on his primacy. After Emperor Henry III eliminated three from the running by backing one who took the name of Clement II, Benedict IX poisoned this rival. Benedict IX was finally run out of Rome in 1048 and died penniless a few years later.

BENEDICT X, Antipope ([?]–1059) A counter-pope, this prelate took the title Benedict X, but was degraded and deposed by Hildebrand after attempting to reign from 1058 to 1059.

BENEDICT XI, Pope (1240–1304) One of the few popes of that period with any genuine piety or Biblical scholarship, Benedict ably administered the affairs of the papacy by skillfully improving relationships between the Vatican and many rulers.

BENEDICT XII, Pope ([?]–1342) Nephew of Pope John XXII, Benedict XII nevertheless refused to practice the nepotism so common in Rome, but made his appointments primarily on the basis of merit. He reformed the monastic orders and tried to negotiate a reunion of the Roman and Greek Churches. He is remembered for his pronouncement that the souls of saints may attain the fullness of the beatific vision before the final judgment.

BENEDICT XIII, Antipope (1328[?]–1422[?]) A wily, resourceful leader of the Avignon faction during the unfortunate period of two rival pontiffs, one at Rome and one at Avignon, Benedict XIII helped prolong the schism thirty years. He pretended to desire a reunion of the papacy, yet persisted in trying to line up support for himself among the princes of Europe and ruined negotiations to end the schism.

BENEDICT XIII, Pope (1649–1730) Well-meaning, but ineffective, Benedict XIII was first known as Benedict XIV. This colorless character must not be confused with the Antipope Benedict XIII (see above) or the scholarly Benedict XIV (see below).

BENEDICT XIV, Pope (1675–1758) One of the more studious popes, Benedict XIV established numerous university chairs, published numerous books, directed archaeological diggings at Rome and organized several schools. Benedict XIV was not a strong commander, however, and was not able to stand up to the growing strength of the Roman Catholic rulers of States in Europe or to mount effective attacks on Protestantism, except in a few predominantly Catholic countries.

BENEDICT XV, Pope (1854–1922) Elected pope shortly after the outbreak of World War I, Benedict XV repeatedly tried to use his offices to end the carnage of 1914–18. He was a gentle, scholarly pontiff to whom the great powers politely listened, but whose pleas for peace were just as politely ignored.

BENEZET (1165–1184) In an age when it was believed to be a great act of piety to erect a bridge across a river, Benezet, although a mere boy, responding to a vision and voice, managed to mobilize a crew of workmen to begin a bridge across the Rhone at Avignon, France, in 1177. The plans, engineering and construction were all under the supervision of the twelve-year old youth, who died a few years later at nineteen.

BENGEL, Johann Albrecht (1687–1752) German Lutheran head of a seminary at Denkendorf, Bengel was the father of modern methods of New Testament exegesis. Bengel was the first to note that New Testament Greek manuscripts fall into groupings, and the first to note that the more difficult version of a reading is likely to be the most authentic. In 1742, he wrote *Gnomon* ("Index"), a comprehensive commentary on Scripture in which he laid down that nothing should be read into the Bible but that meaning should be drawn out of Scriptures, using grammatical-historical insights. Scholarly preachers and theologians such as John Wesley found Bengel's *Gnomon* extremely helpful.

BENNO (1010–1106) A German bishop of Meissen who supported Pope

Gregory VII against the Emperor, Benno is remembered primarily because his canonization in 1523 by Pope Adrian VI was violently criticized by Martin Luther.

BERDYAEV, Nikolai Aleksandrovich (1874–1948) Russian-born theologian-philosopher who broke with the Bolsheviks and was exiled in 1922, Berdyaev moved to Paris and continued his outstanding career as a Christian thinker. He was deeply influenced by Dostoevsky as well as by the events of the twentieth century, and wrote opposing the depersonalizing trends and systems of the modern age. Persons as spiritual entities, he insisted, are of the greatest value.

BERENGAR (999[?]–1088) Medieval theologian and head of the Cathedral School at Tours, France, Berengar was a skeptic who publicly expressed his disbelief in the doctrine of transsubstantiation (that the elements of the eucharist in the mass are changed into the substance of the body and blood of Jesus Christ). His heretical views produced an uproar in the Church in his day. The powerful Hildebrand, first as a papal legate and later as Pope Gregory VII, twice brought pressure to bear on Berengar, forcing him to recant. Each time, however, Berengar later resumed his original position, claiming that his recantations in each case were obtained under duress.

Berengar's teachings both clarified and hardened the position of the Roman Church on the Lord's Supper so that by 1215 transsubstantiation was adopted as dogma at the Fourth Lateran Council. Although Berengar resigned his office under pressure and lived the rest of his life in solitude on a lonely island, his viewpoint on the sacrament was not forgotten. Throughout the Middle Ages

those holding to views similar to his, claiming the Real Presence of Jesus Christ but denying a miraculous change in the substance of the elements, were known as Berengarians.

BERKELEY, George (1685–1753) Anglo-Irish bishop and philosopher, Berkeley was the author of the famous, *The Principles of Human Knowledge.* In his "Principles," Berkeley presented the intriguing notion that matter exists only as we perceive it, that all that exists is actually existing only as ideas, and that these ideas in our minds are the products of the constantly-working mind of God. Berkeley wrote to counter the Deists who had put forth the idea that God was the Absentee Watchmaker, who once set the universe in operation but presently had nothing to do with its continuation. Lost in the smoke of the battles over philosophies is the fact that Berkeley was one of the first to urge foreign missions. He tried to found a college in Bermuda to evangelize American Indians and lived for a while in Rhode Island.

BERNARD of Clairvaux (1090–1153) The most influential spiritual leader of his age, Bernard of Clairvaux founded the Cistercian abbey at Clairvaux, France in 1115 and turned down offers to advance in the Church hierarchy to remain as abbot until he died in 1153. A monk whose reflection was always active and whose action was always reflective, Bernard of Clairvaux was both the evangelical devoted to Jesus Christ (this monk won accolades from Luther and Calvin), and the practical persuader who came up with the solution ending the shameful papal schism. He was the most powerful preacher in his age, as well as the most saintly mystic; his eloquence sparked the disastrous Second Crusade in 1146.

A zealous partisan for orthodoxy, Bernard of Clairvaux led the attack against Abélard. Today he is still remembered for his devotional writings and hymns, such as "O Sacred Head Now Wounded," and "Jesus, the Very Thought of Thee." Bernard's mystic contemplation of Christ not only motivated his own life but deeply affected the writing and art of his own age. He was later canonized.

BERNARD of Cluny ([?]–927) First abbot of the monastery at Cluny, Bernard (or Berno) of Cluny energetically reformed and reshaped monasticism in the grim 10th century. He headed the then-new Cluny monastery, designed to be completely free of local ecclesiastical or princely control and soon made Cluny into a motherhouse with six satellite chapters. Bernard accentuated the trends toward asceticism which had been growing during the preceding years and stamped the medieval Church with his other-worldly pietism. Ultimately, many monasteries, including even the famous Monte Cassino, took up Bernard of Cluny's ideals.

BERNARDINO of Siena (1380–1444) Named in 1957 by the Vatican as the patron saint of advertisers, Bernardino was such a persuasive orator that gamblers frequently threw away their dice and tore up their cards.

BERNO See **BERNARD of Cluny.**

BERQUIN, Louis de (1490–1529) One of the first Protestants in France, de Berquin was burned at the stake in 1529 for his views. He was a pupil of the influential humanist churchman Lefèvre, but eventually broke with the Roman Catholic Church and was one of the first martyrs in the Reformation.

BERULLE, Pierre de (1575–1629) Noted 17th century French cardinal-statesman, de Berulle was the first to discover the philosopher Descartes' greatness and encouraged Descartes to write. De Berulle is also remembered as the founder of the Carmelite Order in France.

BESANT, Annie (Wood) (1847–1933) English-born theosophist and Oriental cultist, Annie Besant for a time was a member of the Fabian Society, an avant-garde group promoting socialism and social change in England, and in 1885 helped as a labor organizer. In 1889, however, she came under the influence of Madame Blavatsky, the colorful creator of the Theosophy Society and dabbler in the occult. Mrs. Besant, a devoted member of the Theosophists, spent much of her life in India, delving into eastern religions and taking controversial positions in Indian politics.

BESSARION, Johannes (1395[?]–1472) The Archbishop of Nicea at the time of the Moslem invasions in the 15th century, Bessarion shrewdly tried to enlist western help against the Moslem onslaught by working to unite his Eastern Church with Rome. He won the friendship and trust of Pope Eugene IV, who made him a cardinal in the Latin Church. Bessarion and Eugene IV worked out a vaguely-worded agreement between the Eastern and Western Churches after long negotiations in 1438 and 1439 at Ferrara and Florence, and joyfully announced a reunion of the two separated branches of Christendom in 1439. When Bessarion returned home, however, he was bitterly denounced by his fellow Greeks as one who had sold out to Rome.

BEUKELSSEN, Jan (also Beukils) ([?]–1535) Follower of the fanatic Jan Mathys, who bloodily took over Munster, Germany, in 1534 to set up an earthly New Jerusalem, Jan Beukelssen was elected "king" of the polygamous, communal group of radical Anabaptists. He died when Lutheran and Catholic troops recaptured Munster in 1536.

BEZA, Theodore (1519–1605) Successor to John Calvin at Geneva, Theodore Beza, like Calvin, was a French humanist law student-turned-Reformer. His student years were spent writing frivolous verse and carousing; his conversion came after a severe illness at the start of his law practice in Paris. In 1558 he joined Calvin's congregation at Geneva and began a brilliant teaching career in Switzerland. When the unscrupulous Catherine de' Medici decided to get political advantage from calling a public discussion between Catholic and Protestant theologians at Poissy in 1561, Beza was selected as a Protestant spokesman and showed immense ability. He willingly subordinated himself to the great John Calvin and assisted Calvin in numerous capacities, including editor and administrator. His conciliatory spirit often offset Calvin's abrasiveness and helped advance Calvinism in Geneva. After Calvin's death Beza became both Calvin's biographer and administrative successor at Geneva.

BIANDRATA, Giorgio (1515[?]–1588[?]) An anti-Trinitarian freethinker from Italy, Biandrata became the founder of a unitarian-leaning sect in what is now Hungary. Biandrata, like many intellectuals of his time, wandered extensively, spending a year in Geneva (where his radical views conflicted violently with Calvin's and made it expedient for him to leave in 1558), staying in Poland (where he served as physician to many leading families) and finally to Transylvania in Hungary. His thinking, influenced more by Renaissance skepticism and humanist rationalism than by orthodox Christianity, led him to join the ranks of those questioning the traditional thoughts of Jesus Christ's person and work.

BIDDLE, John (1615–1662) Father of English Unitarianism, John Biddle was an oft-imprisoned defender of anti-Trinitarian views in an age when little tolerance was permitted. He was a well-educated and articulate person but incurred the ire of nearly everyone, including Parliament and the Westminster Assembly of divines. For years Unitarians in England were known as Bidellians. He died in prison in 1662.

BIEL, Gabriel (1425[?]–1495) Scholastic philosopher and theological professor at Tübingen, Germany, Biel wrote lucidly and compellingly on the limits of human reason and the need for relying on the objective facts of revelation. He influenced Luther and Melanchthon in their emphasis on revelation and distrust of reason.

BILNEY, Thomas (1495–1531) An English martyr-cleric who questioned traditional Roman Catholic doctrines such as salvation by works and the work of saints, Bilney influenced many young fellow Cambridge University students (including Hugh Latimer) to adopt views which corresponded with those of the later Reformers. Bilney preached in London and East Anglia, was tried by the intimidating Cardinal Wolsey in 1527, and forced to sign a humiliating recantation. Released, Bilney immediately publicly repudiated his recantation, resumed preaching his former views at Norfolk, and was rearrested and burned alive.

BILSON, Thomas (1547–1616) An ardent Anglican who became Bishop of Winchester, Thomas Bilson countered claims of the Puritans and Separatists in his noted writing, *Perpetual Government of Christ's Church* in 1593. Bilson took the position that the episcopal form and system were divinely inspired by God and that all other systems were to be abhorred.

BIMELER, Joseph Michael (1778[?]–1853) Born in Germany, where he was a weaver, Bimeler assumed the leadership of a group of 300 pietists at Württemburg. Bimeler and his followers, tired of harassment and persecution, finally emigrated to America and bought a tract of land along the Tuscarawas River in eastern Ohio. Bimeler's sect established the "Kingdom of Zoar" (from the name of the town to which Lot in the Bible fled to safety), a communal-type of religious community. Under the benignly autocratic Bimeler, Zoar flourished. After his death in 1853 (and the digging of the Ohio Canal), the community gradually disintegrated, selling the last of the community property in 1898.

BIRGITTA See **BRIGITTA**.

BLAIR, Samuel (1712–1751) Evangelical Presbyterian in the forefront of the Great Revival of the 1740's, Blair became chief spokesman for the New Side after colonial Presbyterianism split over the Revival. Blair, part of the wave of Presbyterian immigrants from Ulster (popularly called "Scots-Irish"), studied at William Tennent's Neshaminy Log College and later established his own famous Log College at Faggs Manor, Chester County, Pa. An aggressive partisan for warm-hearted personal Christianity, Blair unintentionally fanned controversy in the ranks of mid-18th century American Presbyterians.

BLANDINA (2nd Century) A Roman slave woman of Lyon who was a convert to Christianity, Blandina, in spite of hideous tortures, refused to renounce her faith. Eventually, after being forced to watch her companions brutally slain, Blandina was put through a slow, gruesome execution, partly by being gored alive, burned and stabbed. She is a saint in the Roman Catholic Church.

BLAUROCK, Georg ([?]–1529) An ex-monk who joined the ranks of those who believed only in baptism of believers, or a re-baptisism (which gave them the name "Anabaptist"), Georg Blaurock became a leader in the group in Switzerland who believed the mainstream Reformers were too conservative. In 1525, Blaurock re-baptized the first group of adults by sprinkling and shortly began to baptize by total immersion. Blaurock and the Anabaptists, the radical wing of the Reformation, were distrusted and detested by Catholics and most other Protestants alike. The Zürich government cruelly repressed the Anabaptists but the movement spread throughout Europe. Most early Anabaptist leaders died hideous deaths; Blaurock was burned at the stake in 1529.

BLAVATSKY, Elena Petrovna (1831–1891) Russian-born founder of the Theosophical Society, Madame Blavatsky married one Nicephore Blavatsky at seventeen, left him after a few months, and wandered throughout the world for twenty years. During her travels she claimed to have visited Tibet and spent seven years in a "Himalayan retreat." She returned to the West and created a sensation as a spiritualist, attracting large crowds with her clever stunts and confident lectures about the occult. In 1875, Madame Blavatsky established the Theosophical Society, through which she supplied the faithful with her teachings (an amalgam of

Egyptian, Indian, Buddhist and cabalistic ideas and terms, with heavy emphasis on mediums and the mystical).

BLISS, Daniel (1823–1916) A Vermont-born Congregational missionary to Syria from 1855 until his death, Bliss was a pioneer educator in the 19th century Middle East, founding what became the influential American College at Beirut, Lebanon.

BOEHLER, Peter See **BOHLER**.

BOEHM, Martin (1725–1812) Cofounder with Philip Otterbein of the Church of the United Brethren in Christ, Boehm was an American Mennonite pastor with strong evangelical and ecumenical feelings. Boehm, becoming pastor of a Mennonite congregation at Pequea, Pennsylvania in 1753, felt a deep sense of personal unworthiness until a spiritual crisis in 1758 liberated him to preach "in power." His sermons began to stress repentance and salvation by faith. Boehm began to attract attention and was advanced to Bishop in 1759.

The same year, Boehm made a visit to Virginia, where he came in contact with the "Great Awakening" evangelism fired by George Whitefield and other preachers. In 1767, Boehm took part in the "great meeting," an inter-denominational revival service held in a barn in the Conestoga Valley north of Landis Valley, Pennsylvania, where he met Philip Otterbein, a German Reformed pastor. Boehm and Otterbein worked closely during the next years, making lengthy trips throughout German-speaking communities in the Eastern United States to hold worship service together. Boehm organized a team of like-minded warm-hearted circuit riders, and associated comfortably with leaders in other denominations, particularly the Reformed and Methodists.

Boehm's ecumenism, however, was distrusted by many of his conservative Mennonite brothers. He was excommunicated in 1777 by the Mennonite Conference of Lancaster County, Pennsylvania. Undaunted, Boehm and his circuit-riders continued their work. In 1789, Boehm and his long-time friend Otterbein shook hands atfer prayer one day and declared that in Christ they truly were United Brethren. With six lay evangelists, Boehm and Otterbein formally declared themselves to be a new denomination.

BOEHME See **BÖHME**.

BOGUE, David (1750–1825) A Scots-born Presbyterian-turned-Congregational minister, David Bogue was one of the earliest champions of the modern missionary movement. Bogue convened the group which organized the famous London Missionary Society, the interdenominational agency which began sending brave Christian workers to remote overseas locations in 1796. Bogue personally had hoped to serve in India, but was blocked from going by the powerful East India Company. Bogue also had a hand in founding the British and Foreign Bible Society and the Religious Tract Society.

BOHEMUND, Marc (1058[?]–1111) Commander of the Normans from Italy, the finest fighting outfit to set out on the First Crusade in 1096, Bohemund participated in the butchery at the capture of Jerusalem.

BÖHLER, Peter (1712–1775) A Moravian pietist, Böhler deeply influenced John and Charles Wesley who joined Böhler's "Society" in London. His doctrines were simple and personal: a complete self-surrender, an instantaneous conversion and a joy in trusting. He founded the Moravian Fetter-Lane Society in 1738—a prototype of Wesley's "societies" a few years later. Although the Wesley brothers eventually withdrew from Böhler's "Society" to found their own Methodist "United Society" in 1740, Böhler and the Wesleys continued on a friendly relationship.

BÖHME, Jakob (also Behmen) (1575 –1624) Protestant mystic, Böhme lived during the horrors and devastation of the early part of the Thirty Years War in Germany, and, perhaps, in reaction to the events in the world, turned to an inward religion stressing an immediate personal perception of the divine Presence. In reality, Böhme departed from traditional Protestantism and emphasized as his ultimate authority his direct individual awareness of God. Böhme left a lasting influence on a small but persistent group of Christian mystics, including his modern spiritual heirs, the Quakers. His deep commitment to the living Jesus Christ, as shown in such lovely phrases as "He became what I am and now He has made me what He is," has made him a favorite among devotional classics.

BOLSEC, Hermès ([?]–1585) An argumentative onetime monk from Paris who became Protestant and began to practice medicine in Geneva during Calvin's struggles with city fathers between 1548 and 1555, Bolsec savagely attacked Calvin's doctrine of predestination and charged Calvin with error. Bolsec almost succeeded in toppling Calvin, but was finally rebutted by Calvin and forced to leave Geneva. The main result of his attack was to cause Calvin to place greater emphasis on predestination. Bolsec later rejoined the Roman Catholic Church and tried to retaliate on Calvin by writing a scurrilous and distorted record of Calvin's life.

BONAVENTURA (1221–1274) Baptized with the name, John of Fidanza, this great Franciscan leader was miraculously cured of a serious illness by St. Francis of Assisi and given the cognomen "Bonaventura." Bonaventura, later canonized, one of the Medieval Church's greatest meditative thinkers, rose to become the head of the Franciscan order in 1257 and distinguished himself as a strong administrator. Like his friend Thomas Aquinas, Bonaventura was also a noted teacher and dialectic theologian. Essentially, however, Bonaventura was a mystic, one who believed that by prayer and meditation he could reach a union with God which brings insights of divine knowledge. Bonaventura's conservatism brought him into collision with some of his more progressive contemporaries on occasions; he once issued an interdict prohibiting Roger Bacon from lecturing at Oxford and putting the scientists under surveillance. Bonaventura's reputation as a sound thinker and wise leader, nonetheless, was so great that he was called "Doctor Seraphicus" while he was still living. He was made a cardinal shortly before his death in 1274.

BONHOEFFER, Dietrich (1906– 1945) One of the seminal thinkers for post-World War II theological thought, Bonhoeffer was a creative and courageous young German pastor, professor and patriot who was martyred by the Nazis a few days before the collapse of Germany in 1945.

Bonhoeffer, son of a noted Breslau professor of psychiatry, early earned a reputation for original scholarship, publishing his first book, *Sanctorum Communio*, when only twenty-two. After a brief stint as curate to the German congregation at Barcelona, Spain, and additional graduate work at Union Seminary, New York, Bonhoeffer joined the faculty of the University of Berlin in 1930. He traveled and taught until formally expelled from his teaching post by the Nazi regime in 1936 for denouncing the Führer cult as idolatry. Meanwhile, in 1935, Bonhoeffer took over the direction of an illegal Church Training College to train young German pastors. From his personal experiences, the scholarly young activist wrote *The Cost of Discipleship* in 1937, castigating the easy, culture-religion masquerading as the Gospel, and *Life Together* in 1938, commenting on the means to and the meaning of a disciplined Christian community.

Whisked to safety in June, 1939 by American friends, Bonhoeffer could have remained in safety during World War II. Instead, understanding better than most that being a Christian means taking risks, Bonhoeffer returned to Germany. During the War, he took further risks, passing on details of the German resistance movement to British intelligence and meeting with the ringleaders of the unsuccessful July, 1944 plot on Hitler's life. Until his arrest in 1943, Bonhoeffer assisted the Confessional (anti-Nazi) Church.

Dietrich Bonhoeffer spent the years from his arrest until early 1945 in prison in Berlin, where he exhibited a model calm, courage and compassion, ministering to fellow-inmates and guards alike. During this period, he managed to smuggle scraps of writings from his cell to friends. These scraps were published after the War as *Ethics* and *Letters and Papers from Prison*, and were widely read.

Bonhoeffer insisted that if a person is called by God, he is obliged to make use of his freedom with a sense of responsibility to conserve the divine ordering of life. A Christian, he maintained, must be willing to act, to suffer, and, if necessary, to die. Bonhoeffer advocated a Christian "humanism" whereby, rooted in trust of God's grace, a believer must live a life of radical involvement in God's world as "the man for others." Detesting the selfish piosity which shuts a man away from the world, Bonhoeffer stated that the Christian is not "religious" man or one trying to make himself into a saintly person, but simply a person living in the midst of perplexities, questions and tasks who throws himself on the mercy of God and takes the risks of living responsibly.

Bonhoeffer was transferred from Berlin to Buchenwald Concentration Camp in early 1945, then moved to Flossenburg Prison. On April 9, 1945, immediately after conducting a Sunday worship service for prisoners, Bonhoeffer was led out and hung by the SS Black Shirts by special order of secret police chief, Himmler. The thirty-nine year old churchman who had warned against "cheap grace," exemplified in his own life his own phrase, "When Christ calls a man, He bids him come and die."

BONIFACE, Missionary to Germany (680–754) The Englishman who organized the Church among the Germanic tribes, Boniface was a tireless, persistent monk who was undaunted by poor response in his first missionary efforts in Frisia. In 715 he was sent to Germany by Pope Gregory II to counteract the efforts of the Irish Celtic Church by bringing Christians in Germany under Rome and to evangelize among the heathen northern tribes. Protected by Charles Martel (Emperor Charlemagne's grandfather), Boniface systematically established monasteries, organized congregations, demolished pagan shrines (including the sacred oak at Geismar), and baptized droves of new converts. Boniface imported a steady stream of earnest monks and nuns from his native England as missionary helpers, many of whom became famous leaders in the Church. Boniface had organizational gifts which he exercised by setting up bishoprics and establishing ordered procedures for the institutional Church in Germany. He was recognized for his accomplishments by being named Archbishop of Mainz about 747, the leading German see. Remembering his early failure at Frisia, in his old age, he undertook another evangelistic tour of the area in 754 but was assassinated by wild tribesmen in the course of this final missionary trip. Tradition holds that Boniface (later canonized) originated the custom of the Christmas tree.

BONIFACE I, Pope ([?]–422) Also canonized, Boniface I served as Pope from 418–422.

BONIFACE II, Pope ([?]–532) A Goth by birth, Boniface II (one of nine popes who took the name Boniface) was nominated by his predecessor and tried to make it papal policy for the pope to choose his successor. Neither the Roman clergy nor the Roman Senate would accept the proposal, however. Boniface II endorsed the conclusions of the Synod of Orange called by the Bishop of Arles, which officially ended Pelagian tendencies in the Church's doctrine (that is, the idea that man could save himself by working hard at his own salvation) and adopted Augustinian theology (the traditional theology whereby sinful man is saved only by God's grace).

BONIFACE III, Pope ([?]–607) Although pope only a few months, Boniface III got Emperor Phocas to recognize "headship of the Church at Rome," strengthening the position of the Bishop of Rome in the struggle with the Bishop of Constantinople, named Cyriacus.

Boniface III convinced Phocas that the title "Universal Bishop" belonged to the Bishop of Rome and no one else, and forced Cyriacus to abandon his attempt to call himself Ecumenical Patriarch. In this way Boniface III greatly enhanced the prestige and strengthened the position of the see of Rome and the Western Church.

BONIFACE IV, Pope ([?]–615) Serving as pope from 608 to 615, this Pope Boniface was also made a saint.

BONIFACE V, Pope ([?]–625) Pope from 619 to 625.

BONIFACE VI, Pope ([?]–896) Pope for only fifteen days, Boniface VI died in prison.

BONIFACE VII, Pope ([?]–985) Banished by Emperor Otto II, Boniface VII returned after Otto's death and usurped the papacy from Pope John XIV in 984.

BONIFACE VIII, Pope (1235–1303) Ambitious and arrogant, Boniface VIII's demands for unlimited papal power led him into a long, unfortunate quarrel with King Philip IV, "the Fair" of France. Philip and his fellow rulers represented the growing power of national states in Europe in the late Middle Ages, and resented the totalitarian claims of the Roman see. Philip IV set off the feud by taxing clergy. Boniface VIII protested in vain. Next, Philip arrested the Pope's messenger, charging him with treason. Boniface angrily issued his famous Bull, *Unam Sanctam*, claiming absolute supremacy over every ruler and all territory. Philip shrewdly called the first session of the French States-General the French Assembly, and received backing to oppose the Pope. Boniface obstinately prepared to excommunicate Philip. The cunning

Philip, however, had Boniface kidnapped in 1303. Boniface VIII died a month after his release in 1303 and left the papacy seriously weakened, both in prestige and power.

BONIFACE IX, Pope ([?]–1404) A pope of Rome during the shameful schism which put two rival popes in office, one at Rome and the other at Avignon, Boniface IX helped to recoup some of the lost prestige at Rome by his power-ploys. At the same time, he permissively tolerated most of the faults of Church leaders which so offended the rank and file.

BOOTH, Ballington (1859–1940) One of the sons of General William Booth, founder of the Salvation Army, Ballington Booth was put in charge of Salvation Army work in America in 1887. He and his father disagreed on methods, however; Ballington Booth left the Salvation Army in 1897 and founded the Volunters of America, an American-based organization aimed at helping the poor.

BOOTH, Evangeline (1865–1950) Daughter of the famous William Booth, founder of the Salvation Army, Evangeline Booth served as world leader of the Salvation Army from 1934 to 1939. Previously, she organized Salvation Army work in the Klondike during the gold rush of 1898 and headed the Salvation Army in the United States from 1904 until 1934.

BOOTH, William (1829–1912) Founder of the Salvation Army in 1880, William Booth was a Methodist minister in Wales who withdrew from the Methodist Church in 1861 to conduct revival meetings. Moving to London in 1865, Booth began open-air and street-corner services. He concentrated on evangelizing the poverty-stricken in London's East End and organized his converts into a carefully disciplined group designed along military lines. The name "Salvation Army," with Booth as "General," attracted derision and criticism at first. Sometimes arbitrary and autocratic, Booth nonetheless reached persons ignored by more staid Church bodies. Booth published his best-selling *In Darkest England and the Way Out* in 1890, which showed Victorian England how to deal with poverty and vice. By the time of the turn of the century, Booth and his Salvation Army had won respect for their efforts on behalf of the poor and forgotten, and King Edward VII put the seal of respectability on the movement and Booth by inviting Booth to his coronation in 1902. William Booth was the author of many favorite revival hymns. He was succeeded in the Salvation Army by his able sons and daughters.

BOOTH, William Bramwell (1856–1920) Son of and successor to William Booth, Bramwell Booth was an illustrious leader of the Salvation Army from the time he was appointed chief of the staff in 1880 until his death in 1929.

BORA, Katherine von (1499–1552) Former nun who married Martin Luther in 1525, Katherine von Bora Luther was a saintly helpmeet who brought out some of the more pleasant human traits in her sometimes irascible husband. She somehow managed to look after their six children, several orphaned nieces and nephews and a constant houseful of poor students and student boarders whom Martin invited to stay with the family.

BORGIA, Cesare (1475–1507) Amoral and unscrupulous son of the shamelessly ambitious Pope Alexander VI, Cesare Borgia, made a cardinal by his father, was a soldier and politician more than churchman during the Renaissance.

BORGIA, Francisco (1510–1572) A strict and ascetic Jesuit who turned down advancements to be cardinal and bishop, Francisco Borgia chose to remain in Spain as the head of the Jesuit order, exercising wide influence in the 16th century Roman Catholic Church.

BORGIA, Rodrigo See **ALEXANDER VI,** Pope.

BORIS (852–884) King of the Bulgars, the fierce tribe who two centuries previously had swept from eastern Russia into the Balkans, King Boris introduced Christianity into the Balkan area following his baptism in 864. Boris' Bulgarian Church flourished and became largely self-governing. For some time, Boris wavered in deciding whether to have his Bulgarian Church give its spiritual loyalty to Rome or to Constantinople. The Patriarch of Constantinople won, however, by promising to grant Boris' Bulgarian Church a greater degree of autonomy, and agreeing to recognize Boris as the head of the Bulgarian Church. From that point, the Church in Eastern Europe was oriented toward the Greek rather than the Latin tradition and rite.

BOSSUET, Jacques (1627–1704) The most eloquent Roman Catholic pulpit orator of his age, Bossuet was a French cleric at Metz whose sermons were effective in countering the arguments and appeal of Protestantism for many in France.

BOSTON, Thomas (1676–1732) Scottish Presbyterian pastor at Ettrick, Boston was the center of controversies between legalist Calvinists and Evangelicals in Scotland in the 18th century. In 1718 Boston came across a copy of *The Marrow of Modern Divinity,* a document emphasizing that where Christ is received, repentance will follow. Boston had the book reprinted and added notes of his own which stressed faith in Christ. Conservative, hard-core Calvinists attacked the book as undermining the need for repentance. Boston's defenders came to be known as "Marrowmen," and preached their happy Gospel zealously and effectively to large crowds. Boston and his "Marrowmen" were censured for their views by the General Assembly in 1722. Ultimately, this faction founded the Free Church or Succession Church in Scotland in 1740.

BOURGEOIS, Louis (1510[?]–1561[?]) Well-known composer of hymn tunes at Geneva during Calvin's day, Bourgeois served as choirmaster for the great Reformer. He is generally credited as the one who compiled the Geneva Psalter, one of the earliest and best collections of words and music for congregational singing at worship services ever assembled. Bourgeois' best known tune is "Old Hundredth" (or sometimes used for the "Doxology").

BOUVET, Joachim (1662[?]–1732) An early French missionary sent by French King Louis XIV to China to study Chinese customs in 1685, Bouvet returned to China in 1699 with ten missionaries and devoted the rest of his life trying to build up the Christian Church in China.

BOWNDE, Nicholas ([?]–1613) A Puritan who emphasized Sabbath observance in the easy-going Elizabethan age, Bownde wrote the influential *Doctrine of the Sabbath* in 1595. Bownde's book and career stressed his understanding of God's will to preserve the Fourth Commandment in a strict and literalistic way. Bownde helped Puritanism to lay immense importance to the proper keeping of Sunday and was indirectly responsible for the idea of "Blue Laws" in the colonies and still on the books in many American communities.

BRADFORD, William (1590–1657) Second governor of the Plymouth Colony in New England, Bradford crossed on the Mayflower in 1620 with the group of Separatists known as the Pilgrims. He had united with the then-unpopular Puritan sect in England and had taken refuge with others in the Separatist band in Leiden, Holland after earlier enduring a jail sentence for his views. Bradford was a patient, tactful, self-effacing man who was highly regarded by both Pilgrims and Indians, and served as governor each year, except for five years, from 1621 until his death in 1657.

BRAINARD, David (1718–1747) Connecticut-born apostle to the American Indians, David Brainard endured incredible hardships to carry the Gospel to Indians in the Massachusetts wilderness, in the area near the Pennsylvania Delaware Gap and the vicinity of Newark, New Jersey. As a youth, Brainard was high-spirited and ebullient (and was kicked out of Yale for his high jinks and poking fun at the faculty). As a missionary he was tireless and dedicated. He contracted the dreaded tuberculosis which so ravaged the Indian tribes in those days, but continued heroically in his labors among the Indians until his health failed completely. He died shortly afterward from TB at the home of his fiancee, the daughter of Jonathan Edwards. He was only twenty-nine, but his example and his diary made a deep impact on people of his time.

BRAKESPEARE, Nicholas See **ADRIAN IV, Pope.**

BRANDAN See **BRENDAN.**

BRANDON See **BRENDAN.**

BRAY, Thomas (1656–1730) An efficient, missionary-minded English clergyman, Thomas Bray was appointed as "commissary" (organizer) for Anglican congregations in the New World in 1696 by the Bishop of London. Bray did a commendable job, traveling widely and strengthening the Episcopal Church in Maryland and Virginia. Noting the need for Bibles and religious books, Bray in 1699 founded the Society for Promoting Christian Knowledge and established parish libraries throughout England and America. He was vitally interested in the American Indians as well as the colonials, and in 1701 fathered the Society for the Propagation of the Gospel in Foreign Parts, which evolved into one of the earliest and most illustrious mission boards.

BREAKESPEARE, Nicholas See **ADRIAN IV, Pope.**

BRÉBEUF, Jean de (1593–1649) One of the self-sacrificing early French Jesuits who went to the North American wilderness, Brébeuf arrived at Quebec in 1625 and immediately began living among the Indians. He endured incredible privations while trying to evangelize the savage tribes. After years of painstaking effort to build chapels and develop tiny congregations, nearly all of his work was wiped out in the Indian wars of 1648. Most of his converts and fellow-missionaries were murdered, and, after horrible tortures, Brébeuf himself was slain in 1649. He was later canonized.

BRECK, James Lloyd (1818–1876) An energetic 19th century American Episcopal clergyman who helped open the West, Breck began many churches, started two Seminaries (Nashotah and Seabury) and evangelized the Indians.

BRENDAN (484[?]–578) An Irish saint, Brendan (also known as Brandon and Brandan) was the abbot for twenty years of a monastery which he founded in Galway in western Ireland. Legend has it that Brendan sailed across the Atlantic to the "Promised Land of the Saints" in an epochal voyage, 565–573, and landed on "St. Brendan's Island."

BREWSTER, William (1560[?]–1644) One of the earliest members of the Separatist movement in England, William Brewster served as "elder" (spiritual leader) of the group crossing on the *Mayflower* to found Plymouth Plantation. Brewster, originally a postmaster and bailiff, began the second Separatist congregation in his home at Scrooby, England, about 1602. Severe harassment by the established Church of England prompted Brewster to lead his congregation to Leiden, Holland in 1608 then to Plymouth in 1620.

BRIÇONNET, Guillaume (1470–1534) Bishop of Meaux who had strong leanings toward the earliest Reformers, Briçonnet was trained by the outstanding humanist educators of the age and was an associate of many of Reformer John Calvin's teachers and friends. Briçonnet was sympathetic to much in Reformed thinking, such as salvation being a free gift of God rather than something earned through good works by man, but never broke with the Church of Rome. He was named Bishop of Meaux, France, in 1516, but had no reluctance in permitting the fiery William Farel, Calvin's friend, to preach in his see in 1521. Briçonnet seems to have been a Reformation man intellectually, but a traditional Roman Catholic emotionally.

BRIDGET (452[?]–523) A patron saint of Ireland, Bridget was a legendary Irish lass who was also known as St. Brigid and St. Bride or Bridey. Bridget was uncommonly beautiful and intelligent, but wanted to devote her life to God without being bothered by suitors or a husband. According to the legends, she prayed to become ugly, had her prayers answered, and settled under a big oak tree as a nun. (The monastery of Kildare, located on the site of her oak tree, means "Church of the Oak.") Bridget was reputed to have effected many miraculous cures. Her generosity knew no limits; even as a small girl she persistently gave away family belongings whenever she found anyone in need.

BRIDGMAN, Elijah Coleman (1801–1861) The first American Protestant missionary to China, Bridgman, sponsored by the American Board of Foreign Missions, joined British missionary Robert Morrison in 1830 at Canton, China. Bridgman in 1838 assisted in developing one of the earliest medical programs under mission sponsorship in China. Moving to Shanghai in 1847, he spent useful years in that area, translating (with M. S. Culbertson) the Bible into Chinese.

BRIGET See **BRIGITTA**.

BRIGID See **BRIDGET**.

BRIGITTA (1302[?]–1373) Also known as Birgitta and Bridget (but not to be confused with St. Bridget of Ireland—see above), Brigitta was the favorite and most famous saint of Scandinavia. She lived in Sweden where she married and was the mother of eight children (one of whom, Catherine, was also canonized and is known as St. Catherine of Sweden). After the death of her husband, Ulf Gudmarson, Brigitta, who had already won fame for her charity, committed herself completely to the monastic life. She founded the Order of St. Savious (known popularly as the Bridgettines) at Vadstena in 1350. Brigitta claimed to have visions; records of her numerous "revelations" were widely circulated during the Middle Ages. She spent more than twenty years at Rome, pleading for papal authorization for her new order. Her persistence and her reputation for kindness finally persuaded Pope Urban V to give official sanction to the Brigittines (or Bridgetines). In an age where the moral tone was low, Brigitta stands out.

BRIGGS, Charles Augustus (1841–1913) American Old Testament scholar, Briggs held views in Biblical criticism which seemed heretical to his literalist fellow-Presbyterians in the late 19th century. He served on the faculty of Union Theological Seminary, New York, from 1874 to 1914. His inaugural address when installed in the Chair of Biblical Theology in 1891 boldly stated that errors existed in Scriptural texts, that "Isaiah is not author of half the book that bears his name," that "Moses did not write the Pentateuch," and many other now-accepted facts. Briggs outraged contemporary Presbyterians who persecuted him in denominational trials. The General Assembly of 1893 deposed Briggs as a Presbyterian minister. Briggs became an Episcopalian, was ordained an Episcopal priest in 1899 and continued his scholarly contributions to Biblical study. Briggs' trial touched off a long-running controversy between the ultra-orthodox literalists and those holding enlightened views of Biblical criticism which preoccupied all American Protestant denominations during the first third of the 20th century.

BROGNI, Giovanni de (1342–1426) A French Cardinal who rose from a boy swineherd to become the eminent chancellor of the Church of Rome, Brogni labored to end the disgraceful schism which featured two rival sets of popes, at Rome and at Avignon, vying for power and allegiance. Brogni skillfully worked behind the scenes to bring about the Council of Constance, and in 1417 got a new pope, Martin V, elected, and the Vatican reestablished at Rome. Brogni also headed this Council, which, unfortunately passed the death penalty on the Bohemian reformer, John Hus.

BROOKS, Phillips (1835–1893) Beloved Rector of Trinity Church, Boston, Massachusetts, for twenty-two years, Phillips Brooks was the author of some of the favorite Christmas and Easter music in the American church. He had tried and failed as a school teacher before entering the ministry, and retained a humility and humanity about him, both as a parish rector and as an Episcopal bishop. Brooks was a staunch upholder of the Union cause during the Civil War, and was one of the first to champion the cause of Negro rights.

BROWNE, Robert (1550[?]–1633) The pioneer thinker of English Congregationalism, Robert Browne was embroiled in controversy because of his radical views in his younger days, then settled down as conforming member of the Church of England during his middle years. Browne was the first to spell out Puritan insistence on recovering the simplicity and democracy of the primitive Church. In 1581, he started a Separatist congregation at Norwich, suffered imprisonment, and fled to safety in Holland with most of his congregation. He wrote his influential treatises during his stay in Holland and outlined what became the fundamentals of Congregationalism. Browne held that Church membership was a voluntary covenant uniting members to Christ and to one another, and that each congregation should be autonomous, electing its own leaders. Internal dissensions in Browne's Holland congregation caused him to return to England, where in 1591 he appeared to many to have sold out to the enemy by accepting ordination as an Anglican priest. He served as a rector in the established church in Northamptonshire for forty-two years. His earlier followers, known as "Brownists," resented the title after Browne deserted them, but the English Congregationalists were called by the title for many years.

BRUNNER, (Heinrich) Emil (1889–1966) Influential 20th century Swiss theologian, Emil Brunner lived and taught in his native Zurich, Berlin, and the United States. In 1953 he went to the newly-founded International Christian University at Tokyo, Japan, where he gave an impetus and lustre to theological studies for two years until failing health compelled him to return to Zurich. Brunner was a systematic, comprehensive theological writer who was usually classified as a crisis or neoorthodox thinker. Brunner himself preferred to think that his theology was "missionary theology," as he called it, both in content and in intent. He insisted that the classic Christian faith must lead the Church to relate to the issues and questions of modern man. It was at this point that Brunner differed from his friend and fellow-Swiss, Karl Barth; Brunner maintained that Barth was blind to the responsibility of making theology relevant to modern man's situation. Brunner had a flair for accenting Reformation doctrines in meaningful terms and published influential studies on Christ (*The Mediator*) in 1927; ethics (*The Divine Imperative*)

in 1932; man (*Man in Revolt*) in 1937; the Bible (*Revelation and Reason*) in 1941, and later his carefully-written *Dogmatics*.

BRUNO I (925–965) The son of German Emperor Henry I, and brother of German Emperor Otto I, Bruno was a German prince and bishop noted both for his statesmanship and scholarship in the 10th century Empire. Bruno was later canonized.

BRUNO of Cologne (1030–1101) A brilliant Medieval churchman who turned down numerous offers of advancement in the Church, Bruno withdrew to seclusion to start a monastery in the Chartreuse Valley in 1084. Taking its name from the Chartreuse, Bruno's Order became known as the Carthusians, and were distinguished for their solitude and silence. This Bruno was also canonized.

BRUNO of Querfurt (970[?]–1009) Another Bruno who became a saint, Bruno of Querfurt was a zealous German monk who served as a missionary to Poland, Hungary and Russia. He died a martyr's death in Lithuania in 1009.

BRYAN, William Jennings (1860–1925) A famous American Democratic politician and fundamentalist Presbyterian layman, William Jennings Bryan, after a career as a Congressman, ran unsuccessfully for the U.S. presidency three times, in 1896, 1900 and 1908, and served as Secretary of State from 1913–1915, until he fell out with President Wilson. Bryan is remembered in church history for his sturdy defense of an outmoded Biblical literalism at the famous Scopes Trial at Dayton, Tennessee in 1925, where an anti-evolutionary statute was tested. Although Bryan technically won his case, he revealed a scientific ignorance and a naïve literalistic understanding of the Bible under sharp cross-examination by defense lawyer Clarence Darrow. Bryan, savagely lampooned, died a few days after the trial.

BRUYAS, Jacques (1635–1712) A French Jesuit missionary to the Indians in French Canada, Bruyas was instrumental in ending the bloody Indian wars of 1700. He lived a long, useful life among the Indians, writing the first grammar in the Iroquois language.

BRUYS, Pierre de ([?]–1126[?]) One of Abélard's students at Paris, de Bruys preached proto-Protestant ideas in 12th-century France and attracted a following known as Petrobrucians. De Bruys, who declaimed against the doctrine of transubstantiation and the use of images in churches, was arrested as a heretic and burned alive.

BUCER See **BUTZER.**

BUCHAN, Elspeth Simpson (1738–1791) Scottish religious eccentric, Elspeth Buchan abandoned her husband and family, moved to Glasgow, where she persuaded a gullible minister named Hugh White that she personally was the saintly woman described in the twelfth chapter of Revelation, and that Rev. Mr. White was her son, the "man-child" described in the same chapter. Mrs. Buchan and Rev. Mr. White convinced others of their weird claims, set up a communal sect, naturally known as "Buchanites," and waited for Judgment Day. The last of the Buchanites died in 1848.

BUCHANAN, Claudius (1766–1815) A Scots-born Church of England clergyman who went as a missionary to India in 1791, Buchanan was an excellent linguist and persuasive organizer for the Anglican Church. He translated the Bible into Hindustani and Persian, and arranged to have the first bishop appointed to India.

BUCHANAN, George (1506–1582) Gentle Scottish scholar and teacher in the stormy 16th century, Buchanan lived and taught on the continent for many years where his humanist views increasingly got him into difficulty with Roman Catholic zealots and pushed him into the camp of the Reformers. Eventually, he threw in his lot completely with the Reformation. He returned to Scotland in 1560, took an active role in the Protestant Church of Scotland and gained fame as tutor to royalty and nobility, including young James VI of Scotland. Buchanan wrote the important treatise stating that the source of all political power is the people, which neither his pupil, King James, nor Parliament appreciated and later tried to suppress.

BUCHMAN, Frank Nathan Daniel (1878–1961) Pennsylvania-born Lutheran clergyman, Frank Buchman was the father of the "Buchmanite Movement," the "Oxford Group" and Moral Rearmament. After Y.M.C.A. work in Pennsylvania earlier in the 20th century, Buchman visited Oxford, England in 1921. He organized his first "Group" for mutual confession and commitment to idealistic living among students at Christ Church College, Oxford, and soon branched out internationally with his movement (dubbed the "Oxford Movement" by a South Africa newspaper in 1928). In 1938 Moral Rearmament was organized, to be a "God-guided campaign to prevent war by moral and spiritual awakening," and it tried to "change" dictators. Buchman's moralisms ("absolute honesty, absolute purity, absolute unselfishness and absolute love") and technique of weekend "house parties" in well-staffed mansions continued to bring followers. After the war, Buchman turned MRA attention to opposing communism.

BUGENHAGEN, Johann (1485–1558) German priest and humanist scholar who was converted to the Reformation by Luther, Bugenhagen joined Luther at Wittenberg in 1521 and became a loyal and effective associate. In 1528, he organized Reformed Churches for Luther in Hamburg and Brunswick, and in 1530, in Pomerania and Lübeck. Bugenhagen's pamphlets were often scathing attacks on opponents. He hardened the feeling between the Lutherans and the Zwinglians, who were dismissed as near-infidels because they held the Lord's Supper to be primarily a memorial of Christ's death.

In 1530, when the Emperor called a summit conference between Roman Catholics and Protestants at Augsburg, demanding that the Protestants present a statement outlining their stand and their criticisms of the Roman Church, Bugenhagen took a prominent part in drafting what came to be known as the Augsburg Confession. Bugenhagen was also instrumental in establishing Lutheranism in Scandinavia. In 1537, Bugenhagen went to Denmark, where he ordained seven Lutheran Danish bishops and organized the Danish Lutheran Church within five years.

BULLINGER, Heinrich (1504–1575) An influential Swiss Reformer, Bullinger succeeded Zwingli in 1531 as chief pastor at Zurich after Zwingli was killed at the battle of Kappel in the ill-advised venture to further the Reformation by force of arms. Bullinger, in contrast to his predecessor Zwingli, was conciliatory. Even during his pamphlet war with Luther and others over the meaning of the Lord's Supper, Bullinger avoided polemics and personalities. He was unusual in an age which emphasized differences; Bullinger sought for points of unity, did not demand rigid uniformity, and treated fellow Christians who differed with him with charity. In 1549 he worked with John Calvin on the *Concensus Tigurinus,* a careful study of the Lord's Supper, which was carefully read and had considerable influence. Bullinger's great work is the *Second Helvetic Confession,* completed in 1566. This well-written compendium of Reformed belief was adopted as the official reformed position of the Church in Switzerland, Hungary, Bohemia and elsewhere. Bullinger carried on a voluminous correspondence during his ministry, deeply influencing the Reformation in the mid-sixteenth century, not only on the continent but in England as well.

BUNYAN, John (1628–1688) Author of the widely-read *Pilgrim's Progress* and other religious books, Bunyan was an English Baptist dissenter. Bunyan, a tinker's son, was from the lower classes and lived a reprobate boyhood. At seventeen, he served in the Parliamentary Army against King Charles I and was deeply affected by the death of a comrade and by the pageantry of the military. Returning home in 1646, he went through a severe emotional crisis, part of which was described in *Grace Abounding.* His bad dreams, guilt and mental torment led the illiterate young man to careful religious investigation. Bunyan finally, in 1653, joined a nonconformist congregation at Bedford and began to preach. The death of his first wife in 1656 drove him to deep Bible study and unleashed a zeal in preaching.

Bunyan was at first treated with contempt by the Establishment, then with uneasiness as his speaking made a profound effect in the Bedford area. In 1660, with royalty restored in England, Bunyan was thrown into Bedford jail where he spent most of the next twelve years. He worried about his four small children, including a blind daughter and his new wife, but refused to agree to stop preaching as a condition for his release from jail. He tried to support his family while in jail by making shoelaces and began his writing.

Released in 1672, Bunyan was jailed a second time not long afterward. During this term he wrote his allegorical masterpiece, *Pilgrim's Progress*, which became an immediate best seller when published in 1678. After his final release, Bunyan was respected as an author and preacher. He died in 1688 from a chill incurred during a freezing rain while riding to bring about a reconciliation between a son and an angry father.

BURNET, Gilbert (1643–1715) Scotsborn Bishop in the Church of England who was one of the first broad churchmen, Burnet advocated earnestly for a plan of church union which could include non-conformists in an age more accustomed to imprisoning them. He served effectively for twenty-six years as Bishop of Salisbury. Frequently out of step with fellow Anglican clergy who were hostile to any show of toleration toward those not in the Church of England, Burnet even took the radical step of expressing a willingness to recognize non-episcopal orders.

BUSEMBAUM, Hermann (1600–1668) The German Roman Catholic theologian who wrote the sensational *Medulla Theologiae Moralis* (which went into forty-five editions) Busembaum was blamed by the French Parliament for the assassination attempt on the life of King Louis XV for allegedly giving Jesuit approval to murdering kings.

BUSHNELL, Horace (1802–1876) New England Congregationalist theologian, Horace Bushnell criticized the chilling Calvinistic orthodoxy of his time and stressed faith, while taking emotion and intuition into consideration. During the mid-nineteenth century in America, theology was primarily an exercise in logic and Christianity an appeal to the intellect. Bushnell tried to offset these tendencies but encountered stern opposition from his fellow-Congregationalists and most other fellow-theologians. Writing from Hartford, Connecticut, Bushnell presented fresh ideas on the Atonement, the Trinity, conversion and man. His *Christian Nurture*, published in 1847, was the first serious proposal that Christian conversion could be a gradual growth-process instead of sudden emotional upheaval.

BUTLER, Joseph (1692–1752) Church of England Bishop of Bristol (1738) and later (1750) Bishop of Durham, Joseph Butler was the author of the ponderous but then-influential *The Analogy of Religion, Natural and Revealed, to the Constitution and Course of Nature* (1736). Deism (the idea of God as a sort of Absentee Watchmaker who designed and set in motion the universe, then stepped out of the picture) threatened Christian thought in the 18th century. Rationalism deeply soaked Christian thinking during the same period so that Christianity was reduced almost to a system of do's and don't's based on divine law. Bishop Butler set out to refute the Deists. His *Analogy* took up the then-accepted idea that nature moved in a pre-planned, unchanging course and deduced that the probability was great for moral teachings also to be pre-planned and unchanging. Man has a limited knowledge of the natural world, Butler argued, and therefore he should not rule out the possibility of revelation or the miraculous. Butler maintained that every man had a divinely-implanted monitor over conduct (a conscience). Butler's effort to make the Gospel rationally explainable, and therefore acceptable, appealed to many intellectuals in the 18th century, but never touched people's wills. The masses were unmoved. Butler, a melancholy bachelor all his life, typified English church life before the Wesleyan revival.

BUTZER, Martin (also Bucer) (1491–1551) A peace-loving German Reformer, Martin Butzer effectively served at Strassburg during the controversy-filled formative years of the Reformation. Butzer left the Dominican order after encountering Martin Luther, married a nun and embarked on a career as a Reformer in 1522. He settled in Strassburg, and occupied an influential role, both in the life of that city and in the lives of fellow-Reformers.

When Calvin was banished from Geneva in 1538, Butzer welcomed him to Strassburg for three years. Butzer's thinking left its mark on Calvin. After Calvin's stay at Strassburg, his writings emphasized Butzer's stress on God as the one for whom all things are created, as well as Butzer's ideas on election, and his insistence on man's conformity to God's will.

Butzer used all his persuasive powers to bring about greater harmony among the strong-willed reformers and their followers. In 1531 he tried unsuccessfully to get a joint statement of faith acceptable to Lutherans, South Germans, Zwinglians and other Swiss reformers, and wrote *Confessio Tetrapolitana* to promote Protestant unity after Zwingli's death in the debacle at Zurich.

In 1548, Butzer was among those summoned to Augsburg to sign the *Interim,* an agreement drawn up between Protestants and Catholics which seemed to compromise the Reformed position. Butzer, however, showed backbone this time in refusing to accede to princely pressure. He did not sign. He stirred up opposition by his refusal to sign and accepted an invitation from Archbishop Cranmer of England to come to Cambridge the following year, 1549. Butzer taught with distinction at Cambridge the remaining two years of his life and acted briefly as a consultant on the revision of the English Book of Common Prayer before his death in 1551.

BYINGTON, Cyrus (1793–1868) One of the earliest and most dedicated American missionaries to the Indians, Byington was a Congregationalist working among the Choctaws. He compiled a grammar and a dictionary of the Choctaw language.

C

CABRINI, Frances Xavier (1850–1917) The first United States citizen to be named a saint in the Roman Catholic Church, Mother Cabrini was born in Italy, where she was twice turned down by Catholic orders because of poor health and rejected as an applicant for mission work in China. She finally was admitted to a small, disorganized religious order which she energetically galvanized and re-named the Mission Sisters of the Sacred Heart. Mother Cabrini's winsome personality and persuasive enthusiasm won over Pope Leo XIII, and in 1909 she was sent to the United States to work among the Italian immigrants. Although she traveled widely throughout the rest of her life, Mother Cabrini became a U.S.A. citizen and based her operations in the United States.

CAECILIAN (4th c.) A deacon of the Church in North Africa during the horrible Diocletian persecution and the squabbles known as the Donatist controversy, Caecilian was elected and consecrated Bishop of Carthage in 311.

There was ill feeling toward those who had taken a compromising position during the persecution, and the strict faction refused to accept Caecilian as bishop because the one who had ordained him had been guilty of apostasy (by giving up copies of Scriptures) during the persecution. The strict faction insisted Caecilian's ordination was invalid, and chose an alternate, Majorinus, as bishop. Many, however, felt that the real and unspoken reason for Caecilian's

removal was because he was an obnoxious personality. Caecilian was reduced to deacon and the Church reduced to disorder. Those supporting the stricter faction put in Donatus as Majorinus' successor and came to be known as Donatists. Emperor Constantine finally stepped in to try to put an end to the sorry situation where Christian was persecuting Christian in North Africa.

Caecilian arrogantly continued to exercise his prerogatives as bishop.

CAEDMON ([?]–680) The earliest Christian poet in England, Caedmon was an illiterate pig-keeper at Whitby Abbey who had a vision in which he claimed he was told to sing verses in praise of God. Caedmon astounded everyone by uttering verses of singular beauty. Hilda, the abbess, ordered Caedmon to be received into the Abbey as one of the brethren.

Throughout the rest of his life the learned brothers of the Abbey would recount Bible stories and Christian doctrine to the unlettered Caedmon, who subsequently worked the material into religious verse. His best-known work is his *Paraphrase*, a hymn-rendition of the stories of Genesis, Exodus and a section of Daniel. He died in the same year in which Hilda, his protector and "discoverer," died.

CAESARIUS (469[?]–542) Bishop of Arles in southern France, Caesarius was an educated, dedicated monk from Lerins who promoted the idea of purgatory in the Church. In 502 Caesarius was appointed bishop, soon moved effectively to counteract taints of Pelagianism (the theory that a man could save himself by his own good works and human efforts). In 529 he convened a small synod at Orange and later persuaded Pope Boniface II to endorse the recommendations of Orange against Pelagianism. Caesarius is best known, however, for his rigid views on Purgatory, the place of purging fire after death before judgment, an intermediate state between death and judgment.

Pope Gregory the Great a few years later taught that belief in purgatory was essential to the Christian faith.

CAIUS, Pope ([?]–296) Although a relative of Emperor Diocletian, Pope Caius was among those who died during Diocletian's bloody persecution of Christians at Rome.

CAJETANUS, Thomas Vio (1469–1534) A haughty but learned Roman Catholic theologian, Cajetanus was a cardinal serving as papal legate at Augsburg, Germany when Martin Luther was beginning his call for Church reform at Wittenberg. Cajetanus was noted as an authority on Thomas Aquinas' writings and respected as a power in the Roman hierarchy.

In 1518 Luther's writings had aroused the ire of Pope Leo X, who summoned Luther to Rome for a hearing. Luther's protector, Elector Frederick "the Wise" cannily arranged to save Luther's skin by transferring the hearing from Rome to Augsburg under Cajetanus.

Cajetanus summarily ordered Luther to retract. Luther refused and later wrote that Cajetanus was no more fit to handle his case than an ass to play a harp—a theme quickly taken up by cartoonists who pictured the pope himself as an ass playing an instrument.

CALAMY, Edmund (1600–1666) An English Presbyterian minister who was actively involved in the religious-political turmoil and controversies of his day, Calamy, although sharing the same general theological view with Cromwell, stood for royalty and against Cromwell. Later, however, after the restoration of royalty, Calamy was imprisoned with many others for illegally preaching after the Uniformity Act of 1662.

CALDERWOOD, David (1575–1650) A Church of Scotland Presbyterian so opposed to Episcopal authority that he was banished by James VI in 1617, Calderwood returned to Scotland after James' death and worked on the Scottish Church's *Directory for Public Worship* and an authoritative history of the Kirk.

CALIXTUS I (Bishop of Rome) ([?]–224) An aggressive, domineering early Bishop of Rome during persecutions and controversies, Calixtus I had been born a slave, worked unsuccessfully in banking and been banished to the mines of Sardinia for his faith for a time. Calixtus, on becoming Bishop in 217, pushed the position of Bishop of Rome to unprecedented position and prominence; he was the first to issue in his own name regulations absolving those guilty of certain fleshly sins and readmitting them to Church membership —a step which greatly advanced papal authority. Under Calixtus the Bishop of Rome developed greatly into what came to be the papacy. More politician than theologian, Calixtus I realized the destructive effects of the discord over theological issues in the early Church. In 217 he excommunicated Sabellius for teaching that the Father, Son and Holy Spirit were all one and the same instead of three distinct modes or personae of God and accused the learned Hippolytus, the great exponent of *Logos Christology*, with bitheism (two gods). Calixtus' heavy-handed attempt to produce peace, however, brought more ill-feelings as Hippolytus angrily set himself up as a rival bishop of Rome and established a rival church. Calixtus I died a martyr in 224 and he was canonized. His name today is perpetuated primarily by the famous catacombs under Rome which bear his name.

CALIXTUS II, Pope ([?]–1124) Able statesman and vigorous defender of papal claims, Calixtus II served as pope from 1119 to 1124. He checkmated a counter-pope Gregory VIII in 1120 and, without rivals in the Church, set about to down rivals on the thrones.

For the preceding century the growing claims of national emperors and the claims of the papacy had been causing conflict. Certain German kings insisted on the right of choosing and installing German bishops.

Calixtus II worked out the compromise known as the Concordat of Worms in 1122. This arrangement saved face for both Henry V of Germany and Calixtus, and meant that in Germany any new bishop had to be approved by both crown and Church, but also meant that in Italy, Calixtus' powers were expanded. In effect, Calixtus II won acknowledgment that the papacy was at least on a par with secular states.

CALIXTUS III, Pope ([?]–1458) A grim Spaniard by the name of Alfonso Borgia who took the name of Calixtus III in 1455, this pope tried to rouse Europe to another crusade to throw the Moslems out of Constantinople (which they captured in 1453, two years before Calixtus' elevation as pope). Europe, tired of Crusades and preoccupied with home problems, ignored Calixtus' appeals. His most popular and memorable act during his three years as pope was officially to vindicate the beloved Maid of Orleans, Joan of Arc. Calixtus III

promoted his infamous nephew, Rodrigo Borgia, who ultimately became Pope Alexander VI and the father of the notorious Cesare and Lucrezia Borgia.

CALLUSTUS See **CALIXTUS.**

CALVIN, John (1509–1564) Called "the greatest theologian and disciplinarian of the great race of the reformers" and "the only international reformer," John Calvin (or Jean Cauvin) was born at Noyon, France, son of the secretary and attorney for the bishopric of Noyon. Calvin, a brilliant scholar, trained first for law and studied at Paris, Orléans and Bourges. He sat under some of the most learned humanists and by 1532 published his erudite, humanist book, *Commentary on Seneca's Treatise on Clemency.*

About the time Calvin was twenty-three he experienced what he himself called a "sudden conversion"—an experience he refused to elaborate on except to state that God addressed him through the Bible and had to be obeyed. Calvin from then on was a fervent Christian. Later, he adopted as his crest a flaming heart on an outstretched hand with the inscription, "My heart I give Thee, wholly and freely."

Calvin, after his conversion, however, had no immediate plans of breaking with the Roman Church but desired reform. In 1533 his close associate Nicholas Cop was installed as rector of the University of Paris. Cop's inaugural address (although not ghost-written by Calvin, nonetheless was deeply influenced by Calvin's thinking) asked for Church reform, and stirred up a storm. Calvin and Cop were forced to flee from Paris and, after a brief jail term at Noyon, to get out of France and to safety at Basel, Switzerland. By this time Calvin was compelled to break with

Rome and take his stand with the reformers.

Early in 1535, when Calvin was still only twenty-six years old, King Francis I of France tried to excuse his persecution of French Protestants by trumping up charges of sedition and anarchy against them. Calvin, incensed at the slander being directed against his friends, completed the treatise on which he had been working since his flight from Paris. This treatise, called the *Institutes of the Christian Religion,* was a comprehensive and orderly summary of Christian reformed doctrine. Calvin's *Institutes,* later to go through many editings and enlargements until the final edition, 1559, was and is one of the most influential contributions to Christian literature and western thought.

The *Institutes* were first published in 1536 and, along with a courteously-worded letter, sent to the French King, Francis I, as a systematic presentation of the Protestant position. Calvin's key thoughts were clearly and forcefully spelled out. God is absolute Sovereign in His Creation. As Sovereign, God both foreknows and foreordains all things, including man's destiny. Man, though originally pure, has fallen through Adam's disobedience and is sinful. Man can be saved only by the undeserved grace of God, as mediated through Jesus Christ; man cannot earn his own salvation through good works. Those predestined to be saved by God will not be able to resist God's grace. It is important to note that for Calvin his doctrine of election was a source of comfort, *not* armchair philosophizing about who is or is not predestined to be saved. To Calvin and his readers, predestination meant that God had a plan of salvation, had called them to be His fellow workers, stood by them in the midst of opposition and would

ultimately prevail. Calvinism produced strong, confident men.

On his way to Strassburg, in 1536, shortly after the "Institutes" were published, John Calvin was forced to detour through Geneva because of fighting. He intended to spend the night in Geneva, continue to Strassburg and settle down in a quiet library to devote his life in quiet, scholarly studies. Fiery William Farel, frantically trying to keep the reformed cause alive in Geneva, insisted that Calvin remain. Except for three years' banishment at Strassburg from 1538 to 1541, Calvin remained at Geneva the rest of his life, until 1564.

From the first, Calvin's stay at Geneva was packed with tension and controversy. Calvin, however, had an immediate impact on the city, getting the Little Council of Geneva to adopt his recommendations to stem the immoral practices through rigorous church discipline, to impose a confession of faith on the citizenry, and to accept a catechism. An opposition party, however, undermined all that Calvin had accomplished by passing laws making civil authority binding on all church affairs. Calvin was banished.

Calvin's three years in banishment at Strassburg were happy and productive years. He found time to woo a wife and to begin his exegetical studies of Scriptures. When the opposition party at Geneva was disgraced in 1541 and others invited him to return to Geneva, Calvin was reluctant to leave Strassburg.

Calvin on his return took advantage of his new popularity and had the Council pass his *Ordonnances,* a complete constitution, which completely directed the civil and religious affairs of Geneva. Although Calvin was never more than merely a citizen and pastor, he influenced the *Consistoire* (the committee of laymen and ministers which in reality ruled Geneva) to supervise the activities of each citizen. His public image, unfortunately, was that of an austere autocrat. Although he gained an international reputation and attracted thousands of refugees to Geneva, he was disliked by many in Geneva, especially by the old "first families."

The opposition to Calvin welled up a second time. By 1553, Calvin's fall was imminent when the Servetus episode exploded in Geneva. Michael Servetus, a flamboyant skeptic with exasperating mannerisms, had written a tract denying the Trinity, the efficacy of infant baptism and the accepted orthodox viewpoint on the two natures of Jesus Christ. Servetus moved to Geneva in 1553 and persistently stirred up the opposition against Calvin. Calvin, badgered into a showdown trial between Servetus and himself, won. Unfortunately, however, the authorities insisted on burning Servetus at the stake. Calvin, although perhaps technically not responsible for this severe sentence, nonetheless has the blot on his record of being a party to the death of Servetus.

Servetus' death, however, made Calvin the unchallenged power at Geneva. Calvin corresponded widely with the leading thinkers of Europe. In 1559, he founded what became the University of Geneva. Great numbers of Protestant refugees swelled into Geneva to absorb the Genevan Reformation. These later carried Calvinism home to Scotland, the Netherlands, Hungary, France, England and Poland. Under Calvin, Geneva became what John Knox of Scotland called "the purest school of Christ on earth." Calvin died in 1564. True to the end to his idea that glory belongs to God alone, not to any man, he was buried in such an insignificant, poorly-marked spot that today no one knows the exact location of his grave.

CAMERON, Richard (1648[?]–1680)
A stern, uncompromising pastor in southwestern Scotland during the days when Kings Charles II and James II of England rode roughshod over nonconformists, Cameron incited a group of Covenanters to resist the government. The British government brutally moved to suppress Cameron and his Covenanters. Cameron fled briefly to Holland, returned to Scotland in 1679 and, although it was illegal to hold armed assemblies for worship, rallied his band of followers. The Covenanter force was cut down at the battle of Bothwell Bridge; Cameron and his fanatic guerilla followers were hunted down and brutally murdered. The surviving holdouts among Cameron's supporters bitterly refused to become associated with other worshippers. Taking the name "Reformed Presbyterians," but nicknamed "Cameronians," the doughty Covenanters preserved their identity for three centuries.

CAMPBELL, Alexander (1786–1866)
Son of Thomas Campbell (see below), Alexander, like his father was a deeply evangelical pastor from the Secession Presbyterian Church of northern Ireland who emigrated to the Pennsylvania frontier. Alexander Campbell's father, Thomas, had come to America in 1807, but had incensed fellow Secession Presbyterians by his custom of magnanimously welcoming Presbyterians of all shades and sects to the Lord's Supper. By the time Alexander Campbell joined his father in 1809, Thomas Campbell had withdrawn from the Secession Presbyterians and set up "The Christian Association of Washington" for Washington County, Pennsylvania).

Alexander Campbell was an extraordinarily gifted organizer and effective preacher. He quickly assumed leadership of the new movement, organized "for the sole purpose of promoting simple, evangelical Christianity." The Campbells, father and son, continued to insist that they did not intend to found a new denomination, but to provide an opportunity for fervent Christians to be welcomed without tests of creed or ritual. Nevertheless, in 1811, the Campbells organized the Brush Run congregation, near Bethany, West Virginia.

Eschewing any practice not specifically sanctioned in the New Testament, the Campbells stated, "Where the Scriptures speak, we speak; where the Scriptures are silent, we are silent!" In 1812 both Campbells were baptized by immersion after finding no warrant for infant baptism or sprinkling baptism in the Scriptures. They insisted on baptism by immersion and for a number of years were associated with Baptist associations in western Pennsylvania and eastern Ohio. The Campbells, however, were not altogether happy with the Baptists and the Baptists were not comfortable with the Campbells. The Baptists continued to stress a strict Calvinism and put great emphasis on the Old Testament. The Baptists taught that baptism was a privilege for someone who had already been forgiven. Alexander Campbell maintained that baptism was a condition for God's forgiveness. These theological differences eventually caused the Campbells to sever their connections with the Baptists completely in 1830. The followers of the Campbells, popularly known as Campbellites, were in form, if not in fact, a separate denomination, calling themselves "Disciples of Christ."

Alexander Campbell stated when he was baptized, "I will be baptized only into the primitive Christian faith," and throughout his long, useful lifetime maintained this rugged commitment to recovering the simplicity and spontaneity of the first-century Church. Ahead of his time in many ways, he was one of the first to rescue the Lord's Supper from the obscurity of occasional observance and insisted that the Communion Service should be part of worship each week.

Alexander Campbell founded Bethany College, wrote, traveled and lectured widely in the U.S.A. and abroad. He was a sharp debater and bested many orators in public formal confrontations.

In his later years Campbell preached the imminent Second Coming of Christ. The date he fixed, 1866, was the year in which he died. His remarkable personality had brought into existence an energetic group of congregations which have made a deep and lasting contribution to American church life.

CAMPBELL, Thomas (1763–1854) Father of the illustrious Alexander Campbell (see above), Thomas Campbell was a Secession Presbyterian minister of County Antrim, northern Ireland, who settled in southwestern Pennsylvania in 1807. Thomas Campbell, one of the earliest advocates of Christian unity, in the spirit of the Upper Room, welcomed Presbyterians regardless of denominational background to the Lord's Supper. He brought down the ire of Chartiers Presbytery of the Secession Church in Pennsylvania and was formally censured. Thomas Campbell protested the narrowness of the Presbytery, claiming that Christian discipleship should conform strictly to the New Testament. He broke with the Secession Church in 1809 and preached to those joining his "Christian Association of Washington." Thomas Campbell was the author of the notable document known as the *Declaration and Address,* the "Magna Carta" of the Disciples of Christ.

In 1809 Thomas Campbell's son, Alexander, joined the family in America and rapidly surpassed the father in eminence. Both the Campbells, Thomas and Alexander, insisted on strict adherence to what the Scriptures enjoined, yet showed a breadth and generosity highly unusual for a time noted for its sectarianism.

CAMPEGGIO, Lorenzo (1474–1539) A learned Italian lawyer who took up a career in the Church after his wife's death in 1510, Campeggio became a skillful troubleshooting for various popes. He won wealth and advancement in the worldly-minded 16th century Church—a palace and large sums, a cardinal's hat and the titles (and income) as Bishop of Salisbury and Archbishop of Bologna.

Campeggio was a master diplomat; in 1524 he saved most of southern Germany for the Roman Catholic Church from Lutheranism and set off the Counter-Reformation by organizing the cities of south Germany into the League of Regensburg. His skills also brought peace after Pope Clement VII had been abducted and Rome sacked in 1527. Campeggio's talents were used to the fullest during the trial granting King Henry VIII his divorce from Catherine of Aragon. Carrying a secret "Decretal" or commission from the pope prohibiting the court from sentencing Henry without explicit orders and instructing the Campeggio to drag out the hearings as long as possible, Campeggio cleverly managed to carry out his instructions to avoid (a) offending Emperor Charles V, (b) sentencing King Henry VIII, (c) revealing his secret instructions to the wrong parties.

CAMPION, Edmund (1540–1581) English Jesuit priest during the intrigues and rumors of a Catholic take-over in Elizabethan England, Campion was a learned young priest who clung to Roman theology but not to Roman political schemes. Originally an Anglican deacon, he was hounded from his Oxford teaching post in 1569, forced to take refuge with exiled Catholic Bishop William Allen at Douai, France. In France he formally joined the Roman Catholic Church and at Rome in 1573 took Jesuit orders. Campion and a companion, Robert Parsons, smuggled themselves back to England in 1580, disguised as tea merchants. Campion carried out a ministry clandestinely to those still secretly holding to Roman Catholic views but was discovered, seized and imprisoned in the Tower of London. The anti-Catholic hysteria of the times, fanned by the threat of the Spanish Armada invading England, caused the courts to inflict the death penalty on Campion, although he was completely innocent of any seditious plots.

CANDLISH, Robert Smith (1806–1873) A Scots pastor who, with Thomas Chalmers, insisted on the independence of the Church from civil authorities, Candlish joined the group in the Disruption of 1843 which established the Free Church of Scotland. Candlish became the most respected leader of the Free Church after Chalmers' death in 1847, and from 1862 until his death was the distinguished principal of New College, Edinburgh.

CANNON, James, Jr. (1864–1944) Colorful and outspoken American Methodist Bishop in the early 20th century, Bishop Cannon, active in the Anti-Saloon League, helped promote the Prohibition Amendment in the U.S. Constitution. His zealous prohibition views led him to oppose publicly Alfred E. Smith as the Democratic Presidential candidate in the election of 1928 because of Smith's "wet" position.

CANO, Melchior (or Canus) (1525–1560) Spanish theologian of influence in the Roman Catholic Church during the reaction period known as the Counter-Reformation, Cano was a leading spokesman for the Spaniards at the Church's Council of Trent, 1545–63. Cano insisted that the Church needed reform more than it needed new doctrine. He boldly issued his *Consultatio Theologica* in 1556, advising the Spanish king to resist the temporal claims of the pope by standing up for his rights and handling Church funds in Spain himself. Pope Paul IV never forgave Cano for weakening Spain's dependence on Rome. Cano's reputation rests largely on his massive *De Locis Theologicis Libri XII*, published after his death. *De Locis Theologicis* is a systematic theology with Renaissance overtones which claims that the authority of Scripture rests on the authority of the Church (rather than the other way around, as Protestantism claims), and that both Scripture and Church tradition are to be regarded as authoritative. Cano carefully presented the position of the Roman Catholic Church and outlined what has become normative Roman Catholic doctrine.

CANSTEIN, Karl Hildebrand, Frieherr von (1667–1719) Friend of the great German pietist educator and social worker, Herman Francke, Baron von Canstein lived at Halle, Germany during the great upsurge of awareness of social need in Germany in the early 18th century. In 1710, von Canstein founded the world-renowned Bible House, the father of all Bible Societies, to publish and circulate inexpensive copies of the Bible. Baron von Canstein was one of many German nobles enlisted for philanthropic service by Francke.

CANTWELL, John Joseph (1874–1947) The fearless partisan for cen-sorship of the movies, Cantwell in 1936 was the first Roman Catholic Archbishop of Los Angeles. Bishop Cantwell, also prominent in film industry labor disputes, crusaded against immorality in motion pictures and agitated for the creation of the first watchdog over Hollywood films, The Legion of Decency.

CANUTE IV (1040–1086) A king of Denmark who was murdered by rebels among his own troops during a campaign against England's William the Conqueror, Canute, although an unpopular, built so many churches that he was canonized in 1101. He died kneeling at the altar after an attack by rebellious subjects. He is venerated as the patron saint of the Danes.

CAPITO, Wolfgang (1478–1541) Lesser-known reformer, Capito was a German Benedictine monk who was attracted to the Reformation by Zwingli's preaching and Luther's personal letters. In 1523, he moved to Strassburg where he took an active part in the affairs of the Reformed Church until his death in 1541.

CARAFFA See PAUL IV, Pope.

CAREY, William (1761–1834) Indefatigable pioneer of the modern missionary movement, William Carey began his career as an illiterate cobbler at Northamptonshire, England. Carey became a fervent Christian, joining the Baptist Church when he was twenty-one, tacked a map of the world over his cobbler's bench, and began to educate himself. He meanwhile began to preach.

In 1787, he became the pastor of a Baptist Church at Leicester/ and created the ferment which eventually resulted in the Baptist Society for Propagating the Gospel Among the Heathen. In 1792 he wrote the weighty *Enquiry into the*

Obligation of Christians to Use Means for the Conversion of the Heathens and preached a powerful sermon from Isaiah 54:2–3, which broke the resistance to the idea of going overseas to evangelize.

Carey was among the first to offer his services to the newly-established Baptist mission society in 1792. In spite of powerful opposition among certain merchants, churchmen and government officials, Carey finally reached Bengal in 1793, but immediately lost all of his equipment in the Hugli River. He resourcefully took charge of an indigo factory at Malda, learned Bengali, and began the first of numerous translations of the Bible into Indian dialects. In 1799, Carey moved his operations to Serampore and soon set up a church, school and printing shop to publish translations of the Bible and religious literature. Carey, an exceptionally gifted, hard-working linguist, mastered Sanskirt, Mahratta, Bengali, Punjabi, Telinga and Bhotanta, acquired a working knowledge of numerous local dialects and served as professor of Oriental languages at the Fort William, India, College.

Somehow, Carey also found time to make contributions to science as a competent botanist. His personal life, however, was full of tragedy, with his children and wife all succumbing to the diseases and climate of India. On one occasion, years of painstaking work at producing a Sanskrit dictionary were wiped out one night when a fire destroyed his printing shop. Nonetheless, Carey during his lifetime produced more than 200,000 Bibles and Scripture tracts in forty different languages and dialects.

Carey's reports from India had a great effect in promoting interest in the overseas mission of the Church. His remarkable career stimulated the formation of Missionary Societies and Boards in the late 18th century and early 19th century in nearly every denomination in Britain and America.

CARGILL, Donald (1619–1681) A blunt-spoken Scottish Covenanter minister forced to turn renegade for his criticism of episcopacy and the Stewart kings (who were trying to impose conformity to episcopal forms), Cargill led an outlaw band on the bleak moors of southwestern Scotland until he was finally run down, tried and beheaded.

CARHEIL, Etienne de (1633–1726) A tireless, energetic French Jesuit missionary to North America who, driven from Iroquois territory at Cayuga, patiently started over again at desolate Mackinac.

CARLSTADT, Andreas Rudolf Bodenstein (1480[?]–1541) An erratic and radical German reformer, Carlstadt was a colleague of Luther for a time at Wittenberg until his views grew too radical for Luther.

In 1521, during Luther's absence from Wittenberg, the somewhat unstable Carlstadt tried to turn Luther's reform efforts into a revolution, advocating abolition of confession, the elevation of the host, use of priestly garb, clerical celibacy (he himself married in 1522) and use of pictures and images. Riots against the mass broke out, with much needless destruction of church art and property. Luther returned in March, 1522, and Carlstadt left in disgrace. He lived in obscurity and occasional poverty most of the rest of his life, fulminating against Luther for a time, and then in 1530 settled in Switzerland, where he worked with the Zwinglian reformers until his death.

CAROLI, Pierre (1507[?]–1564) A vain, disputatious opportunist, Caroli was a semi-Protestant who annoyed Calvin and the Genevan reformers, accusing Calvin of heresy. His constant badgering finally brought about a trial in which Calvin was embarrassed by being made to appear to be against the traditional creeds. (Calvin in actuality had stated he accepted the creeds only so far as they were faithful to the Word of God). Caroli's scandalous personal life finally discredited him, while Calvin vindicated himself of the charges of heresy. Caroli went back to France in 1537 and rejoined the Roman Catholics, broke with Rome again in 1539 and rejoined the Protestants a second time but fluttered back into the Roman fold still again in 1543.

CARPZOV, Johann Benedikt (1639–1699) Descended from a distinguished German family of jurists, educators and theologians (several having the same name: Johann Benedikt Carpzov), Carpzov was an arrogant Hebrew expert and Protestant pastor at Leipzig who mercilessly harassed the gentle German pietist, Hermann Francke.

CARROLL, John (1735–1815) American Roman Catholic Archbishop John Carroll was the distinguished leader of Roman Catholicism at the time the American colonies became the United States. Carroll was ordained a Jesuit priest in 1769 in Europe, where he studied and taught for a time, but returned to his native Maryland in 1774. He supported the cause of American independence and accompanied Benjamin Franklin on the unsuccessful mission to enlist French-Canadian support for the American Revolution. Instrumental in getting Rome to recognize the American Roman Catholic Church as a body distinct from the British, Carroll was appointed prefect apostolic in 1775, a few years later, Bishop, and, in 1808, Archbishop. Overcoming anti-Catholic hostility in the predominantly Protestant communities and ameliorating ethnic jealousies between the immigrant Catholic groups, Carroll carefully laid the foundations for a strong Roman Catholic witness in the young Republic.

CARSTARES, William (or Carstairs) (1649–1715) Scottish pastor who was involved in the plots against Charles II and James II of England, Carstares became a friend and supporter of William of Orange in Holland while still a student. Because of his immense influence in William's Court, he was dubbed "Cardinal" Carstares. He used this influence to strengthen the independent position of the Church of Scotland.

CARTWRIGHT, Peter (1785–1872) Rough-hewn but eloquent backwoods Methodist circuit rider, Peter Cartwright was an ill-educated gambling youngster who was dramatically converted in 1801. By the following year he made a name for himself as the "Kentucky Boy" preacher, and was ordained a deacon in 1806 by Bishop Asbury of the Methodist Church. Preaching to frontier congregations in Illinois, and in Kentucky, Cartwright spent a long, fruitful life developing Methodism and furthering education. Cartwright was deeply involved in Illinois politics, serving in the State legislature and unsuccessfully running against Abraham Lincoln for Congress in 1846.

CARTWRIGHT, Thomas (1535[?]–1603) A much persecuted English Puritan who firmly held to the Presbyterian form of Church government (rule by elders), Thomas Cartwright was a learned Cambridge University professor in 1569. He insisted that there was no difference in status between laity and clergy and called for democratic procedure in which elders would govern a local parish, the people would elect their own pastor and the hierarchy of archbishops and bishops would be ended.

Cartwright deeply influenced Puritan thinking but earned the enmity of powerful Anglicans, particularly John Whitgift, Vice Chancellor at Cambridge. Cartwright was fired from Cambridge in 1570 and hounded until he finally fled to the continent. In spite of the fact that Cartwright emphatically opposed separating from the Church of England and criticized the early Congregationalists for separating from the established church, he was imprisoned several times when he tried to return to England.

CARVAJAL, Gaspar de ([?]–1584) A Spanish Dominican who accompanied early explorers (including Pizarro) on expeditions to Peru in 1533 and 1538, de Carvajal founded many towns, Indian missions and Spanish colonies in South America.

CARY, Lot (1780[?]–1828) The brilliant, persistent and resourceful slave from Virginia who worked and saved to buy his own freedom and his family's in 1813, and who educated himself to become a scholarly Baptist minister, Lot Cary joined the emigrant American Negro group which went to the west coast of Africa. Cary was one of the founders of the Republic of Liberia.

CASSIAN, John (360[?]–435[?]) A famous hermit and one of the founders of monasticism in western Europe, John Cassian (sometimes known as Johannes Massiliensis) was born in southern France but spent his most formative years in a monastery at Bethlehem and in solitude among the desert hermits in Egypt. Later returning to his native France, he founded what became large and influential religious orders at Marseilles, which reflected his inclination toward Eastern asceticism.

CASSIANUS, Johann Eremita See **CASSIAN.**

CASTELLIO, Sebastian (also Castalion) (1515–1563) A French humanist who became a Protestant theologian, Castellio was welcomed to Geneva by Calvin in 1541 and installed as rector of the college at Geneva. A few years later, however, 1545, Castellio and Calvin had a falling out over interpreting Scripture (Calvin insisted on allegorizing Song of Solomon; Castellio pointed out that it was an erotic love song). Castellio was banished and took up residence at Basel, Switzerland and became a professor at the university. Appalled at the atrocity in which Servetus was burned in Geneva, Castellio, writing in both French and Latin under the pseudonym "Martin Bellie," denounced Calvin's treatment of Servetus and pleaded for tolerance. The sensitive Castellio was one of the few at the time who did not applaud Servetus' death.

CASTELNAU, Pierre de ([?]–1208) A French Cistercian monk sent as the Inquisitor to root out the Cathari and Albigensi (sects of dissidents holding Protestant views before the Reformation in southern France and northern Italy), Castelnau was murdered, causing the furious Pope Innocent III to unleash atrocities against the Cathari and Albigensi.

CATHERINE of Bologna (1413–1463) An Italian saint, Catherine, although raised in luxury at Ferrara, returned to her hometown of Bologna to found the well-known convent of the Holy Sacrament of the Order of Poor Clares.

CATHERINE of Genoa (1447–1510) A mystic who claimed to see visions, Saint Catherine of Genoa, widowed in her teens, responded to one of her visions and devoted the rest of her life caring for the poor and ill, especially during plagues which decimated Genoa in 1497 and 1501.

CATHERINE of Siena (1347–1380) Popular and famous saint and mystic during the early Italian Renaissance, Catherine of Siena joined the Dominican Tertiaries at the age of sixteen and devotedly tended the ill and the dying most of her life. She claimed to receive divinely-sent visions and became respected as a mystic. Catherine frequently spoke out on contemporary issues, however, and showed exceptional insight and judgment in practical affairs. More than anyone else, Catherine was responsible for the return of the papacy from Avignon to Rome in 1376. Catherine unsparingly denounced the clergy for its greed and immorality, and arranged for a reconciliation between the pope and the city of Florence in 1378. Advisor to popes, kings and other leaders in her time, Catherine of Siena offered political as well as spiritual counsel.

CATHERINE of Sweden (1331–1381) Another saint named Catherine, Catherine of Sweden succeeded her famous mother, St. Brigitta, as Abbess of the Convent at Vadstena, where she performed many charitable acts.

CAUCHON, Pierre ([?]–1442) The odious French prelate who condemned Joan of Arc and handed her over to be burned, Cauchon was later so loathed that after his death Pope Calixtus IV had his body exhumed and dumped into a common sewer.

CECILIA (3rd c.) The patron saint of musicians, Cecilia, according to tradition, was a young Roman noblewoman who converted her husband and his brother and a would-be executioner before finally dying as a martyr. Also known as Cecily, legends abound about her musical abilities.

CELESTINE I, Pope ([?]–432) Pope from 422 to 432 during the heated, divisive and unnecessary contest between Nestorius of Antioch and Cyril of Alexandria, Celestine I became embroiled in the politics of the fight. Celestine I sided with the flattering, ambitious Cyril and excommunicated Nestorius for allegedly denying that there were two natures in Christ and for attacking Cyril's expression *"Theotokos"* for Jesus' Mother, meaning "Mother of God." The two emperors, Valentinian III of the West and Theodosius II of the East, tried unsuccessfully to paper over the differences at the Council of Ephesus. Celestine I emerged as a heresy-hunting Pope; he sent special emissaries to Britain to root out Pelagianism, and had problems with his bishops in North Africa and in the Provence of Southern France. He was later canonized.

CELESTINE II, Pope ([?]–1144) Pope from 1143 to 1144, Celestine II lifted the interdict on France imposed by Innocent II.

CELESTINE III, Pope (1106–1198) Pope from 1191 to 1198.

CELESTINE IV, Pope ([?]–1241) Pope for only fifteen days in 1241, Celestine IV was rumored to have been poisoned.

CELESTINE V (1215–1296) An ascetic hermit, Celestine V was elected as a compromise pope at the age of seventy-nine, and served only a few months before abdicating. He is primarily remembered as the founder of the Celestines, a branch of the Benedictine order. Lacking administrative ability and naively duped by those opposing reform, he, returned to his cell under guard by orders of his successor and died a few months later.

CELESTIO See **COELESTIUS.**

CHALLONER, Richard (1691–1781) English Roman Catholic Bishop Challoner revised the English translation of the Douay-Rheims version of the Bible and wrote numerous devotional tracts, including the long popular *Garden of the Soul.*

CHALMERS, Thomas (1780–1847) Scottish Church leader in the "Disruption" of 1843 when one third of the pastors left the State Church of Scotland, Thomas Chalmers was spokesman for the Evangelical party. Chalmers was a brilliant mathematician and, although licensed as a preacher in 1799, made mathematics his main interest for a number of years. Personal bereavements, illness and disappointment (he was turned down for the Chair of Mathematics at Edinburgh University in 1805) changed his outlook and instead of the mathematician who happened to be a Christian preacher, Chalmers became a Christian who happened to be a mathematician. He moved from the party of cold legalists known as "Moderates" in the Church to that of the spiritually warm, fervent preachers known as "Evangelicals."

In 1815, in spite of opposition by the "Moderates," Chalmers became minister of Tron Kirk, Glasgow, and quickly emerged as spokesman and leader of the "Evangelicals." Noting the absence of neighborhood parish life, Chalmers galvanized the Scottish Church into an intensive church extension campaign to start new congregations in the burgeoning cities. Chalmers energetically revolutionized the pattern of Church life, putting immense stress on visitation by lay leaders and on education for children.

By 1841, a dispute was brewing in the Scottish Church over "patronage"— whether a minister could be installed in a congregation against the wishes of the congregation. In 1843, the civil courts threw out the Chalmers-inspired "veto" rule of the Scottish Church Assembly which stopped installation of pastors in congregations where there was majority opposition. Chalmers and 474 fellow ministers of the Church refused to countenance state interference in the affairs of the Church and withdrew from the State Church, insisting that the Church must be independent of state control. This group forsook salaries, manses and parishes and established the Free Church of Scotland. Chalmers, as Moderator, worked tirelessly to raise funds to sustain the ministers and establish a new denomination.

Chalmers' preaching, as exemplified by his famous sermon, "The Expulsive Power of a New Affection," emphasized the practical rather than theoretical side of Christian response to the Gospel. He also wrote on political science, economics and natural sciences.

CHAMBERLAIN, Jacob (1835–1908) One of the first American medical missionaries in the Dutch Reformed Church, Chamberlain went to India in 1860 where he established hospitals and translated church literature into local dialects.

CHANNING, William Ellery (1780–1842) Unofficial leader of the American Unitarian movement in its earliest days in 19th century New England, William Ellery Channing was scion of an ancient and distinguished New England family. Channing was caught up in the theological struggles in the New England Congregational Church and, uncomfortable with the stiff austere, legalistic Calvinism of the "orthodox" party, moved into and gradually beyond the camp of the "liberals."

Channing had difficulties accepting contemporary teaching on the Trinity and divinity of Jesus Christ. As late as 1808 in a sermon at John Codman's ordination, however, he referred to Jesus as "Divine Master" whose blood was "shed for souls." By 1819, however, Channing's sermon at Jared Sparks' ordination amounted to an attack on the current understanding of the Trinity, which, Channing said, was worded to sound like tritheism. Although few today know it, Channing took issue with the "orthodox" party primarily because it was so obscurantist. Channing criticized the semantics and the unbending refusal of the orthodox to define terms in meaningful contemporary phrases.

Although Channing was a mild and moderate man who shunned controversy, he was pulled into the debates wracking Congregationalism, and participated in the founding of the American Unitarian Association in 1825. Channing was a personal friend of and regular correspondent with many of the leading literary figures of his time, including Wordsworth and Coleridge in England, and Emerson and Horace Mann in America. His only pastorate was at Federal Street Church, Boston.

CHANTAL, Jane Frances, Baronne de (1572–1641) A French nun, later canonized, Mme. de Chantal was left a widow at an early age but with the guidance of St. Francis de Sales founded the Congregation of the Visitation of Our Lady at Annency.

CHARDIN de See **TIELHARD, Pierre de Chardin.**

CHARLEMAGNE (742–814) Organizing genius who welded western Europe's wild, warring tribes into a cohesive empire after fighting fifty-two campaigns, Charlemagne was King of the Franks and first German to bear the title Emperor of the West. Charlemagne backed the Church and introduced Christianity into every province, including the Saxons, the heathen hordes in what is now northeastern Germany and Denmark.

Although a warrior and unable to write, Charlemagne committed himself to spreading education and culture. Schools and monasteries appeared throughout Europe. Theological discussion revived.

Instead of seeing himself as a rival to the pope, Charlemagne looked on himself as Protector to the Pope. Grateful Pope Leo III crowned Charlemagne Emperor of the Romans on Christmas Day, 800, and State and Church seemed to be two sides of same shield which brought protection to Europe.

Charlemagne enabled the Church to minister and grow in unprecedented ways and personally participated in its activities (he inserted the Latin word *"Filioque"* in the Nicene Creed to show that the Holy Spirit proceeds from the Son as well as the Father, reformed the Frankish liturgy, imported singers to improve Church music and made frequent generous gifts).

When this magnetic and many-sided man died his empire disintegrated. Europe, however, for centuries looked back fondly to Charlemagne's rule as a golden age and brief revival of the glory of ancient Rome.

CHARLES I, King of England (1600–1649) Haughty, autocratic believer in the divine right of kings, Charles I succeeded his father, James I, in 1625, called and dismissed three Parliaments in four years because they refused to accede to him, then with typical Stuart stubbornness ruled England without Parliament for eleven years. He arbitrarily tried to impose Church of England forms of worship on Scotland and ignited a revolt in 1639. When he was forced to call the famous "Long Parliament" in 1640, he angrily arrested five leaders because Parliament refused again to be pliable. Civil War erupted. Cromwell and the Puritans took over the government. Charles was tried and beheaded in 1649.

CHARLES II, King of England (1630–1685) Son of Charles I, Charles II was the first King after the restoration of monarchy in England, following Cromwell's Protectorate. Crowned in 1660, Charles II proved to be a spoiled, dissolute weakling whose personal conduct encouraged immorality throughout the kingdom. The Puritan cause of sobriety and morality, and the status of non-conformists to the State Church, were jeopardized through ridicule and persecution during Charles' reign. Charles, a Roman Catholic sympathizer for years, became a Catholic convert on his deathbed.

CHARLES VII, King of France (1403–1461) Charles VII's claim to the throne was disputed by the English in 1422. His defense against the English was lagging, notably when Orléans was besieged. His cause was saved when the French were rallied by the charismatic Joan of Arc, 1429.

Charles VII, an effective ruler of France, in 1438 profited from his quarrel with Pope Nicholas V by appropriating some of the papal tax money taken from France and putting an end to papal interference in the French government.

CHARLES IX, King of France (1550–1574) An indolent, spineless playboy, Charles IX was dominated by his mother, the scheming, devious Catherine de' Medici, who in reality ruled France. Intrigues, plots, counterplots, three savage religious civil wars, assassinations and bitter strife between Roman Catholics and Protestants were the pattern of Charles IX's time. Feeling threatened by the Huguenots' (French Protestants') growing strength in France, fanatic Catherine persuaded Charles to agree to genocide for all Protestants in France. The ghastly St. Bartholomew's Day Massacre, August 24, 1572, took the lives of an estimated 50,000 Huguenot Protestant men, women and children.

CHARLES IX, King of Sweden (1550–1611) Crowned in 1604, after years of humiliations at the hands of his brother who even tried unsuccessfully to have Charles renounce his Protestant Calvinist faith, Charles burned up most of his energies during his reign by beating off attacks by Poland, Russia and Denmark. He is also credited with helping to plant Protestantism firmly in Sweden and prepare the way for the Protestant empire of the great Gustavus Adolphus.

CHARLES the Great See CHARLEMAGNE.

CHARLES the Martel (688[?]–741) The famous leader of the Franks who stopped the Moslem tide from engulfing Europe at the crucial Battle of Tours, 732, Charles earned his title, "Martel" or "The Hammer."

In 711, the Arabs conquered Spain; in 720, they pushed over the Pyrenees and marched on France. European civilization and the western Church were threatened. Charles Martel managed to unite the mutually-jealous factions in Gaul, raised an army and, by brilliant tactics, decisively defeated Abdur Rahman and the fanatic Moslem army, October, 732 (exactly 100 years after Mohammed's death). Martel's rule subsequently developed the feudal system. His grandson was the illustrious Charlemagne.

CHAUNCY, Charles (1592–1672) An influential scholar, preacher and theologian in colonial Massachusetts, Chauncy was born in England and served for a time as a vicar in the established church. He resisted Archbishop Laud's strict regulations for worship imposed on the English Church and was arrested twice and finally, in 1634, was suspended and imprisoned. Worn down by persecution, he allowed himself to be forced into recanting in 1637. Released, he felt such a deep sense of shame and guilt that he fled to America. From 1638 to 1641 he served at Plymouth, until he aroused opposition by insisting on immersing babies at baptism. In 1654, he became the second president of Harvard College.

CHAUNCY, Charles (1705–1787) Great-grandson of the Charles Chauncy who was the Harvard College president (see above), Charles Chauncy was a prominent Boston pastor at the historic First Church from 1727 until his death in 1787. Chauncy denounced the "Great Awakening" of the early 1740's as emotionalism and superficiality and was active in the "Old Light" party in New England which sneered at George Whitfield and the Great Awakening preachers. He briefly engaged in a pamphlet war with the great Jonathan Edwards in 1743 and, by his unitarian leanings, helped pave the way for the creation of the American Unitarian movement in the 19th century.

CHEMNITZ, Martin (1522–1586) A German Lutheran theologian who was converted by Luther to Protestantism at Wittenberg in 1545, Chem-

nitz became one of the first and most articulate adherents of the Reformer Melanchthon's theology. After a brilliant success as a professor at Wittenberg, Chemnitz accepted an administrative position in the church at Brunswick. He participated in the theological controversies in Protestantism but was respected for his tact and charity. He had a hand in writing the *Formula of Concord* in 1577, the last great Lutheran Creed.

CHEYNE, T. (Thomas) K. (Kelly) (1841–1915) English cleric and Old Testament scholar from 1868 to 1908 at Oxford. Cheyne was one of the first British Biblicists to insist on a broad and comprehensive study of the Bible in light of literary, historical and scientific considerations.

CHOWN, Samuel Dwight (1853–1933) A prominent Canadian Methodist clergyman, Chown was influential in bringing about the union of the Methodists, Congregationalists and Presbyterians in Canada in 1925 to form the United Church of Canada.

CHRISTOPHER (3rd c.) Apparently a Syrian baptized by St. Babylas, the Bishop of Antioch, Christopher died as a martyr somewhere in Asia Minor during the 3rd century. Christopher is one of those figures in history about whom few actual facts are known, but whose name is associated with dozens of legends. Because his name literally means "Christ Bearer," he is represented as an enormous person carrying the young boy Jesus on his shoulders across a river. St. Christopher's intercession was often sought during plagues, and his relics are found throughout Europe, particularly Spain.

CHRYSOSTOM, John (345[?]–407) Most popular and celebrated of the

Greek Fathers in the Church, John was such an effective preacher that he was posthumously accorded the title "Chrysostom," meaning "golden-mouthed." Influenced by his pious mother, Anthusa, Chrysostom forsook a promising career in elocution and rhetoric at Antioch in Syria, was baptized about 370, and spent ten years living a life of such rigorous self-denial as a desert hermit that he impaired his health.

For the next twelve years he preached at Antioch and turned out to be the greatest preacher in the Eastern Church. Chrysostom had no use for the pomp, luxury and loose living which were so prevalent in the Church and in the Court, and made enemies in both circles by his moral earnestness and unsparing attacks. (On one occasion, after his elevation as Archbishop of Constantinople in 398, he kicked out thirteen bishops for simony and immorality.)

The Empress Eudoxia, stinging from Chrysostom's public criticisms of her opulent living, teamed up with Chrysostom's jealous, unscrupulous rival, Theophilus, Patriarch of Alexandria, and found a pretext for putting Chrysostom on trial when Chrysostom welcomed four Egyptian monks known as "the tall brothers." Chrysostom's foes conspired to depose and banish him.

Although recalled briefly by the haughty but superstitious Eudoxia (after a public riot protesting Chrysostom's ousting threatened her palace), Chrysostom was formally and permanently exiled in 403. Chrysostom lived in the desolate town of Cucusus in the Taurus mountains in the depths of Armenia, but continued to exert a profound influence by his letters. The Empress then ordered him transferred to the desert town of Pityus. He was forced to walk the whole way bareheaded under the blazing sun and collapsed and died in 407.

Both the western Emperor, Honorius, and Pope Innocent I of Rome recognized his orthodoxy and his innocency, and tried unsuccessfully to intercede for Chrysostom.

CLARA See **CLARE.**

CLARE, of Assisi (1194–1253) Gay, pretty young daughter of the well-to-do Sciffi family in Assisi which opposed her interest in St. Francis of Assisi's life of poverty and service, Clare became a nun over family objections. With Francis she established a convent which developed into a female order embracing Francis' ideals. Her order, the Order of the Poor Clares, quickly won adherents and spread throughout Europe, performing outstanding service in nursing the ill and looking after the destitute. Clare, the Mother Superior, energetically supervised the activities of the Order and once successfully withstood Frederick II's soldiers when they attacked her convent at San Damiano. Clare, regarded by Francis of Assisi as a sister, corresponded with him until his death in 1226.

CLARK, Francis Edward (1851–1927) American Congregational minister, Clark was the founder in 1881 of the Christian Endeavor movement, a popular youth organization in American Protestantism for many years. Clark, a pastor at Portland, Maine, was a dynamic speaker and Church youth worker. By 1885 he had spread his Christian Endeavor movement across the United States into a national body and by 1895 he formed the World's Christian Endeavor Union. With its motto, "For Christ and the Church," and with Clark's driving enthusiasm, the movement ultimately represented eighty denominations and claimed four million members.

CLARKE, Samuel (1675–1729) A bookish Church of England clergyman, Samuel Clarke veered toward a unitarian position in his theology and wrote a careful, rationalist defense of his thinking called *Scripture Doctrine of the Trinity* in 1712. Clarke, respected as a scholar and thinker, commanded a wide audience and contributed to the drift of a large segment of English Protestants—particularly the Presbyterians—into Unitarianism. Clarke, saturated with the 18th century viewpoint, was inclined to see Christianity primarily as moral living, and was prone to accept only what could be rationally proved.

CLAVER, Pedro See **PETER CLAVER.**

CLÉMANGES, Nicholas de (1367[?]–1437[?]) Influential and sensitive Roman Catholic teacher, Clémanges joined other notables in 1408 to try to end the scandalous division in the papacy where two rival Popes claimed authority. Clémanges had previously taught at the University of Paris and served as papal secretary at Avignon papacy from 1397 to 1405, and knew firsthand the weakness and corruption in the Church. Clémanges, convinced that the Church's problems stemmed from its neglect of the Bible, was one of the few throughout the Middle Ages in the Church to emphasize Scriptural study. In 1408 he urged others to support the idea of a Church Council to bring reform to the Church and end the schism. The ill-planned Council of Pisa in 1409 resulted, but accomplished little. His writings were influential, however, particularly at the Council of Constance.

CLEMENT of Alexandria (150[?]–215[?]) Born in Athens to pagan parents, Clement at an unknown time in a manner not disclosed became a Christian and settled in Alexandria, Egypt where he became a presbyter in the Church. Little is known of his life except what can be gleaned from his writings and from a few references in Eusebius' writings. As presbyter, he had ties both to the Church at Alexandria and to the school. Under Clement, the school developed into one of the most prominent in the Church in the East.

Clement and the Alexandrians, unlike many of their Christian contemporaries, looked upon philosophy as the handmaid to Christianity and in no way inconsistent with it. Combining the best of ancient philosophy with the Gospel, Clement built what has been described as "Christian Gnosticism"—the idea that, although faith is enough for salvation, the man who adds knowledge to his faith has an even greater good. Clement of Alexandria wrote extensively. His surviving works give us additional information on the Church's life and customs in the Roman world in his time. His most famous pupil was Origen, the Church Father and scholar.

CLEMENT OF ROME See **CLEMENT I, Bishop of Rome.**

CLEMENT I, Bishop of Rome ([?]–101[?] One of the "Apostolic Fathers," Clement of Rome was probably third successor to Peter as Bishop in Rome (Peter, Linus, perhaps Anencletus, then Clement). He served sometime between 92 to 101 or 102. Clement of Rome should not be confused with the Clement mentioned by the Apostle Paul in Philippians 4:3. Clement of Rome, however, may well be the Clement referred to in the ancient Christian document, *The Shepherd of Hermas,* which tells of a Clement who is responsible for communicating with other Church bodies at the time Clement of Rome was a leader in the Christian community at Rome, and was the author of Epistle to the Corinthians (not to be confused with the New Testament writings by the Apostle Paul to the Corinthians).

Although not claiming jurisdiction over the Church at Corinth, the letter assumes that the Church at Rome has a position of prominence. This same letter gives us excellent glimpses into the pattern of Church life at Rome in the earliest days, showing an order and unity in spite of persecution and hardship.

Clement of Rome was esteemed almost as much as the Twelve Apostles in the early Church, and his Letter to the Corinthians was regarded by many almost on a par with the New Testament canon.

CLEMENT II, Pope ([?]–1047) Pope from 1046 to 1047.

CLEMENT III, Pope ([?]–1191) The organizer of the Third Crusade, Clement III ruled from 1187 to 1191.

CLEMENT IV, Pope ([?]–1268) Rising from layman to priest to pope within ten years, Clement IV reigned from 1265 to 1268.

CLEMENT V, Pope (1264–1314) Weak, immoral and controlled by King Philip IV of France, Clement V was a worldly Frenchman, Bertrand d'Agoust. Clement not only absolved Philip IV of any blame for seizing Pope Boniface VIII, but at Philip's suggestion moved the headquarters for the papacy to Avignon in southern France in 1309. Clement's Avignon papacy triggered a disgusting schism in the Church which lasted seventy years, during which time there were sometimes two and even three rival Popes claiming absolute authority over the Church. Pliable

Clement allowed himself to be persuaded by Philip to abolish the historic Knights Templars, which set off an uproar but considerably enriched King Philip's estate. Clement V further disgraced his office by selling positions in the Church hierarchy and installing relatives in key positions. Clement V's rule from 1305 to 1314 brought disaster for the Church.

CLEMENT VI, Pope (1291–1352) Although he practiced nepotism to a shocking degree during his rule from 1342 to 1352, Clement VI showed charity and courage during the Black Death plague.

CLEMENT VII, antipope ([?]–1394) Elected by the same cardinals who elected the tactless Urban VI only four months earlier but rescinded their choice of Urban to vote in Clement VII, Clement VII resided at Avignon, France.

Urban VI, meanwhile, claimed still to be the pope and lived at Rome. Europe was shocked at seeing the Church torn into two, each pope condemning the other, and lined up in two camps, about half the monarchs supporting Clement VII and half acknowledging Urban VI.

Clement VII, who ruled from 1378–1394, obstinately tried a series of costly, brutal military campaigns to extend his influence, with the hope of ousting his rival pope at Rome.

Europe, which desperately wanted unity and reform in the Church, gradually deserted his cause and blamed Clement VII for the troubles in the Church.

CLEMENT VII, Pope ([?]–1534) Not to be confused with the antipope by the same name (see above), Clement VII served as pope from 1523 to 1534 during Luther's Reformation in Germany, but never understood the causes for discontent or the need for reform in the Church. Clement VII, a member of the de' Medici family, used all the wiles of a wordly Italian prince to suppress the Reformation. Instead of attempting to rectify the glaring abuses in the Church, Clement looked upon the Church as a sort of private fiefdom whose interests were to be furthered. Clement indecisively allied himself with various kings and rulers to promote his cause; his political games eventually brought about Henry VIII of England's break with Rome.

CLEMENT VIII, Pope (1535–1605) A man who loved mass, peace and books and his relatives, Clement VIII, pope from 1592 to 1605, revised the Vulgate (Latin version of the Bible), the Breviary, the Missal and liturgical material in worship. He engineered the Peace of Vervins in 1598, ending a long, smouldering dispute between French and Spanish interests. A scholarly cleric, Clement expanded the Vatican Library and corresponded with many of the intellectuals of his time. Clement also unabashedly practiced nepotism, installing three nephews as cardinals.

CLEMENT IX, Pope (1600–1669) One of the most popular and beloved Popes, Clement IX served from 1667 to 1669.

CLEMENT X, Pope (1590–1676) Pope from 1670 to 1676, succeeding Clement IX.

CLEMENT XI, Pope (1649–1721) Ruling from 1700 to 1721, Clement XI was a capable organizer, starting the Church in the Philippines and beautifying Rome.

CLEMENT XII, Pope (1652–1740) Although he became blind and an invalid shortly after being named pontiff in 1730, Clement XII proved to be an effective administrator, reorganizing Vatican finances, paving Rome's streets and rebuilding churches. He also condemned freemasonry.

CLEMENT XIII, Pope (1693–1769) Pope from 1758 to 1769.

CLEMENT XIV, Pope (1705–1774) Chosen pope after a three-month hassle among the cardinals, Clement XIV served from 1769 to 1774. Ineffective against the strong national powers of the 18th century (most were defying the papacy), Clement XIV adopted a conciliatory policy and even agreed to suppress the Jesuits by abolishing the order, 1773. His main accomplishment was the founding of the Clementine Museum in the Vatican.

CLERC, Jean le See Le CLERC, Jean.

CLODOALD See CLOUD.

CLOTILDA (475[?]–545) One of the first to be named a saint in the Church, Clotilda was the wife of the Frankish King, Clovis I. She was a devout Christian, influencing Clovis to become baptized, and, after his death, lived an exemplary life at Tours, France.

CLOUD (520[?]–560[?]) A grandson of St. Clotilda, Cloud, who barely escaped being murdered when two uncles killed two of his brothers, became a monk. Cloud founded the well-known monastery at Paris which came to be called St. Cloud.

CLOVIS (466[?]–511) King of the rough, pagan Franks in 481 at the age of fifteen, Clovis carved out a large territory of Gaul (now France) for himself. Although not a Christian at first, he showed great deference to the self-effacing monks of Europe. Clovis married a deeply Christian Burgundian princess, Clotilda, in 493, but resisted her request to be baptized until he found himself in a desperate battle with the Alamanni in 493. Vowing to be baptized if victorious, Clovis rallied his troops and decisively won. Clovis and three thousand Frankish soldiers and tribal chieftains were baptized the following Christmas at Rheims, the first Germanic tribe to convert en masse to the Christian faith.

A stalwart defender of the faith for the rest of his life, Clovis continued to extend his kingdom (eventually, it bordered on the Pyrenees near Spain) and add chieftains and tribesmen to the rolls of the Church. Clovis championed the Roman clergy against the Arian kings of the Visigoths and the Burgundians, and was honored as a protector of the Church while exercising considerable authority over it.

COCCEJUS, Johann (1603–1669) A Protestant theologian from Germany who taught in Holland, Cocceius was an Old Testament scholar who developed the theological concept known as the "Covenant of Grace."

Before the Fall of Man, according to Cocceius' teachings, God and man were in a relationship which Cocceius defined as the "Covenant of Works." After the Fall, Cocceius maintained, a new relationship, the "Covenant of Grace" was needed and was fulfilled by the coming of Jesus Christ. This viewpoint gained such popularity among Protestant theologians that they came to be called Cocceians. His Bible-based viewpoint stimulated the study of the Scriptures in the original languages.

COELESTIUS ([?]–431[?]) A lawyer who was a tireless disciple of the heretic Pelagius, Coelestius traveled from Rome to North Africa with Pelagius. Pelagius wandered to the East to present his views, while Coelestius remained at Carthage, seeking ordination and an audience for Pelagius' doctrines known as Pelagianism—a denial of man's total sinfulness and the insistence that man can will that he will be saved, or, in effect, can save himself. The Council at Carthage in 418 formally condemned Coelestius and Pelagius, but Coelestius continued to promote Pelagianism. Although he convinced Nestorius, leading Churchman at Constantinople, of some of his doctrines, Coelestius and Pelagianism were repudiated at the Third Council of Ephesus in 431 by the Eastern Church, as well as the Church in the West.

COFFIN, Henry Sloane (1877–1954) American Presbyterian clergyman-educator, Coffin served as President of Union Theological Seminary of New York City from 1926 to 1945. He showed wit, charity, tact and common sense in his involvement during the fundamentalist controversy which wracked American Protestantism during the first third of the 20th century.

COKE, Thomas (1747–1814) A Church of England curate who was ousted for starting open-air revival meetings in 1776, Coke joined the Wesleys in London, became an intimate disciple of the Wesleys, and devoted the rest of his productive life to promoting Methodism.

At Bristol, in 1784, John Wesley decided to send Coke to America. At Bristol, Wesley and other ordained Church of England clergy "set apart" Coke as a "superintendent" for work among the Methodist societies in the infant republic, then fighting for its independence. In actuality Coke's ordination was the break between Wesley and the Church of England, although Wesley did not think so at the time.

Coke, with letters of introduction from Wesley, arrived at Baltimore in 1774 and energetically set to work. Coke called the first American Methodist Conference in December, 1774, ordained Asbury as a "superintendent," and formally established the Methodist Episcopal Church. In 1787 the American Methodist Conference changed Coke's and Asbury's titles to "Bishop." Coke unsuccessfully tried to persuade English Methodists to adopt the same title. He made numerous voyages across the Atlantic and worked hard to heal the breach between the Methodists and the Anglicans. Coke was remembered as one of the first to encourage mission work and personally pioneered in several missionary efforts. Coke was also one of the first to oppose slavery as an institution.

COLENSO, John William (1814–1883) English Bishop of Natal, South Africa, who championed the cause of the Zulu natives against the colonists and espoused a liberal view of Biblical interpretation, Bishop Colenso was put through the humiliation of a Church trial in 1863 which was widely publicized.

COLET, John (1467[?]–1519) Educated humanist who lectured on Paul's epistles at Oxford and served as Dean of St. Paul's Cathedral, London, John Colet was one of the coterie which prepared England for the Protestant Reformation. Colet was a careful Bible student, rejecting allegorical interpretations and insisting the Scriptures speak for themselves. He upbraided fellow clergymen for their lax morals and poor study habits. A doubter in many ways, Colet even questioned use of confession in the Church and criticized the prac-

tice of celibacy for the clergy. Colet, who first met the great humanist scholar Erasmus in 1499, introduced Erasmus to studying the Bible by reading it in the original languages. Although Colet died before the Reformation took place in England, in most ways he shared the views of the leading Reformers and helped set the stage in England for an acceptance of the Reformers' ideas.

COLIGNY, Gaspard de (1519–1572) French military and naval hero who served with distinction in campaigns from 1543 to 1557 under Kings Francis I and Henry II of France, Coligny became the spokesman for the Huguenots, the French Protestants. Coligny, promoted to Admiral in 1552, used his prestige to protect his fellow Huguenots in France, and when hostilities erupted between Protestants and Roman Catholics in 1562 in a series of bloody civil wars, Coligny became commander-in-chief of the Huguenots. Always anxious to negotiate, Coligny, after a notable victory in 1570, returned to court. Coligny was the first to die, however, in the bloodbath known as St. Bartholomew's Day Massacre, August 24, 1572, when an estimated 50,000 French Protestants were butchered at the instigation of King Charles IX.

COLLINS, Anthony (1676–1729) Friend of the philosopher John Locke, Collins, an essayist in the 18th century, created a stir with his pamphlets arguing for Deism. "Ignorance," he wrote in the *Discourse of Freethinking,* "is the foundation of atheism and freethinking is the cure for it." Collins summed up the school of thought of the era which demanded proofs for everything, rejected anything having to do with faith as "superstition," and insisted that revelation conform to common sense. A sensational writer in his day, Collins today is overshadowed by his more profound and scholarly friend, Locke.

COLMAN (605[?]–676) One of the bold band of missionary-scholars who crossed from Ireland to the tiny island of Iona, off the Scottish coast, to introduce the flourishing Celtic Church to northern Britain in the early 7th century, Colman in 661 became head of the abbey at Lindisfarne, the island-monastery off the Northumbrian coast, and a trusted friend of the Northumbrian King, Oswio. At that time, however, the Roman branch of the Church and the Celtic branch, each with separate traditions, collided in England. The issue was the date on which Easter should be celebrated, and a Council was called at Whitby in 664. Colman eloquently spoke for the Celtic Church. Oswio, however, decided in favor of the Roman. Colman, disappointed, returned to Iona, then to Ireland, where he built another monastery at Inishbofin, off the Irish coast. Colman, one of 215 Irish saints of the same name mentioned in the *Book of Leinster*, must not be confused with two other popular Saint Colmans in Ireland, Colman of Cloyne (522–600) and Colman Ela (553–610).

COLUMBA (521–597) Related to the royal family of Irish kings, Columba, a product of the flowering of learning and missionary zeal in the Celtic Church, was the great missionary to Scotland. After an outstanding career of founding churches and monasteries in Ireland, Columba accepted the invitation of his relative in Argyll, Scotland, King Conall, to work among the wild northern clans of Picts and Scots. Columba and twelve monks crossed the Irish sea in 563 to the island of Iona, off the Scottish coast, and established the monastery which became the headquarters for great Celtic Church in

Britain. Columba fearlessly went to the leader of the Picts, Brude, and won him and most of his followers to the Church.

Columba's monks crisscrossed what is now Scotland and northern England, founding and tending monasteries, congregations and schools. His Celtic Church in Britain, having no allegiance to Rome, looked to him or his successor-abbots at Iona until the Council of Whitby in 664, when the pope at Rome expanded his claims to include all of the British branches of the Church. Under the capable Columba, however, teams of missionaries were sent from Iona Abbey as far away as the continent. Columba, working at transcribing selections from the Psalter until the day he died, was honored by his fellow-Scots and the Picts who were brought into the Church.

COLUMBA the Younger See COLUMBAN.

COLUMBAN (543–615) Like his older contemporary of the same name, Columba (see above), Columban was an Irish monk in the Celtic Church during the amazing period when Ireland was Europe's center for learning and missionary activity. Columban, trained at the famous Bangor monastery in Ireland, took twelve fellow monks in 585 and settled in the Vosges and Burgundy area of France, where they founded the monastery of Luxeuil. Columban was stopped in 602, however, when powerful forces from Rome's Church accused him of keeping Easter in an unorthodox way (that is, according to dates used in the Celtic Church), and King Theuderich ordered him to leave for daring to criticize the king's crimes. Columban went to Switzerland with a few monks, began all over again, but was interrupted a second time. The indefatigable scholar and missionary next settled in Italy, where he established the monastery at Bobbio. Combining deep learning with fervent preaching, Columban was an example of the outstanding contribution made by the Celtic Church from Ireland.

COLUMBANUS See **COLUMBAN**.

COLUMBKILLE See **COLUMBA**.

COMENIUS, Johann Amos (1592–1671) Czech pietist and a bishop of the Moravian and Bohemian Brethren, Comenius was forced into exile to Poland in 1621 when persecutions against Protestants broke out. He became bishop of the remnant of the Church of the Brethren in Poland but supported himself by teaching school. Shocked at the schools, which he characterized as "slaughterhouses of the mind," Comenius soon revolutionized education by introducing progressive methods of instructing children. Comenius was the first to supply picture books for small children, to use the conversational method of learning languages, to introduce singing, art, politics, geography, science, and crafts in children's school curriculum. He completely reorganized Sweden's school system in 1642, wrote some less-influential tomes in theology in which he leaned toward millennialism (he said the world would end in 1672), and is today respected as a pioneer in modern educational methods.

COMGALL (6th c.) Irish monk who was a part of the great upsurge of learning and evangelizing in the Irish Church in the 6th century, Comgall in 558 founded the great monastery at Bangor, Ireland, which exported many missionary-scholars during the flowering of the Celtic Church.

COMPTON, Henry (1632–1713) Church of England bishop who was broadminded toward dissenters and concerned about non-believers in remote areas, Compton was Bishop of Oxford in 1674, of London in 1675. He was suspended for upholding one of his outspoken clergymen when Catholic James II came to the throne, but reinstated in the Revolution of 1689 and asked to perform the coronation of William and Mary, the new rulers. Compton vigorously and consistently supported the then-controversial and liberal cause of foreign missions, appointing Thomas Bray, founder of one of the first missionary societies, to work in the colony of Maryland in 1696.

CONRAD of Waldhausen ([?]–1369) A stirring preacher from Bohemia before John Huss's time, Conrad rigorously opposed the corruption in the Church in his time and insisted that Scripture, not the Vatican, was the rule of life. Conrad helped prepare the ground for Huss' teachings in Bohemia fifty years later.

CONSTANTINE I, The Great, Emperor (288[?]–337) The first Roman emperor to be at least nominally Christian, Constantine was one of four contestants for the throne of Rome after Emperor Galerus' death in May, 311, when a vision of a flaming cross with the legend, "In this sign conquer!" inspired him to become a Christian and move with speed on his enemies. Constantine's brilliant victory at Mulvian Bridge in 312, one of history's decisive battles, won him Rome. Constantine quickly eliminated all rivals, set himself as undisputed master of the Roman world in 324 and attributed his success to Christianity.

He soon moved to make Christianity the State Religion and a uniting factor in the Empire. Under his influence, the Church suddenly changed from a poor and persecuted minority to a wealthy and established majority. By 321 the Church was permitted to receive legacies and Sunday was appointed as an official day of rest. In 330 Constantine shifted his seat of government from Rome to the newly built capital in Asia Minor named after himself, Constantinople, leaving the Bishop of Rome as the most important man in the former capital. Constantine showered the Church with favors and gradually made it his tool. Determined that the Church should help unite the far-flung Empire, Constantine repressed any schism. Both the Donatists and Arians were harshly treated after Constantine's Church Councils condemned them as heretics. Doctrinal questions became political issues; the Emperor emerged as an arbiter of Church affairs. Constantine won the clergy by exempting them from taxes and making them a privileged class. A church-builder, Constantine erected the first St. Peter's at Rome and began St. Sophia, Constantinople.

His mother, Helena, claimed to locate many of the sites associated with sacred history in the Holy Land, and bringing home a piece of the "true cross," encouraged the trend toward venerating objects and saints gaining popularity among the newly-converted masses. Constantine's reign, although a reprieve from persecution for the Church, was not an unmixed blessing for the Church.

Constantine, baptized by Eusebius of Nicomedia shortly before his death, died in May, 337, dividing his Empire among his three sons, Constans, Constantius, and Constantine, II, which created three weak kingdoms instead of one strong, centralized government.

CONSTANTINE, Pope ([?]–715) A Syrian, Constantine ruled from 708 to 715.

CONTARINI, Gasparo, Cardinal (1483–1542) Member of a distinguished Venetian family, Contarini was a reform-minded layman who was appointed a cardinal by Pope Paul III on his election in 1534. Contarini, a conscientious churchman and capable administrator, realized the challenge of the Reformers and joined with others in 1538 in presenting the pope with a list of recommendations to improve the situation in the Roman Church. Contarini, long an advocate of reform in the Church, served as Pope Paul III's legate at the conversations with Protestants at Regensburg, and urged a conciliatory policy by the papacy. Contarini's advice was ignored; in 1542 the Pope decided to adopt a stern policy against those holding doctrinal differences and approved the use of the inquisition. Contarini, deeply disappointed, died soon afterward.

CONWELL, Russell Herman (1843–1925) Founder of Temple University and popular lecturer who delivered his famous "Acres of Diamonds" speech over 5,000 times, Conwell was a prominent Philadelphia Baptist clergyman. Previously, Conwell, a Civil War hero, had a successful career as an attorney in New England before entering the ministry in 1879. While pastor of the huge Baptist Temple at Philadelphia, Conwell started Temple University in 1888 and Samaritan Hospital in 1891.

COOK, John (1805–1892) A well-known Canadian Presbyterian pastor and educator, Cook helped found Queen's University at Kingston, Ontario in 1857, promoted union among the Presbyterian bodies in Canada, and served as the first Moderator of the Canadian Presbyterian General Assembly.

COOPER, Anthony Ashley See SHAFTESBURY.

COORNHERT, Dirck Volckertszoon (1522–1590) Dutch copper-engraver, politician, theologian and translator, Coornhert disturbed many of his contemporaries by his tolerance, refusing to endorse capital punishment for heretics. He wrote critically of the Heidelberg catechism and won Arminius to his views when Arminius was sent to refute him.

COP, Nicolas (16th c.) Member of a distinguished French humanist family, Nicolas Cop was a close friend of John Calvin during Calvin's student days in Paris. Nicolas Cop, leader of the humanist circle of intellectuals in Paris, sympathized with Luther's ideas, but was primarily an intellectual. When elected rector at the University of Paris in 1533, he gave an inaugural address (influenced, if not written in part by John Calvin) so critical of abuses in the Church and so insistent for reform that both Cop and Calvin were forced to leave Paris.

COPERNICUS, Nicolaus (1473–1543) Polish astronomer, physician and canon law expert, Copernicus doubted the ptolomaic theory that the earth was the center of the universe, and advanced the hypothesis that the earth and other planets orbited around the sun. After keeping his manuscript hidden for thirty-six years, Copernicus was persuaded by friends to publish it and dedicate it to Pope Paul III in 1543. Pope Paul III, however, was preoccupied with the Protestant Reformation and gave it little attention. Others disagreed with Copernicus' theories. It was not until Galileo popularized Copernican ideas a century later that Copernicus won wide recognition. Most of his life, he lived inconspicuously, tending the

sick and looking after the business affairs of the Frauenburg cathedral in Poland. His astronomical observations were made with scanty equipment in his spare time.

CORBEIL, William of ([?]–1136) Born in Normandy, France, Corbeil in 1123 became Archbishop of Canterbury. In 1130, he dedicated the lovely cathedral of Canterbury.

CORNELIUS, Pope ([?]–253) Pope from 251 to 253, Cornelius was opposed by Novatian for being too lenient to those who had lapsed from the faith during persecutions.

COSIN, John (1594–1672) Church of England clergyman who was a ritualist, Cosin strictly enforced conformity to the state church. He both gave and received rough treatment from the Puritans during the Royalist-Puritan struggles in the mid-seventeenth century. Cosin is primarily remembered for a minor devotional classic, *Collection of Private Devotions,* which he prepared at the request of King Charles I for the Queen's maids of honor in 1627.

COTTON, John (1584–1652) Known as "The Patriarch of New England," Cotton was born and educated in England. He had immense intellectual ability and served for twenty-one years as a parish clergyman in Boston, Lincolnshire, England from 1612 to 1633. His growing Puritan leanings brought him a summons to appear before the Court of High Commission in 1632. Cotton disguised himself and secretly escaped from Boston, England, to Boston, Massachusetts, in 1633, where he quickly distinguished himself as the teacher at Boston's First Church. In theocratic New England, Cotton emerged as the most influential minister, taking an active part and speaking eloquently on all civil and religious issues. He supported the Church-State's expulsion of non-conformists Roger Williams and Anne Hutchinson, and opposed the idea of religious freedom in Massachusetts. His writings, however, were carefully prepared theological treatises which helped guide the course of New England Congregationalism for generations.

COURTENAY, William (1342[?]–1396) Descended from an illustrious English titled family, William Courtenay rose in the Medieval Church to become Bishop of Hereford in 1370, Bishop of London in 1375, and Archbishop of Canterbury in 1381. A prelate-politician who protected the interests of the English Church, Courtenay frequently clashed with the powerful John of Gaunt, Duke of Lancaster. Courtenay suppressed the roving folk-preachers called Lollards, and called a council in London in 1377 to condemn the early reformer, John Wycliffe. Courtenay disputed throughout his career with his monarchs and his bishops, whom he urged to imprison heretics.

COVERDALE, Miles (1488[?]–1569) English bishop at Exeter, Miles Coverdale made the first translation of the Bible into English in 1535. A Yorkshire-born, Cambridge-educated Augustinian monk, Coverdale in 1525 left monastic life and joined the group of exiled Englishmen with reformation ideas on the continent from 1528 to 1534.

His translation, no scholarly masterpiece, was from German and Latin translations, but its prose style left its mark permanently on the English language and literature. Many phrases were taken directly into the translation of 1611 authorized by King James. Although portions of Scripture had appeared previously in English, Coverdale's translation was the first complete English text of the Bible, and went into three editions. Three years later, Cromwell asked Coverdale to help produce what came to be known as the Great Bible, published in 1539, and ordered to be placed in all English churches.

Changing political fortunes in England forced Coverdale to flee again, and in 1542 his Bible was prohibited. By 1548, he was back in England and busy editing Archbishop Cranmer's Bible. His flair for oratory won him an appointment as Bishop of Exeter, where he took an active part in national affairs. He was imprisoned and exiled a third time when rabidly Catholic "Bloody" Mary became Queen in 1553. Coverdale worked for a time in Denmark and Switzerland, where he assisted in the Geneva version of the Bible. He returned to England in 1559. Although not restored to his seat at Exeter, Coverdale was one of the four Bishops who participated in the Controversial investiture of Matthew Parker as Archbishop of Canterbury, 1559—attacked by Roman Catholics as invalid and defended by Anglicans as valid Apostolic succession.

COWPER, William (1731–1800) Rector's son (his father was also chaplain to King George II) and most famous English poet in the late 18th century, Cowper was trained as a lawyer but spent much of his life suffering from emotional illness. He finally settled down at Olney in 1767, where he wrote poetry which helped spread Evangelical ideas. Many of his poems, known as *The Olney Hymns,* became favorite hymns in English-speaking Protestantism, including "O, for a Closer Walk with God" and "God Moves in Mysterious Ways."

CRAIG, John (1512[?]–1600) Scottish reformer, John Craig began as a

Dominican monk who was forced to leave Scotland for his radical views. After twenty-four years of wandering abroad (including a last minute escape from the Inquisition Prison just before being burned at the stake), Craig returned to Scotland in 1560. In 1561, he was ordained minister at Holyrood and the following year became John Knox's assistant at St. Giles. Craig was deeply involved in the politics which were part of the struggles for religious freedom in Scotland, and for a time even served as tutor to young James VI of Scotland who became James I of England. When the Roman Catholics attempted to regain their hold in 1580 in Scotland, Craig drafted the National Covenant—the first of the "Covenants." Craig also helped write the *Second Book of Discipline,* the *King's Confession,* the basis for the Covenant of 1638 and took a leading part in having episcopacy abolished in Scotland in 1581.

CRANMER, Thomas (1489–1556) A vacillating English churchman who tried to be obliging to English monarchs Henry VIII, Edward VI and "Bloody" Mary during the Protestant-Catholic struggles for control of England, Cranmer served as the first Protestant Archbishop of Canterbury. Cranmer, as soon as he was appointed Archbishop by King Henry VIII in 1533, repaid Henry by annulling Henry's marriage to Catherine of Aragon so that Henry could be married to Anne Boleyn. Three years later, Cranmer again proved cooperative when Henry wished to rid himself of Anne, and pronounced that marriage null and void. Cranmer also helped Henry out of his marital escapade with Anne of Cleves by declaring *that* marriage invalid.

Cranmer assisted Henry VIII in shifting the English Church's allegiance from the pope to Henry by adjusting the liturgy and creed and ordering in 1538 that an English translation of the Bible be installed in each parish. Cranmer was rewarded by Henry for obedience by being named one of the regents for the frail young Edward VI when Henry VIII died in 1547. The following year, the beautifully written liturgies of the Edward VI Prayer Book, composed largely by Cranmer, appeared. By 1553, Cranmer prepared a creed known as the Forty-Two Articles.

In 1553, as the young Edward VI was dying, Cranmer foolishly agreed to support a plot by Warwick to install Lady Jane Grey as Queen instead of Mary, Henry VIII's daughter. Mary became queen and immediately jailed Cranmer for treason and had the pope excommunicate him in 1555. Cranmer abjectly submitted to Mary's pressures, even acknowledging that he recognized papal authority as established by law. He disgraced himself further by signing a recantation in which he denied Protestantism completely. Mary, unrelenting, insisted that he die.

About to be burned at the stake at Oxford in 1556, Cranmer recovered his courage and publicly renounced his earlier cowardice, holding the hand which had signed the recantations in the flames until it was consumed and shouting, "This hath offended; oh, this unworthy hand."

CRESPI, Juan (1721–1782) An early Spanish Franciscan missionary-explorer to Mexico in 1749, Crespi was one of the discoverers of San Francisco Bay, one of the founders of the Carmelite Mission at San Diego, and in 1774 one of the earliest to sail from California to Alaska and back.

CRISPIN and CRISPINIAN ([?]–286) The patron saints of leatherworkers and shoemakers, Crispin and Crispinian (who might or might not have been brothers) are reputed to have gone as volunteer-missionaries to Soissons, Gaul (now France), earning their own expenses by working as shoemakers but devoting most of their energies to preaching. These two worker-evangelists did an outstanding job, but were beheaded during Diocletian's persecution about 286 for their faith.

CROFT, William (1678–1727) A gifted English musician, Croft composed extensive works for worship services, many of which are still used in Protestant hymnals and in the regular Episcopal service. Croft served for many years as the official organist at Westminster Abbey, London and as Composer to the Chapel Royal.

CROMWELL, Oliver (1599–1658) A member of the English Parliament with little military experience who emerged as the military dictator of England after Civil War broke out in 1642, Oliver Cromwell ruled England as Protector from 1653 to 1658. Cromwell, a stern, no-nonsense Puritan, built an army which was an extension of his own personality. Known as the New Model Army, and given to prayer before battle, Cromwell's picked fighting force smashed opposition throughout the British Isles (including a brutal subjugation of Ireland) and backed Cromwell's programs.

When the Puritans divided into two factions, the Presbyterians and the Independents, Cromwell sided with the Independents, while Parliament was primarily Presbyterian. Fearful of a Presbyterian-backed restoration of deposed King Charles I, Cromwell agreed to have Charles beheaded in 1649, and a few years later, 1653, marched his troops into Parliament to disband the Parliament which had been in session

twelve years and is called the Long Parliament. The new Parliament was ineffective and disbanded itself. A later Parliament in 1656 offered Cromwell the title of king, which Cromwell declined.

In spite of his attempts to clothe his rule with constitutional respectability, Cromwell essentially was a strongman backed by a strong army. Anglicans and Catholics were denied freedom of worship, and toleration was extended only to non-conformists, who comprised the national Church at the time. Punishments were meted out even to those using the English Prayer Book. Cromwell personally, however, inclined toward a more broadminded viewpoint, and arranged a government policy of extraordinary tolerance toward Jews and Quakers. About two thousand Anglican clergymen, however, were nearly destitute from being driven from their parishes.

Cromwell was succeeded at his death by his weak, lackluster son, Richard, who stepped aside after two years of ineffectual rule.

CROSBY, ("Fanny") Frances Jane (1820–1915) Blind from the age of six weeks, Fanny Crosby was the author of more than 6,000 hymns. She became a pupil at the New York Institute for the Blind when she was fifteen, and began writing poetry. In 1847, she became a teacher at the Institute, and later married one of her pupils, Alexander Van Alstyne, a blind musician. Fanny Crosby, who began her hymnwriting career in 1864, was the author of such well-known songs as "Rescue the Perishing," "Safe in the Arms of Jesus," "Blessed Assurance" and "What a Gathering."

CROWTHER, Samuel Adjah (1809 [?]–1891) The first Negro Bishop of the Church of England, Crowther had a storybook background: carried away as a slave in 1821 near Dahomey; freed by a British warship in 1822; placed in African mission schools; sent to England for a university education and ordination. Bishop Crowther had a distinguished career in Africa. Named Bishop in 1864, he started many schools and congregations. A life-long student, he found time to publish numerous texts of the Bible, grammars and dictionaries for various African dialects.

CRUMMEL, Alexander (1819–1898) The son of an African-born slave, Crummel became one of the most influential and creative leaders in the American Episcopal Church in the 19th century. This distinguished Negro served for twenty years as a missionary to Liberia, then in 1873, organized St. Luke's Church, Washington, D.C. Later, 1897, Crummel began the American Negro Academy and published several books.

CUTHBERT (635[?]–687) An early bishop at Lindisfarne, the island monastery off the northeastern coast of England, Cuthbert was a saintly monk who was much-venerated in the British Church. He was led to monastic orders because of a vision when Bishop Aidan died, and served at Melrose Abbey and Lindisfarne. He was noted for his missionary zeal, according to the ancient historian, Bede, but had retired to a hermit's life when summoned to become a Bishop, first at Hexham, then at Lindisfarne.

CUTLER, Timothy (1683–1765) Originally a Congregationalist clergyman, Cutler became the distinguished president of Yale University. In 1722, Cutler created a sensation at the Yale Commencement by publicly announcing his conversion to Episcopalianism. He was summarily thrown out of Yale, but devoted his energies to building up the tiny Episcopal Church in Connecticut.

CYPRIAN (200[?]–258) A distinguished teacher of Carthage, North Africa, who became a great bishop at Carthage, Cyprian was beheaded in the persecution of 258. He was raised in a wealthy patrician family, well-educated and a popular lecturer when he decided to vanquish Christianity, which was growing rapidly and seemed to Cyprian at that time to be a threat to the unity of the Roman Empire. Instead, Cyprian in 246 was won to the faith, and two years later elected bishop. He used his wealth to help the needy and his intellectual abilities to resolve thorny questions confronting the Church.

Threatened by the persecution under Emperor Decius in 250, Cyprian fled to safety until Gallus became Emperor. At this time, the charitable Cyprian clashed with Novatian, a presbyter from Rome, who wanted to exclude permanently from church membership any who had weakened during the persecutions. Cyprian wrote notable treatises, the best known of which was *De Catholicae Ecclesiae Unitate*, directed against the schismatic Novatian, which set forth key thoughts in the theology of the Church.

"He can no longer have God for his Father," wrote Cyprian, "who has not the Church for his mother," and, "There is no salvation outside of the Church."

Cyprian stood boldly during Valerian's bloody persecution in 258, but was seized and executed. Throughout subsequent Church history, St. Cyprian has been regarded not only as one of the bravest martyrs but one of the seminal thinkers in Christian theology.

CYRIL, Bishop of Alexander (376–444) Ambitious and disputatious Patriarch of Alexandria from 412 to 444,

Cyril ruthlessly assailed anyone or any cause he suspected of heresy. He encouraged one of the first Church-directed attacks against the Jews, expelling thousands and destroying synagogues and houses. An unscrupulous politician, Cyril perpetuated the Church rivalry between Alexandria and Antioch by conniving to discredit Church leaders at Antioch and to extend his own ecclesiastical influence. The disputes over dogma degenerated into political strife. Nonetheless, in spite of the seamy struggles, Cyril helped the Church clarify its thinking on the nature of the person of Jesus Christ.

When Nestorius, a native of Antioch and the Patriarch of Constantinople, seemed to espouse heretical views of Christology, Cyril, a fair theologian in spite of his unpleasant personal manner, emphasized the divine nature of Jesus Christ, almost to the point where Jesus' humanity was absorbed in His divinity. Cyril, not content with attacking Nestorius in letters, pulled the Eastern emperor, Theodosius II, into the struggle. The Emperor turned to the pope, Celestine I, who sided with Cyril, and the battle became nasty. The two emperors, Theodosius II of the East and Valentinian III of the West, uneasy because the dispute seemed to be getting out of hand, called a Church Council at Ephesus in 431. Cyril cleverly had the Council convene and formally deposed Nestorius before Nestorius' followers even showed up. Proud of being the champion of orthodoxy, Cyril continued to root out Nestorianism the rest of his life. At the Council of Chalcedon in 451, however, the Creed adopted by the Church was more Antiochan than Alexandrian, and some of what Cyril had thought was so orthodox was declared to be unorthodox. He was canonized despite the bitter criticism against him.

CYRIL, Missionary (827[?]–869) This Cyril and his older brother, Methodius, were the apostles to the Slavs. Natives of Thessalonica, Cyril and Methodius were eminent in the Eastern Church. When the Duke of Moravia, Rotislaz, asked for missionaries in 864, the Eastern Emperor, Michael III, sent Cyril and Methodius. Together they won the Slavic tribes for the Church.

Tradition attributes to Cyril the invention of the modified Greek alphabet known as the Cyrillic, which is in use in Eastern Europe and Russia today. Another tradition states that while Cyril was still laboring in the East near Kherson (in present-day southern Russia), he discovered the bones of Clement of Rome, which he carried with him wherever he went and finally deposited at Rome in 867.

D

DABLON, Claude (1619[?]–1677) A French Jesuit missionary to Canada in 1655, Dablon established mission outposts among the warlike Iroquois. He was appointed superior of all mission work for the Roman Catholic Church in Canada in 1670, and dispatched Father Marquette and Father Jolliet on their historic expedition in which they discovered the Mississippi.

DALE, Robert William (1829–1895) Well-known Congregationalist Evangelical preacher and Liberal politician in the 19th century in England, Dale was a much-quoted pulpiteer at Birmingham's Carr's Lane Chapel from 1853 until his death in 1895. Dale held progressive opinions, advocating the disestablishment of the Church of England and taking a personal part on the Birmingham school board to improve education.

DAMASKINOS (1891–1949) The great Greek patriot and Primate of the Greek Orthodox Church during the World War II period, Damaskinos not only looked after the spiritual interest of the Greeks but served as regent of Greece from 1944 to 1946 and briefly in 1945 as Premier. During the Nazi occupation, he was under house arrest for urging his countrymen to hide Jews from the Germans and for helping organize the Greek resistance movement.

DAMASUS I, Pope ([?]–384) Bitterly opposed at his election as pope in 366 by several factions which stirred up riots and lawsuits in protest, Damasus I managed to keep the backing of Emperor Valerian and the Roman aristocrats. When many of the recent converts to Christianity began to worship the martyrs, Damasus obligingly hunted out the tombs of martyrs and decorated them lavishly for shrines. Rome was at that time eclipsed by Constantinople as the capital, and Damasus, outclassed by the Patriarch of Constantinople, was not even invited to the Church Council of Constantinople in 381. His greatest contribution was to commission the great scholar, Jerome, to revise the Latin text of the Bible. He was later canonized.

DAMIANI, Pietro (1007–1072) A peppery controversialist and severe disciplinarian, Damiani was head of the monastery of Fonte Avellana, where he introduced severe forms of discipline, including flagellation or whipping. Damiani excoriated clergy vices in *Liber Gomorrhianus* in 1049. He won the confidence of a series of popes as an uncompromising zealot, and served ably in advancing papal claims as a cardinal-bishop and papal legate. Damiani's piety was particularly directed toward the Virgin Mary, and he was later canonized.

DAMIEN, Father (1840–1889) The religious name of a saintly Belgian priest (born with the name Joseph De Veuster), Father Damien served among the lepers in the Hawaiian Islands until he contracted the dread disease and died from it himself. He traveled to

Honolulu in 1863, intending to take the place of a brother who was prevented from serving as a Catholic missionary because of illness, and was ordained in 1864. Noting the pathetic condition of the lepers who were deported to the island of Molokai by the Hawaiian government, Damien cancelled his plans to minister elsewhere and volunteered to serve as chaplain at Molokai, where he worked until his death in 1889.

DANIEL, Anthony (1600[?]–1648) A French Jesuit missionary who came to Canada with the explorer Champlain in 1633, Father Daniel started some of the earliest schools among the Huron Indians after exploring thousands of miles of North American wilderness. Daniel died when he and some Indian converts were attacked by the warlike Iroquois in 1648. He was later canonized.

DANTE, Alighieri (1265–1321) The greatest Italian poet, Dante popularized in verse form the thinking of the greatest Medieval philosopher and theologian, Thomas Aquinas. Dante's personal career made him world-weary. Born in Florence of an ancient family, Dante took an active part in Florentine civic affairs until he was framed by false charges brought about by papal intrigue and jealous factions. Banished from his beloved native city in 1302 with a death penalty on his head if he tried to return, Dante lived a wanderer's life the rest of his days. His hopes of returning were raised when Henry of Luxemburg became Emperor, but collapsed when Henry died in 1313.

In exile, living in Lombardy, Tuscany and finally Ravenna (where he died in 1321), Dante worked on his great cantos. Best known of his writings, and an all-time classic is *Comedia* (it was not given the title *Divine Comedy* until 1555), an epic in verse form teaching which courses of life lead to rewards and which end with punishment. (His "purgatory" vividly portrayed the horrors reserved for sinners after death.) "On Monarchy" defended the place of both popes and kings on earth as the result of divine plan: the pope to make possible eternal blessedness; the king, temporal happiness, with neither infringing on the other. Dante, the prophet for his age, had an incalculably great influence on the thought of western Christianity.

DARBY, John Nelson (1800–1882) Energetic founder of the Plymouth Brethren, Darby was an Anglican rector at Plymouth, England, who rallied others who were dissatisfied with the cold, torpid formalism of the Church of England in the early 19th century. Darby, a charismatic speaker, established clusters of "brethren" who bound themselves together by faith and love and claimed direct guidance by the Holy Spirit. Although Darby disclaimed any plans to found a denomination and insisted that his "brethren" were informal groups recovering apostolic spontaneity, he quickly found himself busy with an institutional structure. Darby tirelessly promoted the ideas of the "brethren" (no formal ministry because all believers are priests; no creeds; a pentecostal-type of worship) and spread the Plymouth Brethren throughout the British Isles, the Continent and North America.

DAVENPORT, John (1597–1690) Founder of the New Haven Colony, Davenport was a strong-willed, no-nonsense pillar of New England Church and government for over thirty years. Davenport, originally a Church of England rector, held non-conformist views which forced him to flee Archbishop Laud's wrath in 1633 and emigrate to Holland, then to New England in 1637. Davenport, one of the founders of New Haven in 1638, was also its first pastor. Respected for his learning, Davenport was invited to the Westminster Assembly in 1642, but declined. He was deeply embroiled in the controversy in New England over whether or not to baptize children of non-communicant members of the Church; Davenport stood firmly against the practice. In the theocratic colony, Davenport became one of the powers to be reckoned with.

DAVID (5th or 6th c.) National saint of the Welsh, whose biggest holiday is March first, St. David's Day, David is believed to have been descended from Welsh royalty and to have evangelized south Wales, where fifty-three churches are named for him. He presided at the Welsh synod of Llandeewi-Brefi, where his eloquence silenced the advocates of Pelagianism. His shrine at St. David's on the remote headland of Mynyw became a famous pilgrimage place during the Middle Ages.

DAVID, Christian (1690–1751) A Moravian carpenter who was deeply affected by the German Pietism movement, David became the leader of a band of German-speaking Moravians who were forced to worship in secret to avoid arrest and persecution. David in 1722 guided his group to Saxony, Germany, where it found refuge on the estate of Count Zinzendorf and established its own village called Herrnhut. David worked with Zinzendorf to arrange a harmonious relationship with other refugees collecting at Zinzendorf's estate, to maintain a sense of identity among those at Herrnhut, and to identify with the Lutheran State Church.

In 1727, Herrnhut elected David as one of its "elders."

De GUZMAN See DOMINIC.

DEISSMANN, Gustav Adolf (1866–1937) A German Lutheran New Testament scholar and ecumenist, Deissmann was the first to do exhaustive research on the newly-discovered Greek papyri, noting that the New Testament is based on various papyri. Deissmann, no ivory-tower recluse, also labored for closer relationships among the bodies in the world Church, serving at pre-World Council of Churches gatherings at Stockholm in 1925 and Lausanne in 1927.

DELITZSCH, Franz Julius (1813–1890) Precise and pioneering philologist, Delitzsch advanced understanding of Jewish and rabbinical background in New Testament studies. Delitzsch, a German Lutheran of Jewish extraction, was deeply concerned that the Church encounter the Jews in modern times and present the meaning of the Gospel. He opened a training school to study rabbinical material and to engage Jewish scholars in dialogue, and prepared a masterful translation of the New Testament into Hebrew. His commentaries are still widely used.

DEMETRIUS ([?]–232) Bishop of Alexandria in the 3rd century, Demetrius is remembered primarily because he headed the Alexandrian Church during the rise of the great scholar Origen. Demetrius, recognizing the scholarly gifts of the precocious youngster, permitted Origen to gather students and reconstitute the catechetical school in 203. Later, miffed and jealous when Origen had himself ordained in Caesarea in 231, Demetrius called a synod and had Origen banished from Alexandria and refused to recognize Origen's ordination. Demetrius was canonized later.

DENCK See DENK.

DENIS (also Denys) (3rd c.) First Bishop of Paris and the patron saint of France, Denis was sent to Gaul during the reign of the Roman Emperor Decius. Little is known of his career. He died a martyr under Decius' persecutions at the village of Catulliacus, now known as St. Denis, where a basilica over his tomb, a famous monastery and the burial place of many French kings are located. Erroneous traditions appearing during the Middle Ages identified Denis with Dionysius the Areopagite mentioned in Acts 18:34, and falsely attributed to Denis the spurious writing known as the work of "Denis the Areopagite."

DENK, Johann ([?]–1527) An early mystic who insisted that each man possessed an "inner light" whose authority is greater than that of the Bible, Johann Denk influenced an extreme group within the Anabaptists, left his mark on mysticism, and stimulated later freethinkers. Denk was a scholarly humanist in Germany who was attracted to the pre-Reformation Anabaptists. More radical than the already-extremist Anabaptists, Denk held Arian views in which Christ was merely the highest human example of love, and said that a Christian may live a sinless life. Denk, a learned man, assisted Ludwig Haetzer translate the Old Testament prophets' writings into German.

DENNEY, James (1856–1917) A Scottish pastor and professor, Denney served at the United Free Church of Scotland College from 1897 to 1915, and wrote several popular commentaries on New Testament writings and books on theological matters.

DE PAUL, Vincent See **VINCENT de Paul**.

DE SALES, Francis See **FRANCIS de Sales**.

DESCARTES, René (1596–1650) The great French-born philosopher, Descartes, because of intrigue and violence in France, moved to the Netherlands in 1617, where he spent most of his active career. Descartes, a Catholic all his life, was profoundly interested in metaphysics and mathematics, and fashioned a philosophical system which combined these interests. He deeply influenced subsequent thinkers who challenged the traditional ideas in western Christianity. Cartesian philosophy, for example, asserted that all concepts should be doubted until proved true, and that any proof must be mathematically demonstrable. His most famous writings are *Discourse on Method* in 1637, *Meditations on the First Philosophy* in 1641 and *Principia Philosphiae* in 1644.

In western thought, doubt was recognized as the beginning of knowledge, and the consequences for the Church during the next centuries were enormous.

DE SMET, Pierre Jean (1801–1873) A Belgian Jesuit who came to the United States in 1821 as a missionary to the American Indians, De Smet had such phenomenal success that he was one of the few ever able to enjoy the respect and trust of both the Indians and the U.S. Government. Father De Smet's achievements included arranging the Peace Treaty between Sitting Bull, Chief of the Sioux, and the government in 1868.

DICKINSON, Jonathan (1688–1747) An American Presbyterian minister at Elizabethtown, New Jersey, from 1706 until his death in 1747, Dickinson was an education-minded pastor who founded the College of New Jersey (now known as Princeton) in 1746, primarily to train clergymen. Dickinson, the first president, died, however, a year later.

DIEGO, of Acevedo ([?]–1207) The Bishop of Osma, Spain, Diego was a close friend and sympathetic supporter of the great Dominic. In 1203, Diego and Dominic journeyed to France, where they were shocked to discover how the Cathari, an underground movement of "the pure" reacting against the wealth and power of the Roman Church, were undercutting the Church of Rome. Diego devised new strategy for the Roman missionaries in which the missionaries determined to be even more pure than the Cathari.

DIODATI, Giovanni (1576–1649) A noted Italian-born Swiss Protestant theologian, Diodati represented Geneva's clergy at the Synod of Dort in 1618–1619, and assisted in drafting the Belgic Confession. Giovanni Diodati, a gifted scholar, made the excellent Italian translation of the Bible (still being used by Italian Protestants) and a French translation.

DIONYSIUS, Bishop of Alexandria ([?]–264) An administrator rather than a thinker, Dionysius of Alexandria studied under Origen, and later headed the well-known catechetical school at Alexandria before becoming Bishop in 247. Dionysius' writings popularized Origen's teachings so that Origen's theology came to be widespread in the East during the latter part of the 3rd century. Dionysius was one of the first bishops to correspond widely with his clergy—a practice which was copied and used widely as a means of reproving errant clerics and fighting theological skirmishes. A foe of Sebellianism (the Christological heresy which, in effect, made Father, Son and Holy Spirit all one and the same, although three forms) Dionysius also tilted with the abler Paul of Samosata, Bishop of Antioch, Alexandria's traditional rival.

DIONYSIUS, Bishop of Rome ([?]–268) A contemporary of Dionysius, Bishop of Alexandria in 444, Dioscurus Dionysius served as Bishop of Rome from 259 until his death in 268, but, although called "Pope" many years later by the Roman Catholic Church, could claim no authority over other bishops such as Dionysius of Alexandria. Dionysius of Rome, a precise thinker, in 262 put ideas in writing which became the basis for orthodox Christology in 326 at the Council of Nicea and saved the western Church many of the bitter wrangles over words defining the nature of Christ which divided the Church in the East.

DIOSCURUS ([?]–454) Successor to the unscrupulous, ambitious Cyril as Bishop of Alexandria in 444, Dioscurus carried on the bitter feud in the Church between Alexandria and Antioch. As eager to extend his powers as Cyril but less learned a theologian than Cyril, Dioscurus continued to use the threat of the Nestorian heresy as an excuse for battling Flavian, Bishop of Constantinople and leaders in the Eastern Church who represented the school of Antioch. Political intrigues and name-calling grew so nasty that the Eastern Emperor Theodosius II called a general council at Ephesus in 449. Dioscurus manipulated the meeting at Ephesus and had Flavian condemned, but incensed Pope Leo I by his high-handedness.

The tables turned two years later, however, in 451 when following Emperor Theodosius II's death, Pope Leo

I arranged to have a new General Council called at Chalcedon (which is known as the Fourth Ecumenical Council). The Council of Chalcedon rejected Dioscurus' Ephesus Council and deposed Dioscurus.

He died in exile three years later.

DIVINE, Father (1882[?]–1965) Born with the name George Baker, probably in Savannah, Georgia, "Father Divine" was a flamboyant revival preacher and cult leader in the eastern U.S.A., whose fame reached its zenith during the Great Depression. Baker worked briefly as a gardener at Baltimore around the turn of the century, turned to professional revivalism, toured the south with mediocre success, then came north to Sayville, N.Y., in 1919, calling himself "Major M. J. Divine." Changing his title to Father Divine, he developed what he called the Peace Mission Movement (in which the greeting, password and key word was "Peace") stressing temperance, peace and frugality (except for Father Divine himself, who was reputed to have been a millionaire). Father Divine claimed to be the personification of God, having God's "personal body," and divided his time at cult headquarters (called "Heaven") at New York and Philadelphia. He built up a chain of "Peace" Restaurants,, selling wholesome, low-priced meals to poor Negroes, "Peace" Dry Cleaning Establishments, etc., and extensive real estate holdings and investment portfolios. In his hey-day in the 1930's, Father Divine claimed 22 million followers.

DOBER, Leonhard (1706–1766) A Moravian refugee at the famous German pietist Zinzendorf's estate, Dober was one of the founders and leaders of Herrnhut, the village of Protestant monastics which grew into the Moravian Church.

DOD, Thaddeus (1740–1793) The second Presbyterian minister (after John McMillan) to accept a pastorate west of the Alleghenies, Dod in 1782 opened the first classical school west of the Alleghenies, using a small log cabin near his home at Canonsburg, Pa. In 1787, Dod established the Washington Academy, one of the parent institutions of Washington and Jefferson College.

DODS, Marcus (1834–1909) A popular Scots theologian, Dods taught at Edinburgh's New College from 1889 until his death, serving as principal during his last two years. He produced a series of readable but well-prepared commentaries on New Testament Scripture and contributed to leading journals and the *Encyclopaedia Britannica*. Although accused of heresy in 1891 at the Scottish Church's General Assembly, Dods was acquitted by an overwhelming vote.

DÖLLINGER, Johann Joseph Ignaz von (1799–1890) A Bavarian-born Roman Catholic priest who became a distinguished professor of theology and Church history at Munich in 1826, Döllinger became the leader of those disaffected with Rome because of the papacy's attempt to extend its powers. After the authoritarian Pope Pius IX issued his famous *Syllabus* in 1864, pitting the Roman Church against modern science or research, Döllinger spoke out forcefully. During the Vatican Council of 1869–1870 which affirmed the doctrine of papal infallibility, Döllinger wrote his famous *Letters of Janus*. After papal infallibility was declared a doctrine, Döllinger headed the protest movement among liberal German university professors. He was summarily excommunicated by his archbishop for his refusal to conform to the new doctrine. This ignited a resurgence of the Old Catholics, the Jansenist Church of Holland, which tried unsuccessfully to attract Döllinger. Döllinger even refused the offer of the title of bishop in the Old Catholic Church, because he abhorred the idea of schism. He devoted much of the rest of his life working for closer relations between the Old Catholics and the Anglicans.

DOMINIC (1170–1221) A brilliant Castillian Spaniard named De Guzman, who took the name Dominic when he was ordained in 1195, Dominic was a successful and spiritual preacher at the Cathedral in Osma, Spain for several years. In 1203, Dominic and his bishop, Diego, journeyed to southern France, where they were appalled at the way the Cathari—an underground movement of the "pure" reacting against the wealth and power of the Roman Church—were undercutting the Church of Rome. At that time, the Cathari were making great inroads in France, and were turning the local people against missionaries from the Roman Church. Bishop Diego conceived the idea of training an elite corps of Roman missionaries who would out-sacrifice the Cathari leaders by living lives of total poverty and absolute self-denial. Dominic assumed leadership of the company of austere preachers in 1207 which grew into the Dominican Order. Dominic apparently did not sympathize with the bloody efforts by Pope Innocent III to slaughter the protesting sects, although he remained on good terms with Simon de Montfort, the ruthless leader of the forces sent to suppress the Cathari and Albigensian heretics. By 1218, Dominic's group was formally recognized as an Order by Pope Honorius III. Dominic successfully guided his mendicants to grow to Europe-wide status, with sixty monasteries and over 500 friars, by the time of his death in 1221.

DONATUS ([?]–355) A gifted bishop in North Africa, Donatus gave his name to the schismatic group called Donatists which received harsh treatment in the 4th century Church.

Previously at Carthage, a party had protested the ordination of a bishop because of those ordaining him had wavered badly during persecution. Insisting that valid ordination could come only at the hands of sin-free men, this protesting group elected its own bishop, who, in turn, was succeeded by Donatus in 316. What began as a local squabble spread throughout the Church and Empire when the Emperor Constantine refused the Donatus' group financial aid but gave it to Caecilian, Donatus' rival Bishop. Constantine, anxious to keep peace, called a meeting of bishops at Rome to referee the case. The bishops decided for Caecilian.

Donatus appealed. The Synod of Arles, 314, repudiated Donatus' claims, stating that ordination is not dependent on the holiness of those performing the act. Donatus appealed to the Emperor in 316. Constantine, wearying of the wrangle, ordered Donatus' supporters suppressed, and succeeded only in making the Donatists more fanatic. Donatus became Bishop of the schismatics in 316, and energetically led his Donatists in what became a near-civil war in North Africa.

His sect flourished until the Moslem conquest of North Africa.

DONNE, John (1573–1631) Famous sonnet writer, John Donne was born and raised a Roman Catholic but converted to the Anglican communion while a law student. His lyrical poetry was written while he was a young man. At the age of forty-one, broke and in poor health, he accepted ordination in the Church of England as a means of livelihood. His wife's death three years later, 1617, leaving him seven children to look after, produced a spiritual crisis. He became a persuasive preacher of such power that in 1621, he was named Dean of St. Paul's, London.

DORNER, Isaac August (1809–1884) Influential 19th century German Lutheran, Dorner was a professor at Tübingen, Kiel, Königsberg, Bonn, Göttingen and Berlin. He wrote extensively to counter the extremists among German Biblical critics of the time, especially F. C. Baur. Dorner was a representative of the "mediating" school of German theologians and Biblical scholars. His *Doctrine of the Person of Christ* which established his reputation was published in 1835; his massive *System of the Doctrines of Faith*, in 1879–80. Both were widely read in Europe and among scholars in Britain and America.

DOWIE, John Alexander (1847–1907) Sensationalist cult-leader Dowie was born in Scotland, raised in Australia (where as an ordained Congregational minister he held a parish briefly). He drifted into free-lance revival activities, emigrated to the U.S. in 1888, and began a career of starting bizarre sects. With a showman's knack, Dowie attracted followers to his Christian Catholic Apostolic Church in 1896, then insisted the faithful join him at sin-free Zion City (now Zion, Illinois) where he built a tightly controlled, ultra-moralistic community where dancing, card-playing, smoking, drinking and theaters were strictly proscribed. Dowie next grandiloquently announced that he was the prophet Elijah and departed for a costly, headline-making junket to "evangelize" New York City and foreign capitals. In 1906, disgraced by polygamous and fiscal scandals, Dowie was finally dumped from leadership by irate followers at Zion City.

DRIVER, Samuel Rolles (1846–1914) Noted Church of England Hebrew scholar at Christ Church College, Oxford for many years, Driver did careful textual and critical studies of most of the Old Testament writings and served on the Old Testament Revision Committee, 1876–84.

DRUMMOND, Henry (1851–1897) A Scots theological professor who enjoyed immense vogue as an evangelist and writer for the student generation in the late 19th century, Henry Drummond helped many to reconcile their Christian faith with the then-unsettling discoveries of science. He wrote several popular books, including *The Greatest Thing in the World* and *Natural Law in the Spiritual World*.

DUCHESNE, Louis Marie Olivier (1843–1922) French Roman Catholic priest and professor of Church history, Duchesne upset traditionalists by his bold way of teaching history according to the rules of scientific criticism. His erudite and oft-polemical writings on the ancient Church made him well-known in the Church at the turn of the century.

DUFF, Alexander (1806–1878) First Church of Scotland missionary to India, Duff finally arrived after two shipwrecks and losing all of his supplies and equipment in 1830. Instead of addressing his efforts to the lowest classes, Duff was the first missionary to use schools as a means of gaining acceptance by the upper class Hindus. Duff became well-known throughout the English-speaking world and traveled widely, advising mission schools and colonial governments' educational departments.

DUNS SCOTUS, John Erigena (1265 [?]–1308) A leading Schoolman who criticized the works of Thomas Aquinas,

Duns Scotus was a Franciscan who was allegedly from Duns, Berwickshire, Scotland, although other traditions place his birthplace at Dunum, Ulster, Ireland, and Dunstane, Northumberland, England. He studied at Oxford, where he remained for a time as a brilliant teacher, then moved to Paris in 1304, where he excelled as a professor of philosophy. He displayed such great dialectical abilities in defending the doctrine of the Immaculate Conception that he was accorded the title *Doctor Subtilis*. As a Franciscan, Duns Scotus had a strong antipathy toward the rival Dominicans, and was undoubtedly unconsciously antagonistic against the teachings of the Dominican Aquinas.

The dispute over the Immaculate Conception was the hottest between the Thomists (as Aquinas' followers are called) and the Scotists, but other fundamental differences were also present. Duns Scotus denied the Aquinas idea that revelation and reason were both independent sources of knowledge, but insisted that revelation only was the source of knowledge in theology. Duns Scotus also rejected Aquinas' ontological proof for the existence of God, and stoutly maintained the idea of freedom of man's will.

Duns Scotus was such an authoritative teacher that for years the Franciscans looked upon him as their champion thinker and continued their hostility toward the Dominican Thomists. Duns Scotus, after four years at Paris, was ordered to Cologne, but died suddenly shortly after arriving in 1308.

DU PIN, Louis Ellies (1657–1719) A French Roman Catholic professor of church history, Du Pin wrote a book on Church history which appeared to the traditionalists to be faulty interpretations of the Roman Catholic position, if not heretical views. Du Pin, however, avoided being tried for his writings. Anxious to bring his own French Gallican rite into union with other communions, Du Pin corresponded extensively with the Archbishop of Canterbury in 1718 and, later, with Peter the Great of Russia. In neither case, however, was Du Pin successful in bringing about a union.

DWIGHT, Timothy (1752–1817) An American clergyman-educator and theologian, Dwight was the erudite, popular and versatile president of Yale College from 1795 until his death. He was a Congregational preacher who served as chaplain in the American army in the Revolutionary War (at which time he composed the then-famous song "Columbia"). Dwight enjoyed wide influence as a speaker and writer, promoting the theology of his maternal grandfather, the great Jonathan Edwards. The author of many ponderous volumes, Dwight is possibly best known today for some of his hymns, including "I Love Thy Kingdom, Lord."

DYER, Mary ([?]–1660) An English-born immigrant to Boston, Massachusetts, in 1635, Mary Dyer and her husband, William, joined with Anne Hutchinson and John Wheelwright during the Arminian controversy at Boston in the mid-seventeenth century. Mary and William Dyer, unwelcome at Boston, moved to Rhode Island, where they helped found the town of Portsmouth. In 1650, Mary Dyer made a trip to England and became converted to Quakerism. Returning to New England, she zealously and boldly returned to Boston time after time to present Quaker views. Repeatedly jailed and expelled for preaching Quakerism, Mary Dyer refused to desist. She was hanged in Boston, in 1660.

E

ECK, Johann Maier (1486–1543) The cocky and contentious defender of Roman Catholic doctrine and papal supremacy during the rise of the Reformation, Eck was Luther's most tireless and formidable adversary. He served as professor at Ingolstadt, where he distinguished himself for thirty-two years. Eck was early recognized as a powerful debater in the frequent public theological disputations of the time. Invariably, his position was that of a conservative upholder of the traditional medieval church-state establishment.

When Luther, a personal acquaintance, sent Eck copies of his Ninety-five Theses in 1517, Eck answered in a pamphlet, *Obelisci*, blasting Luther as a Hussite. Luther left his defense in the hands of his friend, Karlstadt, who challenged Eck to a debate. For parts of two months, June and July, 1519, at Leipzig, Eck brilliantly defended the traditional Roman stance, forcing Luther to admit similarities between Huss' position and Luther's, and pushing Luther to put himself against the pope's authority and Church Council's decisions.

Eck, incensed that Luther should be permitted to question Roman dogma, devoted his energies to overthrowing Luther and stamping out his followers. In 1520, he returned from Rome with the famous papal bull against Luther's writings—which Luther burned. Eck found himself resented throughout Saxony. Furious, he brought pressure on the emperor to silence Luther, and was even angrier when the Diet of Worms failed to squelch him. In 1522,

he managed to secure an edict in Bavaria which in effect made the University of Ingolstadt senate an enquisitional court. He then turned his attention against Swiss reformers. Before his death, Eck served at various other Church conferences; at Regensburg in 1541, where Roman Catholics and Protestants made tentative gestures toward talking about reunion, Eck violently denounced the Reformers and opposed all efforts at reconciliation.

ECKHART, "Meister" Johannes (1260[?]–1327) A well-known German Dominican mystic, Eckhart studied in Paris and because of his reputation for learning was granted the degree of doctor at Rome by Pope Boniface VIII. In 1304, he headed his order at Saxony, in 1307, in Bohemia. He was noted as an able administrator and gifted preacher. Somewhere in the next years, Eckhart was profoundly influenced by the Beghards and Brethren of the Free Spirit movements emphasizing piety and mysticism in the 12th and 13th centuries in Germany, France and Holland. Eckhart, the first of the speculative mystics, taught that every man had a spark of God in him, and should struggle to allow this indwelling God to dominate all of life. Eckhart, claiming that what is real in all things is the divine, espoused a type of Christian pantheism.

By 1327, opponents of the Beghards sniffed heresy in Eckhart's writings and summoned him to the Inquisition at Cologne. Although he cleared himself at the time by offering to recant anything which was shown to be in error, dying soon after this hearing, two years later, Pope John XXII formally condemned many of his works. Eckhart's teachings, however, deeply influenced his fellow-Dominican and disciple, John Tauler, and a long chain of mystics down to the 20th century, such as Rufus Jones.

EDDY, Mary Baker (1821–1910) Creator of the movement known as Christian Science, Mrs. Eddy emphasized non-medical healing. She was born at Bow, New Hampshire, to Congregationalist parents and spent a sickly girlhood. In 1843, she married George Glover, but was left a widow before the birth of her son (who, because of his mother's ill health, was raised by others and was never close to her). She married a dentist, Daniel Patterson, in 1853 but soon separated from him and eventually divorced him.

Still a chronic invalid, Mary Baker Glover Patterson encountered a flamboyant faith healer named Phineas P. Quimby, of Portland, Maine, from whom she claimed to receive healing. She enthusiastically claimed that Quimby had rediscovered the healing techniques of Jesus Christ. It is still hotly argued how much Quimby influenced Christian Science. Quimby, however, died, and the hapless woman found that her illnesses recurred.

After a bad fall in 1866, she later testified that her case was "hopeless." She began to study the New Testament intensively, and claimed to be given an understanding of what she labelled "Christian Science." Gathering students for private instruction, she wrote down her ideas in 1875 in *Science and Health*, which went through many editings and eventually became *Science and Health with the Key to the Scriptures*. This book, at her insistence, is held to have equal authority with the Bible by adherents to her movement. It teaches that there is one Reality: Mind, God and Good, and that matter, evil and illness are unreal. In 1877, she married Asa G. Eddy, one of her disciples. Mrs. Eddy, who had been holding public meetings for several years, in 1879 founded the First Church of Christ, Scientist, Boston, which as the Mother Church, was carefully supervised by her until her death in 1910. The movement has had a steady growth, and is still governed by the Mother Church, Boston.

EDMUND (1175–1240) One of England's most popular saints, Edmund Rich was an idealistic, outspoken Archbishop of Canterbury from 1233 until his death. Edmund Rich was educated at Oxford and Paris, and preferred the life of a scholar. As archbishop, however, he showed a stubbornness which quickly brought him into conflict with the obstinate, blustering King Henry III.

EDWARD I, King of England (1272–1307) Oldest son of King Henry III, Edward is remembered in Church history as the leader of the last major expedition (1272) in the Crusades. In 1268, Edward, then still a prince, hoped to earn recognition by joining King Louis IX's new crusade. By the time Edward collected money and men, however, Louis was dead and a truce was signed. Determined to carry through his plans, Edward landed at Acre in the Holy Land in 1272 and carried out an energetic but pointless campaign. Narrowly escaping assassination, Edward was glad to return to England in 1272 to be crowned when his father died. The Latin Kingdom in the Holy Land, tottering for years, completely disappeared in 1291.

EDWARD VI, King of England (1537–1553) Frail and sickly son of

Henry VIII and his third wife, Jane Seymour (who died shortly after Edward's birth), Edward VI was a Protestant boy-king, who ruled only six years before his death at sixteen. Much of the time, England was actually governed by Edward's uncle, the Duke of Somerset, who, granting an unusual degree of religious liberty, caused confusion and controversy. In 1549, Parliament tried to secure order and push reform by passing an Act of Uniformity, which imposed the lovely First Prayer Book of Edward VI, the prototype of the famous English Book of Common Prayer, on all Englishmen. In Edward VI's name, most of the English Reformation came to fruition and the basic form of the Church of England was established. Edward VI was succeeded by his fanatic Roman Catholic half-sister "Bloody" Mary.

EDWARDS, Jonathan (1703–1758) America's first (and, in the opinion of many, greatest) theologian, Jonathan Edwards was a New England Puritan pastor whose writings produced an evangelistic, missionary-minded Calvinism which came to be known as the New England Theology. Edwards was descended from illustrious New England families, graduated from Yale in 1720, taught briefly, served as pastor in New York for a time, then in 1729 became associate pastor with his famed grandfather, Solomon Stoddard, at Northfield, Massachusetts.

Edwards' ability as a preacher caused a great revival at Northfield in 1734–1735, when, on one occasion, three hundred professed their faith for the first time. In 1737, Edwards described his work in the publication, *A Faithful Narrative of the Surprizing Work of God*, which became a best seller in America and England (and established Edwards' fame) and contributed to the resurgence of widespread Christian faith known as the Great Awakening. During the beginnings of the Great Awakening in 1740–1745, Edwards' powerful sermons and books stirred the colonies.

Edwards, for all his insistence on personal conversion, abhorred a shallow revivalism and resisted the emotional excesses which marred the Great Awakening in many places. Insisting that a real conversion meant living a responsible, moral life, Edwards tightened the requirements for church membership—which caused opposition in his Northfield congregation. When in 1749, Edwards announced that he would refuse to administer communion to those not living a Christian life, an unpleasant controversy broke out which in 1750 caused him to resign. For the next several years, America's mightiest speculative thinker humbly served as a missionary to Massachusetts Indians while serving a tiny parish at Stockbridge. Meanwhile, he continued writing his influential treatises on freedom of the will in 1754 and on original sin in 1758. In 1758, he was invited to serve as president of Princeton, but died from the effects of a smallpox inoculation shortly after taking office.

Edwards' son and others of his disciples took Jonathan Edwards' ideas and created the theological system known as the New England Theology, which dominated American Protestant theological thinking for generations.

EDWIN, King of Northumbria, England ([?]–632) The most prestigious convert of the missionary, Paulinus, in northern England, King Edwin introduced Christianity to his kingdom of Northumbria. Edwin encouraged Paulinus' work and helped have Paulinus installed as Bishop of York in 627.

EICHHORN, Johann Gottfried (1752–1827) The great German

scholar who was remembered as the "father of Old Testament criticism," Eichhorn taught at Jena and later at Göttingen University. Eichhorn took the French scholar, Astruc's thesis that Genesis was a composite of several accounts, and in 1781 published his monumental study. Eichhorn was the first to point out the similarities between Hebrew literature and other Semitic writings.

EINARSEN, Gisser (16th c.) The father of the Reformation in Iceland, Einarsen studied in Germany where he picked up Lutheran ideas. He returned to Iceland and began a Lutheran reformed movement in 1540 at Skalholt. Einarsen, who became the bishop of the Danish State Church at Iceland (which was a Danish possession), helped subdue the uprising led by the fiery nationalist Roman Catholic, Bishop Jon Areson in 1548–1554.

ELIOT, John (1604–1690) The great Puritan missionary to the Massachusetts Indians, John Eliot was born at Hertfordshire, England, and educated at Cambridge. Turning his back on a promising academic and ecclesiastical career in England, Eliot emigrated to the New England wilderness, arriving in Boston in 1631. He served as pastor at Roxbury from 1632 until his death in 1690, but devoted his energies from 1646 to evangelizing the Indian tribes nearby. Eliot began schools and model villages for the Indians and trained his converts to serve as teachers and preachers.

At great effort, Eliot taught himself the Algonquin language and laboriously translated the Scriptures into Algonquin. He even paid the printing expenses for his Indian Bible out of his own pocket. Eliot's Indian Bible, printed in 1663, was the first Bible in any language to to be published in America.

Eliot created such interest in his Indian work in England that he was the cause of the first foreign missionary group in England, the famous Society for the Propagation of the Gospel in New England, founded in 1649.

ELIZABETH I, Queen of England (1533–1603) Successor to her rabid Roman Catholic half-sister, Queen "Bloody" Mary, Elizabeth received a kingdom torn by religious antipathies and weary of persecutions by fanatics from both camps. Elizabeth, inheriting her father, Henry VIII's astuteness, carefully advanced the Protestant cause insofar as it advanced England's cause. During much of her reign, Elizabeth was threatened by the powerful Catholic, Philip of Spain, and she found it politically expedient to encourage the Church of England. The restless radical Puritans felt Elizabeth never went far enough, while the Roman Catholics felt she went too far. Nonetheless, Elizabeth, although personally indifferent to all religious forms, by 1563 effected a settlement which consolidated the Church of England (including the famous Thirty Nine Articles, the Anglican Creed) and brought stability to England (sparing England the horrible Protestant-Catholic wars which ripped France and Germany). Elizabeth shrewdly staved off Philip of Spain (who hoped to make England Catholic again by force and had Pope Pius excommunicate Elizabeth in 1570). The astounding defeat of the mighty Spanish Armada in 1588 enhanced Elizabeth's prestige everywhere, and ushered in a golden age known as the Elizabethan Period.

ELIZABETH, of Hungary (1207–1231) The daughter of King Andrew of Hungary, Elizabeth became one of the most renowned saints of the Middle Ages because of her charity toward the sick and poor. She married Louis IV of Thuringia in 1221, but was widowed six years later. Joining the Third Order of St. Francis (the order for lay persons), Elizabeth built a hospice at Marburg and devoted her entire fortune and life to caring for the ill, elderly, unwanted and indigent at her hospice. She was greatly beloved and her name is still associated with the nursing profession.

EMBURY, Philip (1729–1775) Born in Ireland of German refugee parents (who had fled Louis XIV's persecution in the Palatinate), Embury began the first Methodist Society in New York City.

Embury was converted by John Wesley's preaching in 1752, and was soon accepted as one of Wesley's most resourceful associates. In 1760, Embury was asked by Wesley to serve in America. Embury landed in New York, preached his first sermon in New York to five people in his own living room, and eventually organized this nucleus into a Methodist Society which founded the John Street Church. He is venerated by American Methodists as one of the founders of American Methodism.

EMERSON, Ralph Waldo (1803–1882) A versatile New Englander, Emerson pursued careers as clergyman, essayist, philosopher, traveler and poet. He graduated from Harvard and began a pastorate at Boston's Second Church in 1829. He quickly found himself impatient with the dry, static thinking in the Congregational Church and opposed the use of traditional forms in the Church, including the Lord's Supper (which he refused to administer).

His wife died in 1831, and a year later Emerson left the pastorate to begin a career as an independent writer-thinker. Emerson soon attracted a following who styled themselves the "Transcendentalists." Emerson and his idealistic Transcendentalists, emphasizing the power of Thought and Will, put great stress in their own intuition and personal moral law. Emerson published *Nature* in 1836, a short book which called for men to be self-sufficient and liberated from a religion of sterile orthodox formalism. Emerson, next only to Channing, may be regarded as the founder and spokesman of American Unitarianism, and was hailed as the most avant-garde intellectual in the 1830's and 1840's.

EMLYN, Thomas (1663–1741) The first Englishman to use the name of "Unitarian" to describe his beliefs, Emlyn also had the distinction of being the last Englishman to be imprisoned for denying the Trinity. Emlyn was a Presbyterian minister in Dublin, Ireland, in 1702 when he rashly published *A Humble Inquiry into the Scriptural Account of Jesus Christ* which set forth his Arian position, supposedly bolstered by a careful study of the New Testament. He was thrown out of the Presbyterian Church, imprisoned for heresy and blasphemy, and joined the ranks of many other Presbyterians and General Baptists who, attracted to an anti-Trinitarian position, adopted Deism.

EMMONS, Nathanael (1745–1840) A well-known disciple of the great American theologian, Jonathan Edwards, Emmons contributed to the flowering of the school of thought known as New England Theology and deeply influenced a generation of younger ministers. Emmons graduated from Yale in 1767, served as an itinerant pastor for a few years, and settled at Franklin, Massachusetts, where he preached and lived the remainder of his life. Although not a dramatic preacher, he was a stimulating teacher and made a deep impression on theological students.

Emmons, an ardent patriot who supported the American Revolution, was also a die-hard adherent of the Federalist political party. When Jefferson was elected President in 1801, Emmons preached a homily remembered as the "Jeroboam Sermon," comparing Jefferson to the man "who made Israel to sin."

ENNODIUS, Magnus Felix (6th c.) Although the Bishop of Pavia, Ennodius' major interests for many years were the rhetoric, stylish literature of the period and pagan Latin poets. He was ordained in 493, and indulged his literary hobbies until a severe illness changed him from a dilettante into a serious prelate. During the struggles between the Emperor and the Bishop of Rome in 502, Ennodius, whose words carried considerable weight, urged that the pope be judged by God alone—and assisted in boosting the claims of the papacy.

EPHRAEM, Syrus (306[?]–373) The most famous of the Syrian Fathers and a favorite saint in the Eastern Church, Ephraem was born at Nisibis in what is now southeastern Turkey. He was ordained a deacon, but never a priest, and settled at Odessa, on the Black Sea. Although an exceptional preacher and writer, during his lifetime he was renowned mostly for his miracles and saintly living. Once, when his hometown of Nisibis was under siege by an enemy, Ephraem allegedly delivered the town by a miraculous intervention. Ephraem's commentaries were widely used in the Eastern Church, and his hymns are still part of the Eastern hymnody.

EPIPHANIUS of Salamis (315[?]–403) An austere and argumentative leading Father of the Eastern Church, Epiphanius was a bishop who, in his zeal to attack heretics, managed to tangle with most of his leading contemporaries. Epiphanius was born in Palestine, educated in Egypt and returned to his homeland to found a monastery near the modern village of Beit Guvrin. Even in those times when asceticism was common, Epiphanius made a name for himself and his monks by being exceptionally ascetic. In 367, Epiphanius was elected Bishop of Salamis (Constantia) on the Island of Cyprus. His pugnacious personality sometimes led him to extreme action, especially when rooting out heresy, and involved him in some unfortunate disputes with such notables as John Chrysostom of Constantinople.

EPISCOPIUS, Simon (1583–1643) Dutch Reformed theologian, Episcopius was the originator of the sect in the Netherlands known as the Remonstrants, which protested the harsh Dutch extreme Calvinism. Episcopius was educated at Leiden under Jacob Arminius, founder of Arminianism, emphasizing man's free will in choosing salvation. In 1610, Episcopius headed the group which presented the States General with a set of Remonstrances against the dogmas of the severe ultra-Calvinists. The group, nicknamed "Remonstrants," developed into a party which quickly hardened into a church body. Episcopius in 1612 left his pastorate to teach theology at Leiden. He was appointed spokesman for the Remonstrants at the Synod of Dort in 1618, but was denied an opportunity to make a presentation, condemned and banished. Permitted to return to the Netherlands in 1626, Episcopius taught at the Remonstrants' college at Amsterdam until his death in 1643. He wrote extensively, systematizing Arminianism. In an age noted for its intolerance, Episcopius was kindly toward all parties, including both the stern Dutch Calvinists and the stiff Dutch Roman Catholic traditionalists.

ERASMUS, Desiderius (1466[?]–1536) Matchless scholar of the Renaissance, Erasmus was a Dutch humanist who tried to steer a course of moderation during the early days of the Reformation when opinions polarized either toward the Roman Church or the Reformers. Erasmus, illegitimate son of a priest, received his early education from the Brethren of the Common Life at Deventer and 's Hertogenbosch. He entered the Augustinian order in 1487 near Gouda, Holland, but was irked at the laziness and intellectual torpor of his fellow monks. Arranging to have himself stationed in more challenging surroundings, he studied at the Sorbonne, Paris (where he learned Greek), and in 1499 traveled to England (where he became friends with Thomas More and John Colet) and throughout the Continent, and from 1509 to 1514 taught at Cambridge in England. Erasmus tried to combine culture and Christianity in his living, and in 1516 published his edition of the Greek New Testament and his translation of the Bible into Classical Latin.

At the rise of Luther's career, Erasmus was in Louvain, Belgium. Although Erasmus was expected by his associates to refute Luther, Erasmus, who had no stomach for fights or dogmatism, shrank from getting into the Church disputes at the time of the Reformation. Although he was sympathetic to much of Luther's thinking, the only time he involved himself in a pamphlet discussion with Luther was in 1524 at Basel, when he took issue with Luther's predestination and wrote on free will.

Erasmus tried to take a position of reasonableness and to encourage moderation. As a result, he was scorned by both Catholics and Reformers in the battles of the 16th century as a timid, equivocating intellectualizer. Erasmus, however, had a deep influence in the Netherlands and England during the following centuries.

ERASTUS, Thomas (1524–1583) A Swiss physician-theologian, Erastus' name is remembered primarily by the term "Erastianism" (the doctrine that the Church is always subordinate to the State), although Erastus never himself held such a viewpoint. Well-educated in medicine, theology and philosophy, Erastus was a Zwinglian-type of Protestant. He practiced medicine in Germany and Switzerland, and disputed at Church conferences at Heidelberg in 1560, and Maulbronn, 1564. Aroused at the way in which the Calvinists were using force to promote their ideas at Heidelberg, Erastus in 1570 published his famous *Explicatio*, a hundred theses asserting that the Scriptures nowhere authorize the Church to punish, even to excommunicate, but relegate these functions to the civil authorities. Erastianism was corrupted from Erastus' attack on the use of Church discipline. Erastus was excommunicated by the Heidelberg Calvinists in 1570, restored in 1576, but when a pro-Lutheran faction took over Heidelberg in 1580, was forced to leave for Basel.

ERIGENA See DUNS SCOTUS.

ERIUGENA See DUNS SCOTUS.

ERNESTI, Johann August (1707–1781) A German philologist and theologian at Leipzig from 1742 until his death, Ernesti gave a great impetus to serious Biblical scholarship. In 1742, he began his illustrious career as professor at Leipzig. He edited the writings of Cicero, Xenophone, Suetonius, Tacitus, Aristophanes and Homer, helping to launch the revival of interest in the classics in the 18th century. A devout Christian, Ernesti took the Bible seriously but insisted that the same careful rules of interpretation used in other ancient writings be applied to Biblical studies.

ERSKINE, Ebenezer (1680–1754) Scottish pastor, Erskine was the founder of the first free (non-State supported or controlled) Church in Scotland. Erskine was one of the earliest "Marrowmen," a party in the Scottish Church which was deeply moved by the re-publication in 1718 of *Marrow of Modern Divinity*. The "Marrowmen," the evangelical wing of the Church, however, were accused by their stiffer brethren of emphasizing faith to the point where repentance was unnecessary. Erskine and his fellow "Marrowmen" were censured by the General Assembly of the Scottish Church in 1722. Erskine, annoyed that patrons (wealthy landowners) were empowered to select ministers for parishes on their property, began insisting that each congregation should have total freedom to select its own pastor. He was disciplined by his Church in 1733 for these views, but with three other ministers from the Stirling area, organized his own "Associate Presbytery." Deposed by the Church of Scotland in 1740, Erskine promoted his schismatic group, which ultimately grew into the Secession Church in 1820. In 1747, Erskine's group split over the question of burgesses taking civil oaths (taking the names Burghers and Anti-Burghers). Erskine sided with the Burghers.

ETHELBERT See AETHELBERHT.

ETHELRED See AETHELRED.

ETHELREDA See **AETHEL-THRYTH.**

ETHELWOLD See **AETHEL-WOLD.**

ETTWEIN, John (1721–1801) A patient Moravian missionary to the Indians on the American frontier, Ettwein eventually became Bishop and head of all Moravians in the United States. He was born at Württemberg, Germany, and while a shoemaker's apprentice in 1738, joined the Moravian Church. Ordained in 1746, Ettwein volunteered for mission work. He accompanied the great Bishop Spangenberg to the American colonies in 1754. After working in the Carolinas and Georgia, Ettwein was asked to settle at Bethlehem, Pennsylvania in 1766. In 1772, Ettwein led a group of Indian converts to the Tuscarawas River in eastern Ohio. (During the Revolutionary War, however, the Indians were brutally massacred.) Ettwein served as a chaplain in a hospital for wounded American soldiers during the Revolution, and in 1784, was appointed bishop. He spent the rest of his productive life in Bethlehem, the leading American Moravian colony.

EUGENE I, Pope ([?]–657) Elected pope in 654 after the emperor, Constans II, exiled his predecessor Martin I, Eugene I refused to be intimidated by Constans, and spent a tense three years as pontiff before his death in 657.

EUGENE II, Pope ([?]–827) Pope from 824 to 827.

EUGENE III, Pope ([?]–1153) A monk from the famous monastery run by Bernard of Clairvaux, Eugene III was forced to flee from Rome several times because of civil turbulence. Eugene III encouraged an intellectual revival and improved the educational standard in the Church.

EUGENE IV, Pope (1383–1447) A nephew of Pope Gregory VIII, Eugene IV served as pope from 1431 to 1447. He tried to dissolve the Council of Basel convened by his predecessor to bring religious harmony to Bohemia, but the participants of the Council defiantly refused to disband. They continued meeting, insisting that a Council's powers are superior to the Pope's, and ultimately elected a counter-pope of their own. Their counter-pope, however, was never able to muster enough support to threaten Eugene, and faded from the scene. Eugene IV, eager for reunion of the Western Church with the Eastern, nearly succeeded in uniting the two branches at Florence in 1439.

EUSEBIUS, Pope ([?]–309) Born in Greece and pope only four months, Pope Eusebius insisted that those who had forsaken the faith during the grim Decian persecution be reinstated as Church members only after doing penance. Eusebius was opposed by Heraclius, who wanted to readmit everyone wholesale without any display of penance. They got into a long, ugly struggle, and both were shipped off to Sicily in exile by the disgusted Emperor Maxentius. Pope Eusebius died shortly afterwards.

EUSEBIUS of Caesarea (260[?]–339) "The Father of Church History," Eusebius wrote a summary of the course of Church history to 325 which is still our best record of the early Church. Eusebius was born in Palestine, educated under the great Pamphilus of Caesarea, trained in Origen's theology and given access to Pamphilus' outstanding library (which provided source material for Eusebius' writings). In addition to his monumental "Church History," Eusebius also wrote many exegetical, doctrinal and polemical works.

During the horrible Diocletian persecution, Eusebius fled first to Tyre and then to Egypt for a time. In 313 or 315, he was elected Bishop of Caesarea. Eusebius took part in the Arian controversy which rocked the Church (the Arians held a position verging on Unitarianism by saying that Christ was something less than completely God).

At first, Eusebius was inclined to side with the Arians, but at the Council of Nicea in 325, joined with others in condemning the Arian creed. Eusebius presented the Creed of Caesarea as a model for the Council of Nicea. which, after some modifications and additions by the Alexandrians, was adopted and named the "Nicene Creed." The Nicene Creed was the first summary of Christian doctrine by the Church, and continues to stand as a succinct, carefully worded statement of the Church's faith.

EUSEBIUS of Dorylaeum ([?]–452[?]) A Greek theologian during the era of titanic doctrinal struggles in the Eastern Church over the nature of Christ, Eusebius of Dorylaeum spent most of his career trying to uphold orthodox Christology. In 428, he opposed the teachings of his superior, Nestorius, Patriarch of Constantinople and suffered unpopularity. Later, as Bishop of Dorylaeum in 448, he accused the leading monastic leader of the heresy of Monophysitism (denying Christ's humanity and insisting Christ had only one nature: divine). Eusebius of Dorylaeum was one of the many who was caught in the political machinations of the notorious leaders of the powerful Church at Alexandria and was condemned at the infamous Council of Ephesus in 449. In the powerful reaction against the Council of Ephesus and the Alexandrians, a new Council was held in 541 at Constantinople which restored Eusebius, condemned Monophysitism and repudiated the Council of Ephesus.

EUSEBIUS of Emesa (295[?]–359[?]) A distinguished writer-theologian in the Eastern Church of the 4th century, Eusebius of Emesa, born in what is now Urla, Turkey, studied under the famous historian, Eusebius of Caesarea. He turned down the offer of Bishop of Alexandria (saying that Athanasius, then in exile, was the rightful incumbent) and in 339 accepted the appointment as Bishop of Emesa (what is now Homs, Syria). He made a reputation as an exegete of Scriptures.

EUSEBIUS of Laodicea ([?]–268) A saintly leader who risked his life to help unfortunates, Eusebius spent most of his career as a deacon in Alexandria under Bishop Dionysius. He exposed himself to deadly infection by caring for victims during a plague, and later, in 260, during a seige, alleviated hardships among the needy. He also participated at the Council which condemned Paul of Samosata for teaching Christ was "mere man." In 263, he was elected Bishop of Laodicea in Asia Minor.

EUSEBIUS of Nicomedia ([?]–342) An ecclesiastical politician who connived to promote Arianism (the heresy which makes Christ less than fully Divine) Eusebius managed to grab prestigious posts in the Church hierarchy. After serving as Bishop of Berytus (modern Beirut), in 318 Eusebius had himself appointed Bishop of Nicomedia, the residence of the Emperor Licinius. At the Council of Nicea in 325, Eusebius was the main spokesman for the Arian position (Arius himself, a mere presbyter, was not permitted to defend his ideas). The Council of Nicea repudiated Arianism because it stated that Christ was the first of created beings and therefore not co-eternal nor of the same substance as God. Eusebius of Nicomedia signed the new creed (the Nicene Creed), but, because he refused to join others in condemning Arius, was banished with Arius.

Recalled in 327, Eusebius politicked against Nicene Christianity. He cleverly ingratiated himself with the aging Emperor Constantine, urging Constantine to depose many of those who supported the Nicene Creed, and baptized the emperor on his deathbed in 337. Still promoting Arianism, Eusebius arranged to become Bishop of Constantinople in 339, and almost succeeded in establishing Arianism as normative Christian doctrine before his death in 342.

EUSEBIUS of Samosata ([?]–379) Stalwart supporter of the Nicene Creed in the Church turmoil over Christology in his lifetime, Eusebius in 361 became Bishop of Samosata (now Samsat, Turkey). He was an associate of the other great Cappadocian Christians, Basil the Great, Gregory of Nyssa and Gregory of Nazianzus, who at the Council of Constantinople in 381 won the day for Nicene Christianity (after years of bitter political wrangling with the Arians, who denied, in effect, the full divinity of Christ). Eusebius of Nicomedia helped make the Nicene Creed the only Creed of the Empire. He upheld the Nicene viewpoint even when the Arian-leaning Emperor Valens banished him to Thrace in 374. Eusebius was recalled and reinstated by Valens' successor, Gratian, but died a martyr's death (killed by a rock hurled by an Arian woman) shortly afterward.

EUSEBIUS of Vercelli (283–371) As the Bishop of Vercelli, Italy, Eusebius of Vercelli so staunchly defended the orthodox Nicene position that he sometimes suffered as the victim of imperial and ecclesiastical politics. At the Council of Milan in 335, Eusebius of Vercelli refused to accede to the surge of Arianism (the heretical doctrine that Christ is not fully divine) by declining to join in condemning Athanasius of Alexandria, the leading anti-Arian. The Arians, holding power and Emperor Constantius' ear, had Eusebius of Vercelli sent into exile. Reinstated by the Emperor Julian in 362, Eusebius continued to oppose Arian teachings until he was martyred in 371.

EUSTACE, The Great ([?]–118[?])
Historical facts are difficult to come by
for St. Eustace, but tradition holds that
he was originally named Placidas and
was a Roman general. Converted to
Christianity, Eustace refused to make
sacrifices to the pagan deities, and paid
the price of being martyred with his
family. Eustace is the patron saint of
hunters, and in Roman Catholic tradition, is one of the fourteen Holy Helpers
invoked in time of dire need.

EUSTACHIUS See **EUSTACE.**

EUSTATHIUS of Antioch (270[?]–
337[?] or 360[?]) A staunchly anti-
Arian prelate (that is, against the powerful heretical party which held the view
that Christ was not fully divine), Eustathius served as Bishop of Beroea
(now Aleppo, Syria) from 320 to 327,
then as Bishop of Antioch from 327.
An astute theologian, Eustathius per-
ceived the dangers in the then-popular
Arian position, and presumed to correct
the great Church historian Eusebius of
Caesarea for his temporary leanings
toward Arianism. Eustathius also noted
the dangers in Origen's technique of
allegorizing the Scriptures. Eustathius
attended the Council of Nicea in 325,
but a few years later, when the Arians
gained the upper hand politically, was
deposed by a synod held in his home
town.

His loyal supporters in Antioch, however, refused to recognize his replace-
ment and formed a schismatic group
known as the Eustathians. The Emperor
Constantine, impatient with the bickering in the Church, banished Eustathius
and many of his followers to Trajan-
apolis.

EUSTATHIUS, St. See **EUSTACE.**

EUSTATHIUS of Sebaste (300[?]–
377[?]) A famous monastic in the

Eastern Church who was born in Sebaste
(now Sivas, Turkey), where he later
served as Bishop, Eustathius was always
regarded by orthodox churchmen with
some suspicion because he studied under
the heretic, Arius, and always showed
cloudy theological thinking. Constantly
in trouble in his early career for signing
nearly every theological statement circulated, for dubious orthodoxy and even
such irregularities as not wearing clerical
garb, Eustathius in 356 surprised every-
body by proving to be an outstanding
Bishop of Sebaste. He organized programs to help the needy, founded one
of the first Christian Church-sponsored
hospitals anywhere, and established a
monastery which so impressed the great
Basil that it became the pattern for all
subsequent Eastern monasticism. Eustathius was gratefully remembered particularly as a loving pastor. His theology,
never well thought out, caused him to
break with Basil in 373 when Eustathius
got the notion that the Holy Spirit was
not divine. He lived to a remarkable old
age, revered for his compassion toward
the sick and poor.

EUSTATHIUS of Thessalonica ([?]–
1194) An outstanding classical scholar
and Byzantine reformer, Eustathius of
Thessalonica, Eustathius served as Bishop of Myra, then in 1175, was appointed as Bishop of Thessalonica. He
was the best scholar of the Greek
classics of his time, and wrote excellent
commentaries on the *Iliad* and the
Odyssey. As Bishop, he determinedly
upheld the rights of the Church, once
even being banished for a time for
standing up to the Emperor. He defended his people against greedy royal
tax-collectors, and, during the siege and
sacking of Thessalonica by the Normans
in 1185, loyally stayed with his flock.
Bishop Eustathius, opposed to the lax-
ness of the monks and empty formalism

so prevalent in the Eastern Church, worked assiduously to improve the Church.

EUTHYMIUS ([?]–1419) A noted Slavic author of the 14th century, Euthymius started the Bulgarian religious writings, which influenced the Christian development of Serbia, Rumania and Russia. Euthymius was deeply ascetic; he established a monastery near Trnovo, in the monastery-studded Mt. Athos area of northern Greece where he worked on the Slavic liturgy. Later, as Patriarch of Trnovo, Euthymius counter-acted the efforts of heretics in the area. When Trnovo was overrun by the Turks in 1393, Euthymius was forced to endure many indignities, barely escaping alive. In exile in Bulgaria, he completed his translation of the Greek liturgy and composed new forms at Backovo, Bulgaria, before he died.

EUTYCHES (375[?]–454[?]) The churchman who began the heresy of Eutychianism (the teaching that Christ was divine but not quite truly human), Eutyches lived "seventy years a monk, thirty years an abbot." In his old age, Eutyches got caught up in the doctrinal-political disputes during the reign of Emperor Theodosius II. Eutyches, rejecting the doctrine of the two natures of Christ, was condemned by Flavian, Patriarch of Constantinople in 448. A disgusting Church squabble followed. Eutyches appealed to Pope Leo I of Rome and Patriarch Dioscorus of Alexandria.

Dioscorus, a wily politician who was itching to get even with his long-time rival at Constantinople, Flavian, engineered a Council at Ephesus in 449 which upheld Eutyches and denounced Flavian. In 451, however, the Council of Constantinople set things right by repudiating the Council of Ephesus, deposing Dioscorus and removing Eutyches from his monastery.

EUTYCHIAN, Pope ([?]–283) Elected pope in 275, Eutychian is reputed to have begun the practice of blessing the crops and established regulations for burial of the dead.

EUTYCHIANUS See **EUTYCHIAN.**

EWALD, Georg Heinrich August (1803–1875) A noted German philologist and Semitic scholar, Ewald as professor at Göttingen helped advance Biblical scholarship during the 19th century.

EWING, Finis (1773–1841) One of three co-founders of the American Cumberland Presbyterian Church, Ewing differed with other Presbyterians by rejecting their rigid view of predestination. Ewing was raised in rural Tennessee near Nashville, converted in 1800 at a frontier revival, and entered the Presbyterian ministry. In 1810, uncomfortable with the inflexible predestination (some predestined by God to be saved, some to be damned) enforced by Presbyterianism of his day, Ewing and three other disaffected Presbyterian pastors formed their own independent presbytery. By 1814, this presbytery formed itself into the Cumberland Presbyterian Church, and adopted a modified Westminster Confession which had been prepared by Ewing. Ewing in later life actively opposed slavery (although he had once owned slaves) and worked for the temperance movement.

EWING, James Caruthers Rhea (1854–1925) American Presbyterian missionary educator in India for forty-three years, Ewing headed Forman Christian College, Lahore, India for many years, beginning in 1888. Ewing, an expert linguist, published the first Greek-Hindustani New Testament dictionary and Hindustani hymnal.

F

FABER, Frederick William (1814–1863) Noted Victorian hymn writer, Faber was deeply influenced by the saintly John Henry Cardinal Newman. Faber, who began as a Yorkshire Calvinist, became an enthusiastic Anglican at Oxford, then followed his mentor, Newman, into the Roman Catholic Church. He founded the Order of the Brothers of the Will of God (popularly known as the Wilfridians), which later merged with the Oratory of St. Philip of Neri, which Newman headed. Faber's hymns include such favorites as "Pilgrims of the Light" and "The Land Beyond the Sea."

FABER, Johannes (1478–1541) A Roman Catholic Bishop whose rigorous efforts to thwart the Reformation earned him the sobriquet, "Hammer of the Heretics" (from his book in 1524 titled, *Hammer Against the Lutheran Heresy*).

FABRE (also Favr) See LE FÈVRE, Pierre.

FABIAN, Pope ([?]–250) During the meeting to elect a Bishop of Rome, a dove reputedly landed on the head of Fabian. Others, interpreting this as a divine sign, immediately elected Fabian.

Bishop Fabian quickly showed organizational genius by dividing Rome into seven districts and assigning deacons to look after each district. He also repaired many of the catacombs. He died a martyr's death during the persecution by the Emperor Decius.

FABIANUS See FABIAN.

FABIOLA ([?]–399) The founder of the first public hospital in western Europe, Fabiola was a woman of a distinguished noble family in Rome who became a Christian convert. She worked closely with the great St. Jerome after joining the Church at Rome, using her great wealth, prestige and energy to try to atone for remarrying after divorcing her first husband. Following the death of her second husband, she started a public general hospital at Rome, the first of its kind in the West, performing the medical and nursing care in person.

FAREL, Guillaume (1489–1565) Fiery French Reformer and preacher, Farel brought the Reformation to French-speaking Switzerland. As a student at Paris, Farel had studied the Bible and had begun to sympathize with the Reformed position. He made his break with Rome and committed himself to the Reformed Church at Basel in 1524. A gifted and forceful orator, Farel persuaded the town fathers of Neuchatel, Switzerland to adopt Reformed procedures in 1530 and Geneva to declare itself Reformed in 1532.

In October, 1536, when Calvin stopped overnight at Geneva while passing through town, Farel thundered at Calvin, demanding that Calvin remain at Geneva to help with the Reformation instead of retreating to a life of quiet study. Farel persuaded Calvin to be his assistant, then, in 1538, made him his colleague. Farel, however, was soon obscured by the mighty Calvin, but had the good grace and sense to recognize

Calvin's superior gifts. More evangelistic preacher than original thinker, Farel was a memorable pulpit personality whose sermons made an impact on all hearers. including the cool, cerebral Calvin.

Farel suffered the humiliating banishment from Geneva with Calvin from 1538 to 1541, but re-settled at Neuchatel where he spent most of his subsequent career. Farel remarried at the age of seventy, taking a young wife, which was frowned on by Calvin.

FARRAR, Frederic William (1831–1903) An influential broad churchman in the Church of England in the 19th century, Farrar rendered distinguished service as an educator at Harrow and Marlborough, as Dean of Canterbury, as a participant in many social and philanthropic causes, and as a writer of fiction as well as theological material.

FAUCHET, Claude (1744–1793) A French Roman Catholic priest active in the Revolution, Fauchet held great sway over Paris street mobs and helped lead the crowd which stormed the Bastille in 1789. Previously, Fauchet, a curate at Paris' Saint-Roch and court preacher, had been dismissed for his revolutionary views. Fauchet later joined the Girondists, however, and was seized with other leaders of that militant group for counterplots, and guillotined in 1793.

FAULHABER, Michael von (1869–1952) The German Roman Catholic cardinal during the odious period Hitler's Germany, Faulhaber was one of the few critics of the Third Reich who survived Hitler's rage. Von Faulhaber, descended from Prussian nobility, was appointed Bishop of Speyer in 1910, served in the trenches as Chaplain in World War I, was tapped as Archbishop of Munich in 1917, and elevated as Cardinal in 1921. An enemy of Hitlerism from the start, von Faulhaber helped prevent Hitler's attempted *putsch* of 1923. After Hitler succeeded in coming to power, von Faulhaber continued his outspoken criticisms. Although a cardinal of the Church, he was almost assassinated in 1934 and attacked in 1938.

FAUSTUS (405 or 409[?]–490 or 495[?]) The ascetic, pious Bishop of Riez in Provence of southern France, Faustus was exiled by Euric, King of the Visigoths, for being anti-Arian, but returned to his seat after Euric's death. Faustus, however, dissented from Augustine's position on salvation, holding a semi-Pelagian position. In his book, on *Grace and Free-will,* Faustus stated that God's grace saves man, but can operate only when man allows his natural impulse toward salvation to utilize that grace. Although Faustus was later canonized because of his saintly character, without being identified by name, he was posthumously condemned for heretical views by the Synod of Orange in 529.

FELIX, Bishop of Dunwich ([?]–647 or 648) An early missionary in ancient England to the East Anglia area, Felix was sent by Honorius of Canterbury to convert King Sigebert and organize the Church. Felix successfully carried out his mission, made the kingdom Christian, and served as Bishop of Dunwich.

FELIX, Bishop of Urgel (or Urgella) (8th or 9th c.) A Spanish Bishop and friend of Elipandus of Toledo, the "Adoptionist" theologian, Felix of Urgel promoted Elipandus' views in the Adoptionist controversy, insisting that Christ, though the Son of God, was in human nature only a son by adoption. Adoptionism was condemned at the Synod of Regensburg, in 792.

FELIX of Valois (1127–1212) One of the founders of the Order of the Most Holy Trinity (Trinitarians) Felix lived as a hermit monk in the French forests until he was urged by a disciple, John of Malta, to establish an order. Felix and the Trinitarians devoted their efforts to rescuing Christians captured by the Saracens, buying their freedom from slavery. Sanctioned by Pope Innocent III in 1198, the order grew to over eight hundred houses by the 15th century, the zenith of its existence.

FELIX I, Pope ([?]–274) Pope from 269 to 274.

FELIX II, Counter-pope ([?]–365) This Felix, who claimed to be pope when Pope Liberius was banished in 356, was denounced as a usurper when Liberius returned in 357.

FELIX III, Pope ([?]–492) Elevated as pope in 483, Felix III excommunicated Acacius, Patriarch of Constantinople in 485 for trying to modify the decision of the Council of Constantinople regarding the nature of Christ. Felix's excommunication of Acacius triggered a schism which lasted thirty-four years.

FELIX IV, Pope ([?]–530) Pope from 526 to 530, Felix IV angered everyone by presumptuously insisting on naming his successor, Boniface II.

FELIX V, Counter-Pope (1383–1451) Selected by the Council of Basel in 1439 during a time of dissension in the Church, Felix V was a half-monastic layman who was the Duke of Amadeus of Savoy. Eugene IV, who had been "deposed" by the same Council of Basel, however, rallied support at Rome and pushed aside interloper Felix V in 1449.

FELL, Margaret (1614–1702) Wife of Thomas Fell, the influential Vice-Chancellor of the Duchy of Lancashire, Margaret Fell, who became a follower of George Fox in 1652, was one of the earliest and most distinguished converts to Quakerism. She generously offered hospitality to visiting Quakers at her comfortable estate, Swarthmore Hall, in northern England, at a time when Quakers were hounded and imprisoned for their views. Some years after the death of Thomas Fell, she married George Fox (1669). She was revered among Quakers for her kindness and gentle spirit.

FENELON, Francois de Salignac de la Mothe (1651–1715) An enigmatic French author, mystic and philosopher, Fenelon was appointed tutor to the heir to the French throne, Louis XIV's grandson in 1689. Shortly afterward, he wrote his influential treatise, *The Education of Girls*, won considerable acclaim as thinker and educator and was advanced to be Archbishop of Cambrai in 1695.

Fenelon, however, began to espouse quietism. His book, *Maxims of the Saints*, in 1697 drew the condemnation of Pope Innocent XII for teaching mysticism. Disgraced and banished from the French court, Fenelon was exiled to Cambrai.

FERDINAND I, Emperor (1503–1564) Ferdinand, actively pro-Roman Catholic from the beginnings of the Counter-Reformation at Regensburg in 1524, succeeded his fanatically anti-Catholic brother Charles V as Holy Roman Emperor in 1556. Although fiercely loyal to the Roman Church, Ferdinand I was willing to show some conciliation toward Protestants.

FERDINAND II, Emperor (1578–1637) Grandson of Ferdinand I, Ferdinand II reigned during the ghastly Thirty Years' War which devastated

Germany. Ferdinand's hostility toward Protestants was partly responsible for the hostilities between Catholics and Protestants.

FERDINAND III, Emperor (1608–1657) Son of Ferdinand II, Ferdinand III ended the bloodletting and destruction of the Thirty Years' War in Germany.

FERDINAND I, King of Castile (1028–1065) Called *"El Magno"* (the Great), this able Spanish ruler led the troops which reconquered Spain from the Moslems. The success of this devout ruler was a major cause for Pope Urban II in 1096 to decide to call a Crusade to expel Moslems from the Holy Land.

FERDINAND V, King of Spain (1452–1516) King of Aragon, who in 1479 married the heiress to the throne of Castile. Ferdinand shrewdly united the two strongest kingdoms into what became the Spanish Empire. Ferdinand conquered Granada in 1492, ending the last Moslem state in Europe, and won the title from the pope, "The Catholic." Ferdinand and Isabella commissioned the Genoese navigator, Christopher Columbus, who opened vast new territories in the New World for Spain, making Spain for a century the wealthiest and strongest power in Europe.

FESCH, Joseph (1763–1839) A French Corsican cardinal, Fesch was in effect an uncle to Napoleon Bonaparte and was propelled to prominence when his nephew became Emperor of France. Fesch enjoyed Napoleon's favor until Napoleon and Pope Pius VII clashed in 1806. Fesch, put in the unenviable position of trying to mediate, was excoriated by Napoleon for weakness for not winning over the pope, and criticized by Pius for daring to suggest submission to an emperor. In 1811, Fesch was dismissed by Napoleon.

FESSLER, Ignaz Aurelius (1756–1839) A colorful Hungarian who started as a Capuchin and converted to Lutheranism, Fessler became a noted defender of Freemasonry in Germany. Fessler, who had a flair for arousing controversy, aroused opposition by suggesting to the Hungarian Emperor ways of improving the Catholic orders and by writing a book criticizing Catholic fanaticism in England. In 1791 he became a Lutheran, wrote extensively and taught in Germany, Poland and Russia.

FICINO, Marsilio (1433–1499) An Italian philosopher and priest, Ficino was the leader of the Platonic Academy at Florence, famous for its part in classical studies during the Renaissance. Ficino, an expert in Plato's writings, revived western European interest in classical origins, influencing scholars such as Jacques LeFèvre in France and John Colet in England (who passed on Ficino's "discovery" of Plato to Erasmus, the greatest humanist-scholar).

FIELD, John ([?]–1588) An English Presbyterian Puritan who was convinced that Presbyterianism was the divinely-ordained way of governing the Church, Field was co-author with Thomas Wilcox of the strongly-worded *An Admonition to the Parliament,* in 1572, demanding that the Church of England be altered from episcopacy to presbyterianism.

FILLMORE, Charles (1854–1948) Founder of the movement known as "Unity," Fillmore promoted his Kansas City, Missouri cult into a flourishing enterprise through intensive mail and radio appeals and widespread sales of his books and tracts. Fillmore and his wife Myrtle, one-time Christian Scientists, were broke and ill in 1889, when they were "miraculously" helped. Fillmore, who had been crippled, was healed. He began publishing the periodical, *Modern Thought,* the same year in Kansas City. In 1903, the Fillmores founded the Unity School of Practical Christianity; in 1906, although disclaiming denominationalism or institutionalism, they erected a church building, publishing house, dispensary and headquarters. Fillmore, a tireless writer, produced over one hundred pamphlets and numerous books for "Unity," promising relief from financial or health woes through a pantheistic "one-ness." Although Fillmore died in 1948, his two sons continued to supervise "Unity."

FINIAN of Clonard ([?]–550) An Irish monk during the amazing surge of piety and learning which made Ireland's Celtic Church the center for saints and scholars during the early Middle Ages, Finian was head of the monastery at Clonard. Finian has the distinction of being the teacher of the great St. Columba, and is canonized in the Roman Catholic Church.

FINNEY, Charles Grandison (1792–1875) One of America's greatest evangelists, Charles G. Finney originally was an attorney who was converted after reading the Bible, which he had purchased to read after hearing the Bible referred to so frequently in lawsuits. He was ordained a Presbyterian minister in 1824 and began his famous revival meetings two years later at New York City, causing Broadway Tabernacle to be erected to handle the throngs.

Finney, unlike many subsequent revivalists invoking his name, was no religious huckster or mentally-shallow haranguer. In 1857, his scholarly abilities were recognized when he was invited to open the department of theology at newly-founded Oberlin University in Ohio and later to serve as president of Oberlin from 1851 to 1866.

Finney, who preached and taught that Christians must demonstrate their commitment by participating in current community affairs, took an active part in the abolition movement.

FINNIAN, St. See **FINIAN.**

FISHER, Edward (1627–1655) The probable author of the anonymous theological tract, *The Marrow of Modern Divinity,* which became a great favorite with the republican-minded Puritans, Fisher personally was an ardent Royalist. Fisher, although born to the patrimony of an English gentleman, somehow got into financial straits and sold his father's estate. He taught school for a time, and wrote theological pieces, but finally fled to Ireland to escape his creditors. Fisher's *The Marrow of Modern Divinity,* widely circulated among Puritans, was the source of the name of the "Marrowmen," an 18th century Scottish evangelical group headed by Ebenezer Erskine and Thomas Boston.

FISHER, John (1469[?]–1535) The only English bishop who had the courage to stand up to King Henry VIII during the divorce from Catherine of Aragon, John Fisher was eventually beheaded for denying Henry VIII supremacy of the Church in England. Fisher, in contrast to the many greedy worldlings in the Church at the time, was of impeccable character. A distinguished humanist scholar, he was a close friend of such notables as Erasmus and Sir Thomas More (who was executed with Fisher).

Fisher infuriated Henry VIII for opposing the plans to shed Catherine of Aragon to remarry. When Henry pushed and supplanted the crown in place of the pope as head of the Church in England in 1534, Fisher politely refused to recognize Henry's new title or role.

He was awarded a cardinal's hat by the pope while in prison, but was martyred in 1535 by King Henry VIII who vowed that Fisher would have no head to wear it on.

FLACIUS, Matthias (Illyricus) (1520–1575) An uncompromising Lutheran theologian and Church historian who held academic posts at Wittenberg, Jena, Antwerp, Frankfurt and Magdeburg, Flacius was prominent in keeping alive Lutheranism during the troublous times of the mid-sixteenth century. At one point, when Magdeburg and a few other northern German cities were the only Protestant centers not crushed by Catholic kings, Flacius' stubborn refusal to admit defeat helped prevent the eclipse of the Lutheran cause. Flacius' personality and positive views sometimes caused him to feud with other Church leaders, particularly the gentle Melanchthon, whom Flacius occasionally accused of being too compromising.

FLANAGAN, Edward Joseph (1886–1948) Irish-born U.S. Catholic priest who founded Boys' Town, Nebraska, in 1917, Father Flanagan gained fame by making good citizens of boys who had been in trouble. Flanagan began his work at Omaha, Nebraska, where in 1916 while serving as a pastor, he established the Home for Homeless Boys. His Boys' Town has served as the model for many centers for boys throughout the world.

FLAVIAN ([?]–449) Elected Patriarch of Constantinople in 446, Flavian stood against the unscrupulous Bishop of Alexandria named Dioscurus, who played politics in the Church to advance the Arian cause (that Christ is not quite fully divine). Flavian, caught in an involved and bitter wrangle between the adherents of the Alexandrian school (the Arian) and the Antioch school, moved to censure an incompetent but influential troublemaker and heretic named Eutyches, who was Dioscurus' follower and a member of the Alexandrian Arian group serving under Flavian. The powerful Dioscurus arranged a Church council, the Council of Ephesus, and contrived to have the Council in 449 condemn Flavian. Flavian, who lived with tension and disappointment, died soon afterward, still loyal to the orthodox idea of the nature of Christ. He was vindicated, however, in 451 when the Council of Constantinople adopted his position on the nature of Christ as normative for the Church and deposed Dioscurus.

FLAVIAN I ([?]–404) One of the Patriarchs of Antioch bearing the name Flavian, Flavian I was an advocate and supporter of the orthodox party opposing the Arians (who taught that Christ was not quite truly divine) during the bitter Church quarrels over the nature of Christ. Flavian's rule at Antioch was troubled by the Eustathians, a sect of dissidents at Antioch protesting the ousting of an earlier Patriarch named Eustatius.

Flavian is honored as the person who originated the art of antiphonal singing when he and his followers and his friend, Diodurus of Tarsus, and his followers met outside the city walls of Antioch to worship, and began singing back and forth to one another.

FLAVIAN II ([?]–518) Another Patriarch of Antioch, this Flavian was a bland leader who tried unsuccessfully to appease all theological parties, but provoked riots in 511 during the disgraceful Church quarrels over Christology. Flavian II was deposed and removed to Petra.

FLIEDNER, Theodor (1800–1864) A German Protestant called as pastor to the village of Kaiserswerth (near Düsseldorf) in 1821, Pastor Fliedner began a useful lifetime of founding institutions to look after people who were being forgotten in the growth of the industrial revolution. Fliedner, one of the first to back prison reform, opened a refuge for discharged women convicts in his manse in 1833. Three years later, in 1836, he established the first of his Deaconness Houses and Hospitals, which came to be widely copied throughout the world. Fliedner's Deaconnesses, although not under irrevocable vows, were a Lutheran nursing order caring for the poor and sick and elderly. In 1842, Fliedner started an orphanage for girls; in 1847, a hospital for mentally-ill women. Traveling extensively in 1849–1851 to establish "mother houses," Fliedner set up centers for creating additional training centers for his deaconnesses. Fliedner was responsible for much of the involvement of the Church in the 19th century in social welfare, such as care of the sick, emotionally ill, prisoners, underprivileged and homeless.

FORMOSUS, Pope ([?]–896) Pope from 891 to 896, Formosus was caught up in the political discord in Rome caused by the rivalry between the princes of Spoleto and the German emperors. Because of questions about the legitimacy of his elevation as pontiff, Formosus' reign was ineffective.

FORSYTH, Peter Taylor (1848–1921) Scots-born English Congregationalist theologian, writer and teacher, Forsyth fused evangelical orthodox Christology with the intellectual qualities of modern scholarship to produce influential books and sermons during the pre-World War I era. At the time when much Christian thinking was drifting from the centrality of Jesus Christ, P. T. Forsyth produced books such as *The Cruciality of the Cross, The Person and Place of Jesus Christ* and *The Charter of the Church*, emphasizing the Crucifixion and Resurrection. Forsyth was one of few to be perturbed at the way churchmen on both sides of World War I descended to jingoistic patriotism and blindly backed the War.

FORTUNATUS, Venantus (530–609) Bishop of Poitiers, France, Fortunatus was the friend of most eminent 6th century churchmen and wrote graceful poems in Latin, many of which were made into hymns. He was later canonized.

FOSTER, Stephen Symonds (1809–1881) One of the 19th century Church's most savage critics, seminary-trained Foster was a radical abolitionist who persistently interrupted worship services to flail the institutional Church for its lack of concern toward the slavery issue. Foster's attacks provoked numerous mob scenes.

FOWLER, Charles Henry (1837–1908) An American Methodist Episcopal Bishop interested in education and missions, Fowler started universities at Nanking and Peking, China and helped found Nebraska Wesleyan University.

FOX, George (1624–1691) The Founder of the Society of Friends (the Quakers), George Fox grew up in Leicester, England during the religious and political upheavals of the 17th century. Fox, a serious-minded, sensitive youth, left home twice, to wander through England to listen to the sectarian squabbles ripping the Church. After concluding that the organized Church was hopelessly absorbed in trivialities, Fox turned inward. In 1647, his "Journal" records, "I heard a Voice which said, 'There is One, even Jesus Christ, who can speak to thy condition,' and when I heard it, my heart did leap for joy."

George Fox immediately began preaching his doctrine (direct perception of God) to the lower middle classes in the English midlands. By 1670, he had fashioned a well-knit network of "Meetings" throughout Britain.

Fox, a mystic, emphasized what he called the "Inner Light," or God's revelation of Himself to every responsive person. He iconoclastically rejected all ecclesiasticism, ignoring titles, ceremony, hierarchical organization, even abhorring paid clergy and church buildings (which Fox sourly referred to as "steeplehouses") in his movement. Fox's ideas on citizenship, prickly notions for the 17th century, led him to refuse to bear arms or to take oaths. (Quakers in court now are permitted to affirm rather than to swear.) He urged his followers to dress simply, to ignore frivolous pastimes and to use plain speech, including "Thee" and "Thou" when addressing each other.

Fox encountered immense opposition from the conventionalists of his day, enduring arrest and jail terms in 1649 at Nottingham, 1650–51 at Derby (at which time one of the judges whom Fox advised to "tremble at the Word of the Lord" angrily used the term "Quaker" as an epithet against Fox and his supporters); other imprisonments were in 1653 at Carlisle, 1656 and again in 1664 at Lancaster, 1666 at Scarborough and finally from 1673 to 1675 at Worcester.

Several thousand Quakers suffered imprisonment as a result of the repressive "Quaker Act" passed by Parliament in 1662. Fox's Society of Friends, adhering to the sufficiency of the Inner Light as matters of faith and conduct, spread to the colonies and the continent, and took the lead in many areas of social reform in succeeding centuries.

FOXE, John (1516–1587) An ardent English Protestant who was forced to flee to safety to the continent during Queen Mary's severe persecution of those holding Reformed views, 1553 to 1558, Foxe eked out a living at Strassburg, Frankfurt and Basel, as a proofreader to writers and printers. He carefully compiled records of those suffering repression under Mary in England, and with woodcuts vividly portraying grisly ordeals, in 1563 published an English version of what came to be known as "Foxe's Book of Martyrs." Actually titled, *Actes and Monuments of These Latter and Perillous Dayes,* Foxe's book became a sensational best seller, fanning the fires of anti-Catholic feeling in England for several generations.

FRANCES CABRINI See CABRINI, FRANCES.

FRANCIS of Assisi (1182–1226) The world's favorite Christian saint, this gentle lover of everyone and everything in God's creation possessed a contagious piety and unaffected goodness which endeared him to everyone from lepers to leaders.

Francis, son of a wealthy cloth merchant, spent a harmlessly frivolous youth, and was transformed after a severe illness and a year's imprisonment as a prisoner of war. Recklessly giving away everything he owned and much of his father's stock (to his father's disgust and anger) Francis began begging to raise funds to restore ruined churches and help the poor. He had an affectionate regard for everyone in need, particularly loathed outcasts such as lepers.

Francis' preaching centered on the need for penance. When he was finally granted permisson by the pope to found a new order, it was first called the Preachers of Penance, but later known, of course, as the Franciscans. Francis traveled widely in his preaching, including one celebrated trip to Egypt and Palestine, where he preached to the sultan.

Deeply ascetic and given to fasting and praying for long stretches, Francis had ecstatic visions and is reported to have had *stigmata,* bleeding wounds on his body at the places where the wounds were on the crucified Jesus' body. He performed numerous miracles and was the brightest personality in the dreary late Medieval period of history.

FRANCIS of Paola (1416–1507) A harshly ascetic Franciscan with little of the effervescent charm of his namesake from Assisi, Francis of Paola retired as a hermit to a cave while still in his teens to live a super-holy life. He gathered some like-minded adherents who, in 1474, were recognized as the Order of Hermits of St. Francis of Assisi, but changed in 1493 to the Order of Minims. The Minims were distinguished for adding to the usual monastic vows the requirement to abstain completely from all meat, fowl, eggs or dairy products.

FRANCIS de Sales (1567–1622) Bishop of Geneva, Francis de Sales recovered great blocs of people in the Savoy near Geneva who had been enticed from Rome by the Reformation, and wrote some of the best devotional reading of the Christian Church. As a student, de Sales was beset by deep doubts, despairing of his salvation and completing a law course before finally entering the priesthood in 1593. He proved to be an extraordinarily adroit administrator and gifted missionary, and quickly advanced to be bishop. Francis de Sales founded numerous monastic communities and participated in Church affairs. He is best known today, however, for his masterpiece, *Introduction*

to the Devout Life, and other excellent writings in Christian mysticism.

FRANCIS XAVIER (1506–1552) The Spanish Jesuit missionary to the Orient in the 16th century, Francis Xavier has been called the greatest missionary since the Apostle Paul. Francis Xavier, descended from Basque nobility, taught philosophy at Beauvais until meeting the charismatic Ignatius Loyola, who induced Xavier to study theology and join the newly-founded Society of Jesus. Ordained a priest in 1537, Xavier heard the appeal of King John III of Portugal for missionaries to India and walked from France to Portugal to answer the call. He was sent to Goa on the coast of India in 1542, and began an amazing career of preaching and organizing a Christian witness in the Far East. In little more than ten years, covering enormous distances and traveling through Ceylon, Hindustan, the Malaccas, parts of China, and Japan (where he founded a particularly flourishing Church), Xavier converted over one million Asians.

FRANCKE, August Hermann (1663–1727) The gifted and influential German Pietist educator and theologian, Francke while teaching at Leipzig University in 1686 founded a Bible study group of university instructors known as the *Collegium Philobiblicum.* The following year, while working on a sermon on John 20:31 at Luneburg, Francke experienced what he described as a "new birth." Moving to Dresden where he spent some time with Spener, Francke became part of the German Pietist movement—the group reacting against the cold, unemotional intellectualizing of the faith and emphasizing an intensely personal awareness of spiritual realities, stressed individual Bible study.

Francke returned to Leipzig and soon

caused a rupture in the university with his popular lectures. Harried by a faculty colleague, Carpzov, Francke moved to Erfurt, where he again stirred up controversy with his preaching, and settled finally in 1691 at Halle, where he exercised a powerful ministry. Under Francke, Halle became the center for German Pietism. One of the first to see the need for missionaries, he inspired over sixty from Halle to go as missionaries in the 18th century.

Francke, concerned for the welfare of poor and orphans, also opened carecenters. His school for underprivileged children in 1695 was so successful an educational experiment that the well-to-do wanted to enroll their children, and led Francke in 1696 to open the *Paedagogium,* which pioneered in educational methods.

FREDERICK I, Emperor (Barbarossa or "Red Beard") (1122–1190) A capable monarch who tried to pattern himself on the great Charlemagne, Frederick I was Holy Roman Emperor from 1155 until his death when he drowned en route to the Holy Land on the illfated Third Crusade. Frederick effectively controlled his German bishops and determined to control the papacy as well. He was defeated by Pope Alexander III's Lombard League of northern Italian cities in 1176, however, and forced to recognize Alexander III as pope. The ablest military leader of his age, Frederick was induced to head one of the three armies in the Crusade which embarked in 1189. Frederick's death, depriving the Crusade of its best strategist, caused the expedition to falter.

FREDERICK II, Emperor (1194–1250) An independent German, Frederick II, like most of his family, had strained relations with the Vatican. He promised to undertake a crusade in

1215, but delayed until 1227, left, but became ill, and returned home. Before Frederick could leave again, however, he was excommunicated by the angry Pope Gregory IX for desertion. Embarking again in 1228, Frederick recaptured from the Moslems Bethlehem, Nazareth and Jerusalem and a corridor to the coast (which were permanently lost in 1244).

FREDERICK I, King of Denmark (1471–1533) An astute ruler who sympathized with the Reformation, Frederick shrewdly respected the privileged nobility (who were mostly traditional Catholics) while introducing Lutheranism to Denmark. In 1526, Frederick quietly arranged to have Danish bishops appointed by the king, and in 1527 presented a statute granting toleration to Lutherans. In 1543, he encouraged Tausen, the German Lutheran Reformer to Denmark, to present the *Forty Three Copenhagen Articles,* the foundation of Scandinavian Lutheranism, to the Danish Parliament.

FREDERICK IV, King of Denmark (1699–1730) A devout Lutheran, Frederick IV sent the first Protestant missionaries to India in 1705, where he established a mission outpost at Tranquebar, then owned by Denmark.

FREDERICK III, Elector Palatine (1559–1576) One of the few rulers to make a personal study of theological issues during the Reformation, Frederick adopted a Calvinist position and instructed theologians to prepare the excellent Heidelberg Catechism in 1562, which he officially adopted in 1563.

FREDERICK IV, Elector Palatine (1574–1610) In 1608 Frederick IV organized and headed the "Union," a group of northern German states determined to safeguard Protestantism in their territories. The "Union" was soon opposed by the "League," a band of south German Roman Catholic rulers who were just as determined to safeguard Catholicism in their territories. Bitter Protestant-Catholic disputes and sporadic warfare ensued, during which each prince tried to impose his belief on his realm, supposedly to unify the population.

FREDERICK "the Wise," Elector of Saxony (1463–1525) The politically clever prince who protected Martin Luther, Frederick, partly out of sympathy to the Reformer's ideas, but mostly out of opposition to Rome's money-hungry agents, permitted Luther to teach his radical ideas at Wittenberg in an age when other rulers would have summarily silenced such speakers. Frederick held sophisticated views, and established Wittenberg University in 1502, to which raw university Luther came as a young instructor and preacher. Frederick saved Luther's career several times, particularly in 1518 when he arranged to shift the hearing of Luther's case from Rome (where Luther would have been doomed) to Augsburg.

FREEMAN, James (1759–1835) The first American to use the title "Unitarian" (in 1782), Freeman was the ultra-liberal lay reader at King's Chapel, Boston. He won over the congregation to his anti-Trinitarian position and succeeded in having it withdraw from the Anglican Communion and install him as pastor, which position he held until his death.

FRELINGHUYSEN, Theodorus Jacobus (1691–1747) Frelinghuysen was a Prussian-born Reformed pastor whose stirring preaching in New Jersey kindled the beginning of the Great Awakening in the American Colonies. Educated in the Netherlands where he came under the influence of the Dutch Pietists, Frelinghuysen came from Amsterdam to Raritan, New Jersey in 1720. He soon affected the entire area with his profoundly stirring preaching, causing vast numbers to be baptized and others to reflect their commitment in changed lives. Frelinghuysen, with others including the great Jonathan Edwards and Gilbert Tennent, was responsible for the remarkable revitalization of the Church in the early 1740's in America. Frelinghuysen in 1737 also began moves which brought about the formal creation of the Dutch Reformed Church in America.

FRIEDRICH, Johannes (1836–1917) A German Roman Catholic priest and theologian who was excommunicated in 1871 for refusing to accept the Dogma of Papal Infallibility issued in 1869, Friedrich, a colleague of von Dollinger, became active in the Old Catholic Church. Friedrich helped organize the Old Catholic Theological Faculty at the University of Berne in 1874 and had a distinguished career as a scholar.

FRITH, John (1503–1533) One of the intrepid band of English martyrs who died in the flames at Smithfield during Queen Mary's repression of Protestants, 1553 to 1558, Frith was a promising scholar who had distinguished himself by assisting Tyndale in the translation of the New Testament. Frith promulgated ideas of the doctrine of the Lord's Supper which eventually in 1559 became part of the Communion liturgy of the Church of England. He was only thirty when he was burned.

FRITZ, Samuel (1654–1728) A German Jesuit who went to the upper Amazon and Maranon River wilderness of South America in 1684, Fritz worked forty-two years with native tribes to establish the beginnings of Christianity in the area. Fritz explored and accurately charted large areas of what is now Peru, Ecuador and Brazil. Arrested as a "Spanish spy" by the hostile Portugese on one mapping tour, he languished two years in a steamy prison.

FROMENT, Antione (1508–1581) A lesser-known Swiss reformer, Froment, an associate of Guillaume Farel (the fiery thunderer who kept Calvin in Geneva) in 1532 was the first to come to Geneva to preach reformed doctrine. Froment had training as a schoolmaster, and came to Geneva to teach. His first sermon in public precipitated a riot. He persevered, however, and laboriously built up a following, paving the way for Farel to come to Geneva, and ultimately for the great Reformer Calvin to make Geneva the center of the mid-sixteenth century reformation.

FROUDE, Richard Hurrell (1803–1836) Until his untimely death leading light of the "Oxford Movement," the Anglo-Catholic group of young Anglicans at Oriel College, Oxford in the 1830's, Froude was a Church of England clergyman who insisted that the Church must recover ancient practices dropped by the reformers, such as fasting, celibacy and reverence for the saints. Although he died at thirty-three, Froude deeply affected the thinking of colleagues who made names for themselves including Keble and Newman. Froude wrote several of the famous "Tracts for the Times," issued by the Oxford Movement.

FRUMENTIUS ([?]–380) Born in Tyre of Phoenicia, Frumentius was the founder of the Abyssinian Church. As a young man on his way to India on a business trip with an uncle and a brother, Aedesius, Frumentius was captured by Ethiopian pirates on the shores of Red Sea. All of the party were murdered except Frumentius and Aedesius, who were sold as slaves to the Ethiopian king, Aksum. Frumentius and Aedesius ultimately rose to positions of responsibility in Aksum's court, secured their freedom and formed a Christian congregation in the kingdom. Aedesius ultimately went to Palestine, but Frumentius, consecrated a bishop by the Alexandrian Church in 328 remained in Abyssinia.

FRY, Elizabeth Gurney (1780–1845) The Quaker minister who was the founder of modern prison reform, Elizabeth Fry, wife of Joseph Fry, was a noted English Quaker in the early 19th century. Mrs. Fry shocked Newgate prison officials by insisting on visiting the inmates. Finding appalling conditions at Newgate where women and children were thrown in with criminals, and where all were treated as animals, the indomitable Quaker lady began a crusade, starting an association in 1817 to improve the conditions for women prisoners. She expanded her interests to found shelters for the homeless, to start an organization to locate jobs for unemployed and an agency to provide for the poor. Her zeal helped push the Quakers into the forefront of the battle for social concerns.

FRYTH See **FRITH.**

FULBERT of Chartres (960[?]–1028) The gifted, cultured Bishop of Chartres, Fulbert began the Gothic masterpiece, Chartres Cathedral, when a fire destroyed the earlier structure. He originated new forms of education and opened the outstanding Cathedral School at Chartres. A conscientious churchman and citizen, Fulbert maintained strict standards among his clergy, participated in political life in France, wrote extensively and practiced medicine. Many of his lovely poems became classics in hymn books.

G

GALILEO Galilei (1564–1642)   One of those who prepared the path for modern science, Galileo was humiliatingly censured by the Vatican in 1633 for advocating Copernican views of the universe (that the earth revolves around the sun and is not the center of the universe), starting the era of distrust between the scientific community and the Church. Galileo, whose work gave modern mechanics and physics its first firm basis, was an independent-minded inquirer whose refusal to accept traditional understandings of nature and the universe made him unpopular at Pisa. He moved to the University of Padua, where he stayed eighteen years, inventing the thermometer and conducting research in motion and gravity.

In 1609, he secured a primitive telescope and quickly confirmed what he had long suspected—that Corpernicus' theory was correct. Galileo immediately antagonized traditionalists, who charged him with opposing the Bible, the Church Fathers, Aristotle, the ancient astronomer Ptolemy, Church tradition and common sense. Galileo made the mistake of trying to reconcile his scientific theory with Scripture.

In 1616, official theologians and the Inquisition met at Rome and declared the Copernican theory contrary to Scripture. Furthermore, the Vatican prohibited any publication of any theories contrary to the ancient Ptolemaic view (that the earth is the center of the universe). Pope Paul V ordered Galileo not to "hold, teach or defend", the heretical teaching that the earth moves around the sun.

Galileo, however, in 1623 published *The Assayer,* pointing out a Jesuit astronomer's errors on comets, and in 1630 wrote the popular *Dialogue on Two Chief World Systems.* In 1633, Galileo was summoned before the Inquisition a second time, forced to sign a statement abjectly recanting his views and shamefully subjected to the indignity of house arrest the rest of his life.

This unjust verdict, regarded by the scientific world as a painful wound by the Church against an honest scientist and against free inquiry, has remained as an obstacle blocking cooperation between many in the university-scientific community and the Church.

GALLITZIN, Demetrius Augustine (1770–1840)   A Dutch-born, American-educated Roman Catholic priest-missionary to the Indians and frontiersmen of western Pennsylvania in 1792, Gallitzin (who used the name Schmet or Smith until his father's death in 1803) founded Loretto (Penna.), and helped open Roman Catholic missionary work on the frontier.

GALLUS (7th c.)   An Irish monk who was a disciple and colleague of St. Colambanus, Gallus lived a hermit life as an Anchorite in the Swiss Alps for many years. The monastery of St. Gall is named for him, although he never lived there.

GAPON, Georgi Apollonovich (1870[?]–1906)   One of the few priests of the Russian Orthodox Church to identify with the restless workers in Czarist Russia, Father Gapon led the peaceful marchers on "Bloody Sunday," January 22, 1905, when Czarist troops opened fire, massacring hundreds. Gapon in 1904 organized a workers' movement at St. Petersburg (now Leningrad) to undermine the appeal of revolutionary socialism. On "Bloody Sunday," he planned merely to present a petition to Czar Nicholas II at the Winter Palace. Gapon, who escaped injury, was forced to flee from Russia for a time. "Bloody Sunday" exacerbated the seething discontent and revolutionary mood of great numbers in Russia. Gapon, contacted by the secret police to return in order to assist in rounding up revolutionary socialists, agreed to return to St. Petersburg in 1906, but was seized and executed.

GARNET, Henry Highland (1815–1882) A prominent Negro radical Abolitionist speaker and pastor, Garnet, who was born a slave but escaped to educate himself, worked for the American Anti-Slavery Society. He led the black abolitionist movement and in 1843 he urged in an address that all slaves rise and kill their masters. After serving as pastor in various Presbyterian congregations and at Jamaica as a missionary, in 1881 Garnet was appointed as U.S. Minister to Liberia.

GARRY, Spokane (1811–1892) American Indian chief and Christian missionary, Garry was converted to Christianity at an Indian school at Winnipeg, and returned to his Spokane tribe to organize a congregation and open a school. Garry was instrumental in preventing many Indians from joining Chief Joseph's insurrection and promoted peace and progress among the tribes in the American Northwest.

GELASIUS I, Pope ([?]–496) An African who served as pope from 492 until 496, Gelasius I rigidly defended his idea of the exalted position of the papacy, insisting that the pope had final authority over all rulers. He inevitably clashed with the Byzantine Emperor Anastasius of Constantinople, who claimed supremacy over the pope. This controversy ran for many years; the papacy continued to hold Gelasius' view for nearly 600 years.

GELASIUS II, Pope ([?]–1119) A pope from 1118 to 1119, Gelasius spent a tragic reign, imprisoned on orders from Emperor Henry V and later forced to flee from Henry's invasion.

GENEVIEVE (423[?]–512) The patron saint of Paris, Genevieve is reputed to have taken religious orders as a young girl and moved to Paris. Legends abound about her exploits. Once, when Attila the Hun threatened an invasion of Paris, Genevieve persuaded the inhabitants not to flee but to pray and remain. Paris was miraculously spared and Attila was crushed in 451. On another occasion during a famine Genevieve is alleged to have brought twelve boatloads of grain up the Seine to save Paris. She urged Clovis, the Bishop, and other churchmen to build a church on the site now occupied by the Pantheon in Paris.

GENTILE, Giovanni Valentino (1520–1566) An Italian radical thinker who held anti-Trinitarian views at the time of the Reformers, Gentile was forced out of Italy and fled to Calvin's Geneva. Gentile's brand of Protestantism turned out to be a mixture of skepticism of Scripture and criticism of doctrine, and he was forced to flee from Geneva to escape punishment. His heretical ideas made him unwelcome anywhere, and after many wanderings, he was tried and beheaded at Berne, Switzerland in 1566.

GEORGE (3rd or 4th c.) The patron saint of England, George is one of those half-legendary, half-historical figures about whom little data is available. He is believed to have been martyred at Diospolis (now Lydda, Israel) sometime before the time of Emperor Constantine, perhaps 303. Somehow, George's fame took hold in England. Even before the Norman invasion of 1066, there were English churches dedicated to St. George. By the 1300's, George replaced Edward the Confessor as England's most popular saint and during the 14th century was officially designated patron saint. The legend of St. George slaying the dragon appeared during the same century.

GERALDINI, Alessandro (1455–1525) The Italian churchman who presented the idea of sending Christopher Columbus to the New World, Geraldini was later the first Bishop of Santo Domingo, where he set up orderly procedures of government after the chaos from the Spanish conquest.

GERARD, Tenque (or **Thom** or **Tum** or **Tunc**) (1042[?]–1120) An Italian monk who joined the Crusades in the 11th century, Gerard found the famous Order of the Knights Hospitallers of St. John of Jerusalem to provide safety and shelter for pilgrims to the Holy Land. The Knights Hospitallers achieved fame and power during the Middle Ages.

GERARDUS MAGNUS See **GROOTE, Gerhard.**

GERHARD, Johann (1582–1637) A German Lutheran theologian who wrote and taught (at the University of Jena)

about a century after Luther, Gerhard hardened Luther's thought into a tight system of high Lutheran orthodoxy. Gerhard's book published in 1622, *Loci Theologici*, a throw-back to the Middle Ages, became the classic of the Lutheran scholasticists.

GERHARDT, Paul (1607–1676) The greatest Lutheran hymn-writer, Gerhardt was a German pastor who wrote over one hundred hymns, including "O Sacred Head Now Wounded" and "Jesus, Thy Boundless Love to Me." Gerhardt, intolerant toward non-Lutherans, was put out of his church at Berlin in 1666 because of his loud disapproval of Elector Frederick William's edict of toleration toward others than Lutherans.

GERMAIN (378[?]–448) Renowned as a saint and famous as the Bishop of Auxerre, Germain, descended from French nobility, was trained as a lawyer but joined the Church and gave all his possessions and inheritance to the poor. In 429, Germain was sent by Pope Celestine I to Britain to combat the Pelagian heresy infecting British clergy and established numerous schools for training monks and priests in Britain.

GERMAINE (496[?]–576) An early Bishop of Paris about 555, Germaine is revered as one of France's most celebrated saints. His bones are buried in the Paris church which came to be known as St. Germaine-des-Près.

GERMANUS OF AUXERRE See **GERMAIN.**

GERSON, Jean Charlier de (1363–1429) French theologian and mystic, Gerson played a prominent part in the affairs of the 15th century Church, joining with d'Ailly to persuade the cardinals to call the Council of Pisa in

1409 to try to end the scandalous schism in the Church which produced two competing papacies, one at Rome, the other at Avignon. Gerson, representing the king of France, attended the Council of Constance, 1414 to 1418, where he promulgated his doctrine that Church Councils are supreme even over popes, which was officially adopted by the Council of Constance. Although reform-minded, Gerson joined in convicting Bohemian reformer, Jan Hus. Gerson lost prestige, however, toward the close of the Council of Constance when the Council upheld the Duke of Burgundy, whom Gerson had condemned for murdering the Duke of Orleans. Retiring to Switzerland, Gerson wrote his influential book, *De Consolatione Theologiae.*

GIBBONS, James Cardinal (1834–1921) Prominent American Roman Catholic churchman for many years during the late 19th and early 20th centuries, Gibbons, a Civil War Union Chaplain, served later as Bishop of Richmond and Archbishop of Baltimore before receiving his cardinal's hat. Cardinal Gibbons was an excellent ambassador of Roman Catholicism to the still predominantly Protestant U.S.A. and an equally able interpreter of the U.S.A. to the Vatican. His *The Faith of Our Fathers,* published in 1876, outlined and explained Roman Catholic doctrines in layman's language, and was widely circulated. Gibbons sometimes antagonized the privileged and moneyed people by his pro-labor stands, but was affectionately regarded by all Americans as the country's favorite Catholic.

GILLESPIE, Thomas (1708–1774) The Church of Scotland pastor who joined with others insisting on the independence of a congregation from civil control to found the Relief Church, a parent body of the Scottish United Presbyterian Church, Gillespie served at Carnock, Scotland. The Scots Kirk at that time was torn by the "patronage" question—whether patrons (wealthy landowners) were empowered to impose their choice of a minister on a congregation situated on their holdings. Gillespie refused to take part in the installation of a pastor to a congregation which was unwilling to accept the man. Gillespie was deposed by the General Assembly of 1752 for protesting the patronage tradition. In 1762, he and a few others established the body which came to be called the Relief Church, which combined with the Secession Church in Scotland in 1847 to form the United Presbyterian Church.

GILPIN, Bernard (1517–1583) The beloved English Protestant clergyman who earned the title, "The Apostle of the North," Gilpin worked among the poor in the desolate north country villages in Yorkshire, Durham, Cumberland and Northumbria from 1556 until his death in 1583. Gilpin, originally a priest, was converted to Reformed ideas but had to flee from England to escape Mary Tudor's persecution of Protestant leaders. He returned in 1556, plunged into the backcountry areas of the northern counties, journeying to forgotten hamlets, organizing charity, founding a grammar school for poor children, dispensing help frequently from his own pocket. Although Gilpin was subsequently offered several lucrative and prestigious posts, he chose to remain in the north country among the poor.

GIRALDUS CAMBRENSIS (1146[?]–1220[?]) A Welsh cleric and historian, Giraldus toured Wales to enlist troops for the Third Crusade and wrote a well-known account of his tour of Ireland in 1185.

GLADDEN, Washington (1836–1918) One of the founders of the Social Gospel movement and one of the early leaders in inter-church cooperation in the United States, Gladden served as pastor of the First Congregational Church of Columbus, Ohio from 1882 to 1914. He was one of the earliest voices insisting that Christian commitment be translated into action related to current social problems. Frequently misunderstood (many still mistakenly think that Gladden operated from a sociological rather than a theological stance) and often criticized, Gladden even participated in politics, serving for a time on the City Council in Columbus. In 1905, he was the center of a much-publicized controversy within Congregationalism when he tried to have his denominational Foreign Mission Board decline a large gift from Standard Oil because it was "tainted money" from "predatory wealth." Gladden, ecumenical in spirit, served as moderator of the young National Council of Churches from 1904 to 1907. His deep commitment to Christ was reflected in his well-known hymn, "O Master, Let Me Walk with Thee."

GODFREY of Bouillon (1060[?]–1100) A French feudal noble, Godfrey was a prominent leader in the First Crusade. He kept comparatively aloof from the many intrigues and rivalries which crippled the campaign, and showed a honest zeal to recapture the Holy Land for the Church. When his troops finally captured Jerusalem, however, he was unable to prevent the pointless, horrible massacre of innocent citizens by his rampaging Crusaders. Godfrey, the only candidate on which the squabbling factions could agree, was elected King of Jerusalem. He declined the title, instead calling himself, "Advocate of the Holy Sepulchre." Godfrey, whose domain covered most of the Holy Land, died of plague a year later before

he was able to carry out his plans for reconstructing the ruined land.

GODIVA, Lady (11th c.) The wife of Leofric, an honorable and compassionate member of the English nobility who carried the respected title of Earl of Mercia, Godiva—with Leofric's blessing—generously aided many English monasteries. She was the benefactress particularly of Stow monastery in Lincolnshire and Coventry monastery, Warwickshire. The legend of her riding naked through the streets of Coventry to carry out an agreement to get her husband to lower taxes has no factual basis and is not in keeping with the character of Leofric, Godiva's husband.

GOMARUS, Franciscus (1563–1641) Uncompromising Dutch Calvinist during the theological controversy which tore Dutch Protestantism during the 17th century, Gomarus opposed the teachings of Jacob Arminius at Leiden, where both served for a time on the faculty of Leiden University. Gomarus insisted on an absolute predestination in which God unconditionally decreed election and reprobation, then permitted the Fall of Man as way by which His decree could be carried out (a position known as "Supralapsarianism"). Bitterly denouncing the irenic Arminius for giving a place to Man's will in salvation, Gomarus engaged in several acrimonius public debates. When Leiden University later appointed one of Arminius' disciples to succeed Arminius, Gomarus resigned in a huff. Gomarus' followers in the Netherlands were known variously as Gomarites, Gomarists and Gomarians.

GOODRICH, Chauncey (1836–1925) An American Congregational missionary to China for sixty years, Goodrich headed the team which translated the Bible into Mandarin Chinese in 1918.

GOODWIN, Thomas (1600–1680) Independent clergyman in England, Thomas Goodwin was among those influenced by the Puritan thinker, John Cotton and in 1634 became a Separatist. He spent some years in exile in Holland with the English Separatist community, returning to England in 1640. Goodwin participated in the Westminster Assembly in 1643 which drafted the great Westminster Confession, heading the party of dissenters preferring congregational policy to a Presbyterian form of government.

GORDON, Adoniram Judson (1836–1895) An American Baptist who had an intense interest in missions and evangelism, Gordon founded the Boston Missionary Training School in 1889, which developed into Gordon College and Gordon Divinity School.

GORE, Charles (1853–1932) The influential Bishop of Oxford and a noted theologian-author, Gore led the modern wing in high church Anglicanism during the first third of the 20th century. Gore, a brilliant scholar, taught at Trinity College, Oxford, in 1884 assumed the headship of Pusey House, accepted the position of Bishop of Worcester in 1902, Bishop of Birmingham, 1905 and Oxford, 1911.

GOTTSCHALK (808[?]–868) A controversy-causing monk from Fulda, Gottschalk's contentiousness was perhaps caused by being placed in monastic life against his wishes by his parents as a youth and later being prevented from being released from his vows by the severe Archbishop Hrabanus. Forced to remain a monk, Gottschalk grimly studied Augustine, then introduced a notion of predestination more radical than Augustine's. According to Gottschalk, God predestined some to life, others to death. Gottschalk's double predestination was condemned as heretical at Mainz in 848, following some nasty disputes stirred up by Gottschalk. Hrabanus then imprisoned Gottschalk in a monastery.

GRANVELLA (1517–1586) A bishop of Arras, France, who was an uncompromising supporter of Spain's harsh, intolerant Catholic Emperor Philip II, Granvella in 1559 was appointed to a commission by Philip to force a political and religious uniformity on the Netherlands similar to Philip's Spain. Granvella, dominating the commission, used his power to try to crush Protestantism and promote Spanish influence. He was finally dismissed in 1564 after Dutch patriots forced Philip to remove the unpopular, propagandizing prelate.

GRATIAN, John See **GREGORY VI, Pope.**

GRATIANUS, Johannes See **GREGORY VI, Pope.**

GREEN, Ashbel (1762–1848) Prominent 19th century American Presbyterian clergyman and professor, Green was one of the founders of Princeton Seminary. In 1812, he accepted the presidency of Princeton College, and in 1822 became editor of the *Christian Advocate.*

GREENE, Daniel (1843–1913) Well-known American Congregational missionary to Japan from 1869 to 1913, Greene helped translate the Bible into Japanese and taught for many years at Kyoto.

GREENWOOD, John ([?]–1593) The non-conformist clergyman regarded by many as the originator of Congregationalism in Britain, Greenwood left the Church of England in 1581. He suffered long prison terms in the Fleet and the Clink prisons for denying episcopacy. Between arrests and imprisonments in 1592, Greenwood organized the independent congregation at Nicholas Lane, London, hailed as the beginning of the Congregationalist Church in England. Greenwood, who persisted in defying the established church, was rearrested and hanged in 1593.

GREGORY, The Illuminator (257[?]–332[?] or 337[?]) The patron saint of Armenia, the facts of the career of this churchman are so laced with legend that it is difficult to know precisely who he was. It seems that he was a pagan converted to Christianity at Caesarea of Cappadocia (Turkey) who brought his ruler, Tiridates III, and the Armenian nobility into the Church. He inspired a massive surge of baptisms, making Armenia the first Christian State. Appointed Bishop, then Metropolitan of Armenia about 302, Gregory stood second only to the king. He is venerated in both the Eastern and Latin Church.

GREGORY I, Pope (the Great) (540–604) This remarkable leader, pope from 590 to 604, perfected the organization, the discipline and the doctrine of the Church, and left his mark permanently on western Christianity. Prior to becoming a monk in 574, Gregory had a notable career as a government official, rising to become prefect of the city of Rome—the highest civic office—by the time he was thirty. He brought immense organizational experience and administrative ability to his assignments in the Church and quickly ascended from monk to abbot to pope.

As abbot of his monastery about 585, Gregory encountered flaxen-haired Anglo-Saxon slaves, who so intrigued him by their appearance that he determined to start a mission program among the English. Thwarted from going in person as a missionary, he sent Augustine of Canterbury to England.

Gregory became pope in 590 at a time when floods, plagues and famines had wracked Rome, but restored order and skillfully administered programs for the poor and refugees. Gregory also issued a text on discipline for the Church which became the basis for subsequent official Roman Catholic government and procedures. Intolerant of laxity among his clergy, Gregory insisted on celibacy. He revised the liturgy for worship, instituting the stations of the Cross and introducing the plain chant known as the Gregorian chant.

During the Lombard invasions, in the absence of the emperor, Gregory assumed the function of governing the city of Rome and made his own peace arrangements with the invaders. Gregory at this period made moves which helped establish the Vatican as a separate temporal power and gained the Bishop of Rome recognition as Head of the entire Church. A generous and fair man, Gregory, although zealously opposed to pagan cults, refused to compel Jews to be baptized and gave away vast sums to help the needy. He was canonized by the Church.

GREGORY II, Pope (669–731) An energetic pope who ruled from 715 to 731 Gregory was the builder who erected walls around Rome against the impending Moslem invasion and rebuilt many monasteries. Gregory II, anxious to convert the German tribes, sent the great missionary, Boniface.

GREGORY III, Pope ([?]–741) A Syrian-born pontiff, Gregory III, Pope from 731 to 741, called on Charles Martel (the "Hammer") as Protector instead of turning to the Byzantine Emperor in the East, beginning the transference of Rome's political alignment with rulers in the West instead of the East.

GREGORY IV, Pope ([?]–844) One of the Roman nobility, Gregory IV ruled from 827–844.

GREGORY V, Pope (970[?]–999) The first German pope, this young man was elected through the efforts of his uncle, Emperor Otto III. He ruled from 996 to 999.

GREGORY VI, Pope ([?]–1048) An honorable, upright man, Gregory purchased the title from his ingrate of a godson, Benedict IX (who wanted to sell the papacy to the highest bidder) in order to get rid of Benedict. Gregory, however, was caught between so many warring factions within the Church that he voluntarily abdicated to try to bring peace. He served one year, 1045–1046.

GREGORY VII, Pope (1021–1083) Also known as Hildebrand, his name for twenty-four years while guiding the Church before being forced to accept the title of pope, Gregory VII was a high-principled Benedictine monk who resisted many earlier efforts to make him pontiff. He had worked behind the scenes, guiding the policies, developing the powers and purifying the clergy as Hildebrand the Monk for nearly a quarter of a century, and had to be ordained a priest, then consecrated pope after his election in 1073.

Gregory VII, disturbed by the moral decadence throughout Europe following the collapse of Charlemagne's Empire, drafted strict standards for priests. He surprised everyone by rigidly enforcing these standards, raising howls of protest from many of his clergy but lifting the moral tone of the Church at a time when greed and immorality were widespread.

The resolute Gregory VII even humbled the swaggering, devious Emperor Henry IV of Germany, who, disregarding Gregory's summons to account for his misdeeds, "deposed" Gregory at Worms in 1076. Gregory promptly excommunicated Henry; Henry came meekly on foot to Gregory's residence at Canossa, where he was forced to stand three days in the snow appealing for permission to beg Gregory to lift the ban. Gregory, however, had to deal further with the shifty Henry when Henry later set up a rival pope and marched on Rome. Gregory, forced to leave, fled to Salerno. He was later canonized.

GREGORY VIII, Pope (1100–1187) This pope ruled only two months, dying in 1187.

GREGORY IX, Pope (1145–1241) Pope from 1127 to 1241, Gregory IX grew angered because Emperor Frederick II had apparently reneged on a promise to lead a Crusade and excommunicated Frederick. (Frederick was provoked into going on the Crusade.) Gregory IX canonized his personal friends, St. Francis of Assisi and St. Dominic, and sent missionaries to Africa, Asia and northern Europe.

GREGORY X, Pope (1210–1276) To prevent a recurrence of the long, three-year vacancy before his own election as pope in 1271, Gregory passed a ruling that no cardinal could leave the enclave to elect a new pontiff until the meeting had chosen the new pope. He died in 1276.

GREGORY XI, Pope (1331–1378) The last of the French popes, Gregory XI, pope from 1370 to 1378, transferred the Holy See from Avignon, France to Rome again, at the request of St. Catherine of Siena. Gregory XI, aroused by the reports of the doctrines of John Wycliffe, condemned Wycliffe as a heretic.

GREGORY XII, Pope (1327[?]–1417)
Ruling from 1406 to 1415, Gregory
XII was caught in a web of intrigues
at a time when two rival parties and a
rival pope, Antipope Benedict XIII at
Avignon, were all maneuvering for
prominence and power. The weary, aged
Gregory XII abdicated at the Council
of Constance in 1415 to try to bring
peace to the Church.

GREGORY XIII, Pope (1502–1585)
An educator, Pope Gregory XIII
founded twenty-three colleges and seminaries during his rule from 1572 to
1585.

Some accuse him of complicity in the
horrible St. Bartholomew's Day Massacre of French Protestants in 1572, but
the point has never been conclusively
proved. Our modern calendar is named
for this pope; his calendar reforms
corrected the older Julian calendar.

GREGORY XIV, Pope (1535–1591)
Pope from 1590 to 1591.

GREGORY XV, Pope (1554–1623)
Pope from 1621 to 1623.

GREGORY XVI, Pope (1765–1846)
Pope from 1831 to 1846, Gregory XVI
held autocratic views which brought him
into conflict with nationalist-minded
heads of state and others at a time when
the tide of anti-clericalism was strong
in western Europe.

GREGORY V, Patriarch (1745–1821)
The favorite Greek hero of the Greek
War of Independence, Gregory V was
Patriarch of the Greek Orthodox
Church at Constantinople from 1797
until his violent death. His sympathies
with the Greek independence movement
enraged the Turkish Sultan, who banished him to Mt. Athos in 1798 and
again in 1808. Gregory refused to flee
from Constantinople when the Greek

War of Independence broke out in 1821.
He was seized and hanged on the door
of the patriarchal cathedral on Easter
Sunday morning, 1821, by the Turks.

GREGORY of Nazianzus (325[?]–389
or 390[?]) A father of the Eastern
Church as well as a saint, Gregory of
Nazianzus (Turkey) found his dreams
of seclusion, silence and study interrupted by the pleas of his father, Bishop
of Nazianzus, and later by the requests
of his closest friend, Basil of Caesarea,
to serve in administrative capacities. He
helped each for brief times, but retreated
to ascetic solitude. In 379, Gregory of
Nazianzus accepted the post of Patriarch of Constantinople, but relinquished
it after two years to return to be Bishop
of Nazianzus briefly before again retiring to meditate and write. His extensive
correspondence and theological discourses, particularly his carefully-done
Defense of the Trinity, carried great
influence in the Eastern Church.

GREGORY of Neocaesarea See
GREGORY THAUMATURGUS.

GREGORY of Nyssa (331[?]–394)
The youngest brother of the famous
Basil of Caesarea (Turkey), Gregory
of Nyssa became Bishop of Nyssa
(Turkey) in 371 or 372. A fair administrator but excellent theologian, Gregory of Nyssa wrote against paganism
and heresies. He attended the Council of
Antioch in 379 and the Council of Constantinople in 381. Much of his career
was spent battling the Arians within the
Church, the group insisting that Christ
was not quite completely divine. Gregory, a saint, is also listed as one of the
fathers of the Eastern Church.

GREGORY THAUMATURGUS
(213[?]–270 or 275[?]) One of the
Fathers of the Eastern Church, Gregory
Thaumaturgus (which literally means

"wonder-worker") hailed from a pagan home in Neocaesarea (Turkey, today), but was converted by the teaching of Origen at Caesarea while traveling to Egypt for study. Gregory Thaumaturgus, ordained and commissioned as Bishop of Neocaesarea, was sent home, where at that time, there were only seventeen Christians. By the time he died, it was claimed that there were only seventeen non-Christians left in the area. So many miracles were attributed to Gregory that the name Thaumaturgus was added. He is regarded as a saint in both the Eastern and Western Churches.

GREGORY of Utrecht (707[?]–755 or 780[?]) The German-born abbot of St. Martin's Monastery, Utrecht, Netherlands, Gregory of Utrecht was the disciple and companion of St. Boniface during many of Boniface's missionary journeys through Germany. Gregory came to Utrecht in 744 at Boniface's request, and built up a school which attracted students from all of Europe and the British Isles and which trained and sent scores of missionaries and preachers.

GRENFELL, George (1849–1906) An English missionary and explorer in the African Cameroons from 1874 until his death, Grenfell opened mission stations up the Congo River as far as Stanley Pool by 1881. He surveyed and charted much of the Congo basin and various tributaries during his ministry.

GRENFELL, Wilfred Thomason (1865–1940) Beloved medical missionary among the Labrador fishermen, Grenfell, after a stint as missionary doctor in the first hospital ship in the North Sea fishing grounds, went to Labrador in 1892. He fitted out a hospital ship, the *Strathcona II*, and labored for forty years to provide medical services for isolated families.

Grenfell, a warm-hearted evangelist as well as skilled physician, founded five hospitals, seven nursing clinics, several orphanages, cooperative stores, local industries and, in 1912, the King George V Seaman's Institute at St. Johns, Newfoundland.

GRIBALDI, Matteo ([?]–1564) An Italian anti-Trinitarian radical thinker whose ideas made him unwelcome nearly everywhere in 16th century Europe, Gribaldi was forced to quit teaching law at the University of Padua. He fled to Geneva, but aroused John Calvin with his unorthodox views, and was driven from Geneva in 1559.

GRIESBACH, Johann Jakob (1745–1812) A German Biblical scholar who taught at the University of Jena, Griesbach carefully classified ancient Greek manuscripts of the Scriptures. He was the first to arrange the first three Gospel accounts as Synoptics.

GRINDAL, Edmund (1519–1583) A gentle Church of England archbishop who displeased Queen Elizabeth and his fellow bishops by being too lenient toward non-conformists, Grindal held strong Puritan sympathies while remaining in positions of top leadership in the Anglican communion. Appointed Archbishop of York in 1570 after serving as Bishop of London, Grindal was made Archbishop of Canterbury in 1576. He was suspended from office in 1577 by the Queen for not being severe enough toward non-Anglicans.

GRINNELL, Josiah Bushnell (1821–1891) A leading Abolitionist in the pre-Civil War Days, Grinnell was removed from his pulpit in a leading Congregational Church in Washington, D.C., in 1851 for his strong anti-slavery preaching. He headed west to Iowa, where he founded the town of Grinnell.

He continued his abolitionist activities in the Mid-west, becoming active in politics in Iowa. Because of his long association and interest in the small college at Grinnell, the college was renamed in his honor.

GROOTE, Gerhard (1340–1384) A great Dutch mystic and founder of lay monastic communities, Groote is reputed by some to be the author of the devotional jewel, *The Imitation of Christ*, translated from Dutch into Latin by his pupil and disciple, Thomas à Kempis. Groote, a wealthy burgher, was led to pious living through the influence of Roysbroeck, the Flemish mystic.

Groote's preaching quickly attracted followers, whom he called "Brethren of the Common Life" and organized into semi-monastic communities throughout the Netherlands and Germany. The Brethren of the Common Life, led by Groote, were characterized by plain unadorned living, practical kindnesses toward others, and constant study of the Scriptures. Their schools, such as at Deventer, attracted outstanding students and attempted to spread Christian education among the laity. Groote's communities were designed as lay academies, not for clergy or monks.

Groote and the Brethren of the Common Life contended publicly that the Bible should be translated into common tongues for laymen to read, and are sometimes called "Reformers before the Reformation." Groote died of the plague in 1384 while nursing the ill.

GROSSETESTE, Robert (1175–1253) An honest, determined English prelate, Grosseteste earned a reputation for justice and courage when he defended the Jews against the king in 1232. He was given the prominent appointment of Bishop of Lincoln in 1235, and gained a reputation for his impartiality in appointments and his insistence on high moral standards among his clergy.

Grosseteste got into a controversy with Pope Innocent IV who wanted Grosseteste to install Italian and French papal cronies in the best-paying posts in the diocese. Grosseteste persistently refused. The matter became almost ugly when Grosseteste was ordered to install the pope's nephew in the lucrative position as canon of Lincoln Cathedral in 1253. Grosseteste, backed by his clergy and the king, stood firm.

GROTIUS, Hugo (1583–1645) A Dutch Calvinist theologian scholar and statesman, Grotius is revered as the father of International Law (he first conceived the idea for a deliberative body of all nations bound together under world law). Grotius, applying his Calvinism to the realms of law and statecraft, has been called "Jurist of the Human Race."

A deeply Christian man, Grotius penned a devotional manual for Dutch sailors (1627), wrote excellent Biblical commentaries, and tried to resolve creedal differences between Protestants and Roman Catholics.

Grotius participated in the political life of his country, representing the province of Holland in the States General until forced into exile. He was captured by Prince Maurice in the religious-political revolution of 1618 and given a life sentence to remote Loevestein Castle. Cleverly escaping, Grotius lived in Paris until Maurice's death in 1631, where he wrote extensively. He served as Sweden's ambassador to Paris during the last ten years of his life.

GUIDO D'AREZZO (also known as **Fra Guittone** and **Guido Aretino** (995[?]–1050) The inventive French Benedictine monk who first reduced music to a system of symbols and introduced the monosyllables *do, re, mi, fa,* *sol, la* (known as the *Solfeggio*, taken from an ancient Latin hymn), Guido was asked to teach Pope John XIII his scales, and found his idea spread everywhere in the Church. Guido is also credited with originating the four-line staff to help monks chant the correct tunes.

GUSTAVUS ADOLPHUS or GUSTAV IV, King of Sweden (1594–1632) Fervent Protestant defender, astute statesman and skilled soldier, Gustavus Adolphus waged successful campaigns against the Danes, Russians and Poles with his small, tightly-disciplined, highly-trained, exceptionally-swift army, which made Sweden for a time the most formidable power in Europe. In Church history, his memory is cherished by German Protestants for his involvement in the devastating Thirty Years' War. Gustavus Adolphus, partly out of sympathy for German Protestantism and partly out of the threat of the Holy Roman Empire touching Sweden's borders, landed in Germany in 1630 to avenge the Edict of Restitution. (The Edict of Restitution in 1629 ordered all Church property which had passed into Protestant hands from 1552 to be returned to Roman Catholic possession, commanded all Protestants to be expelled from territories controlled by Catholic princes, and deprived German Calvinists of all rights throughout all of Germany.) Gustavus Adolphus defeated the Roman Catholic coalition in a series of startling victories, and, although he was fatally wounded in the last battle at Lutren, nullified the Edict, saving Protestantism in Germany.

GUYON, Madame Jeanne Marie Bouvier de la Motte (1648–1717) The French mystic who introduced Quietism to France (worship by waiting on the Spirit so that God may speak directly), Mme. Guyon met with harsh treatment at the hands of the Roman clergy in Paris. She had been left a widow while still in her twenties, and after being introduced to mysticism, became an influential defender of the idea that the individual may have direct apperception of the Divine Will. Opposed by the Bishop of Paris, she suffered imprisonment in a convent, and in 1695 was formally condemned by an ecclesiastical commission, which sentenced her to the Bastille for seven years. Mme. Guyon, a persuasive writer and teacher, even converted the great Fenelon to her ideas.

H

HAAKON I, King of Norway (914[?]–961) Known as Haakon "the Good," Haakon, raised a devout Christian by Aethelstan, King of England, tried to introduce the Christian Church to Norway. He was not notably successful, although he had Harold Bluetooth of Denmark send some missionaries. It was not until King Olaf I, about 1000, that Christianity firmly took root in Norway.

HADRIAN, Popes See ADRIAN, Popes.

HAETZER, Ludwig ([?]–1529) Scholarly Swiss humanist and extremist Anabaptist, Haetzer was part of the radical wing of the Reformation which threw out much of the content of the Christian faith. Haetzer, who did a competent translation from Hebrew of the Old Testament prophets (the first into German), rejected the sacraments and accepted Jesus only as a noble teacher and example. His later career was clouded with charges of adultery. After a long imprisonment, he was beheaded at Constance in 1529.

HAKON, King See HAAKON.

HAMILTON, Patrick (1504[?]–1528) One of the earliest martyrs in the Scottish reformation, Hamilton, descendant of Scottish nobility, was a young Roman Catholic priest who was won to the Reformation while a student at Germany. He returned to Scotland in 1523 to teach at St. Andrews, but soon ran afoul of the treacherous Cardinal Beaton by teaching reformation ideas. Fleeing to Germany in 1527, Hamilton met Luther and Melanchthon at Wittenberg and took up studies again at Marburg. The young Scots Reformer rashly reappeared at Linlithgow, Scotland and resumed preaching late in 1527. Lured to St. Andrews by the wily Beaton with promises of safety, Hamilton was seized, hastily tried and burned at the stake for heresy. He was only twenty-four, but his example fired the courage of others, including the youthful John Knox.

HAMLIN, Cyrus (1811–1900) A New England missionary educator to Turkey from 1838 to 1881, Congregationalist Hamlin founded the Bebek school and Seminary along the Bosporus soon after arriving, and in 1860 opened the world-famous Robert College in Istanbul. Hamlin's efforts to open and direct these institutions were opposed by Turks, Greeks, Armenians, local Christians and Moslems, but his perseverance and vision ultimately won him respect throughout the Middle East. An unfortunate strong difference of opinion between Hamlin and the Congregationalist Board led to Hamlin's resignation from the presidency of Robert College. He returned to the U.S. and continued his distinguished career as an educator by serving as president of Middlebury College from 1881 to 1887.

HANAFORD, Phoebe Ann Coffin (1829–1921) The first woman ordained as a minister in New England, Nantucket-born Mrs. Hanaford held pastorates in Universalist congregations at Hingham and Waltham (Mass.),

New Haven (Conn.), and Jersey City (N.J.). She wrote an extensive assortment of biographical studies which were widely read for a time.

HANNINGTON, James (1847–1885) One of those self-sacrificing Victorians who went from the comforts of England to the living grave of 19th century Africa as a missionary, Hannington was one of the best-known martyrs for the faith in the 1880's. Hannington, an Anglican, pushed into forbidding East Africa in 1882, was forced home nearly dead from illness little more than a year later, but insisted on returning as soon as his health permitted. Appointed Bishop of Equatorial Africa, Hannington trudged from the east coast of Africa to the shores of Lake Buganda to plant churches. In 1885, however, he was seized by superstitious tribesmen and executed. His journal, published later in England, made a deep impact on English church life.

HARDING, Stephen (1109–1134) Austere English monk who served as the third abbot of the great monastery at Citeaux, France, Harding during his brief lifetime made the Cistercian Order one of the most prominent forces in European life during the Middle Ages. Harding, a superb organizer and administrator, opened four subsidiary monasteries, exercised close supervision over the many affiliated Cistercian houses and successfully promoted his order's fame for severity, charity and crops. Harding personally was an extreme ascetic, and stressed practical demonstrations of piety in agriculture, rather than learning.

HARNACK, Adolf von (1851–1930) The leading Protestant Church historian at the turn of the 20th century, Harnack, a friend and disciple of the fellow-German theologian Albrecht Ritschl,

applied Ritschl's critical methodology to the field of church history. Harnack's views, often raising controversies, held that the parts of Christian doctrine which most frequently came into conflict with modern thinking were those which crept into Christian thought from the Greek world, not the Hebrew, and appeared in the first four centuries A.D., rather than being part of the original content of the Gospel. Harnack spent his career on theological faculties at Leipzig, Giessen, Marburg, and finally Berlin. He particularly influenced theological thinking in Britain and America.

HAROLD BLAATAND, King of Denmark ([?]–985[?]) Known also as Harold Bluetooth, Harold, a Christian convert, reigned around 940 and succeeded in establishing a strong Church with its own bishopric in his territory of Jutland. Responding to an appeal from his neighbor in Norway, King Haakon, Harold Bluetooth dispatched missionaries to help introduce Christianity to Haakon's kingdom. Harold Bluetooth, forced out about 983 by an anti-Christian revolt, fled to the Slavic tribes and never regained his throne.

HAROLD KLAK, King of Denmark (9th c.) This King Harold suffered the ups and downs of being a feudal ruler, but introduced the Christian Gospel to Denmark while clinging to the throne. He was banished by an usurper early in the 9th century, and was baptized around 826 at Ingleheim. Returning to power, King Harold Klak brought Anscher, the "Apostle to Denmark" and established the Church. He was forced out, however, before he could complete all of this plans and died in banishment.

HARRIS, Howell (1714–1773) Welsh lay-preacher, Harris founded societies in which later formed the Welsh Calvinistic Methodist Church. Harris, following a conversion experience in 1735, began in 1736 to preach fervent evangelical sermons to Welsh miners and villagers, often in the open air. Never ordained as a clergyman, he taught school to earn his living until he was forced out by those opposing his preaching and message. He was frequently threatened, several times attacked. Although he tried to work within the Church of England, he was forced to establish "societies" to converts. By 1739 Harris had founded thirty societies in Wales. He became associated with George Whitefield, the famous evangelist who worked with John Wesley. In 1811, thirty-seven years after Harris' death, his societies and followers formally organized the Welsh Calvinistic Methodist Church, with a Calvinist theology and Presbyterian form of government.

HARRIS, Thomas Lake (1823–1906) American spiritualist and founder of utopian cult-communities, Thomas Harris was a Universalist pastor who became absorbed in spiritualism following the death of his wife in 1850. He began giving exhibitions of trances and other phenomena in 1859, and in 1860 established a utopian community named the Brotherhood of the New Life which, after several moves, finally was located on a farm at Salem-on-Erie, New York. Harris had a flair for attracting the well-heeled and the well-known, luring the English writer Laurence Oliphant and his wife and others as members of the Brotherhood community. In 1875, Harris moved west and opened a new operation called "Fountain Grove" at Santa Rosa, California. His "doctrines" were a mishmash of Eastern philosophies, Swedenborgianism, spiritualism and utopian socialism.

HARRISON, Robert ([?]–1585) An early English Puritan Separatist preacher, Harrison is revered as one of the fathers of English and American Congregationalism. Harrison, a disciple of the famous Separatist Robert Browne, was co-founder with Browne of a Congregational Church at Norwich, England, in 1581. When the heat of reprisals against Harrison, Browne and the congregation grew intense, the entire group emigrated to the Netherlands. Harrison shared with his colleagues Browne, Barrowe, Greenwood and other early English Separatists the conviction that Congregationalism was the only pattern of Church government authorized in the New Testament.

HARVARD, John (1607–1638) The English-born clergyman who bequeathed his library and half his estate to the struggling college at Cambridge, Massachusetts, Harvard is immortalized by having one of the world's most distinguished universities named after him. Harvard came to Massachusetts Bay Colony in 1637, where he became the teaching elder of the tiny congregation at Charlestown. He lived only one year in the New World, dying of tuberculosis in 1638 as a young man of thirty-one. Harvard generously left his four hundred books and one-half of his inheritance and possessions to the new college founded in 1636. The grateful college took Harvard's name in 1639.

HAWEIS, Thomas (1734–1820) A Church of England rector at Aldwinkle, Haweis held deep convictions about proclaiming the Gospel everywhere. Anglican Haweis joined with Congregationalist David Bogue in 1795 to found the London Missionary Society, which became one of the most distinguished agencies for the overseas mission of the Church in the 19th century.

HATZER See **HAETZER**.

HECK, Barbara Ruckle (1734–1804) The woman who has been called the "Mother of American Methodism," Barbara Ruckle Heck was the daughter of refugees who had settled in Ireland, and were won to Methodism by Wesley's preaching. Mrs. Heck and her husband were part of a contingent which immigrated to America in 1760. Urging her cousin, Philip Embury, to hold the first Methodist services in his living room in New York, Barbara Heck encouraged him and other early Methodists to establish the John Street Chapel in New York City. The Hecks were Loyalists during the American Revolution, and with other Tories were forced to move to Canada where Barbara Heck was active in organizing Methodist Societies in the north.

HECKER, Isaac Thomas (1819–1888) American Roman Catholic convert who founded the Paulist Fathers, Hecker left the Brook Farm Community in 1844 to study for the priesthood at Belgium. After being ordained by the Redemptorists in 1849, Hecker was sent as a missionary for the order to New York. He became noted for his success in converting Protestants to Roman Catholicism and in 1858 was granted papal permission to found a new order, The Missionary Priests of St. Paul the Apostle. Hecker and the Paulists stressed proselyting work among Protestants.

HEDVIG (1174[?]–1243) The patron saint of Poland, Hedvig, the daughter of a Bavarian count, was raised in a convent, and married at twelve to the Duke of Silesia. She founded the Cistercian convent at Trebnitz near Breslau, with her husband's encouragement, and generously built or rebuilt many monasteries and convents. After her husband's death, Hedvig moved to Trebnitz. Although she never took orders, she lived many years performing countless acts of charity.

HEGEL, Georg Wilhelm Friedrich (1770–1831) The leading philosopher of his day, Hegel was a German Protestant who taught at universities at Jena, Nuremberg and Berlin. Hegel, objecting to the fad in philosophy which artificially divided everything into a world of things or a world of mind or spirit, insisted that all things are the result of the growth of spirit toward the ideal. He employed a reasoning method of Thesis, Antithesis and Synthesis.

Applied to theology, Hegel's method made revelation, for example, the Father (Thesis) objectifying Himself in finite humanity (Antithesis) uniting God-Man in love (Synthesis). Hegel's theory of the Absolute held that the universe is a constant development of the Absolute (God) through struggle against opposition, uniting to produce a higher union.

Hegel, doing away with rigid distinctions between world of things and world of spirit, blurred the distinctions between divine and human for Protestant thinking for several generations. His dialectical method was picked up by Marxists, and is part of Communist philosophical thought. Hegel died of cholera at the peak of his fame in 1831.

HEINRICH, Duke of Saxony ([?]–1541) A fervent Protestant, Heinrich, Duke of Saxony was remembered in German church history for making Saxony completely Protestant during his brief, two year reign from 1539 to 1541.

HELENA ([?]–330[?]) The Mother of the Emperor Constantine, Helena was the wife of Constantius Chlorus, who humiliated her in 292 at the behest of the Emperor Diocletian. Helena, understandably hostile to the cult of emperor worship, became converted to Christianity in 313, and had an influence on her son's embracing Christianity. Constantine avenged the earlier insults on Helena by granting her the title "Augusta."

In 325, Helena made her famous pilgrimage to the Holy Land, where she "located" the alleged sites of Jesus' birth, career and death. Archaeologists and historians, pointing out that Jerusalem, for example, had been deserted rubble for two centuries, fear that many of the most sacred sites identified by Helena were the result of pious guesswork.

HÉLOISE (1100[?]–1164) The wife of the famous Scholastic, Abélard, Héloise, the learned and lovely niece of Canon Fulbert of Notre Dame in Paris, was pupil, then lover to Abélard. They secretly married, and fled to Paris to escape Fulbert's wrath. Héloise remained loyal to Abélard after Fulbert's goons emasculated her husband, disgracing him and ending his church career. Joining the convent of St. Argenteuil as a nun, Héloise later (1129) became the Superior of the Convent at the Paraclete, and continued to exchange movingly beautiful love letters with Abélard.

HELWYS, Thomas (1550[?]–1616[?]) One of the co-founders of the first Baptist congregation in England, Helwys was originally one of the English Separatists from rural northern England. Helwys, a member of John Smyth's congregation at Gainsborough, accompanied Smyth and the Gainsborough congregation into exile at Amsterdam in 1607. After there was separatism within the Separatists caused by Smyth's fluctuating theological views, especially over infant baptism, Helwys and John Murton, partisans of baptizing adults only and by pouring instead of sprinkling, led a large number home from Amsterdam to England in 1611 or 1612.

Their congregation in London is honored by British Baptists as the first in Britain and gave rise to the General Baptists because of the Arminian ideas picked up during the sojourn in the Netherlands.

HENDERSON, Alexander (1583–1646) Revered as second only to John Knox in the Church of Scotland, Henderson was a tactful yet firm defender of Presyterianism during the early 17th century when King Charles I obstinately tried to impose episcopal forms on the Scottish Kirk. Henderson helped draft the National Covenant of 1638 when the stubborn Charles demanded that the Scots conform to the liturgy of the English Church. When Charles high-handedly talked of forcing the Church's General Assembly to close, Henderson adroitly negotiated a settlement which preserved the integrity and independence of the Church. A few years later, Henderson's skills again were largely responsible for keeping alive the Church of Scotland. He wrote the monumental *Solemn League and Covenant* in 1643, guided the General Assembly of the Church to adopt the Covenant by serving as Moderator, and persuaded King Charles to agree to it. Henderson was one of few Scottish Presbyterians to win the King's respect and trust.

HENDRIX, Eugene Russell (1847–1927) A well-known Methodist Episcopal Bishop from 1886 until his death, Hendrix, one of the earliest ecumenists, served as first President of the newly organized Federal Council of Churches of Christ in America, from 1908 to 1912.

HENRY I, King of England (1068–1135) Contesting with Church leaders for power, Henry I of England grew irritated when the famous Anselm refused to be installed as Archbishop of Canterbury until Henry relinquished his claim to be the one to invest the Archbishop with spiritual authority. Henry, infuriated, was forced to back down.

HENRY II, King of England (1133–1189) Boisterous but brainy, Henry II determined to bring the Church in England to heel, and installed his crony, the complaisant chancellor, Thomas à Becket, as Archbishop of Canterbury. When Henry rammed through the Constitutions in 1164 to check the authority of the Church and put bishops under Henry's control, he was confronted by Becket, now a steadfast defender of the Church's claims. Henry and Becket, once closest friends, became foes. Henry engineered Becket's murder on the chancel steps of Canterbury Cathedral, 1170. Although forced to rescind the Clarendon Constitutions and do penance at Becket's grave, Henry continued to dominate Church affairs in England.

HENRY IV, King of England (1367–1413) An intolerant usurper from the House of Lancaster and the first to owe his right to rule to Parliament, Henry IV agreed to placate Church hierarchy by passing the statute in 1401 which ordered Lollards hunted down. (The Lollards, followers of the early English pre-Reformation Reformer, John Wycliffe, were barefooted lay preachers who lived in poverty and expounded the Scriptures to a great following.) Henry IV had many Lollards burned.

HENRY V, King of England (1387–1422) Son of Henry IV, Henry V is immortalized in British history by his stunning victory at Agincourt in 1415, when his English bowmen decimated a French force four times as large. Henry accelerated the persecution of the Lol-

lards, and hounded into exile hundreds of English Lollards. He executed dozens more, including the saintly, influential Sir John Oldcastle, most illustrious adherent of Lollard-inspired Reformed ideas.

HENRY VII, King of England (1457–1509) First of the Tudor kings, the able Henry VII achieved immense control over Church affairs in England, paving the way for his successor, Henry VIII to sever the tie to Rome.

HENRY VIII, King of England (1491–1547) The extraordinarily charismatic, controversial and colorful king who broke the English Church from Rome, Henry set himself up as Supreme Head of the Church of England. Henry, disgusted with his wife, Catherine of Aragon, for not bearing him an heir, planned to discard her for an attractive maid of honor, Anne Boleyn, and demanded that Pope Clement VII declare his marriage annulled. When Henry's divorce plans got hopelessly mired in papal court procedures, Henry shrewdly turned the currents of the Reformation and nationalism to serve his own purposes. He dismissed Cardinal Wolsey in 1529, passed a law prohibiting appeals to papal courts, appointed the pliable Cranmer Archbishop of Canterbury in 1533, had Cranmer pronounce the marriage to Catherine null and void, married Anne and crowned her Queen.

By 1534, Henry completed the Church of England's break with Rome by having Parliament pass acts setting aside the pope's authority in England and appointing Henry to replace the pope as Supreme Head of the English Church. Henry proceeded to close monasteries, appropriating their vast wealth and holdings for the crown, and wasting most of it on personal whims.

Henry, who eventually had Anne Boleyn executed, married six wives altogether, two of whom were executed (Anne Boleyn and Catherine Howard), two of whom were divorced by him (Catherine of Aragon and Anne of Cleves), one of which died in childbirth (Jane Seymour) and one who managed to outlive him (Catherine Parr).

HENRY II, King of France (1519–1559) Tendentious Roman Catholic ruler of France during the mid-sixteenth century, Henry II ruthlessly persecuted Huguenots (French Protestants) and greedily acquired bishoprics to line his own pockets.

HENRY III, King of France (1551–1589) A weakling hopelessly dominated by his devious, cruel mother, Catherine de' Medici, Henry III—prompted by Catherine—instigated the barbarity known as the St. Bartholomew's Day Massacre in 1572, killing 50,000 French Protestants. Ironically, Henry was assassinated by a fanatical Dominican monk.

HENRY IV, King of France, HENRY OF NAVARRE (1553–1610) Raised a Protestant by his mother, Henry served during the bloody French religious wars under the doughty Huguenot Admiral Coligny. Henry of Navarre managed to save his life during the bloodbath of St. Bartholomew's Day Massacre (which lasted several weeks) in 1572 by pretending a conversion to Roman Catholicism. In 1576 he escaped from the dungeon where he had been imprisoned and headed the Huguenot armies. He finally wrested control of France and succeeded to the French crown in 1589.

France, however, was so bitterly divided by religious hates that Henry, a Protestant, found he was unable to unite the nation. On the advice of everyone, Henry reluctantly became a Roman Catholic in 1593, and was crowned in 1594. In 1596, Henry published the Edict of Nantes, lifting all restrictions against Huguenots, and extending full religious liberty to all Christians. Henry, a popular ruler, brought some degree of healing to the exhausted nation.

Concerned for the welfare of everyone, Henry of Navarre originated the phrase, "A chicken in every pot for Sunday for every peasant."

HENRY II, King of Germany and Holy Roman Emperor (973–1024) Known as *der Heilige* or Henry the Saint, this German monarch zealously defended the pope, making forays against the Lombards in northern Italy and against the Greeks in southern Italy to protect the pope's interests. Henry established numerous schools and monasteries and was rewarded by being canonized in 1146.

HENRY III, King of Germany and Holy Roman Emperor (1017–1056) Capable, reform-minded Emperor, Henry III saved the papacy but set the dangerous precedent of controlling the Church. At the time when scandalously amoral Pope Benedict IX sold the papacy and three rival popes squabbled for allegiance, Henry III called a Synod at Sutri to settle the mess. The Council at Henry's insistence deposed Sylvester III, prevailed upon Gregory VI to resign and demanded that the Synod of Rome oust Benedict IX. Henry then rammed through the election of his hand-picked choice, the Bishop of Bamberg, as pontiff, who became Pope Clement II. When Clement II died, Henry, determined to avoid a repetition of the earlier controversy, had the Church install another pliable German prelate, who became Damasus II. The no-nonsense Henry followed this procedure four times, putting in his cousin as Pope Leo

IX when Damasus II died, and Victor II when Leo IX died.

Although Henry appointed able men, and although he held together the Church of Rome, Henry's interference seriously undermined the independence of the Medieval Church.

Henry III, personally deeply pious, denounced the glaring abuses of clerical power such as the sale of offices and tried to institute reforms.

HENRY IV, King of Germany and Holy Roman Emperor (1050–1106) Engaged in a lifelong feud with Pope Gregory VII, Emperor Henry IV is remembered as the ruler who was forced to wait barefooted in the snow outside the papal residence at Canossa, begging Pope Gregory VII to hear his plea to restore him from excommunication. Henry IV, an arrogant, vengeful ruler who touched off the fight by insisting on choosing the Saxon bishops and imprisoning intractable churchmen, had previously called his lackey-bishops together at Worms in 1076 to "depose" Gregory VII. After his excommunication and the feigned humility at Canossa (which succeeded in getting the excommunication lifted) the spiteful Henry beseiged Rome, routing Pope Gregory.

HENRY V, King of Germany and Holy Roman Emperor (1081–1125) Another German monarch who tried to bully the papacy, Henry cowed Pope Paschal II, but had to work out a compromise with Pope Calistus II. In 1122 at the Concordat of Worms, Henry agreed to permit his German churchmen conduct their own elections of bishops—with the Emperor in attendance—and to forego the symbols of spiritual authority. In effect, bishops and abbots had to be acceptable from then on to both the Emperor and the Church.

HENRY OF NAVARRE See **HENRY IV, King of France.**

HENRY, of Lausanne ([?]–1145[?]) A pre-Reformation Protestant, Henry of Lausanne, a one-time Benedictine monk who left the cloister to give fiery, street-corner sermons, called for a return to apostolic poverty and simplicity. Henry repudiated the trappings of the slothful, power-hungry ecclesiastical institution, even denying the validity of the sacraments when administered by an unworthy priest. His excoriations of the clergy and strict personal asceticism attracted large throngs, but enraged the Church hierarchy.

HENSON, Josiah (1789–1883) An American slave-born Negro, Henson was the real-life model for the character Uncle Tom in Harriet Beecher Stowe's famous novel, "Uncle Tom's Cabin." Henson, enduring desperate hardships as a boy and young man, escaped from his Maryland owner via the Underground Railroad in 1830 and made his way to Ontario, Canada. He educated himself and became the pastor of a Methodist Episcopal Church at Dresden, Ontario. Henson quickly emerged as a leader of the Abolition movement, making three trips to Britain to present the Abolitionist viewpoint. In 1849, he published his autobiography, which made a deep impression in pre-Civil War America.

HERBERT, Edward, 1st Baron of Cherbury (1583–1648) The Father of English Deism, Herbert was an Oxford-trained onetime diplomat who served both the English Crown and the Dutch Prince of Orange. In 1624, Herbert published his influential volume, *De Veritate*, which urged that Christianity was one of the variety of religions and that all other religions were basically the same thing. All, according to Herbert, were based on the same five general principles enunciated in his book. Continuing to stress the universality of natural religion, Herbert followed up *De Veritate* with *De Causus Errorum* in 1645, pointing out the common denominators in religions, and *De Religione Gentilium* in 1663.

HERMAN ([?]–1837) Russian Orthodox priest who founded the first Orthodox Mission in Alaska, Father Herman headed a group including five monks which arrived at Kodiak Island, September 24, 1795. The missionary band made what is considered the longest missionary journey in the history of the Church, traveling 7,327 miles across Russia and Siberia in two hundred ninety-three days. Father Herman, after twenty years of seclusion following an active missionary life in Alaska, died in 1837.

HERMAS of Rome (115[?]–140) A Christian writer living at Rome who wrote the highly regarded, oft-quoted, near-canonical *Shepherd of Hermas*, Hermas was probably the brother of Bishop Pius I of Rome. Hermas continued the tradition of the Hebrew prophets, delivering piecemeal preachments as God's spokesman. His writings give a clear picture of Church life in the earliest days, revealing that Church members then were also guilty of indifference, hypocrisy and worldliness.

HICKS, Elias (1748–1830) Persuasive and persistent Quaker preacher, Hicks presumed to "correct" more traditional Quaker practices, causing a tragic split in 1827 among American Friends. Hicks, whose fluency made him a well-known speaker by the time he was in his mid-twenties, held rationalist, semi-Unitarian views, which downgraded the place of the Bible and the need for Jesus Christ. His followers in the schism were popularly known as "Hicksite" Friends. Hicks, an active abolitionist, pressed New York State to free all slaves residing within its borders in 1827.

HILARION (291[?]–371[?]) The first to introduce monasticism to Palestine, Hilarion brought his practice of asceticism and solitude from Egypt where he had studied with St. Anthony in the desert. Hilarion, supporting his meager needs by weaving baskets, settled in the Gaza area, and quickly made such an impression with his holy living and startling miracles that he felt constrained to move to Sicily to escape the crowds. Equally popular in Sicily, he tried to escape to Dalmatia, then to Cyprus, but attracted great numbers in each place. Hilarion was eulogized by the learned Jerome, and canonized by the Roman Church.

HILARY of Poitiers ([?]–367) The most learned man in Gaul (France in his day), Hilary stoutly stood for orthodox Christian Christology against the aggressive adherents of Arianism (the idea that Christ was not quite truly God). He grew up in a pagan home, but converted to Christianity and entered the Church, eventually becoming Bishop of Poitiers, Gaul (France).

Vindictive Arians banished Hilary to lonely Phrygia for defending Nicene Christianity so ably. Hilary used his banishment to write *De Trinitate* to convince bishops leaning toward Arianism of the traditional position of the Church toward Christ.

Hilary was active in the bitter squabble over the one letter "i": some with Arian sympathies said that Christ was *homoiousios* (in Greek, "of like substance" with God); Hilary and the Nicene group insisted that Christ was *homoousios* ("of one substance" with

139

God). Following the convocation at Seleucia, Hilary in 361 returned to his see. His rigid anti-Arian stand continued to bring him tensions and problems.

HILDA (614–680) The perceptive, competent woman who served as abbess at Whitby, England, Hilda, consecrated a nun by Bishop Aidan of the Celtic Church, headed the Abbey at Hartlepool, then in 657, founded Whitby Abbey. Hilda made Whitby Abbey the strongest and most influential in Britain.

Observant of others, Hilda encouraged the illiterate boy cowherd named Caedmon to dictate his epics, which became classics.

HILDEBRAND See **GREGORY VII**, Pope.

HILDEGARD (1098–1179) A German Benedictine nun who was raised in the Convent of Disenberg near Speyer, Hildegard headed her home convent for a time, then moved to Rupertsberg to found a new Benedictine community. Hildegard was renowned for her startlingly accurate "visions," which have been recorded in *Scivias* from 1141 to 1150. Her gift of ESP propelled her to fame as an advisor to the great and would-be great and her writings were widely circulated.

HINCMAR (805[?]–882) The Archbishop of Rheims, France, Hincmar carried forward the momentum for learning started by Emperor Charlemagne, and energetically managed the Church in Gaul, directing the course of the entire Frankish kingdom during his lifetime. Hincmar's assertive authoritarian way of operating won him few friends, especially among his own clergy. Hincmar was twice checked by popes for too zealously upholding the rights of his office.

HIPPOLYTUS ([?]–235[?]) A perceptive theologian who refuted many of the ancient heresies, Hippolytus has the distinction of being an antipope who was subsequently canonized by the Church. When Callistus I was chosen pope, Hippolytus' supporters held a separate election, making him a counterpope through the reigns of Callistus I, Urban I and Pontian. During the Emperor Maximius' persecution, both Hippolytus and his rival Pontian were exiled together on the Island of Sardinia and then together executed. Hippolytus reportedly was reunited with the Church before his death, and was honored for his martyrdom and his excellent writings by being made a saint. He is also known as Hippolytus of Rome.

HOCHSTRATEN, Jakob (also Hoogstraten) (1460–1527) The dogmatic, disputatious Dominican who served as Inquisitor at Cologne, Hochstraten was a key figure in the controversy over the quiet, respected humanist Reuchlin, advocate of the new learning. Hochstraten opposed Reuchlin's approval of the use of Jewish books, Hebrew literature in libraries and discussions with Jewish scholars. Hochstraten's narrowminded accusations against Reuchlin exploded into a bitter, witless attack on scholarship. Hochstraten's trial of Reuchlin was appealed to Rome, and the pope in 1520 upheld Hochstraten and denounced Reuchlin as a heretic. Hochstraten's bigotry and ignorance deeply offended the academic world in the 16th century, united the humanists against the conservative Dominicans, and pitted the Church against intellectual inquiry.

HOFFMANN, Melchior (1498–1543) Radical Anabaptist leader who believed himself divinely appointed to lead the faithful to Strassburg, the "New Jerusalem," to await the end of the world which he claimed would take place in 1533, Hoffman, pathetically self-deluded and self-assured, gained wide success by insisting that he had direct inspiration from God as a prophet. An earnest Lutheran before he swung over to the Anabaptists, Hoffman attracted a following in Friesland, in the Netherlands. He prophesied that he, as the prophet of the new dispensation, would be imprisoned for six months in the Spirit-designated Jerusalem of Strassburg, but that when the world ended in 1533, all those who opposed him and his followers, the "saints," would be destroyed. Hoffman confidently went to Strassburg, was arrested and imprisoned as expected but kept in his dungeon until he died in 1543.

HOLMES, John Haynes (1879–1964) The oft-criticized advocate of unpopular causes and outspoken defender of left-of-center social and political causes in 20th century America, John Haynes Holmes was a Harvard-educated Unitarian pastor serving at New York City Community Church from 1907 to 1949. Holmes was an activist who helped found the National Association of Colored People in 1909 and served as Director of the American Civil Liberties Union in 1917; he was also a pacifist during both World Wars who acted as president of the War Resisters' League from 1929 to 1939. Vigorously opposed to denominationalism, Holmes pulled his own New York congregation out of the Unitarian fold in 1919.

HOLTZMANN, Heinrich Julius (1832–1910) Gifted German Protestant Biblical scholar, Holtzmann, professor at Strassburg, introduced the idea in New Testament studies that Mark was the oldest of the Synoptics, and traced the sources of the present Gospel accounts. His meticulous scholarship and cautious conclusions were reflected in a series of outstanding exegetical studies appearing from 1863 until his death. Holtzmann's pioneering work has won almost universal acceptance.

HONORIUS I, Pope ([?]–638) A capable pontiff who ruled from 625 to 638, Honorius I pushed the Celtic Church to bring its date for Easter into conformity with Rome's (and ultimately succeeded in extinguishing the unique witness of the Celtic Church). Although Honorius died respected and honored, forty-two years later in 680, at the Sixth Ecumenical Council, he was anathematized as a heretic on the shaky evidence of a letter written to Sergius in which he seemed soft toward Monophysites (those holding that Jesus had only a divine and no human nature).

HONORIUS II, Pope ([?]–1130) Pope from 1124 to 1130.

HONORIUS III, Pope ([?]–1227) Reigning from 1216 until 1227, Honorius III excommunicated Emperor Frederick II for procrastinating on a promise to mount a Crusade, finally propelling Frederick into action. Honorius confirmed the rules of several of the greatest Roman Catholic Orders, including the Carmelites, the Franciscans and the Dominicans.

HONORIUS IV, Pope ([?]–1287) Pope from 1285 to 1287.

HOOKER, Richard (1554–1600) An influential Church of England theologian, Richard Hooker, in spite of Puritan sympathies, believed in upholding the *status quo*. From 1585 to 1591, Hooker served as Master of Temple, the key ecclesiastical post at the Inns of Court, the distinguished legal societies of Britain. Answering stinging Puritan attacks against Anglicanism in his five volume, *Of the Lawes of Ecclesiasticall Politie* in 1593, Hooker with an astonishing breadth of learning appealed to Scripture, tradition and reason to defend the Anglican establishment.

HOOKER, Thomas (1586[?]–1647) A Cambridge-trained Church of England divine who joined the Non-conformists during the English religious upheavals of the 17th century, Hooker is venerated as one of the founding fathers of Connecticut and as one of the outstanding leaders of early American Congregationalism. Hooker, fleeing from Archbishop Laud, went to the Netherlands about 1630 before emigrating to Boston in 1633 with the famous John Cotton. Hooker served three years as pastor of the Cambridge congregation, but found Massachusetts too inhibiting.

In 1636, Hooker and his congregation resettled at New Haven for greater freedom. Hooker achieved prominence as leader in both ecclesiastical and political realms, helping draft the Connecticut Constitution in 1639 and urging an alliance of the colonies for the purpose of defense in 1643.

HOOPER, John (1495[?]–1555) A stubborn British bishop-martyr, John Hooper left the Cistercian Order after reading the tracts by Reformers Zwingli and Bullinger. He fled to Switzerland in 1539 to escape reprisals, became a Protestant and remained on the Continent in safety for ten years. Returning to England in 1549, he was elected Bishop of Gloucester, but was not consecrated for a year until a prison sentence and the pleading of friends wore down his opposition to wearing "idolatrous" clergy garb. In 1552, Hooper was made Bishop of Worcester, where he effectively furthered the Reformed cause. He was a marked man

when rabidly Catholic Queen Mary came to power in 1553. He was held in jail until Mary got laws passed against "heresy," then tried, convicted and burned alive in 1555.

HOPKINS, Samuel (1721–1803) An American pastor and theologian who studied under Jonathan Edwards, Hopkins while pastor at Great Barrington, Rhode Island from 1769 to 1803 stirred what became known as the Hopkinsian Controversy by opposing traditional ideas of Original Sin and the Atonement.

HORT, Fenton John Anthony (1828–1892) Church of England vicar and Cambridge don, Hort joined with Brooke Foss Westcott in 1853 to produce the authoritative Greek text of the New Testament which has been accepted and used by many exegetes. In 1870, the scholarly Hort was appointed to the committee translating the English Revised Version of the New Testament (published in 1881).

HORTON, Douglas (1891–1968) Leader in the 20th century ecumenical movement, Horton, a Congregational minister, was architect of the merger of the Congregational Church and the Evangelical and Reformed Church in 1957 to form the United Church of Christ. Horton previously headed the General Council of the Congregational Christian Churches from 1938 to 1955, and chaired the Faith and Order Commission of the World Council of Churches from 1957 to 1963. A reputable scholar, Dr. Horton wrote many books, served as Dean of Harvard Divinity School from 1955 to 1959, and taught at Newton, Chicago, Union and Harvard Divinity Schools.

HOSIUS ([?]–358[?]) The steadfast Spanish Bishop at Cordova about 300,

Hosius won fame for remaining faithful to his calling during Emperor Maximian's persecution from 303 to 305. He became an adviser to Emperor Constantius II and at Constantius' request tried to resolve the bitter quarrel between Arius and the Bishop of Alexandria.

Hosius' mediating efforts were fruitless. The quarrel blew up into a disgusting fight involving the entire Church and remembered as the Arian controversy.

Hosius attended the Council of Nicea in 325, which tried to unsuccessfully conclude the Arian controversy (in which the Arians took a position that Christ was not truly and completely God). Hosius used his prestige to urge the Emperor to agree to Nicene Christianity. Hosius, however, lost his standing with Emperor Constantius when the Arians won the Emperor to their cause. Hosius stood firm for Nicene Christianity for a year, but finally under severe pressures from Constantius signed a much-advertised compromise statement drawn up by Arians. Arian partisans gave wide circulation to Hosius' alleged endorsement of Arianism, gleefully misrepresenting him to have joined the Arian camp. Hosius, broken and unable to refute effectively the allegations, retired to Cordova.

HOWARD, John (1726[?]–1790) A fervent Congregational layman, Howard is revered as the Father of Prison Reform. While serving as Sheriff of Bedfordshire, Howard was shocked at the conditions in the jails. He pushed Parliament to pass legislation to improve prison conditions in 1774, and founded the Howard League for Penal Reform, which became a powerful lobby in Britain. His fame took him to Europe and America, where he encouraged partisans to establish the Philadelphia

Society for Alleviating the Miseries of Public Prisons, the first prison reform group in the United States.

Later in his career, Howard tried to find methods of arresting the spread of bubonic plague. He contracted the dread disease while traveling in Russia and died suddenly in 1790.

HRABANUS MAURUS (776[?]–856) Abbot of Fulda and Archbishop of Mainz, Hrabanus was prominent in the resurgence of learning spurred by Charlemagne. His writings were widely read and respected in the Middle Ages, his *Excerptio* serving as the most popular textbook for several centuries. Hrabanus Maurus also produced one of the earliest approximations to an encyclopedia, and penned numerous commentaries on the Bible. His efficiency as an educator made his school at Fulda one of the greatest in Europe. Hrabanus marred his otherwise creditable career by refusing to release the unhappy monk Gottschalk from his vows, ruthlessly shutting him up in a monastery after his lapse into heresy.

HUBERT (656[?]–728[?]) The patron saint of hunters, Hubert is surrounded by the legend that once while hunting in the forest in the Ardennes of France on a Good Friday, he saw a stag with a gleaming crucifix on its antlers, and heard a voice. Hubert, staggered by the vision, immediately determined to devote his life to holy orders. He ultimately in 704 served as the Bishop of Maestricht and Liege. Hubert reportedly performed many miracles, especially with mad dogs.

HUBMAIER, Balthasar (also Hubmeyer) (1480[?]–1528) Onetime pupil and colleague of Eck, Luther's able opponent, Hubmaier was won to Reformation views by reading Luther's works, but was led into the radical wing of the Reformation, and became the leading spokesman of the Anabaptists.

Hubmaier settled in Waldshut, Switzerland, as a pastor, where he became convinced that there was no Biblical warrant for infant baptism. His outspoken views ignited a fierce controversy over baptism. Hubmaier, who had himself re-baptized in 1725 by a colleague, Wilhelm Roubli, and his followers were opposed and denounced by other Protestants and by the Roman Catholic Church. Dubbed "Anabaptists" or rebaptizers, Hubmaier and his community at Waldshut insisted on living with the Bible alone as their law, and joined the peasant revolt. When the revolt was quashed, Hubmaier was arrested, tortured and imprisoned at Zurich, but escaped to Moravia.

With the fanaticism of a persecuted minority, Hubmaier and the Anabaptists propagandized successfully throughout northern Europe, winning vast sections of the populations, especially among the peasantry disenchanted with Lutheranism after the collapse of the peasant revolt. The Anabaptists, with their persistent rejection of princes and governments, seemed seditious and anarchical to everyone, Lutheran and Catholic. Hubmaier, with most of the other Anabaptist leaders, was eventually executed, meeting death bravely by being burned at the stake in Vienna in 1528.

HUGEL, Friedrich von, Baron (1852–1925) Exemplary and erudite German-born Roman Catholic layman who won accolades for his work as a linguist and theologian, Baron von Hugel settled in England in 1873, becoming a British citizen in 1914. He emerged as the spokesman for the liberal wing of the English Roman Catholics, founding the London Society for the Study of Religion in 1902. An expert on Roman Catholic dogma, von Hugel was a loyal but critical Roman Catholic all his life. His most famous writing was an excellent treatise which questioned the traditional attitude toward the Fourth Gospel. Von Hugel corresponded with a wide circle of Protestant and Catholic friends, many of whom revered him as a modern mystic.

HUGH of Avalon See HUGH of Lincoln.

HUGH of Lincoln, Bishop (1135[?]–1200) At the age of eight, Hugh was taken by his father, the Lord of Avalon, to a monastery near Grenoble, France. He formally joined the Carthusians in 1160, and won a reputation as a skillful, tactful administrator. In 1175, Hugh was asked by King Henry II of England to take charge of the faltering monastery at Witham. Hugh's brilliant record at Witham brought him the close friendship of King Henry and advancement to the bishopric of Lincoln in 1186. A genial, even-tempered prelate who could disagree with the king and still retain royal favor, Hugh of Lincoln served Henry as a special envoy, personal adviser and ambassador to France. He has been canonized in the Roman Catholic Church.

HUGH of Lincoln, "Little Saint Hugh" (1246[?]–1255) A nine-year old boy whose battered body was found in the well belonging to a Jewish Englishman named Copin, Hugh's death triggered notorious tales which whipped fanatic anti-Jewish feelings and bloody outbursts against Jews in England. The youngster's body was allegedly found to have wounds similar to those of a crucified person. Pouncing on the hoary, Medieval superstition that Jews practiced human sacrificial rites at Passover time, and erroneously concluding that Copin and fellow Jews had murdered the boy, Christian Lincolnshire citizens frenziedly tortured and lynched Copin and many other innocent Jews, and forced dozens of others to pay outrageous fines. Many lurid, bizarre embellishments of the story of Hugh were repeated, such as the corpse crying from the well, or refusing to stay buried.

HUGHES, John Joseph (1797–1864) Militant Irish-born American Roman Catholic Archbishop of New York from 1850 until his death, Hughes laid the cornerstone of St. Patrick's Cathedral, New York City in 1858 and founded Fordham University in 1841. Archbishop Hughes, fiercely pro-Union during the Civil War, was sent to Europe in 1863 to counteract Confederate propaganda.

HUGO of St. Victor (1096[?]–1141) A French mystic and theologian, Hugo of St. Victor headed the Abbey school at St. Victor at Paris. Although professedly orthodox and a defender of traditional dogma, Hugo of St. Victor arrived at his position through the path of personal mysticism. Although a mystic (one who believed in direct apperception of the Divine), Hugo of St. Victor stoutly defended Christian Church doctrine in his work, *De Sacramentis Christianae Fidei.*

HUMBERT ([?]–1061) A power in papal politics during the 11th century, Humbert was made a cardinal by Pope Leo IX when the Cardinalate was filled with reform-minded churchmen. Humbert, originally a French monk from Lorraine, vigorously opposed lay control in Church affairs or lay participation in Church elections. Humbert wrote the decree adopted by the Roman synod of 1059, regulating the election of popes to this day. Humbert's constitution removed papal election from the hands of clergy and laity in Rome (where the

ruling clique had frequently installed its own candidate) to the cardinalate, giving the papacy an independence from political control which it had not previously enjoyed.

Cardinal Humbert also served as an envoy to Constantinople in 1054 when Pope Leo IX excommunicated Patriarch Michael Cerularius and all his followers, formally separating the Greek and Latin branches of the Church.

HUME, David (1711–1796) Eighteenth century Scottish intellectual and philosopher, Hume blasted both then-popular Deism and the then-current defenses of Christianity.

Hume created a sensation by criticizing the miracle stories in the Bible, which were widely believed to be the main proof for believing in revelation and accepting the Gospel. Hume, stressing experience as the source of our knowledge, pointed out how unlikely it is for nature to alter its course. In addition, he asked how these irregular, unlikely occurrences could be regarded as special disclosures of the divine will. Hume's keen reasoning demolished traditional popular reliance on the miracles as prime proofs of Christianity, and encouraged a destructive skepticism among thinkers.

Hume also helped give rise to historical criticism by pointing out that primitive, polytheistic nature cults preceded Monotheism, which devastated the Deist's cherished ideal of a simple, rational religion of nature. Hume's speculations gave rise to rationalistic thinking, which in the 18th and 19th centuries threatened to wreck the faith of many believers.

HUMPHREY, Laurence (1527–1590) A prominent Puritan intellectual in the 16th century English Church, Humphrey, head of Magdalen College,

Oxford, was forced to flee to the Continent to escape fanatic Queen Mary's death sentence. Later, Humphrey led the heated discussions in the Church over the use of vestments prescribed by Queen Elizabeth's Archbishop Parker, known as the "Vestiarian Controversy." In spite of severe pressure, Humphrey firmly refused to obey Parker's orders to wear vestments.

HUNTINGDON, Selma Hastings, Countess of (1707–1791) Widowed by the death of her husband, the Earl of Huntingdon, in 1746, Countess Selma of Huntingdon became a devout Methodist. She headed the Calvinistic Methodists (guided by her private chaplain, George Whitefield), founded several training schools for clergymen, built sixty-four chapels and gave liberally to support Wesleyan clergymen and her congregations.

HUS See HUSS.

HUSS, Jan or John (1371–1415) Great Bohemian patriot and preacher, Huss raised the curtain on the Reformation on the Continent, adopting Wycliffe's theology and anticipating many of the 16th century Reformers' key ideas. Huss, ordained a priest in 1401, quickly won a wide audience, preaching in Czech and protesting the corruption in the Church. Huss' scathing sermons, however, lost him the support of his onetime ally, the powerful Archbishop Zbnek Zajic of Hasenberg. By 1410, Huss had been excommunicated and his publications publicly burned. Ignoring the ban, Huss continued his influential work at Prague University, where he was rector, and his sermons at Bethlehem chapel.

When counter-pope John XXIII in 1411 placed the city of Prague under the interdict, King Wenceslaus protected Huss and ordered the papal order ignored.

Huss' outspoken criticism of the pope's blatant sale of Indulgences to raise cash for a Crusade (for which Huss denounced the pope as the Antichrist) finally was too much even for King Wenceslaus. Huss at the king's prodding, left Prague in 1412 and busied himself with writing his treatise *On the Church*.

In 1414, the Council of Constance convened to try to untangle the confusion in the Bohemian Church, heal the disgusting schism where counter-popes tried to rule from Avignon, and effect some long-overdue reforms. Huss, ordered to present himself before the Council, was promised safe conduct by Emperor Sigismund. He was seized after he arrived at Constance and ordered to recant. Stoutly maintaining that Scripture is the only guide to belief and practice and that the only true Church is the community of the Elect, Huss refused to retract from his position. He died heroically in the flames after being condemned by the Council of Constance in 1415.

HUT, Hans ([?]–1527) Fanatic Anabaptist (the nickname meaning "rebaptizer" given to the radical wing of the Reformation), Hut was a self-appointed "prophet" who preached a terrifying message of speedy final judgment and Second Coming of Christ, gaining huge following among the lower classes in southern Germany in the 1520's. Hut announced that the trials of the "saints" would be quickly followed by a Turkish invasion which, according to Hut, would end the Holy Roman Empire and usher in the final days. All "saints" would be gathered together to be saved, and all priests and evil rulers would be destroyed, Hut proclaimed, and Christ would appear physically. Hut was imprisoned at Augsburg and died from burns from setting the prison on fire to escape in 1527.

HUTCHINSON, Anne Marbury (1591–1643) English-born non-conformist minister's daughter, Anne Hutchinson was won to the views of Puritan divine John Cotton in England and with her husband and family, emigrated to Massachusetts Colony in 1643 to re-join Cotton. Mrs. Hutchinson joined Boston's Church, but began holding informal meetings of women from the congregation in her home, discussing sermons, religious topics and her own ideas. She quickly turned these meetings into a forum to promulgate her belief that the Holy Spirit is in every believer. She taught that salvation comes without the need for any Church or government but when a believer, by his own intuition, senses God's goodness through the direct inspiration of the Holy Spirit. Her questionable orthodoxy brought her into conflict with the authorities, who harshly denounced her doctrines as antinomianism. After being condemned by the Church Synod in 1637 and ordered banished from the colony in the dead of winter by the General Court, Anne Hutchinson and her family fled to Rhode Island. The Hutchinsons later resettled near present-day Westchester, New York, and were tragically massacred by Indians during the Dutch-Indian Wars of 1643.

HYACYNTHE, Père See **LOYSON, Charles.**

I

IBAS of Edessa ([?]–457) A leading theologian at the Syrian Church school at Edessa, Syria, Ibas stood with Nestorius during the Church squabble over proper wording to define the nature of Christ. Nestorius, banned for opposing the popular term for Mary, "Theotokas" ("Mother of God") because it confused the human and divine nature of Christ, gained many supporters, including Ibas. Ibas was deposed in the notorious Synod of Ephesus in 449, manipulated by the Alexandrians, but restored again at Chalcedon in 451.

IGNATIUS, Bishop of Antioch ([?]– 98 or 117) A devoted pastor, Ignatius was condemned to die because of his faith during the reign of the Roman Emperor Trajan, and hauled to Rome from Asia Minor. He wrote seven letters as a prisoner as he was dragged from city to city to the capital. In these masterpieces, Ignatius expresses his thanks to members of the Christian community who have traveled to bid him farewell and shown him kindnesses, warns them to be faithful amidst future persecutions and urges them to maintain the unity of the Church. In his letter to Polycarp, Ignatius urges this bishop of Smyrna to "stand firm like an anvil under the hammer," and instructs Polycarp on carrying out his duties. Little is known of Ignatius' earlier career. His letters, however, give a matchless record of 1st century Church life. He died in Rome, torn apart by wild beasts, and was canonized.

IGNATIUS of Loyola (1491[?]–1556) The Basque nobleman-soldier (born Imgo Lopez de Recalde) who founded the Jesuits, Ignatius brought the devotion and discipline needed to renew the Church of Rome and reclaim territories lost to Protestantism.

Ignatius, an aristocratic bon-vivant and Spanish officer, suffered grave wounds at Pamplona in 1521, and whiled away his time during a long painful convalescence by reading the life of Christ and records of the saints. He determined to use the same military qualities of obedience and discipline to serve Jesus Christ as he had used to serve Emperor Ferdinand. In the tradition of knightly chivalry, Ignatius, following his recuperation, journeyed to Montserrat, hung his sword and armor on the Virgin's altar, and knelt all night in prayer. He retired briefly to the monastery at Manresa, then in 1523, embarked as a pilgrim to the Holy Land. The Franciscans, however, were uneasy about using him at Jerusalem and sent him home.

Ignatius, meanwhile, began to practice a deep piety with prayer vigils and rigorous devotional exercises. He began to write his famous *Spiritual Exercises,* which became a drill manual for developing intensely steadfast Christian believers.

Realizing his need for education, Ignatius crammed an astounding amount of schooling into the next several years, studying at the University of Paris from 1528 to 1535. His no-nonsense discipleship among the easygoing students won him his first followers, six outstanding young scholars. Ignatius and the six students banded together in the form of a military unit, determined to fight heresy, battle infidels, practice unquestioning obedience, and work under a strict spiritual drillmaster. The seven finally won the approval of Pope Paul III to found the Society of Jesus in 1540.

Ignatius soon organized a powerful army, which he served as "general." By his death in 1556, his Jesuits numbered over 1,000 in over a hundred houses. Ignatius so thoroughly trained his Jesuits that as elite commandos for the pope they were not bound to fixed forms of worship or dress, yet spearheaded the Counter-Reformation, emphasizing excellent preaching, frequent confession and regular communion, and organizing outstanding schools and overseas missions.

IGNATIUS, Patriarch of Constantinople (797–877) A haughty, rude Byzantine Churchman, Ignatius the Patriarch feuded with fellow prelates and moved to expand his jurisdiction. Ignatius, a deposed Armenian emperor's son, was castrated while a boy by his father's enemies and imprisoned in a monastery to prevent him from claiming the throne. Pushing his way to prominence in the Eastern Church, Ignatius had a habit of deposing those who disagreed with him, removing such able churchmen as Gregory Asbestas, the Archbishop of Syracuse, and excommunicating Emperor Bardas. Ignatius was banished by Bardas in 858 and replaced by Photius as Patriarch. A revolution in 867, however, ousted Bardas and restored Ignatius, who had the Fourth Ecumenical Council confirm his standing. He ambitiously tried to take over the Bulgarian Church, Pope John VIII's territory, and was bickering with John at the time of his death.

INGE, William Ralph (1860–1954) Nicknamed the "Gloomy Dean" because of his pessimism over the trends of modern western culture, Inge served as Dean of St. Paul's, London from 1911 to 1934. Inge, a Church of England prelate, was frequently quoted for his outspoken observations and penetrating analyses of many current topics.

INGHAM, Benjamin (1712–1772) A restless English sect-founder, Ingham, originally ordained by the Church of England, joined the Wesleys and traveled to Georgia and Germany with John Wesley. In 1738, Ingham became infatuated with Moravian tenets, left the Wesleys and organized his own group, called the Moravian Methodists, blending Moravianism and Wesley's main points. Ingham's sect, popularly known as "Inghamites," eventually numbered over eighty congregations. Later, however, Ingham began dabbling in the mystical teachings of Robert Sandeman and broke with his own Moravian Methodists. The Inghamite congregations soon died out or melded with Wesleyan congregations.

INGLIS, Charles (1734–1816) Honored as the first colonial bishop of the Church of England, Inglis served at Trinity Church, New York City before the American Revolution forced him, an unswerving Tory, to flee to Halifax, Nova Scotia. Inglis advocated an American episcopacy before anyone else thought of the idea, and was consecrated bishop in Nova Scotia in 1787.

INNOCENT I, Pope ([?]–417) A strong-willed prelate who maintained tight control over his see, Innocent I ruled during the disintegration of the Roman Empire from 401 to his death in 417, guiding the Church when the Barbarians crossed the Rhine in 406 and when the Goths sacked Rome in 410. Innocent claimed that the Roman Church had sole custody of apostolic tradition and primacy over all bishops because of Peter's primacy among the apostles. He insisted that other bishops refer important questions to Rome and advocated celibacy among all clergy. His policies and leadership considerably enhanced the power of the papacy in its formative years. Innocent I was canonized by the Roman Church.

INNOCENT II, Pope ([?]–1143) Pope Innocent II struggled with Anacletus II to be recognized as pope, inasmuch as both claimed to have been legally elected Supreme Head of the Church. Church law was hazy on this point, and each had some basis for a case, but Innocent II eventually won and ruled from 1130 to 1143. His reign was remembered as one which condemned Abélard and Arnold of Brescia.

INNOCENT III, Pope (1160[?]–1216) The pontiff who brought the papacy to the zenith of its earthly power, powerful Innocent III centralized the Church's government at Rome and determinedly, sometimes ruthlessly, tried to dominate princes and kings.

Innocent freely hurled excommunications and interdicts on recalcitrant rulers to strengthen his supremacy. In 1213, for example, he humbled erratic King John of England when John opposed the papal appointee as Archbishop of Canterbury; Innocent bludgeoned John with an interdict, forcing John to become his vassal and yield England as his feudal holding (which was denied by the barons in 1215 when they compelled John to sign the *Magna Carta*).

Innocent III launched the Fourth Crusade and ordered bloody suppressions against the Albigensi, a pre-Protestant sect in northern Italy and southern France.

One of the most influential popes in Roman Catholic history, Innocent III also called the Fourth Lateran Council, which established transubstantiation as official Roman Church doctrine and required confession and communion annually of every faithful Catholic.

INNOCENT IV, Pope (1190[?]–1254) Contesting for power with Emperor Frederick II, Pope Innocent allowed the struggle to degenerate to warfare, resulting in victory by papal troops at Parma in 1247. Innocent IV thought of power in terms of worldly might. He sparked the Crusade by Louis IX of France in 1248, and encouraged the Inquisition, issuing a papal bull in 1252 allowing the accused to be tortured and permitting the authorities to withhold accusers' names and to confiscate the accused's property for the Church. He held the papal throne from 1243 to 1254.

INNOCENT V, Pope (1225[?]–1276) Ruled only six months in 1276.

INNOCENT VI, Pope ([?]–1362) Pope from 1352 to 1362.

INNOCENT VII, Pope (1336[?]–1406) Pope from 1404 to 1406.

INNOCENT VIII, Pope (1432–1492) A weak worldling, Innocent VIII, father of several children, practiced nepotism to advance them to such a shocking degree that the moral tone of the entire Church was pulled down. His dilettante tastes led him to engage the Church's energies and funds on extravagant building programs—at a time when the most sensitive voices were pleading for reform. Innocent VIII's persistent refusal to heed these voices or to make any effort to introduce reforms prepared the Church for the inevitable convulsion in Luther's time.

Superstitious and superficial, Innocent VIII once in 1484 issued a bull (edict) declaring Germany to be full of witches. He ruled from 1484 to 1492.

INNOCENT IX, Pope (1519–1591)
Pope for only three months in 1591.

INNOCENT X, Pope (1574–1655)
An insipid, irresolute cypher, Innocent
X was dominated by his sister-in-law,
whose greed and intrigues made his
reign from 1644 to 1655 one of Rome's
most dismal.

INNOCENT XI, Pope (1611–1689)
Although above reproach as a person,
Innocent XI was indecisive as a pope.
His reign from 1676 to 1689 was a
near-constant clash with France's Louis
XIV over the selection of bishops.

INNOCENT XII, Pope (1615–1700)
A reform-minded prelate who introduced many rules to eliminate abuses
in the Church, such as prohibiting judges
to accept gifts or bribes in ecclesiastical
cases, Innocent XII was regarded as a
personally blameless but professionally
ineffective leader. He managed to end
the long quarrel between Rome and
Louis XIV of France, but became en-
gulfed in doctrinal fights which led him
to try to resolve by condemning the
Jansenists and the Quietists. Innocent
XII served from 1691 to 1700.

INNOCENT XIII, Pope (1655–1724)
Pope from 1721 to 1724.

IRELAND, John (1838–1918) Irish-
born American Roman Catholic leader,
Ireland was instrumental in the founding
of the Catholic University of America,
Washington, D.C., and promoted the
spread of parochial school systems in
the United States. He served in later
years as Archbishop of St. Paul, Minne-
sota, and took an active part in public
affairs.

IRENAEUS (115 to 142–200[?])
Raised in the tradition of the Eastern
Church, Irenaeus was born in Asia
Minor and educated under the illustrious
Polycarp, but settled in the West at
Lyons, Gaul (now France), as a
missionary and later as bishop. Irenaeus
opposed Gnosticism infecting the
Church (salvation through mystical,
supernatural knowledge passed on to
special initiates, blending aspects of old
pagan mystery religions with the
Gospel). Writing a powerful treatise,
Against Heresies, Irenaeus insisted that
the Apostles passed on no private secrets
to insiders. He also urged conformity
with the Church at Rome, where, he
pointed out, Apostolic tradition had
been faithfully preserved.

A deeply spiritual man, Irenaeus
fused the older, Pauline theology with
the newer "Catholic" thinking of his
own day. Irenaeus, primarily concerned
with salvation, emphasized Christ as the
second Adam, the new man, the full
revelation with God, who is united with
us in an almost physical sense through
the Eucharist.

Unlike many others of his time,
Irenaeus continued to expect a speedy
return of Christ to earth. He also
insisted that the New Testament is as
sacred as the Old for Christians. Irenaeus was the earliest theological writer
and leader of distinction in the development of the Old Catholic Church, and
gives us insights into the problems
confronting the Church in the 2nd
century. Tradition holds that he was
martyred at the time of Emperor
Septimius Severus.

IRENE, Sister (1823–1896) Born in
England and christened Catherine Fitz-
gibbon, but as a member of the Order
of the Sisters of Charity she was given
the name Mary Irene. Sister Irene was
sent to America where she took an
interest in foundlings and deserted
youngsters. In 1869 she founded New
York's first home for unwanted children,

which became New York Foundling Hospital.

IRVING, Edward (1792–1834) Unstable Scots clergyman who founded the community known as the Catholic Apostolic Church, Irving was a promising preacher in his early career who served as Thomas Chalmers' assistant in Glasgow and won fame for his polished sermons in a prominent pulpit in London before veering into strange doctrines. Irving began emphasizing his own brand of premillenarianism, stressing the imminent Second Coming of Christ and radical ideas on Christ's human nature. His dubious orthodoxy led the Church of Scotland to remove him from his pulpit in 1832 and depose him for heresy in 1833. Meanwhile, Irving organized the sect which he resoundingly named the Catholic Apostolic Church, but locally dubbed, "Irvingites." Irving, apparently suffering from an emotional disturbance, died in 1834.

ISIDORE (560[?]–636) By far the most learned man of his age, Isidore, Bishop of Seville, Spain, headed the Spanish Church and influenced the thinking of all other churchmen in his day by his writings. Isidore's *Book of Sentences,* a succinct compendium of doctrine, became such a classic that it was the standard theological textbook in the Latin Church until the 12th century. His *Origines* or *Etymologies* was an encyclopedia-like summary of the secular and sacred learning of the Middle Ages, and reflected an immense breadth of learning. He was later canonized.

J

JABLONSKI, Daniel Ernst (1660–1741) German-born, Bohemian descended (his maternal grandfather was the Czech Hussite Comenius) Moravian who took the ancestral name, Jablonski was appointed to the influential post of Court Preacher to Emperor Frederick III at Berlin in 1693, and elected Bishop of the Moravians in 1699. Jablonski tried unsuccessfully to unite Calvinists, Lutherans and other reformed groups into one German Protestant body, but pulled together the remnants of the Bohemian Hussite group exiled in Poland and Germany. In 1737, Jablonski ordained as bishop the saintly Count von Zinzendorf, who helped spread the Moravian Church to the U.S.A.

JACKSON, Sheldon (1834–1909) American Presbyterian missionary to the frontier, Jackson, dubbed "Bishop of All Beyond," was the pioneer Protestant in Alaska. Jackson, disappointed at being rejected for foreign missions because he seemed to be a health risk, went to the Rocky Mountain area in 1870, opening schools and churches and covering vast stretches of the rugged, remote American northwest. In 1884, he shifted his operations to Alaska. As first federal superintendent of Public Instruction in Alaska, Jackson opened schools for Indians, Eskimos and whites. Noting the food shortage for Eskimos, Jackson persuaded the U.S. Government to import reindeer from Siberia.

JACOB, Henry (1563–1624) English Congregationalist, Henry Jacob effectively replanted Congregationalism in England after earlier congregations had been uprooted by authorities. Jacob, who had been forced to flee to Holland with other exiled Separatists, had been a member of devout John Robinson's congregation of English Separatists at Leiden. He returned to England and founded a congregation at Southwark in 1616. Although remnants of the earlier Congregational Church established by Greenwood and Johnson but suppressed by the English government held on in London, Jacob's congregation was the first permanent Congregational Church.

JAMES I, King of England (and VI of Scotland) (1566–1625) Headstrong and haughty, James led the procession of stubborn Stewart kings, imperiously insisting on his divine right to rule. James I held a cavalier attitude toward Puritans and Parliaments, failing to conceal his contempt at the Hampton Court Conference for democratic forms of government in the church of both the established church and Puritans. He stimulated the first permanent English colonization program in the New World at Jamestown in 1607, and lent his name to the renowned English translation of the Bible in 1611. His exalted opinion of his station as supreme ruler put him at odds with nearly everyone during his reign.

JAMES II, King of England (1633–1701) Son of Charles I, the only English monarch to be beheaded, James inherited all the authoritarian arrogance of his Stewart ancestors. He returned with his brother, Charles II, when the monarchy was restored in England in 1660, and succeeded Charles as king in 1685. James II, obsessed with restoring Catholicism as the state religion of England, avowed his Catholicism in 1672 and as King rapidly took measures to establish Roman Catholic power. After a series of bloodily-repressed revolts and the refusal of seven brave Anglican bishops to knuckle under to his demands, James was forced to flee in 1688, following a wholesale uprising by the nobility. James, living in exile in Louis XIV's France, plotted to regain the throne. He invaded Ireland, collected Catholic sympathizers, but was spectacularly defeated at the Battle of the Boyne, July 1, 1690 by King William of Orange's British forces.

JANSEN, Cornelius (1585–1638) Dutch Roman Catholic theologian and Bishop of Ypres whose strong Augustinian views gave rise to the viewpoint known as Jansenism in the Roman Church, Jansen tilted against the powerful Jesuits, whom he accused of Pelagianism. Jansen emphasized Augustine's doctrines of sin and grace which he elucidated in his treatise, *Augustinus*, published posthumously in 1640. By accusing the Jesuits of Pelagian leanings (the heresy where man chooses to save himself by his own efforts), Jansen brought down Jesuit cries of "Extremist" on his head and the condemnation of Pope Urban VIII.

JEANNE D'ARC See **JOAN OF ARC.**

JEROME (340[?]–420) One of four great Church scholars recognized as "Doctors" by the Church during the Middle Ages, Jerome translated the Old Testament from Hebrew into Latin, and founded monasticism in the Latin Church. Jerome, raised a pagan, was

drawn to Christianity by seeing the tombs and catacombs of Christian martyrs at Rome as a student, gradually renounced his zeal for pagan philosophies and was baptized into the Church. After four years as a hermit monastic in the East, he studied some years at Constantinople then returned to Rome as teacher and as literary secretary to Pope Damasus. Jerome, in spite of his crusty disposition and strict asceticism, found a large audience among Rome's wealthy, upperclass women, several insisting on accompanying him later to the Holy Land.

In 386, Jerome founded a convent at Bethlehem, where he retired to work on his translation of the Scriptures. He was a meticulously careful scholar, insisting on translating from the original language and from the best available manuscripts. The Vulgate, Jerome's Latin Bible, became the fountain for Ecclesiastical Latin, the language used by the Church and throughout European universities for over a millennium.

Although a gifted preacher and expositor, Jerome was better remembered as a churlish controversialist in the doctrinal disputes of his time.

JEROME of Prague (1360[?]–1416) An early Czech reformer and companion of John Huss, Jerome of Prague inflamed the unrest stirred by Huss in Bohemia by his intemperate oratory and probably hastened the reprisals against Huss and his movement. Learned (he was asked by the King of Poland to set up the University of Cracow) and loquacious (he was asked by the King of Hungary to preach at the palace), Jerome frequently aroused the Prague populace to public disturbances, When the pope issued a bull (edict) calling for a crusade against Ladislaus of Naples, Jerome publicly burned the bull. Jerome rushed to the defense of his associate John Huss when Huss was arrested at Constance in 1415, and was seized and tortured for eighteen months until he agreed to recant. Huss was burned, but Jerome was kept imprisoned for another year. Jerome repudiated his recantation, was hauled out of his cell on orders of the Church Council at Constance, and burned at the stake.

JEWEL, John (1522–1571) One of the many Church of England clergy who were forced to flee to the Continent during Queen Mary's grim anti-Protestant reign, Jewel returned to England following Mary's death, became Bishop of Salisbury in 1560 and emerged as the leading defender of the Anglican establishment. Jewel's *Apologia pro Ecclesia Anglicana* in 1562, carefully refuting the attacks on Anglicanism by Roman Catholics, carried great weight among Church of England thinkers in the late 16th century.

JOACHIM of Floris (1145[?]–1202) A Cistercian abbot at Fiore on Monte Nero in southernmost Italy, he styled himself something of a prophet and founded his own rule and his own monastery. Joachim helped inflame a bitter feud within the Franciscan Order in the 12th century by his polemical treatises. One which gained wide circulation stated that all human history was divided into three periods: the age of the Law, or age of the Father; the age of the Gospel, or age of the Son; the age of Contemplation, or the age of the Holy Spirit. This was the monastic age, he declared, in which the Roman Church would be purified and the Church hierarchy would fade in importance as the truly spiritual men—the monks—gained ascendancy. The rigorists among the Franciscans, regarding themselves as the "Spirituals" or the Elect, assumed that they were the

initiators of the last age, and took Joachim's writings most seriously. Joachim's treatises were formally condemned at the Council of Arles in 1260, but spurious documents attributed to Joachim (especially attacks on the papacy) and Joachim's fame continued to be circulated and taken seriously for many years.

JOAN OF ARC (1412–1431) The peasant girl regarded as France's greatest heroine, Joan rallied the French forces when France was occupied by the English and Burgundians in 1429. She claimed to have experienced visions in which the voices of saints confirmed the legitimacy of King Charles VII's claim to the throne, which was then disputed in France and dividing the nation. Other visions commanded her to fulfil a mission to rouse the French to regain control of their country from the English. Joan convinced the dubious Charles to put her at the head of 10,000 troops in 1429, and astounded everyone by relieving the besieged city of Orléans. A few weeks later, Joan stood beside Charles at Reims Cathedral for his coronation.

Joan, however, was not given sufficient forces to try to recapture Paris, and was captured by the English. Accused of witchcraft by Bishop Cauchon (at the instigation of the English) and condemned by a Church court, Joan was publicly burned at Rouen, 1430.

Her death touched off a surge of patriotism in which her words were popularly interpreted as divine prophecies. In 1456, the Church officially rescinded its condemnation, but it was not until 1930 that it finally formally canonized the Maid of Orléans as a saint.

JOHN of Antioch ([?]–441) The Patriarch of Constantinople, John supported his friend Nestorius during the disgusting ecclesiastical-political-theological disputes at Ephesus in 431, where each side condemned members of the opposing faction in the Church —while arguing over the nature of Christ.

JOHN of Asia (505[?]–585[?]) A leader in the Monophysite group (which argued only one nature in Christ—the divine one) in the Syriac-speaking Church and a noted historian in the 6th century who was driven by plagues and persecutions from Palestine to Constantinople about 535, John of Asia was put in charge of the finances of the Monophysite Church and appointed bishop by Emperor Justinian. He energetically set out to establish over ninety monasteries and baptized over 70,000 converts in Asia Minor. His career was ended when Emperor Justin and Patriarch Paul of Asia began rooting out and persecuting the Monophysites.

JOHN of Capistrano, or SAN GIOVANNI da Capistrano (1386–1456) An Italian who left his new bride following a vision to join the Strict Observance of the Franciscan Order, John of Capistrano became a renowned missionary-preacher in Italy and eastern Europe. He served as legate for a series of popes and became an Inquisitor noted for his severity toward Moslems, Jews and Hussites.

JOHN CASSIANUS See **CASSIAN.**

JOHN CHRYSTOSTOM See **CHRYSOSTOM.**

JOHN of the Cross (1542–1591) Spanish Carmelite priest, mystic and poet, St. John of the Cross wrote the haunting, meditative lyrical poems, *The Dark Night of the Soul, The Living Flame of Divine Love* and *The Spiritual Canticle* which expressed a mysticism in lofty symbolism. His personal career in the Spanish Church was deeply unhappy. After founding several monasteries of Discalced Carmelites, John (born Juan de Yepes y Alvarez) tried to introduce reforms in the Carmelite Order suggested by St. Teresa but was caught in a furious dispute between rival Carmelite factions. John was thrown into prison by opposing Carmelites, escaped, but driven out by the winning faction. Broken by persecution, he sought out a desolate hideout in Andalusia, where he spent the remainder of his life meditating and writing.

JOHN of Damascus, JOHANNES DAMASCENUS, JOHN DAMASCENE (675[?]–749) A Syrian churchman honored as a Doctor in the Eastern Church, John of Damascus was the last great theologian produced by the Eastern Church. John, raised a Christian, succeeded his father as a key administrator on the staff of the Caliph at Damascus, but left to become a monk at St. Sabas monastery at Jerusalem. His eloquent preaching earned him the label "Chrysorrhoas" (literally "gold-streaming"); his hymns gained him fame in the East; and his monumental compendium of Eastern doctrine, *The Fountain of Wisdom,* made him the most honored theologian in the Eastern Church.

JOHN DUNS SCOTUS See **DUNS SCOTUS.**

JOHN of Ephesus See **JOHN of Asia.**

JOHN the Faster ([?]–595) Such an ascetic that he went spectacularly long periods without food, John became known for his fasting and was elected Patriarch of Constantinople. John the Faster insisted on assuming the title

"Ecumenical Patriarch," which infuriated the popes of Rome. He was denounced by Popes Pelagius II and Gregory I who maintained that this distinctive title may never be used by any bishop.

JOHN FIDANZA See BONAVENTURA.

JOHN of God (1495–1550) Also known as Juan Ciudad, this Portuguese-born layman founded the lay group known as the Brothers of Charity. John, a shepherd boy who became a mercenary in the Austrian army, settled at Granada, Spain, where he was stirred by sermons and the human need in the city. In 1440, he rented a house, opened it to the sick and poor and attracted a handful of willing helpers. Following his death in 1550, the movement spread to Madrid, where its hospital was well endowed by gifts from royalty. John of God's group was formally created an Order with the Augustinian Rule in 1572 known as Brothers Hospitalers. John himself was canonized in 1690.

JOHN of Jandun ([?]–1328) A radically "modern" thinker and writer who helped write *Defensor Pacis*, John of Jandun proposed that the powers of all rulers are based on the sovereignty of the people. John of Jandun with co-author Marsilius of Padua wrote their famous treatise in 1324, stating the then-heretical idea that even popes and kings are granted their rights to rule by the consent of the governed. John of Jandun and Marsilius were forced to flee wrathful Pope John XXII, who excommunicated them in 1327. Fortunately, however, they were protected by Emperor Louis the Bavarian.

JOHN of Leiden See Beukelssen.

JOHN of Monte Corvino (1246–1328) A courageous Italian Franciscan who heard of the Polos' odyssey to China, John embarked for China to carry the Christian Gospel in 1291. He traveled to Peking, laboriously founded a congregation about 1300 and was recognized when Pope Clement V appointed him archbishop over six bishops in China. John of Monte Corvino and his tireless bishops established a strong Church in China which flourished until 1368, when the xenophobic Ming Dynasty suppressed Christian worship and expelled all foreigners.

JOHN of Nepomuk, or POMUK or NEPOMUCEN (1340[?]–1393) The patron saint of Bohemia, John served as Vicar-General of Prague until he was ordered drowned in the Moldan River by King Wencelaus IV in 1393. The facts of the cause of his execution are covered with a heavy veneer of legend, but seem to indicate that John refused the King's demand to turn an abbey into a cathedral and declined to reveal the Queen's confession to the King. John was canonized in 1729.

JOHN of Pomuk See JOHN of Nepomuk.

JOHN SCOTUS ERIGENA See DUNS SCOTUS.

JOHN I, Pope (470[?]–526) Pope John I was forced by Emperor Theodoric to travel from Rome to Constantinople to ask Justin grant leniency to Arians in the Church (the group teaching that Christ was not quite fully divine). John went reluctantly and was not very persuasive. When he returned home to Rome after only partial success, he was imprisoned at Ravenna by the angry Emperor. John I served from 523 until his death in prison in 526.

JOHN II, Pope ([?]–535) Pope from 533 to 535.

JOHN III, Pope ([?]–574) John III, pontiff from 561 to 574, ruled during the anarchy in Italy caused by repeated invasions by the Lombards.

JOHN IV, Pope ([?]–642) Remembered as a determined and orthodox pope, John IV tried to end the angry Church dispute in which a noisy group called the Monothelites insisted that there is only one will in Christ by condemning them as heretics. He served from 640 to 642.

JOHN V, Pope ([?]–686) John V, from Syria, was the first pope from the Middle East, and ruled from 685 to 686.

JOHN VI, Pope ([?]–705) Pontiff from 701 to 705, John VI settled the disagreement in England between Wilfred of York and the Archbishop of Canterbury, deciding in favor of Canterbury. John VI was one of the few Greek popes.

JOHN VII, Pope ([?]–707) Pope from 705 to 707.

JOHN VIII, Pope ([?]–882) John VIII had to buy off the Saracen invaders who had marched up to the very gates of Rome. Ruling from 872 to 882, this pope tried unsuccessfully to unite the Eastern and Western Churches and tighten the lax discipline among his clergy, especially the top leaders.

JOHN IX, Pope ([?]–900) A Benedictine monk originally, John IX reigned from 898 to 900.

JOHN X, Pope ([?]–928) A better general than politician, John X personally led an army which drove the Saracens out of Italy in 916. However, he made the error of antagonizing the powerful daughter of Theodora named Marozia, wife of the Margrave of Tuscany, who imprisoned him and probably murdered him. John X was in office from 914 until his death in 928.

JOHN XI, Pope ([?]–936) The son of the notorious Marozia, wife of the Margrave of Tuscany, John XI, elected pope in 931 even though he was not of age, was merely a mouthpiece for his mother. After his mother was jailed by his brother, Alberic II, young John XI was controlled by Alberic. His death in 936 ended this tragic farce in the Church.

JOHN XII, Pope (938[?]–964) Dubbed "the boy pope" because he was only eighteen when elected, John XII brought disgrace to the chair of Peter by his unbridled immorality and is recalled as one of the worst pontiffs. The first pope to change his name on becoming the Church head, he was originally called Octavian, and was the son of Alberic II, the Italian nobleman whose family controlled the papacy for nearly fifty years. John XII was also the first pope to call on the German Emperor for help, working a deal to get Emperor Otto I to oppose Berengar II (who had taken over a large slice of Italy) but starting the precedent whereby the papacy became beholden to emperors for protection. John XII, a fickle type, turned on Otto, who angrily deposed John and installed his own choice, Leo VIII. As soon as Otto went home, John returned and excommunicated Leo. John XII's scandalous reign lasted from 955 to 964.

JOHN XIII, Pope ([?]–972) The papacy was somewhat of a revolving door as popes came and went during the 10th century. John XIII was the twenty-first pope in the period from Stephen V's death in 897 until John's elevation in 965. The nephew of Marozia, the Italian noblewoman whose family dominated the papacy for most of that period, John XIII was the hand-picked choice of German Emperor Otto I. John, however, was thrown out by the Roman nobles, but restored by Otto. Although John XIII and the papacy had been rescued by the emperor, the office of pope had become subservient to the powerful emperor. John XIII was pope from 965 to 972.

JOHN XIV, Pope ([?]–984) Emperor Otto II's selection as pope in place of Counter-pope Boniface VII, John XIV unfortunately lost his benefactor when Otto died. John XIV was either starved to death or murdered in prison by the vengeful Boniface after reigning little more than a year, from 983 to 984.

JOHN XV, Pope ([?]–996) Hopelessly and completely controlled by the Roman prefect, Crescentius, and his faction, John XV held the title of pope from 985 to 986.

JOHN XVI, Antipope ([?]–1013) An Italian named John Piligato, John foolishly allowed himself to be installed as a pope in 997 by the prefect Crescentius II even though Pope Benedict V occupied the papal throne at that time. When Emperor Otto II, who backed Benedict, rushed back to Rome to crush opposition and reinstate Benedict, John XVI was deposed, blinded, castrated and imprisoned.

JOHN XVI and XVII, Pope ([?]–1003) Actually, no legitimate pope ever called himself John XVI, and the pope who sometimes is called John XVI actually numbered himself John the seventeenth. Named John Sicco, married and the father of three children, he was made pope through the influence of the powerful Roman prefect Crescentius III, son of the man who installed John Piligato as John XVI. Not wanting to offend or antagonize Crescentius, John Sicco called himself John XVII, throwing the numbering of popes named John into confusion. Some later historians at Rome tried to bring order by labelling this pontiff named John (who ruled five months in 1003) "John XVI."

JOHN XVIII, Pope ([?]–1009) Another pontiff installed through the machinations of the Crescentius faction at Rome, John XVIII held office from 1004 to 1009, abdicated wearily to spend the last few months of his life in a monastery.

JOHN XIX, Pope ([?]–1032) The brother of Pope Benedict VIII, John XIX, although a layman, contrived to get himself elected pope in 1024, and used the title for eight years until his death. He lived in lavish splendor, and was the first to grant the sale of indulgences (payment of alms for release from sins) to replenish papal coffers.

JOHN XX There was never any pope named John XX. Through an error in papal record-keeping, the number was somehow omitted in the succession.

JOHN XXI, Pope (1215[?]–1277) Sometimes called John XX (to compound the confusion in numbering popes named John!) John XXI was the only Portuguese pope, ruling from 1276 to 1277. He dabbled in scientific matters, writing a medical treatise which received considerable attention, and died from injuries when the roof of his laboratory in the papal palace at Viterbo collapsed and fell on him.

JOHN XXII, Pope (1249–1334) The third Avignon pope, John XXII was a French prelate with an executive flair and an avaricious streak. He successfully opposed Emperor Louis IV of Bavaria who tried to replace John XXII with an antipope, Nicholas V, and amassed a large private fortune during his tenure as pontiff, 1316 to 1334.

JOHN XXIII, Counter-pope (1370[?]–1419) One of three rival pontiffs ruling simultaneously during a schism from 1410 to 1415, Counter-pope John XXIII thought that he would resolve the situation by calling the Council of Constance in 1414. To his chagrin, the Council asserted its authority, accusing John of some seventy charges, deposing him and choosing Martin V as rightful occupant of the throne of Peter. John XXIII died in prison.

JOHN XXIII, Pope (1881–1963) The personable, peasant-born pontiff who stunned the world by calling an Ecumenical Council on December 24, 1961, John XXIII, elected in 1958, was expected to be an "interim pope" because of his advanced age. Previously, as Cardinal Roncalli, he had served many years with distinction in numerous ticklish positions. Displaying immense energy and originality (even by choosing "John"—unused for 500 years) John XXIII galvanized the papacy which, during the last years of the long (1939–1958) incumbency of the somewhat indecisive, scholarly Pius XII, had become creaky and conservative. He filled long-empty posts, created twenty-three cardinals, raised the College of Cardinals to seventy-five, and revived discarded customs such as personally visiting Rome's prison and hospital. The greatest achievement of this popular pope was to summon the gathering known as the Second Vatican Council, which convened in October 1962.

JONES, George Heber (1867–1919) An American Methodist Episcopal missionary to Korea beginning in 1887, Jones founded forty-four congregations and brought over two thousand Koreans into the Church. He helped translate the Bible into Korean and served as president of the Biblical Institute and Union Seminary, Korea.

JONES, Rufus Matthew (1863–1948) Winsome American Friend, modern mystic and longtime (1893–1947) professor at Quaker-sponsored Haverford (Pa.) College, Rufus Jones served as unofficial spokesman for the Society of Friends for over a half century. Rufus Jones, with a background of a practical Maine farm upbringing, turned his mystical piety and profound learning into down-to-earth demonstrations of compassion, such as instituting feeding programs among the starving, destitute Germans and Belgians following World War I. Jones helped found the American Friends Service Committee, and served as its chairman for many years. His many books reflected his cheerful optimism, unswerving pacifism and radiant love of God.

JONES, (Samuel Porter) "Sam" (1847–1906) A successful attorney ruined by alcoholism, following a dramatic conversion in 1872, he became one of America's most colorful and popular revivalists. Sam Jones was a well-known Methodist tent-preacher in the late 19th century in the South and Midwest America.

JOSEPH II, Patriarch of Constantinople ([?]–1439) Threatened with an invasion by the Moslem Turks and pressed by the Eastern Emperor John VIII and Bessarion, Archbishop of Nicea, to find allies, Joseph II turned to the pope at Rome, offering to start negotiations for the reunion of the Greek and Latin branches of the Church. The reunion plans were scuttled by the chauvinistic Mark of Ephesus, who accused Joseph and the other Eastern churchmen of selling out to Rome.

Tragically, the fall of Constantinople in 1453 ended the dreams of reunion for many centuries.

JUAN DE LA CRUZ See JOHN of the Cross.

JUDSON, Adoniram (1788–1850) Pioneer Baptist missionary to Burma, Judson settled at Rangoon in 1813, patiently overcame hostile Burmese Buddhist governmental officials and unfriendly villagers, although making only twenty converts in his first eleven years. He endured imprisonment for seventeen months, beginning in 1824, and began over again in lower Burma following his release, finally founding a congregation. Driving himself until his health broke, Judson returned to the United States for two years, but by 1847 was back in Rangoon. Judson worked on Burmese translations of the Bible, and prepared a Burmese grammar and dictionary. Some think his greatest contribution was building up feelings of toleration and good will toward Christians by the suspicious Burmese.

Judson has the additional distinction of being one of the first five missionaries sent by the famed American Board of Commissioners for Foreign Missions. A Congregationalist at that time, Judson went to India, but joined the Baptists in Calcutta, helping to form the Baptist Missionary Union.

JULIUS I, Pope ([?]–352) Pope Julius I provoked resentment among leaders in the Eastern Church by welcoming Athanasius, who had just been pushed out of Alexandria by the Arian faction then trying to take over the Eastern Church. Julius I, who ruled from 337 to 352, tried to damp down Arianism (the heresy that Christ was not quite fully God) and promote Rome's primacy by calling together fifty Italian bishops in 340 to vindicate

Athanasius. Julius followed up his Italian conference by calling churchmen from everywhere to the Council of Sardica in 343.

The leaders from Constantinople and other Eastern sees, however, boycotted the Sardican Council. Irked at Julius' "interference," they rejected western Church rules passed by Julius' Council which enunciated the right of appeals to Rome from any local Church Council, and restored Athanasius to his old post at Alexandria.

JULIUS II, Pope (1443–1513) A wily politician and cunning military strategist, Julius II resorted to bribery, bargaining and force to maintain the independence of the papal state. Julius II successfully subdued all opponents, including a dissident faction of cardinals which tried to trim his powers by calling a Council at Pisa. Julius neatly checkmated the rebel cardinals by calling a Council of the Lateran in 1512.

Pope from 1503 to 1513 during the years immediately preceding the Reformation, Julius ignored the pleas for reform, busying himself with protecting papal political interests and prettying papal property. Julius, an art patron, commissioned such artists as Michelangelo and Raphael to beautify the Vatican.

JULIUS III, Pope (1487–1555) A cultured, indolent pontiff, Julius III reigned from 1550 to 1555. He reconvened the Council of Trent in 1552, after prodding by Emperor Charles V, and later blandly agreed to strengthen the powers of the Jesuits.

JUNIPER, Father See SERRA JUNIPERO.

JUSTIN MARTYR (100[?]–165[?]) Awarded the name "Martyr" for his heroic witness under the Roman Prefect Rusticus who put many Christians to death, Justin was one of the early Church's ablest defenders. Justin, raised a pagan, was so saturated with pagan Platonic philosophy that he saw the Gospel as the truest and most perfect philosophy rather than the Resurrection experience or awareness of divine grace. Taking up the then-current idea that *Logos* or divine word-idea is operating always everywhere, Justin carried the Fourth Evangelist's idea much further in maintaining that the *Logos* became incarnate in Christ.

Although Justin Martyr can be accused of minimizing the Jesus of History, his "Apology" (addressed to Emperor Antoninus Pius) and "Second Apology" (addressed to Emperor Marcus Aurelius) explained Christian practices and argued the philosophical truth of Christianity to a world used to subtle philosophical presentations.

Justin also effectively battled Gnosticism, the notion that secret knowledge imparted to select initiates can bring salvation. He lived at Rome as a Christian teacher from about 150 until his death.

JUSTINIAN, Emperor (483–565) The "theological politician," Justinian was a peasant-born victorious military commander who rose to rule as Roman Emperor in the East at Constantinople. Justinian, one of the most sophisticated theologians of his day, was also a shrewd dictator who in effect made the Church a department of his government. Careful not to tamper with the wording of the Chalcedonian Creed, yet anxious to produce a policy which would conciliate all Church factions, Justinian, a partisan of the Cyrillic school's interpretations of theology, called the Fifth General Council in 553 at Constantinople. Justinian's Fifth Council, condemning Theodore of Mopsuesta's works, Origen's writings and Theodoret of Cyprus' teachings, effectively played down Chalcedonian Christianity, slammed the Antioch school and pushed Cyril of Alexander's Christology.

Justinian also commissioned ten scholars to produce a new legal code: the body of civil law today known as the Code of Justinian. An energetic ruler who kept his finger on all phases of his Empire, Justinian rebuilt numerous churches, including the glorious St. Sophia in Constantinople.

K

KAGAWA, Toyohiko (1888–1960) Saintly Japanese Christian, Kagawa identified with the poor and outcasts in industrial Japan, promoting most of the first Church-sponsored social programs in 20th century Japan. Kagawa, born into a wealthy Buddhist family, became a Christian during his university days but, unlike most Asian Christians who have been drawn from the professional classes, chose to live in the festering slums of Kobe.

He endured slander, beatings, and imprisonments, and contracted trachoma. Kagawa, carrying the Gospel to lower class Japanese, founded settlement houses, peasant farm cooperatives, folk schools, and blueprinted plans for social work at Tokyo. Sometimes encountering violence for his efforts to stop the custom of selling daughters into prostitution and efforts to counter alcoholism, Kagawa was jailed for supporting labor in the industrial conflict of the 1930's. Kagawa, a pacifist, was also imprisoned for a time during World War II.

Following the war, he brought his influence to bear in urging the Japanese to accept democracy.

His books and poems, combining a profound Christian commitment with an Oriental sensitivity, were widely circulated.

KANIS, Peter (also Canisius) (1521–1597) The earliest German Jesuit, Kanis was a ferociously anti-Protestant theologian who held great influence on the later proceedings at the Council of Trent, 1545–1563, which unequivocably rejected Reformed doctrine. Kanis was canonized in 1925.

KANT, Immanuel (1724–1804) Raised in a strict German Protestant Pietist home, Kant wrote and taught at Königsberg, where he held numerous academic distinctions.

His philosophical writings, beginning with *Critique of Pure Reason* in 1781, vindicated man's deepest feelings as the basis of practical religious conviction and moral conduct. Breaking with rationalism (which, said Kant, can organize knowledge but cannot take the place of experience as the best teacher), and attacking traditional speculative metaphysics (which Kant maintained cannot penetrate to ultimate reality), Kant insisted that the mind classifies what comes to it from without under its own laws.

In *Critique of Practical Reason,* Kant tried to combine empiricism and rationalism to state that man, with a sense of moral "ought," had a duty to provide the greatest happiness for the greatest number.

Religion, for Kant, became the "apprehension of all duties as divine commands" in which God's existence is a postulate based on trust, not proofs. Kant's intellectualism and rejection of traditional props for the Church's dogma brought about strong reactions pro and con in his 18th century and immeasurably influenced all subsequent philosophical and theological thinking.

KARLSTADT See **CARLSTADT.**

KEBLE, John (1792–1866) The Church of England cleric who sparked the Anglo-Catholic or "High Church" wing of the Anglican Church, Keble was one of a circle of brilliant young clergymen (including Froude and Newman) at Oriel College, Oxford, who tried to revive ancient traditions such as fasting, clerical celibacy and reverence for the saints which they regretted had been dropped by the Reformers.

Keble, a gifted poet and bright scholar, preached a sermon July 14, 1833 at Oxford which is credited with inaugurating the "Oxford Movement," which ultimately led Newman and others to become Roman Catholics. Keble remained Anglican, but represented the Anglo-Catholic position.

Keble College, opened at Oxford in 1869, stands as a memorial to his influence.

KEMNITZ See CHEMNITZ.

KEMPIS, Thomas à (1380[?]–1471) Author of the devotional classic, *The Imitation of Christ,* the world's most popular Christian treatise next to the Bible, Thomas lived a long (ninety-one years) life as a shy, bookish Augustinian priest at a poor monastery at Zwolle. He grew up in a peasant's family at Kempen, near Düsseldorf, and was sent at twelve to the great school founded by Gerhard Groote, the Dutch mystic, at Deventer, where he was called simply Thomas of Kempen or Thomas à Kempis instead of Thomas Hammerken, the family name. Thomas imbibed deeply of the mystics' sense of the presence of God at Deventer. Although he entered the Augustinian Order in 1399 at the monastery of Mount St. Agnes near Zwolle, where his older brother, John, was Prior, Thomas à Kempis retained the simple, mystical devotion to the person of Christ of the Deventer school. He was ordained as a priest in 1413, but had to earn his living by copying manuscripts throughout his life in the poor monastery at Zwolle. Thomas' personal life was uneventful; apart from an unhappy and brief term looking after the business affairs of the monastery, he lived a retiring existence.

His masterpiece, *The Imitation of Christ,* ascribed by a few scholars to Gerhard Groote his mentor at Deventer, has been translated into more languages than any other book except the Bible.

KENTIGERN (518 or 527[?]–603 or 618[?]) Also known as St. Mungo, Kentigern was an ancient British missionary-preacher who founded a monastery on the River Clyde on the site of modern Glasgow, Scotland. Kentigern's name (meaning "Great Chief" in Celtic) hints that he was descended from early British royalty, and his alternate name, Mungo (meaning "My dear friend" in Celtic) suggests pleasant personal characteristics. He preached and taught for thirteen years on the banks of the Clyde at Cathures (now Glasgow), becoming Bishop of the kingdom of Strathclyde about 540. He was forced out, however, when an anti-Christian uprising deposed his protector, the king of Strathclyde. Fleeing to Wales, Kentigern founded a monastery near Llanelwy, where his most famous disciple was Asaph and the monastery came to be called "St. Asaph's."

Kentigern returned to Scotland about 573, and after a sojourn at Dumfries, came back to Cathures to his monastery. Later, he was visited by St. Columba.

Glasgow Cathedral, located on the site of Kentigern's monastery, is named St. Mungo's in his honor, and the Glasgow coat of arms honors his memory as founder of the city.

KETHE, William ([?]–1608) One of the horde of refugees to the Continent from England during Protestant-baiting Queen Mary's reign, Kethe (or Keith?) was a Scots Protestant who fled to Frankfurt in 1554. He joined fellow-refugee William Whittingham and moved to Geneva when Whittingham succeeded John Knox as pastor of the English-speaking congregation. Kethe and Whittingham published a service book in 1556 containing fifty-one metrical psalms in English, including "Old Hundredth" and many other familiar psalms sung in Protestant worship. Kethe's words and tunes, renowned for their theological integrity and musical dignity, were incorporated in the Scottish Psalter of 1564. Kethe, returning to England in 1561, served a parish near Oxford for some years.

KHOMIAKOV or **KHOMYAKOV, Aleksei Stepanovich** (1804–1860) The father of modern Russian theology, Khomiakov led a Slavophile movement of devotees to the culture, language and literary possibilities of the Slavic peoples. Khomiakov, an earnest adherent to the Eastern Orthodox Church, was certain that the West was decaying and forecast an eventual takeover by the Slavs in which the Eastern rite would play a crucial part. He blasted both the Roman Catholics and Protestants as apostates for breaking the unity of the Church, and glorified the Eastern Church, with its mystical insights and liturgy as the one real hope of Christianity.

KIERKEGAARD, Søren Aaby (1813–1855) Melancholy Danish thinker whose insights have lingered both among the existentialists such as Sartre and among theologians such as Niebuhr, Søren Kierkegaard demanded such a radical Christianity in 19th century Europe that he was shunned as an eccentric but later revered as a Protestant revolutionary thinker.

Kierkegaard, a curious recluse who never married after breaking his engagement to Regine Olsen in 1841, nor ever was ordained after studying theology, excoriated the Danish Church of the day as a mockery of Christianity. Pointing to its self-righteous sham, stuffy formalism and superficial piety, Kierkegaard appears peculiarly modern.

Kierkegaard opposed the philosopher Hegel's notion that absolute knowledge is possible and rational, and also opposed Aristotle's and Plato's idealism whereby man has truth in himself and need only to become conscious of it. Insisting that truth comes from outside, Kierkegaard stated, "To be what one is by one's own act is freedom."

Beginning with *Either/Or* in 1843, Kierkegaard set a new trend by raising questions and posing alternative viewpoints rather than pretentiously trying to give final answers. In *Concept of Dread,* he wrote of the anxiety which "eats away all the things of the finite world and lays bare all illusions," leaving man to decide whether or not to take the "leap of faith" without proofs of God's existence. Kierkegaard, obsessed with the meaninglessness and futility of life, which he explored in *Sickness Unto Death* in 1849, proposed a real, radical Christianity as the only alternative.

Kierkegaard's other notable works include *Fear and Trembling* in 1843, and *Concluding Unscientific Postscript* in 1846, in which he lambasts the orthodox, rationalist theologians for their pretentiousness in "demonstrating" that God's will is shown in history or can be "proved." Kierkegaard bitingly commented that these thinkers would have to be God to know what only God can know.

KILIAN ([?]–689) A 7th century Irish missionary to Germany, Kilian became bishop of Thuringia and Franconia, but was cruelly put to death on the orders of the prince, Gosbert. Two co-workers, Colman and Totnan, died with him. Kilian is honored as the favorite saint in the Wurzburg area of Germany.

KING, Martin Luther, Jr. (1929–1968) Martyred American Negro Civil Rights leader, King spearheaded efforts by southern U.S. Negro churchmen to arouse the nation's conscience to bring redress for social injustice. King, venerated by some but vilified by others, dominated the era of race relations in the United States between the 1954 Supreme Court ruling ending school segregation and the rise of the black militants in 1968.

King, a young Ph.D.-holding Baptist pastor, mobilized the Negro citizens of Montgomery, Alabama to wage a bus boycott in 1956 which ended segregation on the city buses and catapulted King into national prominence. The following year, King and a group of black pastors organized the Southern Christian Leadership Conference, which grew to become the most active Civil Rights group in the U.S. in the early 1960's.

King's charismatic leadership and the Southern Christian Leadership Conference's insistence on non-violence rallied powerful support but also frequently detonated intense opposition by their tactics of sit-in's and massive demonstrations. King led the 200,000-strong "March on Washington" in August, 1963 to plead for stronger Civil Rights legislation, and the Selma-to-Montgomery, Alabama March in March, 1965 to emphasize the need for a Federal Voter Registration bill.

In 1964, Martin Luther King, Jr. was presented with the Nobel Peace Prize, the youngest person ever to be so honored. King, who had endured beatings, bombings, threats and imprisonments for his peaceful efforts to secure rights and respect for black Americans, died from an assassin's bullet in Nashville, April 4, 1968.

KIRKLAND, Samuel (1741–1808) An American Congregational missionary to the Seneca and Oneida Indians, Kirkland persuaded many tribesmen to join the cause of the colonies during the American Revolution. In 1793, Kirkland founded a mission school for Indian boys, Hamilton Oneida Academy, which became the illustrious Hamilton College.

KITTEL, Rudolf (1853–1929) Meticulous German Lutheran philologist, pastor and Old Testament scholar, Kittel painstakingly compiled the best possible Hebrew text of the Old Testament. Now published under the title *Biblia Hebraica*, Kittel's masterpiece and lifework is universally used by Biblical students who want the most reliable Biblical text in Hebrew.

KNOX, John (1515[?]–1572) Prickly father of the Scottish Reformation and Scottish nationalism, Knox, originally a Roman Catholic priest, was won to the Protestant cause when George Wishart was burned at St. Andrews by Cardinal Beaton. Knox became spiritual teacher to the hunted band of early Protestant sympathizers.

Knox, after serving nineteen months as a galley slave following his capture at St. Andrews, settled in England (then under Protestant regents ruling for Edward VI) where he became a royal chaplain and was offered (but declined) the post of Bishop of Rochester.

Forced to flee when fanatic Catholic Queen Mary ascended the throne of England in 1553, John Knox found refuge in John Calvin's Geneva, where he became a devoted disciple of Calvin's theology and form of Church government.

Knox returned to Scotland in 1559 at the urgent plea of the coalition of those supporting Scottish Protestantism and Scottish independence, which were in imminent danger of being snuffed out by Mary Queen of Scots' marriage to the heir of the French throne. Knox's preaching had an immediate incendiary effect on the masses. By 1560, through Knox's leadership, Scottish independence was assured. That same year, Knox established a presbyterian system throughout the kingdom, adopted a Calvinistic confession, abolished the pope's jurisdiction and called the first General Assembly.

In 1561, however, Mary Queen of Scots returned to Scotland as a lovely, prudent and charming young widow (her husband, Francis II of France had died in December, 1560) freed from commitments to France. She aroused widespread popular sympathy and divided Knox's supporters among the Scottish Protestant nobility.

Knox, unmoved by the winsome Queen, for a time found his gains threatened as Mary won support, reintroduced Roman Catholic practices and flirted with the notion of marrying a foreign Catholic prince. Knox, from Mary's return in 1561 until her downfall through shameless matrimonial adventures and imprudent intrigue in 1567, kept alive the cause of Scottish Protestantism. His triumph was complete when he preached the sermon at Mary's year-old son's (James VI) coronation following Mary's forced abdication.

In addition to fiery oratory, Knox had gifts as an organizer. Through the *First Book of Discipline,* Knox laid out an ecclesiastical system based on Scripture which provided nearly every part of Scotland (except some areas of the remote Northwest Highlands) with a plan for a minister and elected "elders" constituting a "Session" to exercise church rule in each parish. Knox also arranged programs for public education of all children and relief of the poor in each parish. Knox's liturgy, *The Book of Common Order,* approved in 1564 and modelled on Calvin's Genevan liturgy, was intended as a model or guide, not a compulsory order of worship.

A modest unassuming man personally, Knox's grave today appropriately is marked merely by small initials on a paving stone in Edinburgh's High Street. He is honored as the man who influenced not only the faith but character of the Scottish nation more than any other in Scottish history.

KNUT   See **CANUTE.**

L

LABADIE, Jean de (1610–1674) A one-time French Jesuit priest who broke with the Jesuits and then with the Roman Catholic Church in 1650 to become a Reformed pastor at Geneva, Labadie moved on to the Netherlands where he was suspended by the Protestants as a schismatic. Labadie established his own sect and communal society near Middleburg, which moved to Amsterdam for a few years until it was expelled. Transferring his operation to Westphalia, where Princess Elizabeth encouraged him until the excesses of his Labadists soured her. Labadie's last stop was Denmark.

His cult, the Labadists, was a communal group holding all property in common and clinging to beliefs which were a mishmash of mystical piety and Calvinist deviations, such as claiming that children of the Elect are free from original sin. The Labadists died out in the mid-eighteenth century.

LACTANTIUS, Firmianus (260[?]–340[?]) Dubbed the "Christian Cicero" because of the resemblance of his style to the great Roman orator's, Lactantius was an early Christian apologist or writer. He was born and raised as a pagan in Nicomedia (now Izmir, Turkey), and was converted to Christianity at the age of thirty while serving as a teacher in the Emperor Diocletian's school. Fired from his post during Diocletian's persecution in 303, Lactantius later was protected by the Emperor Constantine and asked to act as tutor for Constantine's son. Lactantius, in

spite of a skimpy knowledge of the Bible, was a persuasive and earnest defender of the Christian faith in his numerous works.

LAINEZ, Diego (1512–1565) One of the seven charter members of the band of Paris students which formed the Society of Jesus, Lainez joined his fellow-Spaniard Ignatius Loyola at the University of Paris. Lainez, like Ignatius, was an intensely disciplined believer and astute thinker. He served as a papal theologian at the Council of Trent, 1545 to 1563, helping influence that Council take action to reject Reformed doctrine. Following Ignatius' death, Lainez was selected to become the second General of the Jesuits. He led the Jesuits so effectively that he was asked to succeed Pope Paul IV. Preferring to head the Jesuit Order, he declined the papacy.

During Lainez's term as General, the Jesuits began their famous emphasis on education.

LAKE, Kirsopp (1872–1946) An English-born Biblical scholar with strong liberal leanings, Lake taught at Harvard from 1914 to 1938. He participated in a series of archaeological expeditions to the Middle East and wrote several books, including the five-volume *Beginnings of Christianity*.

LAMENNAIS, Felicite Robert de (1782–1854) A French religious-political radical who left an imprint on French thinking throughout the 19th and early 20th centuries, Lamennais served as a Roman Catholic priest from

1816 to 1834, when his left-of-center views stirred so much controversy and opposition inside and outside the Church that he broke with Rome. He endured a year's prison sentence for his political activities, but later served on the French National Assembly.

As a priest, Lamennais had attracted many bright, young scholars and priests —a sort of Oxford Movement in France—by advocating democratic ideals and early Church simplicity.

LAMY, John Baptist (1814–1888) The model for American authoress Willa Cather's "Death Comes to the Archbishop," Lamy, an immigrant priest from France in 1839, served in a series of assignments in the American West before being elevated to a see covering a vast expanse of the southwest in 1850. Lamy founded dozens of congregations and schools, in spite of opposition by some of his Spanish priests and hardships in covering his diocese. Made archbishop in 1875 in Sante Fé, Lamy acquired a reputation for courage, honesty and dedication.

LANFRANC (1005–1089) An efficient and forceful Norman prelate who as a friend of William the Conqueror was brought to England in 1070 after the Norman invasion of 1066, Lanfranc quickly dominated English Church affairs. He insisted that York be subservient to Canterbury, giving the see of Canterbury unquestioned supremacy in the Church in England, rapidly replaced British bishops with French churchmen, and rebuilt Canterbury Cathedral. A traditionalist, Lanfranc strictly enforced Pope Gregory's rules on celibacy for the clergy and opposed Berengarius in 1050 in the row over transubstantiation.

LANGHAM, Simon ([?]–1376) A powerful English churchman-statesman,

Langham won prestigious appointments while in King Edward III's good graces, serving as Treasurer of England (1360), Chancellor (1363) and Archbishop of Canterbury (1366). Langham, however, lost favor with the touchy Edward when he accepted a cardinal's hat without consulting the King.

Sometimes called the "second founder of Westminster Abbey" because he left the bulk of his considerable estate to the great Abbey, Langham's tomb is the oldest of the tombs of any ecclesiastics in Westminster Abbey.

LANGTON, Stephen ([?]–1228) An archbishop of Canterbury who was frequently caught in the quarrels between the crown and the pope in the early 13th century, Langton was appointed by his friend from Paris school days, Pope Innocent III. His installation in 1213 was delayed by King John, however, until the pope clapped John under excommunication and England under an interdict. Langton joined the English barons at Runnymede in 1215, forcing King John to sign the *Magna Carta*. He was suspended, however, for three years by the autocratic Innocent, who disliked the democratic trends in England.

Returning to office under King Henry III, Langton helped patch up the differences between the nobility and the crown. In 1222, Langton presided at the Synod of Osney, where his *Constitutions* became part of English canon law.

A serious Bible scholar, Langton was the first to divide the books into chapters.

LA SALLE, JEAN BAPTISTE de (1651–1719) The patron saint of school teachers, La Salle was a leading French priest and educator who opened some of the earliest schools for the poor in France. By 1680, La Salle interested several others in educating the underprivileged, and founded Brothers of Christian Schools. La Salle's institutes or training schools innovated many new pedagogical techniques, including group teaching, the inductive method, and classes in French instead of Latin. La Salle insisted that none of the Community of Brothers could be priests and no priests could be full-fledged members of the Brothers to prevent any cliques or castes from forming. He won fame and acclaim, and later founded numerous schools throughout France and elsewhere in Europe. La Salle was canonized in 1901.

LAS CASAS, Bartolome de (1474–1566) The first Spanish churchman to champion the Indians oppressed by the Spanish *Conquistadores,* Las Casas left a law practice in Spain to sail for the New World's Spanish Antilles as an advisor to colonial governors in 1502. Las Casas, influenced by Dominic de Montesinos (the first to oppose the Spaniards' brutality toward the natives), began speaking against the colonial system which gave large tracts to settlers and enslaved the Indians. In 1514, he gave up his own land, freed his Indians, and tried unsuccessfully to start a settlement for Indians at Cumaná on the Venezuelan coast. He became a Dominican, and wrote to urge humaneness instead of harshness and example instead of enslavement to convert the Indians, proving his ideas in 1537–1538 in Guatemala. After immense effort, Las Casas succeeded in 1542 in getting the "New Laws" passed, outlawing the old *encomiendas* system of serfdom for Indians.

The "New Laws" were soon changed, however, by the powerful colonial landowners, government officials and church officials, who accused Las Casas of meddling, not understanding the problems, exaggerating the evils of system, misrepresenting the Spanish interests, and proposing unrealistic solutions.

LASKI, Jan (1499–1560) In spite of having relatives in high places in the Roman Catholic hierarchy and being an ordained priest frequently sent on important diplomatic missions for the Roman Church, Laski broke with Rome and helped introduce the Reform movement to Emden, Germany. In 1546, Laski drew up the Emden Catechism. Asked by Archbishop Cranmer to help organize the Anglican Church in 1550, Laski lived in England until rabidly anti-Protestant Queen Mary came to the throne in 1553. He returned to his native Poland, where he worked to reconcile and unite the Lutherans, Calvinists and Hussites.

LATIMER, Hugh (1485[?]–1555) Stalwart of 16th century English Protestantism who suffered martyrdom under rabid-Catholic Queen Mary, Latimer stood up to despotic monarchs and steadied fellow sufferers. Latimer, converted to Protestant ideas in the early 1520's, lived for several years under suspicion by traditionalist clergy until 1529, when because of his support of Henry VIII's divorce, he was pushed into prominence by the grateful Henry. Latimer served ten years as Bishop of Worcester.

He resigned in 1539, however, because the Act of Six Articles made doctrinal dissent a capital offense, and Latimer refused to countenance such a reprisal. Imprisoned off and on for several years because of his stand for conscience and the right to dissent, Latimer was finally reprieved when Edward VI succeeded to the throne.

Latimer served as Court Preacher during Edward's reign, where he exhibited exceptional courage in speaking out on current social and political issues and helped set the future course for English Protestantism.

Although he could have fled when Queen Mary came to the throne, Latimer insisted on remaining at his post in England and suffered inevitable arrest. He was tortured but refused to recant. Dragged to the pile of faggots to be burned with Nicholas Ridley, Latimer calmly told Ridley as the flames licked around them, "Be of good comfort, Master Ridley, and play the man; we shall this day light such a candle by God's grace in England as I trust shall never be put out."

LAUD, William (1573–1645) The martinet Church of England Archbishop of Canterbury who attempted to impose a rigid uniformity in religion throughout Britain, Laud antagonized the nonconformists so deeply that an estimated 20,000 left England for Puritan New England during one ten-year period.

Laud, an uncompromising royalist, served as one of King Charles I's top advisers from the beginning of Charles' reign in 1625. After the dissolution of Parliament in 1629, Laud became one of the most powerful men in the realm. His outspoken royalist sentiments and anti-Calvinist bias aroused fanatic resentment. Determined to standardize worship throughout England and Scotland, he forced his own liturgy on all congregations, with stiff punishments for those refusing to conform. Laud's narrow-minded, heavy-handed rules ignited civil uprisings in Scotland and an exodus of some of England's best minds to the American colonies.

Long suspected of Roman leanings and despised for his despotism, Archbishop Laud was impeached by the Long Parliament of 1640 and beheaded for treason in 1645.

LAURENTIUS Andreae See **ANDERRSON, Lars.**

LAW, William (1686–1761) A Cambridge don and Church of England clergyman whose loyalty to the Stewart line of kings cost him his position, Law wrote the devotional classic, *A Serious Call to a Devout and Holy Life.* Law refused to take the oath of allegiance to the House of Hanover after James II was removed as King in 1689, and, denied his post as a cleric, was forced to take a job as private chaplain and tutor to the household of Edward Gibbon, grandfather of the famed historian.

Law, admired by a wide circle of friends who looked to him as a spiritual adviser, wrote his "A Serious Call" in 1728 to show the ideal of a consecrated Christian.

A high church controversialist who vigorously opposed Deistic ideas then in vogue in the English Church, Law later became an admirer of the mystic, Jakob Boehme. Law veered toward mysticism toward the end of his career, causing a break in his relationship with John and Charles Wesley, with whom he had been close friends.

LAWRENCE ([?]–258) One of the earliest martyrs in the Church, St. Lawrence served as a deacon in the Church in the city of Rome. He died during Emperor Valerian's persecution, which took the lives of many leaders at Rome. According to legends, St. Lawrence was roasted to death on a gridiron, which subsequently became his symbol.

LAWS, Robert (1851–1934) A Scottish Free Presbyterian Church missionary to Africa, Laws opened the first schools in Nyasaland. He had educated himself largely by self-instruction, and was a skilled physician and theologian. During his lifetime, Laws founded over seven hundred schools in Nyasaland. He is also remembered for his feat of designing and building a steamboat which he sailed up the Zambesi River, dismantled, carried overland, and reassembled on Lake Nyasa.

LE CARON, Joseph (1586–1632) A French Franciscan missionary who landed at Quebec 1615, Le Caron holds the honor of saying the first mass in the French New World. He worked among the Huron Indians until deported by the English after they captured Quebec in 1629.

LE CLERC, Jean (1657–1736) A Swiss-born Protestant theologian who moved to Amsterdam, Le Clerc, an Arminian in theology, joined the Dutch Remonstrants, the group within the Reformed Church in the Netherlands wanting to liberalize its rigid ultra-Calvinistic stance. Le Clerc, a careful exegete, won respect for his insistence on seeking to find what Scripture was trying to say, rather than using the Bible to fish for proof-texts, as was so common.

LEE, Ann (1736–1784) A poorly-educated but magnetic Englishwoman street-preacher, with eccentric views against sex, Ann Lee founded the sect known as "Shakers." Mrs. Lee, the wife of a blacksmith, was stirred by a Quaker woman preacher, Jane Wardley, in 1758 who forecast the imminent end of the world and the reappearance of Jesus Christ in the form of a woman. Ann Lee took up preaching herself, and was thrown into the Manchester jail for disturbing the peace. Claiming that Christ had come to her in her cell and became one with her in form and spirit, Ann Lee dubbed herself "Ann the Word." Her claims were believed by a coterie of fanatically faithful followers, who reverently addressed her as "Mother Ann."

Ann Lee and her following were severely harassed, however; with seven disciples, she fled to America and settled near Albany, New York, where she formed the first Shaker community.

Ann and her Shakers, insisting that absolute celibacy was necessary for the Christian life, demanded that no member ever marry, forbade those already married from living together as husband and wife, and even prohibited from their diet anything which they thought was associated with the reproductive process, such as eggs, meat or fowl.

Establishing other Shaker communities at Hancock, New York, and New Lebanon, New York, Ann Lee inculcated frugality, industry, sobriety and pacificism along with celibacy and vegetarianism.

Her Shakers were sometimes persecuted during the American Revolution for refusing to support the war and, with no children born into the communities, gradually died out. Today, Ann Lee's Shakers are noted also for their austere, unadorned but functional furniture.

LE FÈVRE D'ETAPLES, Jacques (1450–1537) An early Reformer, scholar and theologian at Paris who influenced John Calvin, Le Fèvre D'Etaples made one of the earliest translations of the Bible into French, 1523 to 1530. He was frequently forced to flee for his life when those suspected of Reformed sympathies were attacked or jailed in France.

LE FÈVRE, Pierre (1506–1546) One of the seven original founders of the Jesuits with Ignatius Loyola, LeFèvre burnt himself out by the age of forty to further the Counter-Reformation. LeFèvre and his roommate, Francis Xavier, were both students at the University of Paris when they met Ignatius. As one of the nucleus of the Society of Jesus, LeFèvre helped spearhead an intense resurgence of devotion to the

Church of Rome in the mid-sixteenth century. LeFèvre attended important Roman Catholic assemblies at Worms in 1540 and Speyer, Regensburg and Mainz in 1541. In 1544, he launched an effective movement in Germany and Belgium which won back vast numbers once lost to the Protestant cause. Transferring his operations to Spain and Portugal in 1545, LeFèvre traveled on foot to nearly every province to rekindle allegiance to the pope.

LEIBNITZ, Gottfried Wilhelm (1646–1716) A profound speculative German philosopher, Leibnitz also received recognition as a mathematician, statesman, historian, librarian and tireless promoter of reunion between Protestants and Catholics.

Leibnitz, anticipating modern scientists who theorize that the universe is full of an infinite number of indivisible centers of energy (which he called "monads") stated that God is the original monad or power-center. The monads, like atoms, do not occupy space, but do, however, have all ideas wrapped up in them and are innate to men. Knowledge, according to Leibnitz comes from drawing out to greater clarity those innate ideas. These refined speculations later had considerable influence on later thinkers.

LEIGHTON, Robert (1611–1684) A Scots-Presbyterian pastor named head of the University of Edinburgh in 1653 and Bishop of Dunblane in 1661 following the restoration of Monarchy in Britain, Leighton tried desperately to reconcile the feuding Presbyterian and Episcopal parties in Scotland. He used his offices in every way to effect more harmonious relationships, especially after Charles II appointed him Archbishop of Glasgow in 1670. His efforts were unsuccessful, however; deeply disappointed, he resigned in 1674.

LEO I, Pope, "The Great" ([?]–461) A respected and responsible administrator during some of the most troublesome days for both the Church and the Roman Empire, Leo I ruled from 440 to 461. Leo, a staunch supporter of orthodoxy, acted to counteract the Pelagians and the Manichaeans, then in 448 became involved in the ruckus in the Eastern Church when Arians led by Dioscorus of Alexandria and Eutyches, abbot of Constantinople, condemned Flavius, a Trinitarian. The Council of Chalcedon in 451 vindicated Flavius, deposed the Arians, and enthusiastically heard a letter on the incarnation written by Leo I.

Leo I had gifts as a mediator which were brought into play on numerous occasions, including once when Emperor Valentinian III and the Roman Senate were at odds, and another time when the city of Rome was beseiged by the invading tribes. Leo successfully negotiated with Attila and the Huns, but in 455, he unsuccessfully tried to avert an attack by the Vandals. The Vandals sacked Rome in a two-week orgy of fire, rape, looting and slaughter. Leo led the citizenry in restoring government, order, relief and rebuilding the devastated city. Acclaimed by Christians and pagans alike, Leo I was later canonized.

LEO II, Pope ([?]–683) Pontiff from 682 to 683, Pope Leo II confirmed the decision of the Sixth Ecumenical Council at Constantinople in 680–81 to condemn the Monothelite heresy. Leo II was subsequently declared a saint.

LEO III, Pope ([?]–816) Leo III began his reign in 799 in a dramatic way when he was attacked and badly injured by a hostile faction of churchmen led by former Pope Adrian's nephew, who had hoped to be pope. Leo, however, recovered in a surprisingly short time and was believed to have received miraculous help.

In 800, Leo III crowned Charlemagne as Emperor, then knelt before the Emperor, symbolizing his homage in temporal affairs. Leo III's alliance of papacy and empire enhanced papal prestige and patrimony, but set a precedent which caused many of his successors difficulties with headstrong emperors. Leo III was later officially recognized as a saint.

LEO IV, Pope ([?]–855) Elected in the midst of the Saracen assaults on Italy in 847, Leo IV was selected as the strong man to save the city of Rome. Leo energetically organized defenses and fortified the Vatican Hill with a wall. Further Saracen invasions were temporarily halted, however, when the Saracen fleet was broken up at sea by a severe storm.

LEO V, Pope ([?]–903) Leo V, who reigned only one month, was deposed by a priest named Christopher, and died in prison.

LEO VI, Pope ([?]–929) This pope served for only six months, 928–929.

LEO VII, Pope ([?]–939) Pope from 936 to 939.

LEO VIII, Pope ([?]–965) A layman selected by Emperor Otto I in 963 to displace Pope John XII, Leo VIII received all orders, including ordination as a priest, in just one day, and was elevated as pontiff the following day. Leo was pushed out by John XII as soon as Otto returned to Germany in 964, and kept out of office after John XII's death by the determined Romans, who immediately elected Benedict V as Pope. Leo VIII, however, was reinstalled when Emperor Otto rushed back to Rome and dumped Benedict. Leo VIII, as the emperor's lackey, obliged Otto by granting him sweeping powers over the Church, even to selecting bishops and choosing popes.

LEO IX, Pope (1002–1054) A conscientious pontiff who worked hard to improve the morality of the clergy by enforcing celibacy and eliminating simony, Leo IX also tried to enlarge papal territories, opening a series of wars with the Normans which resulted in Leo's capture and imprisonment and lessened prestige.

Leo IX tried to arrest the drift toward a complete break between the Eastern and Western Churches after the Patriarch of Constantinople accused the Latin Church of heresy because of differing ritual and discipline. Leo, who sent emissaries to Constantinople to try to conciliate the Patriarch, died before accord could be reached.

Leo IX is also remembered for proposing that the cardinals and not clergy and laity elect a new pope. After Leo's death, this proposal became policy. Leo IX was subsequently canonized as a saint.

LEO X, Pope (1475–1521) A cultivated esthete, Leo X found himself so preoccupied with the trifles of Vatican art and politics that he was oblivious of the spiritual crisis in the Church. Leo X, pope at the start of the Protestant Reformation, never comprehended the meaning of Martin Luther. A layman at the time he was elected pope on March 11, 1513, Leo was ordained a priest on March 13, promoted to bishop on March 17, finally elevated as pontiff on March 19. His reign was distinguished primarily for a sordid series of intrigues and conspiracies (Francis I of France schemed to move into Italy; Cardinal Petrucci plotted to kill Leo, while the Franciscans noisily squabbled among themselves).

LEO XI, Pope (1535–1605) Leo XI, Pope in 1605, served less than one month.

LEO XII, Pope (1760–1829) A coolheaded politico, Leo XII busied himself with signing Concordats between the Papal States and various European courts during his reign, 1823 to 1829.

LEO XIII, Pope (1810–1903) Blessed with the unusual gifts of being a competent administrator, a scholarly teacher and a personable human, Leo XIII did much to change popular attitudes in Europe toward the papacy from antipathy or amusement to acceptance or admiration. Leo XIII concluded the conflicts between the German government and the Vatican and urged French Catholics to support the Republic. In addition to being a statesman, Leo was a scholar whose encyclicals covered a wide range of contemporary topics, from Socialism (*Quod Apostolici* in 1878) to Scripture (*Providentissimus Deus* in 1893).

LEONTIUS of Byzantium (485[?]–543) A Nestorian Christian in his youth who was converted to Nicene orthodoxy as a young man, Leontius of Byzantium penned theological works trying to explain the union of the human and divine natures in Jesus Christ. Leontius was devotee of Aristotle, and applied Aristotelian philosophy to Christological problems. Although the human element in Christ is real, said Leontius, it is so subordinated that the ultimate reality is divine. The teachings of this monastic thinker delighted Emperor Justinian who was then trying to satisfy Eastern Churchmen subscribing to Cyril of Alexandria's views and Western Churchmen holding to Nicene Christianity.

LESSING, Gotthold Ephraim (1729–1781) A noted German classics schol-

ar, drama writer and literary critic, Lessing introduced new forms to German literature and enjoyed immense stature in German intellectual circles. In 1780, he published his *Education of the Human Race*, regarded by some as the writing which liberated German thought and by others as the book which taught that Christianity belonged to a past, inferior period of human development.

LEWIS, C. S. (Clive Staples) (1898–1963) The gifted, imaginative Oxford (1924–54) and Cambridge (1954–63) don who wrote popular satire on profound subjects, C. S. Lewis aptly described his conversion at the age of thirty in the title of his autobiography as *Surprised by Joy*. Lewis' witty *Screwtape Letters*, the purported correspondence between a junior devil and wily old Uncle Screwtape, has become a devotional classic. The Irish-born Christian literary figure also wrote *The Great Divorce, Miracles, The Abolition of Man, Christian Behavior, Letters to Malcolm, Mere Christianity*, and several space novels and children's books.

LIBERIUS, Pope ([?]–366) A Roman deacon who during his reign as pope, 352 to 366, showed theological agility to cling to his title, Liberius was accused of heresy while pope and banished by Emperor Constantius II for refusing to agree with the Arian-controlled Council of Arles in 353 that Trinitarian Athanasius was a heretic. Liberius decided to go along with the Emperor and the Arians, however, and regained his position. Later, after Constantius' death when it was safe to return to the Nicene viewpoint, Liberius resumed his orthodox stance.

LIGUORI, Alfonso Maria de' (1696–1787) The Italian priest who founded the Congregation of the Most Holy

Redeemer (the "Redemptorists"), Liguori practiced law for eight years before studying for the priesthood, was ordained in 1726, then served six years as a missionary. He founded the Redemptorists in 1732, but later, 1762 to 1775, took up the duties of the Bishop of Sant' Agata Dei Goti. Liguori originated "equiprobalism," the process permitting either of two courses as "moral" when it is not possible to determine which is the "right" course.

LIVINGSTONE, David (1813–1873)

The famous Scottish missionary doctor and explorer of Africa, Livingstone epitomized missions for many in the 19th century with his romantic exploits and silent suffering.

Livingstone, put to work in the mills of Blantyre, Scotland, as a boy of ten, was largely self-taught. Finally graduating with degrees in medicine and theology from Glasgow, Livingstone was commissioned by the London Missionary Society in 1840, joining the well-known fellow-Scot, Dr. Robert Moffat in South Africa.

Livingstone combined doctoring with exploring for a time, discovering Lake Ngami in 1849 and penetrating the upper reaches of the Zambesi River in 1853. He broke his tie to the London Missionary Society in 1857 and after 1866 gave all of his energies to exploring Africa. His prodigious journeys took him across the entire continent on foot through uncharted areas, discovering Lake Banweulu, Lake Mweru, Lake Nyasa and other wonders. Presumed lost and dead after total silence for three years, Livingstone was located by New York newsman Henry M. Stanley in 1871, following a sensational search. He died two years later in the African bush, but his body was interred in Westminster Abbey as one of Britain's revered heroes.

LLOYD, Charles (1784–1829)

A Church of England clergyman who taught theology at Oxford, Lloyd profoundly and permanently influenced a generation of divinity students, who formed the Oxford Movement. Lloyd, emphasizing the tradition and theology of the high church wing of Anglicanism, lamented the loss of many Roman Catholic practices at the time of the Reformation, including celibacy, confession and apostolic succession. Any reform within the Church, he insisted, would have to include a return to these emphases.

Lloyd's disciples, including Pusey, Newman, Manning, Keble, Palmer, Rose and others, formed the nucleus of the Anglo-Catholic party in 19th century Anglicanism.

LOCKE, John (1632–1704)

Influential thinker and philosopher, John Locke taught at Oxford, practiced medicine (without a degree), held various public offices which took him out of England and also gave him time to write from 1675 to 1689.

Locke's fame rests on his *Essay Concerning Human Understanding* in which he denied there are such things as innate ideas and insisted that the mind is like a sheet of clean paper on which experience makes its mark. All ideas, said Locke, originate either in sensation or reflection. Locke stated that even the existence of God and morality can be demonstrated like the truths of mathematics, and that religion must be reasonable or provable.

Locke furthered the cause of tolerance by teaching that religion's only weapon is its reasonableness. His ideas on government in which each individual is granted the rights of life, property, liberty and revolution when the preceding are denied influenced reflective people in the American colonies and were written into the American *Declaration of Independence* and other documents.

LOEHE, Johann Konrad Wilhelm (1808–1872) A 19th century German pastor deeply concerned about the welfare of fellow-countrymen emigrating to the United States, Loehe established missionary training centers to train men for work among Germans in America. Loehe, a persuasive preacher and promoter, also founded the Lutheran Society for Home Missions in 1849, a deaconess training center, a mental hospital and several other hospitals in Germany.

LOISY, Alfred Firmin (1857–1940) The storm-center of the "Modernism" movement in the Roman Catholic Church in Europe at the turn of the century, Loisy, a competent scholar, aroused the opposition of the tradition-minded Vatican by his writings and teachings in Old Testament criticism. Loisy, an ordained Catholic priest, was dismissed from his teaching post at Institut Catholique and denied the right to publish in Church-sponsored journals. A spate of books followed in the early 1900's, all of which were put on the Index in 1903. Loisy remained loyal to the Church until he was excommunicated, then taught at the Collège de France. The papacy continued to denounce his oft-rationalistic writings in Biblical studies.

LOMBARD, Peter (1100[?]–1164) A student of Abélard, Bishop of Paris (1159) and the first Doctor at the University of Paris, Lombard wrote the much-studied *Sententiarum Libri Quatuor*, earning him the sobriquet, "Master of Sentences." Lombard's masterwork was a compilation of sentences from the writings of various Church Fathers, particularly Augustine, ar-

ranged by topics and listing objections and defenses of the doctrines listed under each topic. It was widely studied and quoted through the centuries until the Reformation.

LOUIS IX, King of France, Saint (1214–1270) Deeply pious, Louis IX steadfastly defended medieval Roman Catholic Church ideals, squelching heretics and heading crusades during the last gasps of the crusading spirit in Europe. His disastrous march on Egypt in 1248 to 1250 ended when Louis was taken prisoner; his expedition to Tunis cost him his life. Louis, much admired for his religiosity, showed administrative skills when he worked at governing France.

LOUISE DE MARILLAC See Marillac.

LOVEJOY, Elijah Parish (1802–1837) Young American Presbyterian minister-turned-Abolitionist editor who became a martyr, Lovejoy stirred feelings throughout the North against slavery. His bold, outspoken editorials in his Alton, Illinois, *Observer* aroused mobs to wreck his presses four times. Trying to protect his presses during a fifth attack in 1827, Lovejoy was killed. He is revered by newspapermen as a fearless champion of a free press and honored by partisans of righteousness as a determined advocate of justice.

LOYOLA See IGNATIUS.

LOYSON, Charles (1827–1912) Known also as Père Hyacynthe (his monastic name), Loyson, a French Carmelite priest and eloquent preacher, was excommunicated in 1869 for his dubious orthodoxy and stinging criticisms of Vatican methods. Loyson founded the Christian Catholic Church of Switzerland, a break-away sect similar to the Old Catholic Church, and opened congregations in Geneva and Paris.

LUCIAN of Antioch ([?]–312) A presbyter at the city of Antioch, Lucian founded the school of theology which came to have immense influence in the Eastern Church in the 4th and 5th centuries and which came to have an intense rivalry with the school at Alexandria. Lucian, mentor of such illustrious pupils as Eusebius of Nicomedia and Arius, taught at Antioch from about 275 to 303, and died a martyr's death in 312. Disliking the allegorizing of Scriptures so commonly done at Alexandria, Lucian advocated a grammatical and historical treatment of Scriptural texts. His theological views are thought to have been similar to Arius', whose ideas on the nature of Christ gave rise to the heresy called Arianism (teaching that Christ was not quite truly divine).

LUCIUS I, Pope ([?]–254) Pope for little more than a year, Lucius was deported shortly after his election in 253. He returned after Emperor Gallus died, and won affection for his leniency toward those who had lapsed from the faith during Emperor Decius' persecution. He subsequently was canonized.

LUCIUS II, Pope ([?]–1145) Although Lucius II had an outstanding career in the Church prior to his elevation as pope in 1144, he lost papal territory and prestige during struggles with Roger II of Sicily and contentious Romans. He died of wounds suffered from a campaign against Roger in 1145.

LUCIUS III, Pope (1097[?]–1185) A despotic pontiff who summarily excommunicated Waldo and his Waldensians (reform-minded, evangelical preachers in northern Italy), Lucius III proved to be so inept and so unpopular that he

was forced to leave the city of Rome. His dismal term from 1181 to 1185 found him wandering throughout Italy and squabbling with Emperor Frederick Barbarossa.

LUCAR See **LUKAR.**

LUKAR, Cyril (also Lucaris) (1572–1638) A unusual and resolute Eastern Orthodox Church leader, Lukar tried desperately to keep the Eastern Church from being exterminated by the Ottoman Turks in the 17th century. Lukar, born in Venetian Crete, studied in the West, including Geneva, where he picked up Calvinist views and evangelical sympathies. He taught at a Russian seminary, was elected Patriarch of Alexandria about 1602, and in 1621 became Patriarch of Constantinople. He endured constant harassment by the Turkish government, often encouraged by the Jesuits who operated out of the French embassy.

In Constantinople, the Turks confiscated one of his churches after another, forcing him to move repeatedly and finally leaving him with only one. The Jesuits carried on intrigues against Lukar with the Sultan and with various Christian, national-language bodies in the Turkish Empire, causing Lukar to be deposed on five different occasions. The Sultan finally condemned him for treason, had him strangled by the Janissaries and dumped into the sea. Lukar's printing press, which he'd used to print his creed and catechism, was destroyed at the urging of the Jesuits who hoped to bring the Eastern Church closer to Rome.

LULL, Raimon or Raymond (1235–1315) The indolent, spendthrift son of a rich Mallorcan, Lull experienced a startling conversion and a vision commanding him to convert the Moslems. He became a Franciscan, studied the

Arabic language and lore for nine years, founded an academy to train missionaries to the Moslems, and for thirty years pestered everyone who would listen with schemes to bring Moslems to the Church. Dismissed by most as peculiar, Raimon of Lull tried three times to preach to Moslems at Tunis, and was imprisoned or thrown out each time, the last time being left for dead after being savagely stoned.

Lull also attracted attention by contriving a method to "prove" matters of faith by using a curious device, the *"ars magna"* or great art, to give immediate solutions to any question.

LULLY See LULL.

LUTHER, Martin (1483–1546) Martin Luther shattered the structure of the Medieval Church by demanding that the authority for doctrine and practice be the Scriptures rather than popes or Councils, and ignited the Protestant Reformation.

Although the winds of reform were blowing when Luther was born at Eisleben, in Saxony of Germany in 1483, his parents, a poor peasant miner and wife, had a simple, unaffected piety. The Luthers, in spite of their poverty, insisted that young Martin get a good education, sending him to schools at Magdeburg and Eisenach, where Martin helped support himself by singing, and in 1501 to the University of Erfurt.

Complying with his father's wishes, Martin planned to study law. In 1505, however, the sudden death of a close friend and a narrow escape from being killed by lightning during a severe electrical storm stirred Martin Luther to heed the religious revival then sweeping western Europe. Young Luther, feeling a deep sense of sinfulness because of this revival, abruptly left his legal studies and entered the Augustinian monastery at Erfurt.

Luther's spiritual development was painful. Overwhelmed by a feeling of guilt, Luther nearly ruined his health by practicing ascetic excesses to try to achieve some sense of inner peace. He was fortunate in having a sensitive, sympathetic supervisor at the monastery, Johann von Staupitz, who helped point Luther from cringing terror before a vengeful Deity to a joyous response to the loving forgiveness of God through Jesus Christ.

Luther, still plagued by his sense of sinfulness and still determined to achieve a right relationship with God through stringent efforts at being "religious," was ordained a priest in 1507. On the orders of his superiors, he was sent to Wittenberg to study theology. About 1510, on business for the Augustinians, Luther made a trip to Rome, where the pious, rustic young Saxon priest was shaken by the crass commercialism and ostentatious splendor fostered by the Vatican. He returned to Wittenberg, was recognized as a doctor in theology in 1512, and began lecturing on the Bible.

His intensive studies of the Scriptures, beginning with his lectures on the Psalms from 1513 to 1515, and continuing with Romans, Galatians, Hebrews and Titus in 1516, convinced Luther that salvation is a new relationship with God, based not on merit accrued by man's efforts but by complete trust on God's promises. Although man continues to be a sinner, Luther came to understand that he is a forgiven sinner because of the new relationship with God through Jesus Christ. The full meaning of the Gospel burst on Luther late in 1516 when the phrase, "the just shall live by faith" from Galatians 3 released him from his haunting sense of guilt to the freedom of relying on God's grace.

Luther quickly had to decide to put his newly-found idea of salvation to work. In 1517, he discovered that a Dominican huckster named Johann Tetzel was selling indulgences to his parishioners. Luther, incensed at both the shabby methods and the bad theology of the sale of indulgences (not to speak of the outflow of cash to erect a costly new St. Peter's at Rome for Pope Leo X), preached eloquently against buying pardon and loquaciously for relying on God's grace for salvation. On October 31, 1517, Luther offered to debate the question and tacked Ninety-five Theses to the door of the Castle Church, Wittenberg.

The Theses were intended for academic discussion, not as a revolt against the pope or the Church of Rome. They were translated into German, circulated throughout Europe and thrust Luther into the maelstrom of controversy. Tetzel and the formidable Eck attacked Luther, labelling him a heretic. The Archbishop of Mainz and the Dominicans protested to Rome that Luther's attack on indulgences was undermining the faith. By June, 1518, Pope Leo X ordered Luther to appear at Rome. The intervention of Elector Frederick "the Wise" changed the hearing from Rome to Augsburg. At Augsburg, the learned papal legate, Cajetanus, summarily demanded that Luther retract all his criticisms of the papal system of indulgences. Luther refused. Pope Leo X, meanwhile, issued a papal bull in which he defined indulgences in precisely the way which Luther had criticized. Luther's survival at this time was due to the protection of Frederick the Wise.

In 1519, Luther debated publicly with the skilled Eck, and was forced to admit that he rejected both the authority of popes and councils when these did not conform to Scriptures. Luther appeared to many to have taken the sensational stand of rejecting the entire structure of the Church, if not the entire authority of the Church, in favor of private opinion. Luther in 1520 tried to present his position in greater clarity by writing three tracts, *An Address to the Christian Nobility of the German Nation, The Babylonian Captivity of the Church,* and *The Liberty of a Christian Man.* These pamphlets, laying out his theological system and the implications for worship and practices in the Church, circulated widely.

Presented with a papal bull threatening to excommunicate him, Luther publicly burned it and a copy of the canon law, December 10, 1520, openly defying the pope's authority and refusing to renounce any of his viewpoints. The Wittenberg civil authorities looked on approvingly. Germany was in a rebellious mood. Luther became the national hero. Although Luther was excommunicated shortly afterward by the pope and summoned by Emperor Charles V to an Imperial Diet at Worms, Germany, he refused to budge from his position. He was confronted with the awesome assembly of German princes, nobles and churchmen, and ordered to recant. "Unless I am refuted and convicted by testimonies of Scripture," Luther answered, "or by clear arguments, my conscience is bound in the Word of God: I cannot and will not recant anything. I cannot do otherwise. Here I stand. God help me, Amen."

Luther's protector again was the Elector Frederick, who undoubtedly saved the reformer from martyrdom several times. While returning home from Worms, Luther was abducted by Frederick's men and held secretly at Wartburg Castle for ten months. Luther used the time productively, translating the Bible from Greek into German, which introduced "high" German and set the pattern for all subsequent literary expression in the German language. Luther also wrote a tract attacking monastic vows.

Returning to Wittenberg, in March 1522, Luther took up the task of organizing the Reformation, which had nearly foundered under the erratic leadership of unstable enthusiasts such as Carlstadt and Zwilling at Wittenberg. Luther denounced their excesses (in which they had whipped up crowd rampages, wrecking statuary and artwork) ousted the radicals and set about to produce orderly forms for instruction, worship and church government. Even the terrible Peasants' War, which erupted in 1524, did not deter him from his main task. He penned catechisms for the children and common people; he composed hymns, including the stirring "A Mighty Fortress Is Our God," sometimes called the battle hymn of the Reformation.

Martin Luther, who had taught that priests could marry, was induced to marry a former nun, named Katharina von Bora. His home life was happy and boisterous, with six children, a constant houseful of student boarders and guests, and several orphaned nieces and nephews.

Luther continued to write, teach and preach as long as his health permitted. By 1534, he completed the translation of the Old Testament from Hebrew to German. By the end of his life, he had produced over four hundred works and one hundred twenty-five hymns. He is hailed and honored today by Roman Catholics as well as Protestants as one of the few who not only affected the course of history but who gave the Church a deeper insight into the meaning of the Gospel and the response of the Church to the Good News.

M

MACHEN, J. (John) Gresham (1881–1937) Expert New Testament Greek scholar and New Testament professor at Princeton Seminary from 1914 to 1929, Machen, perturbed by the trends away from fundamentalism in the Board of Foreign Missions of the Presbyterian Church, U.S.A., founded an independent mission board. Machen's solicitation of funds among Presbyterians for his independent board (in money-scarce depression years) and continuing criticisms of the denomination's mission program finally brought about his suspension from the Presbyterian ministry after a long, difficult trial. Machen withdrew from the Presbyterian Church, U.S.A. in 1936, taking sixteen pastors and laymen with him, and founded the Orthodox Presbyterian Church, of which he became the first Moderator. A zealous defender of the Virgin Birth, and a partisan of traditional conservative theology, Machen was instrumental in establishing Westminster Theological Seminary, Mt. Airy, Philadelphia.

MACKINTOSH, Hugh Ross (1870–1936) Longtime (1904–1935) and greatly beloved professor of theology at Edinburgh, Scotland's New College, Mackintosh emphasized the forgiveness mediated through the Gospel in widely read books, such as *The Christian Experience of Forgiveness, The Doctrine of the Person of Jesus Christ,* and *Types of Modern Theology.*

MACLAREN, Alexander (1826–1910) Scots-born Baptist pastor at Manchester, England from 1858 until his death, Maclaren became respected for his carefully prepared sermons and expository study of the Bible. He commanded a wide following in Britain during the last part of the 19th century.

MACLAREN, Ian See **WATSON, John.**

MACLAY, Robert Samuel (1824–1907) The pioneering American Methodist mission leader in the Far East, MacLay worked from 1846 to 1872 at Foochow, China, then moved to Japan in 1872 where he opened the first Methodist mission program in that country. In 1884, MacLay transferred his operations to Korea, developing Methodist missions there.

MAGNI, Peter (16th c.) Swedish Bishop of Västeräs, Magni agreed to consecrate King Gustav's newly appointed Lutheran bishops in 1528, at the time of the Swedish Reformation, transmitting Apostolic succession to the Lutheran episcopate in Sweden.

MAJORINUS (4th c.) Caught up in the bitter quarrel in the Church in North Africa over readmission of apostates to the Church after the Diocletian persecution, Majorinus was one of the rigorists who refused to recognize the more lenient Caecilian, newly elected bishop of Carthage. Majorinus and his party, proclaiming that the sacraments were invalid when administered by anyone who had once been apostate, broke off with a schismatic group which came to be known as the Donatists. Majorinus, elected bishop of Carthage in 311 by the schismatics, tried to undermine the rightfully elected Caecilian.

MAKEMIE, Francis (1658–1708) The founder of American Presbyterianism, Makemie came to America in 1682 from Ireland via the Barbados, where he had served as a missionary. Makemie, a scholarly itinerating preacher, covered much of the wilderness of the American seaboard through Maryland, Delaware, Virginia, the Carolinas and the Barbados on foot and on horseback. In 1684, he established what is regarded as the first American Presbyterian congregation at Snow Hill, Maryland, followed by Rehoboth Beach (Del.) and other early churches.

With financial backing from the United Brethren in London, Makemie brought two other Scottish-trained Presbyterian pastors to the colonies in 1706 and organized the first Presbytery, at Philadelphia, Pa.

Makemie also became a hero in the cause for religious liberty when he was arrested by Lord Cornbury for preaching without a license in a private home at Newtown, Long Island, in 1707. Makemie was imprisoned and finally tried and acquitted. He was assessed the staggering costs of the trial by the vicious governor, Cornbury, which broke Makemie financially but brought both favorable publicity to Presbyterianism in the colonies and new laws preventing such injustices in the future.

Makemie, respected for his intellectual gifts as well as his organizational energies, corresponded regularly with Increase Mather and many other New England thinkers.

MALACHY (1094[?]–1148) One of Ireland's better-known saints, Malachy, a monastery abbot who became Bishop of Connor (1132–1136) and Down (1136–1148), brought the Irish Church into conformity with Roman Church practices and stiffened discipline among Irish monks and clergy. He made a pilgrimage to Rome in 1140 and met Bernard of Clairvaux, with whom a deep friendship ripened. Some 112 "prophecies," supposedly penned by Malachy predicting events about later popes, are now regarded as fakes by modern scholars.

MANNING, Henry Edward Cardinal (1808–1892) A high church Anglican who moved from Tractarianism and a long flirtation with Roman Catholicism to convert to the Church of Rome finally in 1851, Manning joined John Henry Newman and other illustrious and scholarly Englishmen who embraced Catholicism in the 19th century. Manning threw himself into work in the run-down Westminster section of London, starting mission and education programs for slum children. Eventually named Archbishop of Westminster, Manning built Westminster Cathedral and headed the ultra-monanist group in England. Manning, a vigorous defender of papal infallibility, was given a cardinal's hat in 1875.

MANNING, William Thomas (1866–1949) Outspoken English-born American Episcopal bishop of New York in the early 20th century, Manning frequently found himself in the headlines for his controversial opinions, such as opposing the remarriage of divorced persons and urging the firing of Bertrand Russell from his New York teaching post for supporting adultery and atheism. In 1892 Bishop Manning started work on the expensive, enormous and yet-unfinished Cathedral of St. John the Divine in New York City.

MANWARING, Roger (1590–1653) An ardent supporter of monarchy,

Manwaring was a Church of England clergyman who quickly caught King Charles I's attention and secured appointment as a royal chaplain. Manwaring in 1627 preached that the king ruled as God's representative and that those refusing to pay taxes levied by the monarch were in danger of God's damnation. Although fined and imprisoned by Parliament in 1628, Manwaring was protected, pardoned and even promoted to bishop by King Charles, angering the Puritan-dominated Parliament and causing further deterioration in relations between Charles and Parliament.

MANZ, Felix (1490–1527) A radical Anabaptist, Manz, scion of a well-known Zurich family, promoted extreme reformation views at Zurich, including rejecting infant baptism in 1524 as scripturally unwarranted. Manz and others known as Anabaptists (because of their insistence on baptizing believers only, hence the title "re-baptizers" or Anabaptists) got into acrimonious debates with other reformers, including Zwingli (whom Manz dismissed as too conservative) beginning in 1523. Manz and his fellows were ordered by the Zurich civic authorities to desist from disputes in 1525. Their fanatic insistence on baptism for believers and by immersion aroused the Zurich government to cruel mocking of the Anabaptists: Manz and many of his fellows were put to death by drowning in 1527.

MARCELLINUS, Pope ([?]–304) Bishop of Rome from 296 to 304 during the grim times of Emperor Diocletian's persecution, Marcellinus was falsely accused by the Donatists (the schismatic heretics in North Africa) of apostasizing. Marcellinus, with many other faithful churchmen, died a martyr's death. He was later declared a saint in the Roman Catholic Church.

MARCELLUS, Bishop of Ancyra ([?]–374) A theologian prominent in the rancorous church debates over Christology in the 4th century, Marcellus, Bishop of Ancyra, tried to defend orthodox, Nicene Christianity.

Heresy-hunting, hair-splitting fellow churchmen in Asia Minor, however, sniffed out dubious theology, such as Marcellus' questionable distinction between the Logos (the Word) and the Son. Marcellus taught that before the Incarnation, the Logos, but not the Son, had existed, and that following Christ's work of redemption, the Son had returned to reside with the Father, implying that the Trinity ceased to be. Marcellus was condemned and deposed but reinstalled by a series of synods from 336 until his death. In 380, after his death, Marcellus was formally denounced by Pope Damasus.

MARCELLUS I, Pope ([?]–309) Pontiff from 308 to 309, Marcellus I was elected after the severe persecutions of the Church by Emperor Diocletian had badly mauled the Church. Marcellus I organized the city of Rome into twenty-five districts, and appointed a presbyter to take charge of each district to revive the teaching and discipline of the Church. He sternly insisted that any church member who had lapsed under the pressure of the persecution had to do penance before being readmitted to the Church. Banished by the Roman Tyrant Maxentius during the turmoil in the empire before Constantine took control as Emperor, Marcellus died in exile, but was subsequently canonized.

MARCELLUS II, Pope ([?]–1555) A pope with one of the shortest reigns on records, Marcellus II served only twenty-two days, in 1555. Previously, Marcellus had a notable career as a Vatican diplomat, presiding at the

Council of Trent for a time, where he angered Emperor Charles V for putting the interests of the Church ahead of Charles' Empire.

MARCION ([?]–160[?]) A Christian teacher at Rome about 140, Marcion promoted the heretical idea that the New Testament completely contradicts the Old, and broke off from the Church, starting his own schismatic group and formulating his own canon of Scripture.

Marcion, separating the God revealed in Jesus Christ from the God revealed in Creation and the events of Israel, insisted that the Gospel totally displaced the Old Testament and excluded the thirty-nine Old Testament Books from his "Bible."

A stern ascetic who rejected marriage as well as the Hebrew origins of the faith, Marcion tried to "spiritualize" the Gospel by stating that Christ was not actually in human flesh, but only appeared to be.

Marcion's canon spurred the Church to form its own collection of canonical Scripture.

MARGARET, of Antioch ([?]–275[?] or 307[?]) The daughter of a pagan priest, Margaret became a popular saint in the East after she allegedly worked many miracles and died a martyr. She is known as Marina in the Greek Church, and is classified as a saint in the Roman Catholic Church, although her story is generally considered fictional.

MARGARET, Queen of Scotland (1045[?]–1093) The wife of Malcolm Canmore, King of Scotland, Margaret brought the Church in Scotland into conformity with the Roman Church in the rest of Europe. Her exemplary piety and purity caused her to be made a saint in the Roman Church in 1251.

MARILLAC, Louise de (1591–1660) The self-sacrificing founder of the Sisters of Charity of St. Vincent de Paul, Louise de Marillac after her husband's death in 1625 devoted herself to work directed by St. Vincent de Paul, caring for the ill, the neglected and the poverty-stricken of Paris. In 1633, she set up a training in her home, and began receiving recruits, although formal approval was not granted until 1655. Sister Louise's order was given the overseeing of many Paris hospitals and institutions. Canonized in 1934, she was named patron saint of Social Workers by Pope John XXIII in 1960.

MARINA See MARGARET of Antioch.

MARINUS I, Pope ([?]–884) Pope from 882 to 884, Marinus I previously had been sent as a deacon three times on an embassy to Constantinople, where in 869 he had presided at the Eighth Ecumenical Council.

MARINUS II, Pope ([?]–946) Served as pope from 942 to 946.

MARSHMAN, Joshua (1768–1837) A boy weaver in a poor village in England who educated himself to become an outstanding Oriental scholar, Marshman joined the first contingent of missionaries accompanying William Carey sent by the Baptist Missionary Society to India in 1799. Marshman laboriously learned Indian dialects and worked with Carey in founding mission stations and publishing a Sanskrit grammar. In 1818, Marshman was instrumental in publishing the first newspaper in a non-European language in the East. He also studied Chinese, and in 1814 printed the first complete edition of the Bible in Chinese.

MARSILIUS of Padua (1270[?]–1343) One of the first to speak out against the power of the papacy, Marsilius, an Italian-born scholar serving as rector of the University of Paris, and another radically-minded scholar named John of Jandun wrote the widely-discussed *Defensor Pacis*. Marsilius' book protested the pope's abuse of power in excommunicating Emperor Louis of Bavaria and propounded the then-radical notion that all authority should be lodged in the people. Marsilius was excommunicated by Pope John XXII in 1327 but protected for the rest of his life by the grateful Emperor.

Defensor Pacis, although denounced by a succession of irate popes, was taken seriously by thinkers in Europe, including Wycliffe and Luther.

MARTIN of Tours ([?]–397[?]) The great advocate of monasticism in France in the 4th century, Martin of Tours established a monastery near Poitiers about 362. He was born in Hungary of pagan parents who moved to Italy. Following a stint in the army, Martin at the age of twenty joined St. Hilary of Poitiers, served as a monk at Milan until he was expelled by the Arians, then founded his own monastery at Ligugé, France. Martin was chosen bishop of Tours in 371, and gained wide fame for his kindnesses and miracles. He was subsequently canonized.

MARTIN I, Pope ([?]–655) Consecrated as pope in 649 without the approval of Emperor Constans II, Martin I soon found himself facing serious opposition from many in the Church who were incited by Constans. Eventually Martin I was put through the humiliation of a trial for treason, condemned and banished. He died in exile, and was regarded as a martyr and saint in the Latin Church.

MARTIN II, Pope See **MARINUS I.**

MARTIN III, Pope See **MARINUS II.**

MARTIN IV, Pope (1210[?]–1285) Actually the second pope to be called Martin, Martin had the misfortune to have the record-keepers get his name mixed up in the list of Pope Martins with Marinus I and Marinus II. Martin IV was a French prelate who was elected pontiff in 1261, and spent most of his reign outside of Rome because of the deep antipathies toward the French at the time. Testy and temperamental, Martin IV excommunicated the Bzyantine Emperor Michael VIII Paleologus, smashing the fragile unity existing between the Greek and Roman churches.

MARTIN V, Pope (1368–1431) Elected pope in 1417 after a long career in papal politics, Martin participated in the Council of Pisa which finally ended the disgraceful schism between rival popes in Rome and Avignon, and the Council of Constance, where he agreed that a Council's power exceeds that of a pope. As pope, however, Martin V vigorously promoted the papacy's powers and downgraded the Council's. He signed numerous concordats with nations, rebuilt the run-down city of Rome, and dispensed favors to his relatives in the Colonna family (opening the door to widespread nepotism by many of his successors).

Martin, easing some of the cruel restrictions against Jews, abolished the practice of baptizing Jewish children under twelve without parental approval.

MARTIN, Gregory ([?]–1582) An English Biblical scholar who remained passionately loyal to Rome during the tempestuous religious struggles of the 16th century, Martin fled to Douai, France in 1570. He was ordained as a Roman Catholic priest in 1573, settled in Reims, France, and began translating the Bible from the Latin Vulgate into English, publishing the New Testament in 1582.

The revision of his translation by Bishop Challoner in London in 1750 was called the Douay or Douai Bible, and for many years was the only authorized Roman Catholic version of the Scriptures in English.

MARTINEAU, James (1805–1900) A 19th century leader of English Unitarianism, Martineau, a teacher and theological philosopher, summed up liberal thinking in the 19th century. In 1830, he founded the Irish Christian Unitarian Society.

MARTYN, Henry (1781–1812) The brilliant Cambridge student who left both a promising career in law and the classics and a frail and somewhat faint-hearted fiancée to carry the Gospel to India in 1806, Martyn died after only six years in the East following intense and exhausting efforts to establish congregations and translate Scriptures into local tongues. He encountered opposition from the powerful East India Company, indifference among fellow missionaries and the massive apathy of the East, but completed a translation of the New Testament into Hindustani and founded a congregation by 1810 in India.

In 1811, he moved to Persia, partly to try to regain his shattered health and partly to improve his Persian translation of the Bible. He died of fever at Tobriz, Persia, age thirty-one.

His diary inscription, "Now let me burn myself out for God," and his example made a profound impact on the 19th century Protestant Church.

MARY STUART, Queen of Scotland (1542–1587) The lovely and charming young "Queen of Scots," celebrated in folklore, Mary also inherited many of the unlovely character traits of the de' Medici family, from which her mother, Mary of Guise, had descended. The winsome Mary nearly succeeded in undoing the Reformation in Scotland brought about by the dour, determined John Knox. She slipped from popular favor, however, when a conspiracy led by her lover, the Earl of Bothwell, killed her husband, the weak Lord Darnley. Mary married Bothwell, but the shocked nation forced her to abdicate in 1567. After further adventures, Mary was finally imprisoned and executed by Queen Elizabeth in 1587 for plots against Elizabeth and anti-Protestant intrigues.

MARY TUDOR, Queen of England (1516–1558) Rabid Romanist, Mary I became Queen upon the death of her half-brother, Edward VI, in 1553. In 1554, she married Prince Philip of Spain, son of the ardent Catholic Emperor of Spain, and forced Parliament to restore papal authority in England.

At Mary's urging, ancient laws against heretics were re-enacted, and harsh measures, including a rash of burnings at the stake, employed against Protestants. Three hundred suffered martyrdom and thousands fled the country. The unhappy Mary died in 1558, mourned by none.

MASON, John Mitchell (1770–1829) An American Presbyterian pastor and educator in New York City, Mason founded a theological seminary in 1804 which became known as Union Seminary of New York. Mason, a distinguished pulpit orator and astute administrator, became Provost of Columbia University in 1811, and president of Dickinson College in 1821.

MATHER, Cotton (1663–1728) The erudite scholar and Puritan divine who dominated the ecclesiastical and intellectual scene in New England during his lifetime, Cotton Mather, son of the illustrious Increase Mather, served as pastor of Boston's Second Church following his graduation from Harvard in 1678 until his death fifty years later.

Mather, a conscientious citizen as well as churchman, participated in the 1689 rebellion against the dictatorial royal governor of Massachusetts, Sir Edmund Andros, and penned the views of the revolters.

When the witchcraft hysteria hit New England Mather, although not yet thirty years old, wrote the statement warning the judges against accepting "spectral" evidence against those accused of witchcraft, and urging prayer and fasting instead of harsh laws, fines, imprisonment, torture or death.

Mather's opus, *Magnalia Christi Americana* published in 1702, presented a careful history of the Church in New England, but was only one of some 450 books and treatises produced by Mather.

Gifted with an inquiring, scientific mind and progressive outlook, Cotton Mather advocated inoculations against smallpox at a time when most feared or denounced it. He was even elected as a fellow of the Royal Society of London and recognized in England as the best-known American then living.

MATHER, Increase (1639–1723) Scholarly Puritan preacher, Massachusetts-born Increase Mather, like his famous son, Cotton Mather, influenced political and ecclesiastical affairs in New England during his long life. He served as pastor of Second Church of Boston from 1664, bringing his son, Cotton, on the staff as his colleague in 1678.

Increase Mather, sent to England in 1688 to petition the Crown to restore the Charter of Massachusetts revoked by Charles II, appealed unsuccessfully to both King James II and King William.

During the infamous witchcraft scare, Increase Mather denounced the use of "spectral" evidence to "prove" the guilt of suspected parties. He wrote *Cases of Conscience Concerning Evil Spirits* which moved Royal Governor Phips to take steps to end the witchcraft trails.

An avid amateur scientist, Increase Mather founded the Scientific Society of Boston in 1683.

MATHER, Richard (1596–1669) The English Puritan who emigrated to Massachusetts, where his son and grandson dominated church and civic affairs for many years, Richard Mather was suspended from his pastorate in England in 1633 because of his Puritan views. He preached at the Dorchester Church in Massachusetts for thirty years, from 1636 until his death.

In 1640, Mather and others published the famous *Bay Psalm Book,* an outstanding collection of words and tunes for worship. Richard Mather also framed the original wording in 1669 for what became the summary of Congregational polity and belief in New England, *A Platform of Church Discipline.*

MATHYS, Jan ([?]–1534) Fanatical Anabaptist iconoclast who tried to bring in the New Age by armed force in the city of Munster in 1533, Mathys set back the cause of the Anabaptist (or "re-baptizers," although they stressed baptism only of believers and by immersion) for a time. Mathys, a Dutch baker from Haarlem, got caught up with Anabaptist extremists at Strassburg. Announcing himself to be Enoch, the second witness named in Revelation 11:3, Mathys followed the lead of Melchior Hoffmann, leader of the radical

Anabaptists who had proclaimed himself the first witness. After Hoffmann's imprisonment in 1533, Mathys took charge, moved the hot-eyed group to Munster and captured the city government.

Mathys' Anabaptists' wild excesses at Munster appalled both the Reformers and Catholics alike. Mathys died in a skirmish in 1534 when the Bishop of Munster laid seige to recapture Munster.

MATTHIAS of Janov ([?]–1394) A stirring preacher from Bohemia, Matthias was one of the early forerunners of the Reformation. He denounced the corruption, immorality and greed then so prevalent in the Church, and emphasized the Bible as the only authority for belief. Matthias, warning that the Antichrist was near and was to be seen in wicked clergy, helped arouse Bohemia to receive Huss a century later.

MAURICE, John Frederick Denison (1805–1872) Ultra-liberal Anglican and early Christian Socialist, Maurice helped spread the influence of broad church ideas, although he persistently disclaimed being part of the movement. Maurice aroused a controversy by publishing *Theological Essays* in 1853, forcing him to resign from his teaching position at King's College, London. The following year, he founded St. Martin's Hall, a workingman's college and helped start the Christian Socialist movement in England.

Maurice's theology, a sunny optimism about human nature and hearty rejection of anything hinting at God's wrath, enjoyed great vogue. He taught theology at Cambridge from 1866 until his death.

MAXFIELD, Thomas ([?]–1784) The first regular lay preacher enlisted by John Wesley, Maxfield helped set the pattern in Methodism in which laymen were used widely in the Movement.

Maxfield, however, grew conceited and ambitious. He ignored the pleas of John Wesley and brazenly asserted he was gifted with visions which told him that the world would end on February 22, 1763. Gathering a schismatic group of followers, Maxfield, an eloquently persuasive preacher, made life miserable for the Wesleys by denouncing and opposing them.

MAXIMILLA ([?]–179) One of the original "prophets" in Montanism, Maximilla was an ascetic heretical woman in Asia Minor who claimed to have special communication directly from the Holy Spirit. With Montanus, the founder of the sect called Montanists, Maximilla as one of the Spirit's mouthpieces proclaimed the imminent end of the world and demanded a strenuous asceticism. The Montanist movement grew to outstanding size, but was finally condemned by early Church synods.

MAXIMUS (580[?]–662) Known as the "Confessor," Maximus was a noted writer, theologian and leader in the Byzantine Church. Maximus, after twenty years' service as secretary to the Emperor Heraclius, embraced the monastic life in 630 at Chrysopolis, and soon rose to become abbot. He participated in the Monothelite controversy, defending the orthodox position and primacy of the see of Rome.

Maximus was instrumental in persuading Pope Martin I to call the first Lateran Council, which denounced the Monothelites (who claimed Christ had only a divine nature). In 653, Maximus fell into disrepute with the emperor, was imprisoned, banished, hauled back to Constantinople, tortured and mutilated, then re-exiled.

A prolific writer, Maximus touched on a wide range of Biblical, liturgical and theological subjects.

MAYHEW, Experience (1673–1758) American missionary to the New England Indians in 1709, Mayhew translated the Fourth Gospel and Psalms into Indian dialects for his six congregations.

MAYHEW, Jonathan (1720–1766) A prominent New Englander whose extreme liberal views lost him his membership in the Boston Association of Congregational Ministers, Mayhew took an active part in the theological battles of his day, daring even to criticize such accepted institutions as the respected British Society for the Propagation of the Gospel.

Mayhew, a staunch American patriot, was accused of fomenting the Stamp Act Riots by his inflammatory preaching and is generally believed to have been the first to have suggested that the colonies unite to throw off the British yoke.

McBURNEY, Robert Ross (1837–1898) The developer of the Y.M.C.A. movement in the United States, McBurney, an immigrant from Ireland, built the first American Y.M.C.A. building and initiated most of the programs and leadership patterns still in use in the American branches.

McGIFFERT, Arthur Cushman (1861–1933) The distinguished scholarly American Church historian and president of Union Theological Seminary, New York from 1917 to 1926, McGiffert excited controversy within his own Presbyterian Church by publishing *A History of Christianity in the Apostolic Age* in 1897. The threat of a heresy trial induced him to withdraw from the Presbyterian Church and unite with the Congregationalists.

McGLYNN, Edward (1837–1900) A controversial American Roman Catholic priest in the 19th century, McGlynn brought down the wrath of his superiors and ultimately an excommunication by backing public schools instead of parochial schools in the state of New York and by promoting Henry George (originator of the single tax on land) as mayor of New York. McGlynn, in spite of his excommunication in 1887, helped found the Anti-Poverty Society and worked among the slum-dwellers. Reinstated as a priest in 1892, he returned to parish work.

McGREADY, James (1758[?]–1817) The American Presbyterian frontier preacher who originated the idea of the camp meeting, McGready helped spark a revival in Logan County, Kentucky, which in turn led to the Great Revival throughout the U.S. in 1800. McGready, trudging throughout the backwoods to reach isolated settlements of settlers, decided to bring them together for several days for intensive instruction and preaching. The camp meeting quickly became a popular social event as well as meaningful teaching form, and became part of American folklore. McGready devoted his entire ministry to reaching lonely families and unchurched villages in the raw frontier.

McMILLAN, John (1752–1833) The first Presbyterian pastor to serve in a congregation west of the Alleghenies, McMillan came to southwestern Pennsylvania in 1776 to Pigeon Creek Presbyterian Church. In spite of Indian disturbances, unbroken wilderness and raw conditions on the frontier, McMillan energetically and fearlessly organized congregations.

McMillan, a great exponent of education and a graduate of the College of New Jersey (now Princeton) opened a "log college" or academy at Canonsburg, Pa., in 1791, which grew to become one of the parent institutions of Washington and Jefferson College.

McPHERSON, Aimee Semple (1890–1944) Colorful woman revivalist in America during the 1920's and 30's, Aimee Semple McPherson founded the International Church of the Foursquare Gospel. She began her career in China, where she and her husband, Robert Semple, served as Pentecostal missionaries. After Semple's death, she returned to the U.S., married Harold McPherson, but separated from him to pursue a full-time itinerant revival-healing meeting schedule.

Sensational and successful, Mrs. McPherson settled at Los Angeles, where she drew immense crowds for over twenty years. In 1926, she organized her fundamentalist Pentecostal-oriented Foursquare Gospel Church, employing her physical attractiveness, flamboyant personality and headline-making methods to promote her sect. Mrs. McPherson also gained notoriety by a third marriage and divorce following, and unproved-charges of affairs. She died in 1944 from an overdose of sleeping pills.

MELANCHTHON, Philip (1497–1560) The gentle, sometimes timid, but learned German scholar who stands with Luther and Calvin as the great trio of Reformers who launched the Protestant movement in the 16th century, Melanchthon produced such masterful theological statements as the *Augsburg Confession*.

Melanchthon, unsurpassed in the classics, especially Greek, Latin and Hebrew, brought a superb Humanist training to theological and Biblical studies. Arriving at Wittenberg in 1518 to teach at the recently-founded university, Melanchthon quickly fell under the influence of the powerful Luther. Although personally retiring and never ordained, Melanchthon quickly emerged as one of the most capable minds in the Reformation, aiding Luther in the tumultuous controversies in the Church and writing treatises glistening with style, clarity and insights. In 1521, Melanchthon published *Loci Communes rerum Theologicarum* ("Commonplaces of Theology"), a collection of addresses on Romans which became the earliest Reformed manifesto and projected Melanchthon as a leading thinker.

Melanchthon, deeply concerned about education, organized numerous schools, revamped the German university program, set up written standards for educational institutions throughout Germany, and helped found the universities of Marburg, Königsberg and Jena. He was sometimes called the "Preceptor of Germany" for his work in education.

Always conciliatory and self-effacing, Melanchthon was frequently sneered at for appearing to vacillate or suspected of selling out to Roman pressures. What appeared to be weakness was actually anguish over the break in the Church. Attending the Diet of Speyer, at which others vehemently protested the Roman Catholic moves to eliminate Protestant rights, Melanchthon angered some of his fellow reformers by his irenic spirit. During the bitter doctrinal disputes which wracked the Church from 1530 to 1560, Melanchthon, weary of controversy, seemed sometimes to compromise with the Roman position on minor matters of faith and practice. He was accused of being a Judas by his sterner colleagues especially in 1548 during the Leipzig-Augsburg Interim, when he acquiesced to many Roman Church demands in order to try to preserve harmony.

Melanchthon occasionally differed with Luther on theological matters, most notably on the Lord's Supper in which

Melanchthon leaned toward claiming Christ's presence in the elements themselves. Tired of attacks and battles, the gentle Melanchthon expressed his willingness to depart this life to escape "the rage of the theologians" and died soon after, April 19, 1560.

MELETIUS, Bishop of Antioch ([?]–381) A Syrian prelate at Antioch during the acrimonious feud between the Orthodox and the Arian Christians, Meletius was exiled by Emperor Constantius II, an Arian, three different times before a non-Arian Emperor, Gratian, finally declared that Meletius to be the duly installed Bishop of Antioch. Meletius died while presiding at the Council of Constantinople in 381.

MELETIUS, Bishop of Lycopolis ([?]–325[?]) Irked at Peter, Bishop of Alexandria, for being too lenient toward apostates during the first of Emperor Diocletian's persecutions. Meletius stirred up so much opposition that he was finally excommunicated. When the persecution was renewed, Meletius was sentenced to the mines and Peter was executed. During the next lull, Meletius and some fellow rigorists founded the schismatic group known as Meletians. Meletius and his followers in Egypt were given special permission to continue operating at Lycopolis, Egypt, but forbidden to ordain or organize elsewhere. In 328, when Athanasius was elected Bishop of Alexandria, Meletius broke off from the rest of the Church again. His followers, the Meletians, an ultra-strict monastic sect continued in Egypt until the 8th century.

MELITO ([?]–190) Bishop of Sardis in Asia Minor, Melito, one of the earliest Christian apologists (or "defenders of the faith" in writing) wrote between 169 and 180 to refute the accusations made against the Christian Church by the Roman government and some of the Roman intelligentsia.

MELVILLE, Andrew (1545–1622) Doughty second-generation Scots reformer, Melville stood up to King James VI of Scotland when that headstrong monarch tried to take over control of the Scottish Kirk.

Melville, after a distinguished academic career in France and Switzerland, returned to Scotland to head Glasgow University, and later served as principal of St. Mary's College, St. Andrews. When the King attempted to substitute royally-controlled episcopacy for self-governing Presbyterianism in Scotland in 1581, Melville led the General Assembly of the Church of Scotland to grant authority to local presbyteries to act as ecclesiastical courts, forcing the irate James to recognize Presbyterianism as the religion of the realm. Melville, however, had to flee across the border to England after presenting the Kirk's petition to King James.

The obstinate and devious King persisted in trying to wrest control of the Church of Scotland by insisting that the King alone was authorized to convene the Church's General Assembly, and supplanting presbyteries' powers with two high commission Courts, each headed by an archbishop.

Melville, summoned to London in 1606 by King James (who by then was also King of England) to discuss Church affairs, was treacherously thrown into the Tower of London on James' orders. The great champion of the freedom of Scots Kirk to govern itself languished in the Tower for five years until the French Duke of Boillou intervened and took him to France, where he lived and taught as a professor at Sedan until his death in 1622.

MEMNON, Bishop of Ephesus (5th c.) Memnon was an Arian-leaning participant in the bitter battles in the Church between Orthodox (Nicene Christians) belonging to the school of Antioch, and the Arians (stating in creeds in effect that Christ was not quite divine). Memnon and his henchmen and Cyril of Alexandria rigged a Church Council at Ephesus in 431 to condemn the orthodox, Antioch group. Memnon, who had cunningly convened the Council before the Antiochians had arrived in full voting strength, in turn was denounced when the full contingent from Antioch came to Ephesus. Although imprisoned for a time by the exasperated Emperor, Theodosius II, Memnon, a wily politician, managed to be released and reappointed to his old see at Ephesus.

MENDOZA, Pedro Gonzales de, Cardinal (also **Mendez**) (1428–1495) A Spanish churchman who exerted a powerful influence on Spanish Emperor Henry IV's domestic and foreign affairs, Mendoza, Archbishop of Toledo from 1482, was a formidable presence in Spain for many years. Mendoza furthered the career of Ximenes, the Spaniard who raised the moral tone of the Spanish Church and encouraged the great intellectual awakening in Spain in the early 16th century.

MENNO SIMONS (1496[?]–1561) A respected and moderate Anabaptist, Menno was a Dutch Reformer whose followers became known as Mennonites. Menno, a Roman Catholic priest whose studies of Scripture led him to break with Rome and become an evangelical preacher in 1530, joined the Anabaptists because of doubts over the Scriptural validity of infant baptism. As a roving evangelist through Germany and the Netherlands, Menno frequently encountered persecution from Roman Catholics and hostile Protestant groups alike. His

deeply moving conversion experience led him to emphasize a profound personal commitment to the living Jesus Christ.

Menno, unlike some other Anabaptist leaders, avoided the extreme dogmatism and fanaticism which led certain Anabaptist groups, such as the faction at Munster, to wild excesses. A thoroughgoing theocrat, Menno flatly refused to bear arms for any state, rejected the use of oaths in civil courts, refused to allow civil authorities to belong to his church.

The Mennonites, a union of various Anabaptist groups in Germany, Switzerland and the Netherlands welded together by the saintly pacifist Menno, gained the respect of everyone by the high quality of their personal piety and practical living, as exemplified by Menno himself.

MERSWIN, Rulman (1307–1382) Part of the group of 14th century mystics in southwestern Germany and Switzerland who dubbed themselves "Friends of God," Merswin wrote numerous letters and tracts which won a wide reading audience. Merswin, a layman, was originally a banker and merchant at Strassburg. He became an intimate friend of the great mystic, Tauler, and left his business to spend all his time and energy on religious affairs. His books and letters, purportedly from an anonymous "great Friend of God" in Switzerland, were assumed to have been written by someone else, but are now believed to have been penned by Merswin himself.

METHODIUS ([?]–885) One of the pair of brothers who left the status and security of their home city of Thessalonica where they had achieved success and position in the Eastern Empire, Methodius and his brother Cyril went as missionaries to the Slavs. Cyril and Methodius, requested by Emperor Michael III to take the Gospel to the Slavic tribes, achieved outstanding success, spreading the Church among thousands of Slavs in the 9th century. Both Cyril and Methodius are recognized as saints in the calendars of both the Eastern and Latin Churches.

MICHAEL CERULARIUS, Patriarch of Constantinople ([?]–1058) Head of the Eastern Church at the time of the final rupture between Rome and Constantinople in 1054, Michael resented the interference of Pope Leo IX with churches, particularly in Sicily, which had an allegiance to Constantinople instead of Rome. Michael, determined to hold on to congregations traditionally under his jurisdiction, retaliated by closing congregations holding to the Latin rite which were located in his territory. Adding fuel to the flames, Michael lashed out at the pope for continuing to hold to heretical notions, such as including an improper clause regarding Christ in the creed, and for practicing incorrect forms of worship, such as using unleavened bread for the Sacrament.

The irascible Michael was promptly excommunicated by the touchy Leo, who immediately sent emissaries to Constantinople to lay the writ of excommunication on the high altar of St. Sophia. Michael, firing back a counter-excommunication of Pope Leo, completed what has been usually regarded as the formal separation of the Eastern and Western Churches in 1054, a tragedy which continues until this day.

MILICZ, Jan ([?]–1374) One of the bold preachers who stirred Bohemia about one hundred years before John Huss appeared, Milicz, who lived and taught at Kremsier, lamented the corruption among the clergy, pleaded for more frequent communion services and insisted that the Bible was sufficient authority for belief. Milicz, certain that the Antichrist was about to come, announced that the unworthy clergy were evidence of the Antichrist's coming.

MILLER, William (1782–1849) Leader of the Adventists, Miller was a Hampton (N.Y.) farmer who sensationally forecast the end of the world in 1843 and again in 1844. Miller, following an emotional conversion experience in 1816, carried on an intense study of apocalyptic passages in the Bible for the next years, and confidently announced that his calculations from Scripture study meant that the Second Coming and the End of the Age would take place in 1843. In 1831, Miller began preaching this message, luring huge audiences and convincing hundreds. Miller wrote down his spectacular predictions in 1836 in *Evidence from Scripture and History of the Second Coming of Christ About the Year 1843*, which was widely distributed. With the help of a skillful promotional agent named Joshua Himes, Miller brought a national movement into existence known as the Adventists, or more popularly the "Millerites."

When 1843 passed without incident, Miller calmly re-checked his calculations, and announced a new timetable for the Eschaton (Second Coming). October 22, 1844, Miller asserted, was to be The Last Day. As the fateful day drew near, thousands of terrified people abandoned jobs and responsibilities. On the night of October 22, 1844, the faithful by the droves gathered on hilltops, many in white robes, anticipating the dramatic climax to history.

Although many were disillusioned and forsook Miller's movement, Miller himself stoutly continued to maintain that the time was still soon. In 1845, after prolonged conflict between his movement and other Protestant groups, the Millerites became a separate denomination. Miller himself, however, unhappy with the strife within the Adventist Church, faded from prominence and died in 1849.

MILLS, Samuel John, Jr. (1783–1818) Driving force behind the spread of the missionary movement in American Protestantism in the early 19th century, Mills led in the formation of the American Board of Commissioners for Foreign Missions in 1810. While still studying at Williams College, Mills and several fellow students were caught in a rainstorm in 1806 and took refuge in a haystack, where they held an impromptu prayer meeting. The "haystack prayer meeting" group organized into the Society of the Brethren at Williams, committing itself to Christian service.

Mills, after graduating from Williams and Andover Theological Seminary, made long missionary tours through the American West in 1812–1813 and 1814, reporting the need for pastors on the frontier. Through Mills' drive and leadership, the first permanent pastor was sent to the Mississippi Valley in 1816, and the first missionaries sent by the American Board to India in 1812.

MILLS, Susan Lincoln Tolman (1826–1912) American missionary and educator who married Cyrus Taggart Mills and accompanied him on his mission assignment to Ceylon in 1854, Mrs. Mills served faithfully in Ceylon and Hawaii with her husband until 1865, at which time they returned to the U.S. to take leadership of a faltering girls' school. Mrs. Mills skillfully guided the school, which developed into Mills College, Oakland, California.

MILMAN, Henry Hart (1791–1868) The Dean of St. Paul's and English scholar who wrote *History of the Jews*

(1829) and *History of Latin Christianity* (1855), Milman encouraged and furthered Biblical criticism by applying careful, critical methods to studying the Old Testament.

MILNER, Isaac (1750–1820) A Cambridge professor for many years, Milner held profoundly Evangelistic views. Isaac Milner completed work interrupted by his brother Joseph's death on *History of the Church of Christ*, stressing the development of Christian biography rather than the disputes which had rent the Church. Isaac Milner had a deep influence on Cambridge University life in the late 18th and early 19th century.

MILNER, Joseph (1744–1797) Brother of Isaac Milner, the distinguished Cambridge scholar, Joseph Milner, a clergyman at Hull, England, with Evangelical views, made Hull a center for Evangelism in the 18th century. Joseph Milner wrote much of the significant *History of the Church of Christ*, completed after his death by his brother, Isaac.

MILTIADES, Pope ([?]–314) Also known as Melchiades, Miltiades served as Bishop of Rome about 310 to 314. At the request of the Emperor Constantine, Miltiades presided at a synod at Rome to hear the protest of a group of angry rigorists who thought the Church was being too lenient in readmitting apostates and clergy who had given up the sacred books during persecutions. Miltiades and the Synod, unable to mollify the protesters, were dismayed to see the group turn schismatic and set up a rival faction, known as the Donatists.

MILTON, John (1608–1674) The great Puritan poet and advocate of religious liberty, Milton achieved great success and salary during his public career. His government service ended abruptly, however, when the monarchy was restored in England in 1660. In the preceding years, Milton had an unhappy first marriage, lost his infant son (1651) and first wife (1652), became totally blind (1652) and responsible for raising three young children, the eldest of which was a helpless cripple, then lost his second wife (with whom he was happy) and baby (1657). Milton, who had written many political and religious polemical pamphlets earlier in his career, found himself penniless and suspected of treason after the Restoration. He completed his epic poems, *Paradise Lost* in 1665, and *Paradise Regain'd* in 1671, in spite of personal tragedy and hardship, and stands as one of the giants of Christian literature. His third wife survived him.

MOFFAT, Robert (1795–1883) A Scots missionary to South Africa from 1816 until 1870, Moffat served much of that time in Bechuanaland. He translated the Bible and many hymns into the local dialect. One of his daughters married David Livingstone, the missionary-explorer.

MOFFATT, James (1870–1944) Learned and likeable Scots Presbyterian Bible scholar, Moffatt served on faculties at Oxford, Glasgow and Union Seminary of New York. His fresh, readable accurate translation of the entire Bible from the original languages into English became a best seller. In addition, he wrote several excellent books.

MOLAY, Jacques de (1243[?]–1314) The last Grand Master of the Knights Templar, de Molay tried to re-equip troops to resume the Crusades in 1310 from Crete. He was summoned by Pope Clement V to France and turned over to French King Philip IV, who feared and resented the strength of the Knights Templar. De Molay, tried as a heretic, was tortured and imprisoned for five years until a forced recantation was wrung from him, then burned at the stake.

MOLINA, Luis (1535–1600) A Spanish Jesuit author and teacher who spent most of his career in Portugal, Molina published *Concordia Liberi Arbitrii*, an attempt to explain the contradictions between the doctrines of man's free will and God's foreknowledge. Molina's tome, accepted by the Jesuits, was blasted by the Dominicans on the grounds that it downgraded the teachings of Thomas Aquinas (who had been a Dominican). A doctrinal squabble ensued which took a papal decree to settle in 1607.

MONTANUS (2nd c.) Founder of the heretical sect known as Montantists, Montanus about 156 announced that he was the mouthpiece for direct revelations from the Holy Spirit. Montanus claimed that the Spirit directed him to proclaim that the promise of Christ had been fulfilled and that the dispensation of the Spirit had begun. The end of the world, Montanus shrilled, was at hand, and the most strenuous asceticism was to be practiced. Montanus, a priest of the pagan cult of Cybele before his conversion, according to a tradition remembered by Jerome, found ready ears for his startling proclamations in Asia Minor, an area noted for its ecstatic forms of religious observations.

His movement swelled to enormous size, threatening the authority of many orthodox bishops. Although Montanism was condemned in several of the earliest Church synods in the 2nd century, it spread to Europe and Africa and flourished through the 4th century.

Montanus, reacting from the secular tendencies already at work in the Church, tapped the latent uneasiness among many faithful Christians in his home province of Phrygia and elsewhere over the growing worldliness of the organized Church.

MONICA (332[?]–387) A prayerful, patient and persevering parent, Monica, daughter of devout Christians in North Africa, married Patricius, a pagan government official, bore a son, Augustine, and struggled for years to bring her husband and son to a response to the Gospel. Monica's persistent prayers and the great Ambrose's persuasive preaching finally won Augustine to the Church at Milan, where she had followed her studious son. Monica, however, died at Ostia, Italy, on the return trip to Africa. A saint in the Roman Church, Monica is the patroness of many associations of Christian wives and mothers.

MOODY, Dwight Lyman (1837–1899) Successful shoe-salesman-turned-preacher, Dwight L. Moody became one of the effective evangelists in the 19th century English-speaking world. In 1860, Moody resigned from his well-paying position to devote all his energies to Sunday School work, speaking engagements and social service. During the next thirty-nine years, this remarkable man built a church at Chicago (1863), served as a chaplain to Union troops during the Civil War, built the first Y.M.C.A. building in the United States (1866), founded a girls' school, Northfield Seminary (1879), a boys' school, Mt. Hermon (1881), and a Bible institute, Moody Bible Institute (1889), and conducted thousands of services.

In 1873, Moody took a singer-composer named Ira D. Sankey to Britain, where they held a series of astoundingly successful evangelistic meetings. Moody and Sankey, renowned figures after their British tour, conducted similar revivals in the U.S. and returned to the British Isles for a second round of meetings.

Moody preached a forthright appeal for Christian commitment, but refused to indulge in high-pitched emotionalism, preferring to emphasize the love of God instead of divine wrath and avoiding histrionics in the pulpit. Unlike some others, Moody refused to capitalize personally on his success, but turned over the receipts from his meetings to an endowment fund for the schools he had founded. Many of the catchy Gospel songs used in Protestantism were introduced by Moody and Sankey.

MORE, Hannah (1745–1833) English writer and philanthropist with deep sympathies for the movement known as Evangelicalism, the informal fellowship of those affected by the Wesleyan revival, Hannah More organized numerous Sunday Schools, wrote over fifty tracts, promoted the Bible Society and the cause of missions and supported the abolitionist cause. She endured the enmity of many in the Establishment during the "Blagdon Controversy" from 1800 to 1803, when she refused to fire a teacher accused of Methodism. Hannah More, a popular playwright of her day, had entree to Samuel Johnson and his circle of leading literary figures.

MORE, Sir Thomas (1478–1535) The distinguished and determined statesman and scholar who refused to take an oath acknowledging the Supremacy Act of 1534 in which Parliament declared King Henry VIII "the only Supreme Head in earth of the Church of England," More was beheaded for his integrity. More, friend of such learned men as Erasmus and Colet, probably had the finest mind in England in his day. He enjoyed a long, brilliant career as a lawyer and civil servant, receiving a knighthood and numerous prestigious appointments, including Lord Chancellor of England in 1529.

During the Reformation, the devout More desired to have the Church purified but, abhorring schism, flinched from breaking with Rome. He disagreed with Henry VIII's divorce from Catherine of Aragon to marry Anne Boleyn. Resigning from his post as Chancellor as a matter of conscience, More refused to swear to recognize Henry instead of the pope as head of the English Church. Although Sir Thomas More had never written or spoken anything against Henry, he was arrested by the angry Henry for declining to acquiesce to the Parliamentary Act on a matter of faith. After a year in prison, he was executed in 1535. Four hundred years later, More was canonized.

MORISON, James (1816–1893) A Scots Presbyterian pastor who had deep reservations about the ultra-Calvinistic views on election then in vogue in the Scottish Church, Morison insisted that Christ's death atoned for all men's sins. Morison was finally suspended in 1841 from the ministry in the United Secession Church, but took his own congregation, his father and two other pastors and established the Evangelical Union.

The Evangelical Union, popularly known as Morisonians, eventually totaled about one hundred congregations. After Morison's death in 1893, it merged with the Congregationalists.

MORRISON, Robert (1782–1834) Great hero of the Protestant Foreign Mission movement in the 19th century, Robert Morrison was the first Protestant missionary to China. Morrison, from a poor Northumbrian family, worked as an apprentice to a last and boot tree

maker and educated himself, learning Latin, Greek and Hebrew. Under the auspices of the London Missionary Society, Morrison finally got to the East in 1809. His labors were unspectacular and discouraging; he ministered patiently at Canton for ten years without making a single convert. At the same time, he diligently worked on a careful translation of the Bible into Chinese, completing the New Testament in 1814, and the Old Testament in 1819. In 1818, Morrison founded the Anglo-Chinese College at Malacca. Working alone much of the time, and enduring opposition and privation, Morrison paved the way for the tide of Church workers who poured into China later in 19th century. He died in the Far East while still at work, and is buried at Macao.

MORRISON, Charles Clayton (1874–1966) Prominent Protestant journalist, publisher and ecumenist, Charles Clayton Morrison in 1908 founded and edited *The Christian Century*, the progressive interdenominational, much-quoted magazine of Protestant thinking. Morrison, a Disciples minister, used his magazine as his pulpit and became the liberal voice of American Protestantism, exercising a great influence for fifty years.

MOSHEIM, Johann Laurenz von (1694[?]–1755) The Father of Modern Church History, von Mosheim, a German preacher, professor at Gottingen, and noted scholar, was the first to attempt to write Church history objectively. Instead of publishing history to produce propaganda, von Mosheim tried to examine the development of the Church without bias or party line. His *Institutiones* in 1726 told the entire sweep of the Church's development; *Commentarii de rebus Christianorum ante Constantium* detailed the first four centuries, A.D. Von Mosheim helped encourage a new attitude of thought in Germany.

MOTT, John Raleigh (1865–1955) One of the architects of the World Council of Churches, John R. Mott helped coordinate the efforts and bring deeper understanding among world Protestant groups during the first half of the 20th century.

From 1888 until 1920, Mott headed the Student Volunteer Movement. From 1920, he served as General Secretary of the International Council of the Y.M.C.A. Mott, one of the first ecumenical churchmen in this century, presided at the World Missionary Conference at Edinburgh, in 1910, and served until 1942 as Chairman of the International Missionary Council which grew out of the Edinburgh Conference.

Mott's commitment to missions and to young people was also reflected when he helped organize the World Student Christian Federation. During World War I, Mott tirelessly worked to help Allied prisoners of war and to send relief supplies to devastated areas.

This outstanding Christian world citizen's dedication and effort to serve mankind were recognized in 1946 when he was named as a co-recipient of the Nobel Peace Prize. As revered elder statesman in the world Church, Mott was elected an Honorary President of the World Council of Churches at its organization at Amsterdam in 1948.

MUHLENBERG, Heinrich Melchior (1711–1787) The sturdy, studious and saintly German missionary to Lutheran immigrants in colonial Pennsylvania, Muhlenberg arrived in 1741 and brought organization to scattered, dispirited Lutheran families on the East coast. Although called as pastor of three tiny congregations at Philadelphia, New Hanover and New Providence, Pa., Muhlenberg assumed responsibility for clusters of German-speaking Protestants within a wide radius, becoming an ex-officio bishop. Muhlenberg organized the first Lutheran Synod in America in 1748.

During the American Revolution, Muhlenberg, an ardent patriot, supported the colonial cause, rallying the Lutherans to the American side.

MUHLENBERG, John Peter Gabriel (1746–1807) American-born son of the illustrious Heinrich Muhlenberg, John Muhlenberg, although raised a Lutheran, accepted Episcopal orders in Virginia in order to collect tithes in his parishes and won fame during the American Revolution by accepting a commission as colonel and enlisting 300 of his parish to serve in the colonial army. John Muhlenberg later took an active part in national politics, serving in both Congress and the Senate.

MULLER, George (1805–1898) A German-born pastor he was invited to serve in London in 1829 by the Society for Promoting Christianity among the Jews. Muller, following a pastorate in which he shocked traditionalists by abolishing pew rents and compulsory tithes in favor of voluntary contributions, then switched to the Plymouth Brethren. In 1835, Muller moved to Bristol, where he opened his remarkable orphan houses. Depending completely upon contributions for support, Muller looked after 2,000 children at a time by 1875.

MUNGO See **KENTIGERN.**

MUNZER, Thomas (1489[?]–1525) Fanatical Anabaptist demagogue, Munzer served briefly with Luther at Wittenberg in 1519, but disgustedly broke with Luther because Luther's type of Reformation was not radical enough. Munzer, claiming to instruct directly by the Holy Spirit, incited a series of peasant uprisings at Zwicken, Allstedt and Mulhausen. Although thrown out of all three towns, he returned to Mulhausen, seized control and set up a theocracy in which all property was held in common. He outraged Protestants and Catholics alike by his senseless destruction of Church property and preaching civil turmoil. Finally defeated in battle by Philip Landgrave of Hesse in 1525, the unstable radical was executed. Munzer helped give the Anabaptists a bad name in many parts of Europe for many years.

MURRAY, John (1741–1815) The founder of the Universalist movement in the United States, John Murray, earlier a Calvinist Methodist follower of George Whitefield in Ireland, was attracted to the Universalist position espoused by James Relly in Britain. Murray was expelled from Whitefield's movement in 1770, and emigrated to America. After several years as a wandering preacher, Murray served as a chaplain in the Continental Army (with Washington's personal approval), then took a pastorate in Gloucester, Massachusetts.

In 1793, Murray accepted the position of pastor of the Universalist Society of Boston. He eloquently taught that all people ultimately would be saved, stating that Christ had atoned for the sins not only of the elect but all men, and that at judgment, all unbelief would disappear and every person would receive immediate blessedness.

MURTON, John ([?]–1625) A north-country Englishman won to the Separatists by preacher John Smyth, Murton and others of Smyth's Gainsborough congregation, feeling the pressures of opposition, fled to Amsterdam about 1607. When Smyth, an unstable dabbler in church forms, quarrelled with the congregation and left, Murton and Thomas Helwys led many of the original congregation back to England. In 1612, Murton and Helwys founded the first permanent Baptist Congregation in England.

N

NASSAU, Robert Hammill (1835–1921) American Presbyterian medical missionary to West Africa, Nassau distinguished himself as an able linguist and perceptive observer of the African scene.

NATION, Carry (1846–1911) Née Carry Amedia Moore, Carry Nation, saloon-smashing prohibition fanatic, helped rally American Protestantism to attempt to curb alcoholism by a constitutional amendment stopping the sale or the manufacture of alcoholic beverages. Carry, embittered by a miserable first marriage to an alcoholic, Charles Gloyd, in 1867, left Gloyd and married the Rev. David Nation in 1877. Beginning her crusade against illegal retail sales of liquor in Medicine Lodge, Kansas, in the 1890's, the muscular matron finally took the law into her own hands in Wichita one day in 1901. Mrs. Nation marched into a saloon, and swinging a hatchet, began a systematic destruction of bottles, furniture and equipment before the startled assemblage of customers and barkeepers. The same year, her mousy husband finally divorced her for desertion.

Although her neurotic personality made her the butt of many jokes, her grim obstinacy, most agree, helped promote the cause of Prohibition in American churches at the turn of the century.

NAUMANN, Friedrich (1860–1919) A German Lutheran pastor who left the pastorate to enter politics in 1894, Naumann in 1896 helped found the National Socialist Party in Germany (which had no connection with Hitler's Nazi party) and served as its first president. In 1915, Naumann, anticipating Hitler's dreams of a German Empire in Europe, published *Mitteleuropa,* a grandiose scheme for German expansion in Central Europe. Naumann after the 1918 Revolution became one of the founders of the German Democrat Party.

NEANDER, Johann August Wilhelm (1789–1850) Given the name David Mendel by his Jewish parents, this great Church historian left Judaism to be baptized Neander (meaning "new man") in 1806. Neander, a devout Lutheran the rest of his life, taught as a professor at Heidelberg and Berlin. His six-volume history of the Church, a classic in its field for many years and translated into several languages, treated Christianity not as a system of dogma to be defended, but as evidence of God at work in the world through history. Many of Neander's ideas germinated in later thinkers such as Henri Bergson and William James.

NERI, Philip or Filippo Romolo (1515–1595) Best known and esteemed saint in Italy since Francis of Assisi, Philip of Neri practiced an apostolic poverty and founded new forms of worship and ministry in the Roman Catholic Church. In 1548, Neri organized the Confraternity of the Most Holy Trinity. A few years later, as the priest at San Girolamo della Carita, Neri built an oratory over the sanctuary to hold prayer and musical services, developing the musical form now known as the oratory (which took its name from Neri's *"Oratorio"* constructed over the sanctuary). Neri, transferred to San Giovanni dei Fiorentini in 1564, founded what became known as the Congregation of the Oratory, a special order responsible directly to the pope and given papal sanction in 1575. Neri was canonized in 1622.

NESTLÉ, Christof Eberhard (1851–1913) A German Lutheran orientalist, Semitic scholar and pastor, Nestlé made his life's work the preparation of the most authentic Greek text of the New Testament he could possibly present. Nestlé's first edition of his *Novum Testamentum Graece* appeared in 1898. He repeatedly revised it, however, until his death. A professor at Maulbronn, Germany, Nestlé also found time to serve as director of the Seminary and work on numerous committees of learned societies.

NESTORIUS ([?]–440[?]) A presbyter and monk from Antioch who had a reputation as a preacher, Nestorius was elected Patriarch of Constantinople in 428, where his teachings on the person of Christ caused controversy and schism. Nestorius stated that there were two natures in Jesus Christ: the human (Jesus) and the Divine (the Word of God). From this basis, Nestorius argued that Mary, Jesus' mother, should be called the Mother of Christ, but not *Theotokos* or "Mother of God." Accused by the unscrupulous and ambitious Cyril, Patriarch of Alexandria, of heresy, Nestorius was hounded from city to city until he finally died, excommunicated and forgotten, in lonely exile in Egypt about 440.

Nestorius' followers, however, clinging to Nestorius' emphasis on the reality and completeness of Jesus' human nature as well as divine, became a schismatic group known as the Nestorians, spreading as far East as China and India, where remnants continue to exist today. Nestorius' ideas, although finally vindicated at the Council of Chalcedon, were distorted and maligned by Cyril in a repulsive political struggle within the Church and Empire which raged for many years in the 5th century.

NEVIN, John Williamson (1803–1886) An outstanding American theologian, scholar and educator, Nevin, with his colleague at Mercersburg Seminary, Philip Schaff, created what became known as the Mercersburg Theology— a dynamic devotion to Christ coupled with a brainy, critical look at contemporary conditions.

Nevin, originally a Presbyterian, taught at Western Theological Seminary of Pittsburgh for ten years, 1830–1840, before joining the faculty of Mercersburg (Pa.) Seminary and joining the Reformed Church.

In 1843, Nevin published his controversial *The Anxious Bench—A Tract for the Times,* in which he opposed the highly-charged revivalism then gaining acceptance among all Protestant bodies. He unleashed another storm of criticism in 1845 when he preached a warm, open, thoughtful sermon on Catholic Unity. Nevin with Philip Schaff answered the bigots and critics with a series of articles, tracts and books, which collectively compose what is called the "Mercersburg Theology."

In addition to extensive writing, Nevin established and edited the "Mercersburg Review" in 1849, served as acting president of Marshall College from 1841 to 1853, and carried a heavy teaching load at Mercersburg Seminary for many years.

NEWMAN, John Henry, Cardinal (1801–1890) A sensitive, scholarly

Englishman, Newman moved from mild Evangelicalism to liberal Anglicanism to high church Anglicanism to Roman Catholicism.

Newman, a brilliant classics scholar and don at Oriel College, Oxford, became associated with Hurrell, Froude, Keble and Pusey and others in the start of the Anglo-Catholic wing in the Church of England. Desiring a return to a purer, more primitive form of the Church, they urged fasting, celibacy, confession and other Roman usages which had been dropped at the time of the Reformation.

In 1832, Newman experienced a near-fatal fever and deep spiritual crisis during a Mediterranean tour. His hymn, "Lead Kindly Light," describes his personal uncertainty at this time.

Returning to England in time to hear Keble's sermon which launched the Oxford Movement, Newman, the intellectual leadership of the Movement and his Oxford friends produced a stream of "Tracts," defending their Anglo-Catholicism as the middle way between the extremes of Protestantism and Rome. Newman, however, touched off a furious controversy in the ninetieth "Tract" by maintaining that the Thirty-Nine Articles of the Church of England rejected the political supremacy but not the spiritual supremacy of the pope.

Forbidden by the Anglican Bishop of Oxford to publish additional "Tracts," Newman left the Anglican communion in 1843, officially became a Roman Catholic in 1845 at the age of forty-four, and was ordained a priest in 1847. Subject to severe criticism by Protestants and suspicion by many Catholics, Newman's difficulties were compounded by a sequence of personal disappointments including failure to found a National Roman Catholic University in Ireland, failure to make a new translation of the Bible in English, failure to

edit a periodical. After vicious smears by Charles Kingsley, in 1864 Newman felt constrained to write *"Apologia pro Vita Sua,"* explaining his personal change of position.

Eventually, the attitude of the English public changed. Newman won acceptance and honors, including a cardinal's hat in 1879. A master of English, both written and spoken, Newman published works in theology, philosophy, patristics, church history, poetry and novels.

NEWTON, John (1725–1807) One-time English ship captain who ran slaves for four years, Newton left the sea in 1755, experienced a conversion and became an Anglican priest in 1764, serving parishes in Olney, Buckinghamshire, and London. Newton, a friend of poet William Cowper, published a popular hymn book, the *Olney Hymns,* containing for the first time such favorites as "Glorious Things of Thee Are Spoken," "How Sweet the Name of Jesus Sounds" and "Amazing Grace—How Sweet the Sound."

NEWTON, Joseph Fort (1880–1950) American pastor and preacher with literary gifts, Newton served pastorates at City Temple, London, and in New York and Philadelphia. In 1926, after many years as a Baptist, he received ordination as an Episcopal priest. Joseph Fort Newton, a prolific writer, published thirty books.

NICHOLAS I, Pope (800[?]–867) An adroit administrator who was elected pope in the difficult days following the collapse of the Frankish Holy Roman Empire after Charlemagne's death, Nicholas, ruling from 858 to 867, artfully staved the power-hungry princes and kings and stiffened discipline among his tolerant, indulgent clerical hierarchy.

Nicholas successfully outmaneuvered the wily Hincmar, Bishop of Soissons, forcing that prelate to recognize that papal permission was necessary for major appointments. Nicholas also deposed the Archbishops of Trier and Cologne for approving the adulterous marriage of the Emperor's brother. Nicholas, however, drawn into the nasty political struggle in the Eastern Church between the learned Photius and the Emperor's toadies, foolishly deposed Photius.

Nicholas' condemnation of the wrong party at Constantinople exacerbated the bad feeling between Rome and the Eastern Church, which eventually resulted in a complete break in 1054.

NICHOLAS II, Pope (980[?]–1061) A decisive pontiff who was handpicked by Hildebrand, the power behind the papacy for over twenty years before becoming pope himself, Nicholas II, reigning from 1059 to 1061, restored discipline and tightened procedures in governing the Church. He called the Lateran Council of 1059, at which the Church adopted rules for electing popes and pared down the privileges taken over by kings which belonged in the hands of the papacy.

The decision regarding the selection of popes made in 1059 is the oldest written constitution now in effect, and still governs the election of popes.

NICHOLAS III, Pope (1216[?]–1280) The first pope to make the Vatican his permanent residence, Nicholas III, pope from 1277 to 1280, struggled to keep Rome free from foreign control and sent missionaries east to Persia and China.

NICHOLAS IV, Pope ([?]–1292) The first pope to be elected from among the Franciscan Order, Nicholas IV, ruling from 1288 to 1292, managed to check the powerful Colonna family but failed to arouse a war-weary Europe

to still another Crusade against the Moslems.

NICHOLAS V, Pope ([?]–1455) Known as the "Great Humanist," this bookish esthete seemed most interested in beautifying Rome, where he started an elaborate and expensive program to rebuild St. Peter's and established the great Vatican Library. Nicholas also succeeded in ending the long-festering schism by bringing the last antipope, Felix V, to heel. Closing the Council of Basel in 1449, Nicholas quashed hopes of turning the papacy into a constitutional monarchy whereby councils could effect reforms.

Nicholas, who for all his qualities as the perfect Renaissance Man, also liked traditional pageantry, and crowned Frederick III, the last Emperor to be crowned at Rome.

NICHOLAS, Saint ([?]–345 or 352[?]) The real-life saint whose name and career have been corrupted into the symbol of a commercialized, secularized holiday on December 25, Nicholas hailed from Patara in Asia Minor. Although later legends have obscured most of the facts about his career, Nicholas reportedly entered the monastery of Sion, near Myra, where he became abbot and later bishop. Some think that he attended the Council of Nicea in 325. He is believed to have been cruelly tortured and jailed during Emperor Diocletian's persecution. Long after his death, sometime in the 1200's his bones were carried to Italy by merchants and were claimed to effect miraculous cures. The legends about Nicholas and his alleged miracles circulated widely in the late Medieval period, making him one of the most popular saints.

Nicholas, the patron saint of Greece and Russia and several cities, is also the guardian of sailors, merchants, scholars, children, unwed maidens, pawnbrokers and thieves.

In the Medieval Church, nonsensical customs surrounding his feast day sprang up, such as the mock election of a boy bishop on St. Nicholas' Day in parts of England who dressed up in splendor and paraded through the streets into houses dispensing cheer. Elsewhere in Europe, festivities of St. Nicholas' Day, such as St. Nicholas coming down the chimney to leave presents, were gradually incorporated into Christmas celebrations.

Santa Claus, a corruption of the Dutch "Saint Nikolaas," was brought to the New World, where he has become part of the folklore of the American holiday and tended to overshadow the celebration of the birth of Jesus.

NICHOLAS of Clemanges See CLE-MANGES, NICHOLAS DE.

NICHOLAS of Cusa (1401–1464) A German-born Roman Catholic thinker and papal legate in the 15th century, Nicholas of Cusa wrote *De Docta Ignorantia* to combat the twisted scholasticism in European universities. A faithful Vatican official, Nicholas of Cusa performed numerous chores for Pope Nicholas V.

NICHOLAS of Hereford ([?]–1420[?]) Early English translator of the Scriptures, Nicholas worked with John Wycliffe between 1382 and 1384 to translate the Bible from the Latin Vulgate into readable English. Most scholars think that Nicholas did the bulk of the translation of the Old Testament, while Wycliffe did the New. Their Bible, a vivid, readable translation, helped both English piety and the English language.

NICOLL, William Robertson (1851–1923) Scottish journalist and cleric,

W. Robertson Nicoll, following pastorates in the Free Church of Scotland, served as editor of the *Expositor* in 1884, and in 1886 founded the prestigious, influential, non-denominational church magazine, *The British Weekly*. The erudite Nicoll helped mold progressive thinking in the British Isles for many years. In 1891, Nicoll started publishing *Bookman,* and in 1897, edited *The Expositor's Greek Testament.*

NIEBUHR, Helmut Richard (1894–1962) American theologian and Evangelical and Reformed pastor, H. Richard Niebuhr brought an inquiring, disciplined mind to examine traditional theological matters in the light of sociology, history and psychology. Professor at Yale Divinity School for many years, Niebuhr wrote many noted books, including *The Social Sources of Denominationalism* (1929), *Christ and Culture* (1951), and *Radical Monotheism and Western Culture* (1960).

NIKON (1605–1681) Arrogant, insensitive Patriarch of Moscow who headed the Russian Orthodox Church from 1652 until he was deposed in 1666, Nikon enraged most of his laity and clergy by stubbornly ramming inconsequential changes down the throats of the Russian believers.

Nikon, while a monastic and Metropolitan at Novgorod, caught the eye of Czar Alexis, who elevated Nikon to Patriarch and leaned on him for counsel in affairs of state. Nikon, with his hold over the Czar and immense prestige, became in effect co-ruler of Russia, even presuming to take the title "Sovereign."

Determined to update liturgical practices to bring them into conformity with the Greek Church, Nikon published a manual instructing all Russians to change such trivial traditions as using two fingers instead of three to make the sign of the cross. Nikon tried to enforce his proposed changes with a heavy hand, arousing furious opposition among the masses of ignorant but faithful priests and laymen and causing a schismatic group known as the "Old Believers" to split off from the State Church.

Nikon was finally removed in 1666 by the Czar, who grew tired of the officious Patriarch.

NITSCHMANN, David (1696–1772) First Bishop of the Reorganized Moravian Church, Moravia-born Nitschmann traveled widely, planting Moravian congregations throughout Europe and North America. Nitschmann, deeply influenced by von Zinzendorf, lived at the Herrnhut community of pietist expatriates from Moravia, and went as one of the first Moravian missionaries. After a brief missionary tour in 1732 with Leonard Dober in the West Indies among the black slaves, Nitschmann returned to Europe, where in 1735 he was consecrated bishop. The same year, he sailed with twenty-five other Moravians to Georgia.

Nitschmann's and the other Moravian's cheerful confidence during a severe storm at sea so impressed two priggish young Anglicans, Charles and John Wesley, that the Wesleys later spent some time in the Moravian communities in Germany.

Nitschmann continued his tireless labors throughout Europe and America until his death in the Moravian colony at Bethlehem, Pa., in 1772.

NOAILLES, Louis Antoine de (1651–1729) A prestigious Cardinal Archbishop of Paris, Noailles, sympathetic to Jansenism, inflamed Church tensions in France by demanding that a Church Council rather than the pope resolve the argument. (Jansenist doctrines taught a rigid predestination, emphasized man's hopelessly corrupt nature, left no place for the efficacy of good works, and denied that it was God's will that all be saved.) De Noailles endorsed Quesnel's Jansenist book in 1687, but was pressured to withdraw his endorsement after Pope Clement XI condemned Jansenism. Instead, de Noailles and four other bishops appealed to Clement to call a General Council. De Noailles was not only turned down but excommunicated for his impertinence in suggesting a Council. De Noailles, eighteen bishops and 3,000 priests angrily broke off in a schism. The conflict raged for many years, but de Noailles finally submitted to the Pope in 1728.

NOEL, Baptist Wriothesley (1798–1873) A London Anglican priest with deep evangelical zeal, Noel helped found the Evangelical Alliance in Britain in 1846 and finally left the Church of England in 1848 to become a Baptist pastor. Noel twice headed the English Baptist Union and spurred social causes in London during the mid-nineteenth century.

NOETUS (2nd c.) Although facts about Noetus' life are obscure, Noetus, a teacher in Asia Minor (possibly at Smyrna), originated the theological viewpoint whose adherents were called Modalistic Monarchians. Noetus, surrounded by a heathen polytheism, tried to emphasize the unity of God the Father (hence the term "Monarchians"). At the same time, Noetus feared that the Logos Christianity then in vogue undermined that unity. He taught that the "Mode" of that unity was that in Christ was the Father Himself, and that the Father Himself was born and crucified. Teaching in Asia Minor from about 180 to about 200, Noetus had his ideas carried by such pupils as Praxeas, Epigonus and Cleomenes to Rome, where Bishop Zephyrinus of Rome was brought to Noetus' position.

NOGARET, Guillaume de (1265[?]–1313) A tough-minded tool of King Philip IV of France during the French power struggles with Pope Boniface VIII, de Nogaret humiliated Boniface by forcibly preventing him from sending a bull to curb Philip's authority in France. Later, in 1305, de Nogaret, a master politician, contrived to have a pliable French cleric, Clement V, elected pope, starting the Avignon papacy to end Rome's domination of French affairs. Knowing Philip's desire to get his hands on Knights Templar wealth, de Nogaret displayed great ingenuity to discredit the Order, framing leaders such as de Molay of immorality and heresy, to give Philip a pretext curbing Templar powers and seizing the Order's property.

NORBERT (1085–1134) An ascetic French churchman who founded the Premonstratensian Order near Laon, Norbert subsequently became Archbishop of Magdeburg, 1126. His order emphasized penitence and preaching. Norbert was canonized in 1582.

NOTKER ("The Thicklipped" or "*Labeo*") (950[?]–1022) This extraordinarily learned monk at St. Gall in Switzerland translated many Latin classics into Old High German, enhancing the development of German literature and language. Notker, among his several nicknames, was also called "*Teutonicus*" or "The German," hinting that his origins were in Germany.

NOVATIAN ([?]–258[?]) The second antipope, Novatian, a Roman theologian converted to Christianity from Stoicism after a near-fatal illness, caused a split

in the Church over whether or not to readmit church members who had lapsed during Decius' persecution from 249 to 251. Novatian took a hard, uncompromising line, maintaining that apostates had no place in the Christian fold, and excoriated Pope Cornelius for being too lenient. Bitter feelings followed, and Novatian rallied other rigorous dissenters and had himself elected as a rival pope. Novatian not only excluded the lapsed but also all others who had been known to sin, according to his definition.

Although Novatian died during the Valerian persecution (253 to 260), his super-pious Novatian followers held out and, in spite of repeated condemnation by popes and councils, lingered as a separate sect as late as the 7th century.

Novatian, an able theologian and thinker who did the first great theological writing in Latin, wrote the widely read treatise on the Trinity *De Trinitate*, and gave the Latin Church standing in the eyes of the Eastern Church for the first time.

NOVATUS (3rd c.) Lenient presbyter at Carthage in North Africa, Novatus grew irate when Cyprian was elected Bishop of Carthage because he regarded Cyprian as too severe on those who had lapsed from the Church during persecutions. Novatus and an associate, Felicissimus, formed a schismatic group in 250, welcoming any and all who had fallen away from the faith without asking any questions or making any demands.

Although excommunicated in 251 for holding such lax views, Novatus reportedly later joined the ultra-strict Novatian sect, reversing his stand completely.

NOYES, John Humphrey (1811–1886) Erratic, eccentric cult leader, Noyes announced in 1834 that he had achieved a state of sinless perfection. He was promptly fired from his teaching post at Yale. In 1839, proclaiming that Christ's Second Coming had occurred in A.D. 70, and that the faithful had to live in a perfectionist communal gathering, Noyes founded a group calling itself the Bible Communists. Noyes and his Bible Communists finally located near Putney, Vermont.

Noyes then shocked sensibilities by introducing the notion that wives in the community as well as all other items were to be held in common. Although arrested for adultery, Noyes skipped bail and promptly opened a new community near Oneida, New York. Despite opposition and harassment, Noyes and his community continued their practices of free love and communal living for thirty years. Noyes, however, grew increasingly unpopular within his "religious" community, and fled to Canada in 1879 to escape arrest warrants and law suits.

O

OBERLIN, Jean Frederic (1740–1826)
A self-sacrificing Alsatian Protestant pastor who labored nearly fifty years in a backward valley, Ban-de-la-Roche, in France, Oberlin showed both competence and compassion in his long ministry. He organized a savings and loan program, started a cotton industry, introduced modern farming, helped improve the roads and opened orphanages as well as preached three sermons monthly in French and one in German. Oberlin was posthumously honored by having the distinguished college in Ohio named for him in 1833.

OCCAM, William of (also Ockham) (1285[?]–1349[?]) Earnest English Franciscan monastic and competent Oxford scholar, Occam is referred to as the last great Medieval philosopher. Occam, a pupil of the great scholar Duns Scotus, divorced philosophy from theology even more than his teacher, insisting that there is much in theology which is philosophically improbable, but which must be accepted on the authority of the Church.

Caught in the intense arguments within the Franciscan Order over whether the poverty of Christ and the Apostles was complete, Occam sided with the strict party. When Pope John XXII intervened and ruled in favor of the laxer view of poverty for the Franciscans, Occam found himself imprisoned from 1322 to 1328.

Escaping from prison, Occam took refuge with Emperor Louis of Bavaria at Pisa, then at odds with the papacy. Occam stoutly defended the independence of the state from Church control for the rest of his life.

OCHINO, Bernardino (1487–1564)
An unstable Italian reformer whose startling views, such as advocating polygamy, made him a fugitive most of his life, Ochino began his career as a Franciscan monk before switching to the Capuchins. He had a flair for scholarship and leadership, became head of the order in 1538, but began having misgivings about the efficacy of works to achieve salvation. Called before the Inquisitor in 1542, Ochino fled to Calvin's Geneva where he lived contentedly for two years before accepting a pastorate at Augsburg. Wars and civil turmoil forced Ochino to skip from country to country for safety during most of the rest of his life. Hounded out of Switzerland after he began defending plural marriages and other heretical ideas, Ochino tried to settle in Poland, was uprooted because of his heresies and died in Moravia.

OCKHAM See OCCAM.

O'CLERY, Michael (1575–1643)
Irish Franciscan monk and literary genius, O'Clery was one of the four masters who wrote *The Annals of the Kingdom of Ireland by the Four Masters*, a magnificent and comprehensive sweep of Church history, beginning with the Flood and continuing down to 1616.

OCTAVIAN See JOHN XIII, Pope.

ODILO, Abbot of Cluny (994–1048)
Fifth abbot of the great monastery at

Cluny, Odilo advanced the centralized control of other monasteries founded or reformed by Cluny, bringing them under the complete supervision of the Abbot of Cluny. Odilo appointed the heads of the other "congregations" or houses, holding them responsible to him personally and making Cluny in effect a separate order rivalling the Dominicans or other monastic groups.

ODO, Abbot of Cluny (927–942) Adroit administrator of the great monastery at Cluny, Odo made Cluny so outstanding that numerous other houses asked to accept Cluny's rules and become satellites. Odo eventually supervised a collection of sixty-five "congregations" or houses obedient to the Cluny discipline.

ODORIC (1286[?]–1331) A Franciscan monk who served as a missionary in Asia from 1316 to 1329, Odoric traveled extensively through China, penetrating as far north as Peking and returning home via Tibet. Odoric, although regarded with indifference by his fellow Franciscans, was treated as something of a popular hero among the laity when he returned, and was beatified in 1755.

OECOLAMPADIUS, Johann (1482–1531) A capable German scholar and reformer he argued for the "Memorial" view of the Lord's Supper during the heated debates over the Sacrament in Lutheranism. Oecolampadius, born Hussgen or Heussgen, left St. Bridget's monastery at Altemünster near Augsburg after reading Luther's material. He joined the Reformation cause at Basel, where his vigorous preaching and writing quickly singled him out as a champion in the controversies. Oecolampadius served at Basel, Baden, Berne and Ulm as pastor and teacher.

Siding with Zwingli during the Lord's Supper debates, Oecolampadius differed with Luther. In an age when tempers and tensions were often in evidence, he was respected by everyone for his charity and cheerfulness.

A capable scholar, Oecolampadius in 1518 aided Erasmus to put together a good text of the Greek New Testament.

OENGUS (8th–9th c.) An Irish monk at Clon Enagh in Leix and later a student at Tallaght near Dublin, Oengus "the Culdee" was closely connected with the reform movement among Irish monastics known as "Fellows of God." About 800, Oengus assembled his "calendar" in Irish, the *Felire,* a type of prayer book listing names and biographical material for Irish and foreign-born saints under each day of the year. This devotional piece came to have an important place in early Irish liturgy.

OLAF I, King of Norway (969[?]–1000) Converted to Christianity in 993 during a sojourn in the British Isles before seizing the Norwegian throne, Olaf I married Gyda, a Christian Irish princess, then returned to Norway in 995 to push out Earl Haakon, the pagan ruler. Olaf I zealously introduced the Christian faith, often forcing reluctant subjects to be baptized. An ambitious monarch who projected a great pan-Scandinavian empire, Olaf I was drowned during a sea battle with the joint forces of the Danes and Swedes in 1000.

OLAF II, King of Norway and Saint (995–1030) Patron saint of Norway and idealized popular hero in Norwegian history, Olaf II returned to his native land after service with English King Ethelred's troops to repel the Danes. Olaf, becoming King, continued the aggressive proselyting program initiated by his father, Olaf I.

In 1028 when Canute of Denmark attacked, Olaf II was forced to flee and, during an attempt to regain his throne two years later, was killed in battle. A posthumous hero, Olaf II came to symbolize Norwegian independence. He was canonized in 1164.

OLAF Sköttkonung, King of Sweden (995[?]–1024[?]) Baptized a Christian in 1008, King Olaf Sköttkonung of Sweden established the Church in his kingdom. A tolerant ruler, Olaf of Sweden encouraged the spread of the faith without resorting to threats or cruelty to force his subjects to convert. Wary of the powerful Norwegian kingdom to the west, Olaf of Sweden joined with the Danes to smash Norway in 1000.

OLDCASTLE, Sir John (1378[?]–1417) A leading Englishman belonging to the Establishment who threw in his lot with the Lollards, pairs of lay preachers sent by John Wycliffe to live in apostolic poverty while preaching reform, Oldcastle was the most prestigious martyr during the grim repressions of the Lollard movement. Oldcastle held a series of prominent posts in the English government and enjoyed deep respect for his high principles. A Lollard from 1410, Oldcastle, as Lord Cobham, became the leader of the devout band. Accused of heresy in 1413, with the permission of King Henry V (who agreed to stamp out the Lollards in return for Church support), Oldcastle was thrown into the Tower. He escaped and, driven into rebellion, was finally recaptured, hanged and burned as a traitor and heretic.

This stern and upright Christian somehow became transformed by Shakespeare into the character of Falstaff.

OLDENBARNEVELDT, Johann van (1547–1619) A resolute Dutch states-man who sided with the Arminian-leaning Remonstrants during the super-heated struggles within Dutch Protestantism in the early 16th century, he earlier rallied fellow Dutchmen to throw off the Spanish yoke and support Prince Maurice of Orange. Oldenbarneveldt, however, later broke with Maurice. When Oldenbarneveldt joined the moderate Calvinist group, the Remonstrants, Maurice supported the rigid Calvinist Counter-Remonstrants. When Oldenbarneveldt felt that he had to set up his own private army in the province of Holland, the Remonstrant stronghold, he was attacked, captured, condemned in a rigged trial and executed.

OLEVIANUS, Kaspar (1536–1587) A devout German reformer with a flair for writing, organizing and administering, Olevianus brought the Presbyterian form of church government to the Reformed Church in the Palatinate and in 1562 worked with Ursinus to prepare the Heidelberg Catechism. Olevianus, an exceptionally gifted Calvinistic theologian, and Ursinus wrote one of the ablest summaries of the Calvinist position and one of the most Christ-centered, personal expressions of Christian experience of any of the creeds produced during the Reformation.

Olevianus also originated the idea of the "covenant of grace" in theological thinking, the doctrine that God's "covenant of works" having failed, God offered a new covenant based on love through Christ.

Like Luther and Calvin and other reformers, Olevianus originally studied law but switched to theology, and used his training to prepare tidy, carefully reasoned materials for the Church.

OLGA, Queen of Russia ([?]–969) A peasant who became a princess by marrying Prince Igor, and became queen after Igor's sudden death in 945, Olga ruled Russia until her son came of age in 955. In 957 she went to Constantinople to be baptized and took the name Helena. On her return to Russia she worked so tirelessly to promote the Christian faith that she was canonized.

ORIGEN (185[?]–254[?]) Pious, popular and persuasive, Origen stands out as one of the great figures of the ancient Church. He was raised by devout Christian parents, and, after the death of his father during a persecution, stepped in as leader of a group of catechumens. With the approval of Demetrius, Bishop of Alexandria, Origen, although only eighteen, did spectacularly well as a teacher. In misguided obedience to Matthew 19:12, Origen even emasculated himself, and later regretted the act.

Origen, still a layman, made a trip to Greece and Palestine about 227 to 230. He was ordained a presbyter by a group of bishops at Caesarea in order to permit him to preach. Origen's ordination infuriated the testy Demetrius, bishop of Origen's home city, who excommunicated Origen and banned him from preaching. Origen, however, found wide support throughout the East, although an ugly Church squabble erupted over Origen's ordination.

Origen stayed at Caesarea, teaching and writing and making occasional journeys. He wrote prolifically. His *"De Principiis"* systematically laid out Christian doctrine in terms of Hellenic thinking, and set the pattern for most subsequent theological thought in the East for many years. *Against Celsus* written between 246 and 248 was the ablest defense of Christianity against the accusations of a pagan thinker. Origen produced a stream of sermons and commentaries although he was frequently guilty of allegorizing Scripture.

He was seized with hundreds of other Christians during the Decian persecution, imprisoned and severely tortured. He died from the effects of the experience shortly afterward.

OSIANDER, Andreas (1498–1552) The first scholar to publish a harmony of the Gospels (1537) Osiander was a Lutheran who preached at Nuremberg. He refused to support the Augsburg Interim, was fired and moved to Königsburg, where he continued sparring with other Lutheran leaders.

Osiander's insistence that the sinner receives actual righteousness from the in-dwelling Christ and not merely the declaration of righteousness seemed to most others to do away with the place of showing any evidence of salvation, and he was opposed by many.

OSSIG von Schwenckfeld See SCHWENCKFELD.

OSWALD of Northumbria, King and Saint (605[?]–642) Converted to Christianity on the Isle of Iona where he had taken refuge during civil upheaval, Oswald established himself as King of Northumbria in what is now northern England and southern Scotland in 634. He enthusiastically introduced Christianity to his realm and begged Iona to send him a bishop. When Iona sent him the famous Aidan, Oswald installed Aidan at Lindisfarne, and zealously backed Aidan's endeavors. Oswald successfully spread both the Church and his borders from the Midlands to the Lowlands.

OSWALD of Worcester, Archbishop and Saint ([?]–992) A nephew of both the Archbishop of Canterbury and the Archbishop of York, Oswald founded many monasteries in England and labored to upgrade the moral tone among clergy. Oswald, an earnest and ascetic churchman, died while washing the feet of the poor. He was later canonized.

OSWY, King (612[?]–670) An early British King, Oswy summoned the synod at Whitby to resolve the conflict between the ancient Celtic Church and the newer Roman Christianity over the authority of the pope.

The Romanists, ascribing an authority to the pope which the Celtic Christians were not prepared to grant, insisted that all practices such as dates for Easter, types of tonsure (how the monks cut their hair) and form of administration conform wtih Rome's. Oswy's Synod in 664 decided in favor of Rome.

OTTERBEIN, Philip William (1726–1813) Co-founder of the United Brethren Church, Otterbein, born in Germany, arrived in America as a German Reformed missionary in 1752. He served at Lancaster, Pa. where he went through a conversion experience which he described as a "change of heart." Fervently evangelical from then on, Otterbein worked closely with like-minded pastors from among the Methodists and Mennonites to conduct open-air meetings and prayer services.

Otterbein and Martin Boehm, a neighboring Mennonite pastor, became particularly closely associated, joining to make lengthy trips throughout the German-speaking settlements to hold worship. The two friends finally shook hands after prayer together one day in 1789, declaring that in Christ they truly were United Brethren.

With six lay evangelists, Otterbein and Boehm considered themselves a new group. The United Brethren held their first conference in 1800, electing Otterbein and Boehm the first Bishops.

OTTO I, Emperor (912–973) The greatest military and political figure in Europe in his day, Otto I unified the feuding German duchies, shoved out the invading Magyars and Slavs, saved Italy from the tyranny of Berengar II, and got himself crowned with the title Emperor of the Holy Roman Empire by Pope John XII. When John refused to serve Otto's ends and internal dissension within the Church threatened to ruin the papacy, however, Otto installed his own hand-picked choice, Leo VIII, as pope, taking over the papacy as a German province. When a flurry of revolts and plots to oust Leo followed, Otto harshly put down the rebellious parties and restored Leo. Otto probably saved the papacy but set the bad precedent of causing the Church to be subservient to the emperor.

OTTO II, Emperor (955–983) A son of Otto I, Otto II followed the same policies toward the Church, but lacked the firm touch of his gifted father.

OTTO III, Emperor (980–1002) The last of the Saxon line, Otto III subdued the troublesome Roman nobles who tried to control the papacy. Otto III installed his cousin Bruno in the papal chair as Pope Gregory V, the first German pope. After Gregory's death, Otto III selected the learned Silvester II, the first French pope.

OTTO, Rudolph (1869–1937) A German Lutheran thinker who taught at Gottingen, Breslau, and for the last twenty years of his life at Marburg, Otto found his interests shifting from philosophy and theology to the history and psychology of religion. His monumental *Idea of the Holy,* published in 1917 and translated into a dozen languages, presented a penetrating psychological analysis of human religious experience and awareness of the divine. Otto, widely quoted and discussed by subsequent 20th century philosophers, attempted to have liberal Protestantism recover its sense of the otherness of God.

P

PACHOMIUS (292[?]–346[?]) An early Egyptian Christian, Pachomius founded the first Christian monastic community in Egypt. Pachomius, raised a pagan, was so touched by the kindness of Christians while serving as a soldier at Thebes that he was baptized after serving in the army. He joined the hermit, Palaemon, for a time, but about 318, in response to a vision, Pachomius gathered other monks into an organized community, the first in the history of the Church. (Previously, the pattern of monasticism had been for each individual monk to live separately.) Pachomius located his monastery Tabennisi on the Nile near Dendara and drew up a set of written regulations for the community. By the time of Pachomius death, the order had spread to include nine monasteries and two convents.

PAGE, Kirby (1890–1957) American Disciples of Christ minister with a passion for pacificism and social reform, Page left the pastorate to work for the Y.M.C.A. in France during World War I. His experiences in France made him an indefatigable worker for peace in the period between the two Wars. He travelled and lectured widely for the American Friends Service Committee and the Fellowship for Reconciliation, and wrote nearly a dozen books promoting pacificism.

PAINE, Thomas (1737–1809) The outspoken English-born radical political and religious thinker of the late 18th century, Paine came to America in 1774 after meeting Ben Franklin in London. Paine published *Common Sense* in 1776, the first of a series of fiery political polemics which steeled the colonies to continue the struggle for independence. Although acclaimed in the new republic, Paine moved to France in 1792 to participate in its political struggles. After writing the influential *Rights of Man,* Paine wrote the controversial *Age of Reason,* completing the first part in 1794, the second in 1795, and the final section in 1807. *Age of Reason* offended many, losing Paine much of his support in America. Although not espousing atheism as popularly supposed, Paine's *Age of Reason* defended the deistic position. Freethinker Paine is recognized as one who helped open the way for Biblical criticism.

PALEY, William (1743–1805) A keen 18th century mind who tried to prove the existence of God by appealing to arguments from design, Paley wrote the widely-read (fifteen editions) *Principles of Moral and Political Philosophy* in 1785, *View of the Evidences of Christianity* in 1794 and *Natural Theology* in 1802. Paley introduced the idea of a watch implying a watchmaker, and the human body implying a Designer. Paley's popular mechanical explanations were largely demolished by Darwinian theories in the 18th century.

PALLADIUS (368–431) A desert monastic who was made bishop of Bithynia by John of Chrysostom, the great Patriarch of Constantinople during the political tumult in the Eastern Empire, Palladius suffered imprisonment twice for supporting John. Palladius was finally banished to Ancyra in Upper Egypt, where he wrote the history and biographies of ancient monastics.

PALMER, William (1803–1885) A high church Anglican in the 19th century, Palmer took an active part in the Oxford Movement with Newman, Pusey, Keble, Rose and other sensitive young Englishmen who came under the influence of Oxford divinity professor, Charles Lloyd. Palmer, emphasizing apostolic succession, a return to a celibate clergy, and confession, lamented that the English Church had dropped these practices at the time of the Reformation.

PAMPHILIS of Alexandria ([?]–309) An outstanding Christian scholar who amassed one of the finest libraries in the 4th century and enjoyed an excellent reputation as a teacher at Caesarea and Alexandria, Pamphilis numbered the historian Eusebius among his distinguished pupils. Pamphilis was imprisoned and tortured in 308 for refusing to sacrifice to pagan deities, and beheaded the following year.

PAPHNUTIUS ([?]–350 or 360[?]) An early desert hermit, Paphnutius was a disciple of St. Anthony, the monastic, and suffered mutilation during Emperor Maximinius' persecution. Paphnutius won wide respect for his unswerving commitment under incredible stress. Later, at the Council of Nicea, Paphnutius opposed the Arians and urged that clergy be permitted to keep their wives if married before ordination.

PAPIAS ([?]–120[?]) One of the earliest writers in the Church, Papias was the author of the now-lost *Exposition of the Lord's Oracles*, which is believed to have had five volumes. Fragments of Papias' works are preserved in the Christian historian Eusebius' writings, hinting that Papias' writings contained numerous legends about Jesus' career and many of the oral tradtions about Jesus' life. Papias, a fervent pre-millenarian, helped fan the hopes of a speedy Second Coming of Christ through the early centuries. Little else is known of Papias, although Irenaeus states that Papias was a friend of Polycarp at Smyrna, and Eusebius maintains Papias served as bishop of Hierapolis in Phrygia. A legend, usually rejected as being without any factual basis, states that Papias died a martyr with Polycarp.

PARKER, Joseph (1830–1902) English Congregational preacher-orator, Parker became pastor of the Poultry Chapel, London, in 1869 which grew to become the world-renowned City Temple in 1874. Parker traveled widely on lecture tours, headed the Congregational Union of England and Wales twice, and wrote extensively, including the twenty-five volume *Peoples' Bible*.

PARKER, Matthew (1504–1575) The second Protestant Archbishop of Canterbury, succeeding Thomas Cranmer, Matthew Parker combined sense, scholarship and spirituality to a degree which won him the respect nearly of all Englishmen. Parker, as chaplain to Anne Boleyn, was so trusted by the doomed queen that she left her young daughter, the future Elizabeth, to his keeping. Parker was also so respected by Henry VIII that he was made royal chaplain and given influential posts in Henry's English Church. Parker was appointed Archbishop of Canterbury in 1559 by Elizabeth. The doughty prelate wrote competent Bible commentaries and edited a new psalter to counterbalance Puritan zealots.

PARKER, Theodore (1810–1860) An American Unitarian whose extreme liberal views even at the time of his ordination earned him the title, "the infidel," Parker preached his bombshell sermon in 1841 called "The Transient and the Permanent in Christianity." Parker's sermon, denying the authority of the Scriptures and the divinity of Christ, caused the doors of nearly all church bodies to be slammed on him, including the Unitarians. In spite of the chilly reception among organized Christian bodies, Parker as a semi-independent preacher went to Boston's Twenty-eighth Congregational Society in 1846, and filled halls to capacity for many years. A spirited defender of most reform movements and humanitarian causes, Parker actively promoted the abolitionist cause before the Civil War.

PARKHURST, Charles Henry (1842–1933) An American Presbyterian pastor, Parkhurst served at New York city's Madison Square and First Presbyterian Churches for many years. His outspoken preaching against the corruption in City Hall touched off the Lexow investigation, which uncovered evidence of collusion between the police and crime rings in New York City.

PARRIS, Samuel (1653–1720) The superstitious, hysteria-causing, English-born cleric at Salem, Massachusetts, Parris touched off the disgraceful episode in colonial history known as the Salem Witch Hunts. Parris, in 1692, took seriously the accusations of a few neighborhood busybodies that his West Indian slave girl Tituba had an "evil hand" which caused the illnesses of his daughter and niece. Parris wrenched a "confession" from the terrified Tituba and ignited hysteria in Salem which eventually resulted in twenty people executed and fifty others horribly tortured in attempts to extract confessions. Parris personally served as prosecutor

in many instances, introducing what was called "spectral evidence." He was finally forced to resign from the ministry, and in 1696 was thrown out of Salem.

PARSONS, Robert (also **Persons**) (1546–1610) Tireless English Jesuit, Parsons left a promising career at Oxford's Balliol College to journey to the continent to be baptized as a Roman Catholic in 1575 and then to be ordained a priest in 1578. Parsons and a fellow-Jesuit, Edmund Campion, returned in disguise to Elizabethan England to carry out an undercover ministry among those still secretly Roman Catholics. For two years, the pair held clandestine meetings and secret masses. Campion was arrested, but Parsons managed to escape alive in 1581. Remaining on the continent, Parsons tried to engineer a Roman Catholic takeover of England by urging Philip of Spain to send the ill-fated Armada in 1588. He founded several schools for English Catholic refugees.

PASCAL, Blaise (1623–1662) One of history's most brilliant minds, this Frenchman abandoned scientific research in his mid-twenties to commit himself to the Biblical God, "not the God of the philosophers and scientists." Pascal, a child mathematical genius at twelve and inventor of a computer at eighteen, pioneered in physics (particularly hydrostatics) and calculus, formulating the creda of modern physics that experiments are the true teachers which one must follow.

A sudden conversion convinced young Pascal that he could "live only for God and to have no other aim than Him." A second inner cataclysmic experience in 1654 led him to forsake his career in physics and mathematics entirely and withdraw to the Convent of

Port-Royal. He devoted himself to writing to refute the claims of the French atheists, producing the *Provincial Letters* in 1657 and a collection of essays published posthumously under the title *Pensées (Thoughts)*.

Pensées, intended as Pascal's polished masterpiece to win indifferent sophisticates to trust in God, emphasized that "the heart has its reasons which reason does not know" and that "it is the heart which experiences God, and not reason; that is what faith is: God felt by the heart, not reason." Pascal's epigrams and emotion have profoundly influenced thinkers in every part of the spectrum from mystics to existentialists.

Never robust, and debilitated by constant pain and illness from the time he was in his late teens, Pascal died at the age of thirty-nine.

PASCASIUS See **RADBERTUS.**

PASCHAL I, Pope ([?]–824) The Pope who received a document from Emperor Louis I confirming privileges and possessions of the Church, Paschal I ruled from 817 to 824. Paschal stood by Theodore the Studite in opposing Theodorius of Constantine during the controversy over images and icons in the Church, and later was canonized.

PASCHAL II, Pope ([?]–1118) Paschal II, caught in bitter wrangles with Emperors Henry IV and Henry V over whether the Emperor could name Church officials, proposed a face-saving compromise whereby highly-placed churchmen would relinquish their titles and holdings in return for the emperors' giving up their claims of the right to select prelates in their territories. Paschal's suggestion so enraged everyone that he was dumped into prison by Emperor Henry V. Paschal gave in and crowned Henry V Emperor, turning over to him the right of investitures.

Subsequent Synods at Rome and Vienna in 1112, however, excommunicated Henry and prohibited laymen to choose prelates.

Paschal occupied the chair from 1099 to 1118.

PASCHAL III, Counter-pope ([?]–1168) Successor to Antipope Victor IV, this Paschal claimed to be the real pope during the reign of Pope Alexander III. Paschal for a time managed to prevent Pope Alexander from coming to Rome. Under pressure from Frederick Barbarossa, Paschal III, a pawn of the Emperor, announced the canonization of Charlemagne—a claim, however, which was never supported by the Church.

PASSAGLIA, Carlo (1812–1887) An Italian Jesuit writer and thinker who left the Society in 1859 to take part in politics, Passaglia publicly questioned the supremacy of the pope on matters of temporal power and was finally urged to leave the Society of Jesus. He joined the Italian Nationalist movement and accepted a teaching post at the University of Turin. Later, Passaglia was elected a member of the first Italian Parliament, where he tried to organize a liberal Catholic party.

PATRICK (389[?]–461[?]) The legendary hero and celebrated patron saint of the Irish, Patrick actually was born either in Dumbarton, Scotland, or in Glamorganshire, Wales, or possibly near the Severn in England, but not in Ireland. His father, Calpurnius, was a deacon in the Church, his grandfather was a priest, and the family was devoutly Christian. Kidnapped by Irish pirates when he was about sixteen, Patrick was sold as a slave in Ireland and subjected to humiliating ill-treatment. Young Patrick, however, apparently remembered his Christian upbringing. He managed to escape to France by boat and finally made his way home to Britain.

In response to a vision, however, Patrick returned to Ireland to carry the Gospel to the wild, heathen Celtic tribes about 457. He was an energetic worker and expert organizer, planting over 200 congregations, and baptizing over 100,000 converts.

Patrick, however, had his critics in the Church and opposition among the Irish. His *Confession* is an attempt to clear himself of the charges that he was poorly educated and that he came to Ireland for personal gain. Patrick was actually turned down as a candidate for bishop of Ireland at first. (Earlier, in 431, the first Bishop of Ireland had been named.)

Patrick's vigorous personality and administrative gifts, however, brought him great prestige and ultimately the appointment as bishop. He introduced the diocesan episcopate to Ireland. Patrick spawned dozens of legends, leading some scholars to think that there might have been two Patricks who were so popular that all the stories in Irish folklore about early churchmen have clustered around "Patrick."

PATROCLUS ([?]–259[?]) A respected citizen and beloved churchman at Troyes in Gaul (now France), Patroclus staunchly stood by his commitment to Jesus Christ during Emperor Aurelian's persecution. Patroclus survived the attempt to execute him by drowning, and was finally beheaded after ghastly torture. He was made a saint in the Roman Catholic Church.

PAUL of the Cross (1694–1775) Founder of the Congregation of Discalced Clerks of the Most Holy Cross and Passion of our Lord Jesus Christ (usually known as the Passionists), Paul

was a fervent mystic and fearless missioner. He established his penitential community in 1720 after a long period of rigorous self-denial and meditation. Greatly revered for his holiness, Paul was canonized in 1867.

PAUL the First Hermit See **PAUL of Thebes.**

PAUL I, Pope ([?]–767) Successor to his brother, Pope Stephen III, Pope Paul I with the help of Pepin, King of the Franks, consolidated papal power over Central Italy. Paul I welcomed the monks who were run out of the Eastern Church during the icons-images controversy during his reign from 757 to 767 and won a reputation for personal kindness. He was later canonized.

PAUL II, Pope (1417–1471) The nephew of Pope Eugene IV (who advanced him up the ladder to cardinal), Paul II tried unsuccessfully to line up a league of Christian powers to offset the possibility of a Turkish attack. Although as a cardinal he had signed a pact with other cardinals to curb powers of the pontiff, as pope, Paul II repudiated the pact and forced the cardinals to acquiesce to his will. He served from 1464 to 1471.

PAUL III, Pope (1468–1549) A tough-minded worldling, Paul III was the first Pope to appreciate the gravity of the situation caused by the Protestant Reformation. Paul III permitted the Inquisition to handle Protestants in Italy, punished King Henry VIII of England by excommunication, and promulgated reform by calling a long-overdue Council which opened at Trent in 1545. During his office from 1534 to 1549, Paul III purchased manuscripts to improve the Vatican, patronized the arts (hiring Michaelangelo to grace the

Vatican with his great art) and promoted members of his own family to key posts in the Church.

PAUL IV, Pope (1476–1559) A member of the Caraffa family in Italy, Paul IV had previously won some sort of reputation as the barbarically brutal supervisor of the Inquisition before his elevation as Pope in 1555. Paul's somber qualities made him one of the least-likeable pontiffs. A martinet, he founded the *Index Librorum Prohibetorum*, the "Index" listing books forbidden to Roman Catholics. Under Paul IV, the Counter-reformation reached its greatest strength.

PAUL V, Pope (1552–1621) Although personally gentle, Paul V's reign from 1605 to 1621 was marred by nepotism. In 1616, Paul V ordered the scientist Galileo not to "Hold, teach or defend" the then-heretical idea that the earth moves around the sun, exacerbating the hostility of many scientists toward the Church.

PAUL of Samosata ([?]–272) Helped by a good income and good connections after serving in a high government post under Queen Zenobia of Palmyra in Syria, Paul of Samosata was the politically powerful and theologically gifted bishop of Antioch from about 260 to 272. Paul of Samosata was the most outspoken advocate of the heresy known as Dynamic Monarchianism, the teaching which tried to emphasize the unity of God's nature, but which implied that Jesus' divinity was merely delegated by the Father. Between 264 and 269, three Synods debated Paul's views, and finally concluded that Jesus was not raised to divine status by God. Paul was astute and strong enough to cling to his position at Antioch until he was ousted when Emperor Aurelian toppled Queen Zenobia in 272.

PAUL of Thebes (234[?]–341[?]) Traditionally known as the first Christian hermit, Paul fled from Emperor Decius' persecution and subsisted in the desolate fastnesses of Upper Egypt for nearly a century. Legend has it that the great St. Anthony sought out Paul in his solitude, and later buried the saint in Athanasius' cloak.

PAUL of Venice See SARPI, Paolo.

PAUL, Vincent de See VINCENT de Paul.

PAULINUS of Nola (353–431) A French-born Roman consul who after the death of his son turned his back on the glitter of wealth and position to become a monk, Paulinus settled at Nola, Italy, near the tomb of St. Felix, on whose feast day Paulinus decided to become a monastic. Paulinus won wide approval for his asceticism and generosity to pilgrims and the poor. In 409, he was elected bishop of Nola, and used his wealth to help the entire area, even to repairing the viaduct bringing water to the town. He was later canonized.

PAULINUS of York ([?]–644) The first bishop of Northumbria and Archbishop of York, Paulinus was sent to ancient Britain by Pope Gregory I to work with Augustine, the missionary to Southern England. Paulinus, highly successful in working with early British chieftains, baptized King Edwin of Northumbria in 627, advancing the cause of the Roman Church in northern Britain.

PAULUS, Heinrich Eberhard Gottlob (1761–1851) Extreme rationalist theologian in the German universities of Jena from 1789 to 1811 and Heidelberg from 1811 to 1844, Paulus led the attack on anything smacking of the supernatural in the Bible or the career of Jesus. He published his *Life of Jesus* in 1828, in which he attempted to give plausible explanations for all miracles, even going so far as to insist that Jesus was not dead when removed from the cross and revived in the tomb. In the 19th century such ideas were widely accepted in many circles.

PAZMANY, Peter (1570–1637) A Hungarian archbishop and educator, Pazmany was influential in restoring the standing of the Roman Catholic Church in Hungary after the Reformation. Pazmany, born a Protestant, entered the Roman Catholic Church in his teens, joining the Jesuits, and rose to become Cardinal Primate of Hungary. He founded what became Trnava University in present Czechoslovakia, which later gave rise to the University of Budapest.

PELAGIUS ([?]–419[?]) A British monk who probably hailed from Wales, Pelagius arrived in Rome around 400, teaching the heretical doctrine which came to be associated with his name. Pelagianism, with its shallow, sunny view of human nature, in essence denies the need for divine grace. According to Pelagius, Adam as a mortal man would have died whether or not he had sinned. Any man if he merely tries hard enough, Pelagius insisted, could lead a sin-free life, and does not need God's intervention to save him. Sin, by Pelagius' standards, was merely a solitary act, and had nothing to do with one's nature.

Traveling to North Africa in an unsuccessful effort to call on Augustine, the great bishop of Hippo, Pelagius expounded his views to everyone who would listen.

Although Pelagius and Augustine never met, Augustine was aroused to object violently to Pelagius' teachings,

insisting that Adam's falling away has affected us all and that only God's act can save us. Pelagianism, as defended by such eloquent and persuasive spokesmen as Pelagius and his disciple Coelestius, was condemned by a series of Synods from 412 to 418.

In 418, Pelagius was banished from Rome, along with his followers. He is believed to have died before 420, probably in the East.

PELAGIUS I, Pope ([?]–561) Elected in 555 at the insistence of Emperor Justinian over the objections of many churchmen, Pelagius I spent an unhappy career as pontiff feuding with most of the bishops in the western Church. As Justinian's man, Pelagius I promoted the theological policy known as "The Three Chapters," in which Justinian had blasted the person and writings of Theodore of Mopsuestia, Theodore of Cyrus and Ibas of Edessa, and thereby undercut the Council of Chalcedon.

PELAGIUS II, Pope ([?]–590) Pope from 579 to 590.

PENN, William (1644–1718) Son of a famous British Admiral, Sir William Penn, young William upset his family and shook England's Establishment by leaning toward Quakerism as early as 1661 and joining the Friends by laying aside his sword in 1666. Penn quickly became one of the Quakerism's most effective and eloquent defenders. Determined to find freedom for the members of his sect, Penn first sent eight hundred Quaker emigrants to New Jersey in 1677–1678, then negotiated with King Charles II to secure a large grant of land in 1681 to settle a debt owed Penn's father by the crown.

Pennsylvania ("Penn's woods") quickly attracted hundreds of persecuted Quakers. In 1682, Philadelphia was laid out, and Penn's experiment begun.

William Penn was one of the first to extend religious and political freedom to all comers.

PEPIN See **PIPPIN.**

PETER ABÉLARD See **ABÉLARD.**

PETER of Alcantara (1499–1562) A dour Spanish mystic and ascetic, Peter of Alcantara stressed the penitential side of St. Francis of Assisi's life, usually to the neglect of the more winsome qualities of the beloved saint. Peter of Alcantara's friars, whom he organized into a tautly-disciplined band which eventually came to be known as the Discalced or Alcantarine Friars Minor, won renown for their insistence on solitude and discomfort. Peter was canonized in 1669.

PETER of Alexandria ([?]–311) Head of the great catechetical school at Alexandria, Egypt, and respected for his knowledge of Scriptures, Peter became Patriarch of Alexandria in 300. He issued decrees to receive lapsed heretics back into the Church, excommunicated Bishop Miletus for stirring up schism, and stoutly opposed the heretical ideas of Origen and Arius. During Emperor Diocletian's terrible persecution, Peter fled to safety for a time, but returned to supervise his see, was seized and put to death.

PETER of Amiens See **PETER the Hermit.**

PETER d'Anghiera ([?]–1526) An influential Italian cleric stationed at the Spanish Court at the time of Ferdinand and Isabella's reign and Columbus' epochal voyages, Peter d'Anghiera in 1505 was appointed dean of the Cathedral at Granada. In 1516, he wrote the first account of the discovery of Amer-

ica. Peter d'Anghiera is sometimes known as "Peter Martyr," one of three called by this name in English.

PETER of Bruys ([?]–1140[?]) Probably from Bruis, France, and a pupil of the famous Abélard, Peter of Bruys tried to introduce reform into the Medieval Church, rejecting prayers for the dead, transubstantiation, most of the ceremonialism of the Church and even the use of buildings. Peter's stern simplicity and radical preaching in southern France in the early 12th century aroused immense controversy. After publicly burning crosses at St. Gilles, Peter was seized and burned by a mob about 1140.

His followers, calling themselves Petrobrusians after their iconoclastic leader, allied themselves for a time with the disciples of Henry of Lausanne, and were finally absorbed by the Waldensians in southern France and northern Italy.

PETER CANISIUS See **KANIS Peter.**

PETER of Castelnau ([?]–1208) A French-born Cistercian who was appointed Inquisitor of the hapless Albigensians in 1203 by Pope Innocent III, Peter was murdered at the instigation of Raymond III of Toulouse after brutally suppressing the "heretics."

PETER Chrysologus (400[?]–450[?]) Italian-born cleric who in 433 became bishop of Ravenna, the residence of the western Emperor, Peter Chrysologus (literally, the "golden orator") with the backing of Empress Regent Galla Placidia erected many church buildings. His reputation for eloquence and orthodoxy reached even to the East, where Eutyches, the Monophysite, appealed to Peter to intercede to have his condemnation by the pope annulled. Peter Chrysologus was honored posthumously by being canonized and later, 1729, declared a Doctor of the Church.

PETER CLAVER (1581–1654) A self-sacrificing Spanish Jesuit known as the "Apostle of the Negroes," Peter Claver (Pedro Claver) worked tirelessly for forty years among the suffering slaves in Colombia. He arrived at Cartagena, Colombia, in 1615 immediately after his ordination, and spent his entire career nursing, teaching, feeding and helping helpless blacks landed by the slavers to work the mines and plantations of South America. In spite of valiant efforts, Peter Claver was unable to end the traffic in human lives. His ministry was recognized, however, when he was canonized by the pope in 1888.

PETER DAMIAN See **DAMIANI, Pietro.**

PETER FABER, FAVRE See **LE FÈVRE, Pierre.**

PETER the Hermit (1050[?]–1115) Apparently originally a French soldier who tried to make a pilgrimage to the Holy Land but was prevented from reaching Jerusalem by the Moslems and brigands, Peter the Hermit is the man who reportedly first suggested the idea of a Crusade to capture the Holy Land to Pope Urban II, the father of the First Crusade. Peter, after the Council of Clermont, dressed as a hermit and rode a mule throughout northern Europe, arousing zeal for the projected Crusade. When the undisciplined ill-equipped horde of thirty thousand set out, Peter marched at the head of the column. Peter, who was among the few who survived the grim journey, participated in the bloody orgy in 1099 when Jerusalem was captured, and preached on the Mount of Olives. Returning to France, he organized a monastic com-

munity at Neufmontier, where he served as abbot until his death.

PETER LOMBARD See **LOMBARD, Peter.**

PETER MARTYR Three churchmen are sometimes referred to as "Peter Martyr" in English. They are:

(1) **PETER MARTYR,** also known as "Peter of Verona" See **PETER of Verona.**
(2) **PETER MARTYR,** also known as "Peter of d'Anghiera" See **PETER d'Anghiera.**
(3) **PETER MARTYR,** also known as "Peter, Martire Vermigli" See **PETER, Martire Vermigli.**

PETER, Martire Vermigli (1500–1562) An Italian Augustinian who left the Roman Catholic Church after reading Luther and Zwingli, Peter traveled to Zurich to join the Reformation in 1542, then, at the invitation of Archbishop Cranmer, emigrated to England in 1547. Peter served as a professor of theology at Oxford, where he exercised considerable influence on the English Reformation. Forced out by rabid Catholic Queen Mary in 1553, Peter fled to Zurich to teach. He participated in the fruitless talks between Protestants and Roman Catholics at Poissy, France in 1561. He is one of several variously called Peter "the Martyr."

PETER of Montboissier (1092[?]–1156) A French Cistercian monk and later abbot of the great monastery of Cluny from 1121 for the following thirty-five years, Peter tightened the discipline in an order which had grown lax, dictating strict procedures but bringing new luster and power to Cluny. Peter, also known as "the Venerable," had a reputation for sagacity and scholarship, even making the only known translation of the Koran in the western world for many years. He vigorously opposed all non-Christian groups, including the Jews and Moslems, and fiercely denounced heretics in a series of tracts. After his death, Cluny's prestige declined, never to rise again to the heights it enjoyed under Peter.

PETER NOLASCO (1189[?]–1256) Founder of the Order of Our Lady of Ransome, Peter Nolasco, born of wealthy French nobility, spent most of his inheritance and energies ransoming Christians held as slaves in Spain by the Moors. His order raised funds and bought freedom for hundreds of captured Christians. Peter personally made two trips to Africa to bring back enslaved believers. He was canonized in 1628.

PETER des Roches ([?]–1238) Up to his bishop's hat in English politics during most of his career, Peter des Roches, bishop of Winchester, won a reputation as a doughty soldier and diplomat as well as prelate. He supported King John against the Magna Carta-minded barons, joined the Crusade to the Holy Land in 1227 and nimbly participated in the political games in Rome and England in the 13th century.

PETER the Venerable See **PETER of Montboissier.**

PETER of Verona (1206–1272) A fiery Italian Dominican who exhibited intense zeal in wiping out the heretics known as Catharists in Italy, this Peter Martyr came to head the Inquisition in Italy in the 13th century. His fanaticism aroused counter-fanaticism, and he was assassinated by a group of Catharists on the road to Milan in 1252. Canonized the following year and given the

sobriquet "Martyr," Peter became the patron saint of the Spanish Inquisition.

PETERSSON, Lars See **PETRI, Laurentius.**

PETERSSON, Olaf See **PETRI, Olaus.**

PETRARCH (1304–1374) The earliest Italian for whom the spirit of the Renaissance became a consuming passion, Petrarch, a learned and literate scholar-cleric, dominated the international literary scene for many years. Petrarch revived interest in Latin literature by prowling monastic libraries to seek ancient scripts, discovering several forgotten works by Cicero and Quintilian. Petrarch's graceful Italian verse and zest for learning excited other Italians to bring about the rebirth known as the Renaissance.

PETRI, Laurentius (1499–1573) A Carmelite monk who was studying with his brother, Olaus, at Wittenberg at the time Martin Luther was teaching there, Petri and his brother were won to the Reformation. Laurentius and Olaus Petri both returned to Sweden in 1518 and began a spectacular career in which they convinced most fellow Swedes to follow Lutheran doctrine. After serving as a theology professor at Upsala in 1531, Laurentius Petri became the first Lutheran Archbishop of Sweden. He wrote many translations of Psalms in the Swedish liturgy and helped his brother translate the Old Testament into Swedish.

PETRI, Olaus (1493–1552) One of the pair of brothers who brought the Reformation to Sweden, Olaus Petri, like his brother, Laurentius, was converted to Lutheran ideas while studying at Wittenberg, Germany, in 1517. After his return to Sweden, Olaus eventually was appointed chancellor to King Gustavus Vasa in 1531, where his overbearing attempts to promote the reformed cause finally led to his removal in 1539. In 1542, Olaus Petri became the first Lutheran pastor in Stockholm.

PFEFFERKORN, Johann (1469–1522) A convert to the Church from Judaism, Pfefferkorn sparked a controversy in Germany in ecclesiastical and academic circles by demanding suppression of all Hebrew literature as an affront against the Gospel. Pfefferkorn convinced Emperor Maximilian to issue an order confiscating Jewish books in 1509. A famous case resulted in the Church when the theologian John Reuchlin opposed the order, insisting that a knowledge of Hebrew was necessary and that discussion with the Jews was more useful than book burning. Pfefferkorn's narrowness caused the humanists and other advocates of the new learning to unite, so that they were ready to listen to Luther a few years later.

PFLEIDERER, Otto (1839–1908) German Protestant theological professor at the University of Jena from 1870 to 1875, and Berlin from 1875 to his death in 1908, Pfleiderer considerably influenced theological thinking by continuing the Hegelian metaphysics begun by the famous New Testament critic F. C. Baur.

PHILIP II, Augustus, King of France (1179–1223) A vain opportunist, Philip II decided to join King Richard the Lion-hearted of England and King Frederick Barbarossa on a campaign to wrest the control of the Holy Land from Moslem forces after the disastrous defeat of the Latin forces in 1187. King Philip II and the two other kings each led an elaborately equipped army on what came to be known as the Third Crusade (1189–1192). Philip, however, pouted and squabbled with the other leaders, particularly Richard of England after Frederick accidentally drowned en route. Although he reached the Holy Land, Philip quickly found excuses to return to France to look after his interests at home.

The Third Crusade collapsed, and Jerusalem remained in Moslem hands.

PHILIP IV, "the Fair," King of France (1285–1314) Pompously imperious, Philip IV, absolute ruler of a powerful France, entered into a long, disgusting power match with stubbornly ambitious Pope Boniface VIII over powers and prerogatives. Philip levied heavy taxes on his French clergy to raise money to fight his wars. Boniface threatened excommunication on anyone who taxed Church properties without papal permission. Philip retaliated by refusing to permit any Church money to leave France, and in 1301 arrested the pope's *nuncio*, charging him with treason. In 1302 he called the first assembly of the States-General in France. Boniface angrily issued his famous bull, *Unam Sanctan*, asserting papal supremacy over all civil powers. Philip sent a force which made the pope his prisoner, puncturing the pretentious claims of Boniface.

PHILIP, Landgrave of Hesse (1504–1567) The strong German prince who supported the Lutheran cause in 1524 in Germany, Philip bolstered the political strength of Lutheranism, organizing Lutheran powers to counteract the confederation of Catholic princes. Philip, remarkably progressive in many ways, called a synod to draw up plans for an annual representative-type synod, which, however, was rejected by Luther who had come to distrust democratic organization. In 1529, Philip, determined to unite the Protestant minority in Germany and Switzerland, called a colloquy at Marburg, bringing together the two main Reformed parties headed by Luther and Zwingli to harmonize their doctrinal differences.

In spite of Philip's prodding, however, the German Lutherans and the Swiss evangelicals remained divided. Philip's political genius, however, saved Protestantism in Germany; in 1531, he brought together fellow Lutheran princes at Schmalkalden to create the Schmalkaldic League, a powerful union of five princes and eleven cities.

Philip's bigamous marriage, however, in 1540, with the tacit approval of Luther and Melanchthon, scandalized Europe, weakened his position and brought disastrous division in the Schmalkaldic League.

PHILIP Neri See NERI, Philip.

PHILIP II, King of Spain (1527–1598) Married to Queen Mary of England in 1554 while he was still a prince, Philip left Mary and England in 1555, but as King of Spain from 1556 to 1598 constantly plotted against her successor, Queen Elizabeth. Philip II, ferociously anti-Protestant but politically cunning, headed a united Catholicism in Europe which made the period from 1559 (when the Treaty of Cateau-Cambresis forced France to relinquish leadership of Europe in favor of Spain) to 1588 (when the Spanish Armada was defeated) an era of extreme peril in the history of Protestantism. The inflexible Philip tried to impose his brand of religious and political conformity on the Netherlands, igniting a passionately dedicated Dutch independence movement led by Dutch Calvinists.

PHOTINUS See POTHINUS.

PHOTIUS (820[?]–891[?]) The outstanding scholar and writer of his age and related to the Emperor because of his descent from a noble family, Photius, although a layman, was elected Patriarch of Constantinople because he was the only candidate satisfactory to two feuding parties. One group of hold-outs, however, continued to back the deposed Patriarch, Ignatius, even managing to win the support of Pope Nicholas I, who summarily excommunicated Photius. Stung by the excommunication, Photius insisted that the Eastern Church was not bound to Rome, and chilled relations between the Eastern and Western Churches. A sudden shift in the political situation sent Photius into exile for several years, during which time a series of synods pronounced condemnation on Photius.

Photius, however, was eventually reinstated and cleared of the condemnations; Photius and Ignatius became reconciled, and Photius even opened communications with Rome. He sent missionaries to Bulgaria, Moravia and Russia, wrote extensively and ended the last traces of icon worship.

PICO della Mirandola Giovanni (1463–1494) An erudite scholar of Hebrew and the Cabala, Pico confidently offered to debate all-comers on any of nine hundred subjects or theses but was forbidden to do so by the disapproving pope. Pico was later investigated but cleared of heresy charges.

Deeply influenced by the Florentine preacher of reform, Savanarola, Pico planned to become a missionary preacher, but died suddenly at Florence at the age of thirty-one. His studies in Hebrew helped influence the Italian Renaissance.

PIPPIN the Short, King of Franks (741–768) Father of King Charlemagne, Pippin supported Boniface, the great missionary to the German tribes in baptizing German chieftains and tribes into the Christian faith. Pippin defended Pope Gregory III from the invading Lombards and was rewarded by being crowned King of France, starting the interplay between papacy and empire which composed so much of the history of the Middle Ages.

PIUS I, Pope (90[?]–157[?]) A murky figure in history, Pius I is alleged to have been a brother to the author of the non-canonical book, *Shepherd of Hermas,* and is referred to in the Muratorian fragment. Pius I has been a long-time saint in the Roman Catholic calendar.

PIUS II, Pope (1405–1464) Known for years as a worldly opportunist who shifted allegiances whenever it was expedient and who penned clever verses under the pen name Aeneas Sylvius, Pius II had a remarkable spiritual awakening in 1444. He was ordained in 1446, rose rapidly in the Church and was elected pope in 1458.

As pope, he retracted many opinions expressed during his earlier literary career, including his caustic comments on the Council of Basel and many frivolous literary pieces. A strong-willed pontiff, Pius forbade appeals of papal decisions to Church Councils, insisting in his decree *Execrabilis* in 1460 that a Pope's pronouncement is final.

An excellent poet and recognized literary figure throughout his life, Pius II was the only pope to write an autobiography. He tried to expell the Turks from Europe, and died at Ancona where he was assembling Christian troops for his campaign.

PIUS III, Pope (1439–1503) A nephew of Pope Pius II, Pius III although of exemplary character, had the misfortune of surviving only twenty-six days after elected pope in 1503.

PIUS IV, Pope (1499–1565) A welcome contrast to his predecessor, Paul IV, Pius IV extended amnesty to many indicted for heresy by Paul, limited the Inquisition, and freed many suspected of disloyalty to the Church (although he let the death sentence stand against Cardinal Carlo Caraffa and his brother). Pius IV reconvened the Council of Trent in 1562 and promulgated Trent's decrees by a papal bull in 1564. Anxious to prevent further deviations from the faith, Pius formulated what is known as the Creed of Pius IV, to which all ordained to any office in the Roman Church must subscribe.

Pius, a patron of the arts during his reign from 1559 to 1565, commissioned Palestrina to compose many of his greatest musical works and established the Vatican press to publish materials.

PIUS V, Pope (1504–1572) An austere ascetic who rejected any hints of luxury and levity, Pius V spent his energies as pope from 1566 to 1572 trying to stamp out any signs of deviation from Roman Catholic dogma anywhere in Europe. This testy pontiff excommunicated Queen Elizabeth of England, backed Mary Queen of Scots, supported the League opposing the Huguenots in France, urged suppression of all Dutch Protestants, and encouraged armed intervention against the Turks, resulting in the stunning naval victory at Lepanto in 1571.

Pius V also revised the missal and breviary in Roman worship. He frequently encountered resistance by adamantly reiterating the ancient papal claim of supremacy over all states and rulers, but was canonized later for his stand.

PIUS VI, Pope (1717–1799) Pius VI's twenty-four year reign (1775–1799) was packed with problems because he insisted on clinging to claims which the jealous 18th century kingdoms were trying to usurp for themselves. This autocratic pontiff failed utterly to understand the winds of democracy and egalitarianism which were beginning to shift in Europe. After the French Revolution, which Pius abhorred, he turned down the Civil Constitution of Clergy in France, causing thousands of clergy to be thrown out of France and stimulating the anti-clericalism which became part of the French ethos. Pius VI, finally humiliated by Napoleon, lost five papal states, enormous sums as indemnities, and numerous art treasures to France. In the ensuing civil disorder which broke out at Rome, Pius was carried off to France by Napoleon, who occupied the city to restore order. Pius died a captive.

This pope is also remembered as the pontiff who acceded to John Carroll's petition and removed American Catholics from the jurisdiction of an English vicar, establishing the first American see at Baltimore, where Carroll was appointed the first American bishop in 1789.

PIUS VII, Pope (1740–1823) Trying to alleviate the thorny relationship with France created by his stubborn predecessor, Pius VII signed a Concordat in 1801 with Napoleon. Pius, however, refused to recognize Joseph Bonaparte as ruler of Naples, and was carted off as a prisoner to France for five years by the exasperated Napoleon.

Pius VII, conservative to the core, lifted the ban against the Jesuits, condemned the efforts of all Bible Societies and reorganized the Congregation of the Propaganda. During his reign from 1800 to 1823, such well-known American dioceses as New York, Boston, Philadelphia, Cincinnati and Richmond were organized.

PIUS VIII, Pope (1761–1830) Pontiff less than two years, 1829 to 1830, Pius VIII is remembered as the author of the letter requiring those seeking blessing on their marriages to promise to educate their children as Roman Catholics.

PIUS IX, Pope (1792–1878) The strong-willed but insensitive pope who centralized the government of the Roman Catholic Church and demanded uncompromising obedience to the person of the pope, Pius IX sharply changed the character of the Roman Catholic Church in the 19th century, creating the modern papacy. Astonishingly inept at managing the papal states, especially during the revolutions convulsing Italy in 1848, Pius' bungling produced such chaos that he finally ended as virtually a prisoner at the Vatican after French-Austrian military and diplomatic machinations.

Pius' reign of thirty-two years, 1846 to 1878, the longest of any pope in history, was also notable as a reactionary period in Catholic history. Pius IX tried to strengthen the prerogatives of the papacy with a series of pronouncements which showed few insights into modern thinking. In 1854, accenting the trend away from any intellectualism toward an introspective devotionalism, Pius IX announced the dogma of the Immaculate Conception, declaring the Virgin Mary free from all taint of original sin from the moment of her conception.

Concentrating authority in the person of the pope, and extinguishing hopes among liberal Catholics for greater freedom of inquiry and expression, in 1864 Pius IX issued *Quanta Cura*, with the accompanying *Syllabus of Errors*, totaling eighty. A few years earlier, in 1861, Pius had issued his encyclical *Jamdudum Cerninius*, denouncing all modern political doctrines, pitting the Roman

Church against all dominant political forces and estranging many intelligentsia.

In 1870, in spite of strong opposition by French, German and American bishops, Pius IX announced the dogma of Papal Infallibility, declaring the Pope's *ex cathedra* pronouncements to have divine authority. This announcement marked the triumph of the ultramontane party within the Roman communion, and the beginning of the modern Roman Catholic papacy.

Pius IX canonized more as saints than any previous pope.

PIUS X, Pope (1835–1914) A staunch traditionalist, Pius X condemned any attempts to liberalize or introduce change in the Roman Catholic Church as "Modernism." Pius issued decrees regarding daily communion by the laity (1905) and first communion by children (1910). In 1954, he was canonized.

PIUS XI, Pope (1857–1939) Although he signed the Lateran Treaty with Mussolini in 1929, Pius XI later boldly opposed the pagan aspects of Mussolini's, Hitler's and Franco's totalitarian regimes. Pius XI reached an agreement with the Mexican government to end the persecution of priests in Mexico.

PIUS XII, Pope (1876–1958) A gentle scholar by training and temperament, Pius XII served during the holocaust of World War II, probably the most trying time in papal history since the struggles with Napoleon. Pius heroically organized relief efforts and attempted to persuade the belligerents to curtail the slaughter.

In the post-war "Cold War" era, Pius XII firmly stood against Communism, particularly when the Hungarian government brought Cardinal Mindszenty to trial in 1949.

Pius in 1950 issued an encyclical deploring new "inhuman weapons" of war and proclaimed the dogma of the corporal assumption of the Virgin Mary. A devoted adherent to the cult of Mary, Pius specified 1954 as a Marian Year, commemorating the one hundredth anniversary of the dogma of the Immaculate Conception.

PLACIDUS ([?]–550[?]) Son of a Roman patrician named Tertellus, Placidus was miraculously saved from drowning as a boy and sent to live at the famous monastery of Monte Cassino with St. Benedict. Placidus allegedly founded the monastery of St. John at Messina, Sicily, where, according to some legends, he, his two brothers and a sister and thirty-three others were martyred by pirates. He was later declared a saint.

PLUTCHAU, Heinrich (1678–1747) One of the students of the great German Lutheran Pietist August Hermann Francke at Halle, Plutchau was sent to Tranquebar, India, in 1705 by King Frederick IV of Denmark. Plutchau and Ziegenbalg, also from Halle, were two of the earliest Protestant missionaries to India. They translated Lutheran hymns, prayers and catechism into Tamil and Portuguese, and attracted converts from Hinduism and Roman Catholicism.

POLE, Reginald (1500–1558) A loyal but reform-minded Roman Catholic from England, Pole, refusing to look favorably on King Henry VIII's divorce from Anne Boleyn, left England to study on the Continent. Pole was appointed by Pope Paul III to a commission which made recommendations for improving the Roman Church, and was disappointed when no action was taken on the commission's work. Although still a layman, Pole was given a cardinal's hat in 1538. In 1545 Pole was one of three papal legates appointed to preside over the Council of Trent. Readmitted to England in 1554 to bring papal absolution to the English Parliament, Pole worked closely with Queen Mary from 1555 to 1558 to reestablish Catholicism in England. He was made Archbishop of Canterbury, but endured the humiliation of being suspected of heresy by the papacy he had so faithfully served.

POLYCARP (69[?]–156[?]) Traditionally described as a disciple of John the Apostle, Polycarp served for many years as the benign and beloved bishop of Smyrna, in what is now western Turkey, his home town. Polycarp, revered for the quailty of his life rather than the profundity of his teachings, was seized during the Emperor Marcus Aurelius' severe persecution. Urged to renounce his faith in Christ before a large crowd in the city square, Polycarp, an elderly man, stoutly refused, proclaiming, "For eighty-six years I have served Him, and He never did me any wrong. How can I blaspheme my King who has saved me?"

A letter which Polycarp wrote to the church at Philippi is still extant, revealing Polycarp to be a sweet-tempered, honest person. He once journeyed to Rome in an attempt to heal the breach between the Eastern and Western branches of the Church over the date for Easter. Although he and Pope Anicetus could not resolve their differences over fixing the date to observe Easter, Polycarp won the respect of everyone for his kind and gentle ways.

POLYCRATES (125[?]–195[?]) A prominent and powerful bishop of Ephesus, Polycrates led the Eastern Churches in their squabble with Rome and the Western Churches over the date for celebrating Easter. Although a series of synods were held around 190 in Palestine and Rome which decided in favor of the Roman procedure for fixing the date, Polycrates and his supporters insisted on retaining the ancient usage of observing Easter with the Lord's Supper on the evening of the fourteenth of the month Nisan, the night of the Jewish Passover, maintaining that Jesus died the afternoon the Passover lambs were slaughtered (as intimated in the Gospel of John). Polycrates and many other hold-outs were summarily excommunicated by the imperious Victor, Bishop of Rome, which made the controversy more bitter.

POLYEUCTES ([?]–250[?]) A tough, pagan trooper who soldiered with the much-decorated Thunder Twelfth Legion of the Roman army, Polyeuctes was attracted to the Gospel by a buddy in his outfit named Nearchus who was a devout Christian. While they were stationed at Melitene, Emperor Decius ordered harsh reprisals against Christians. Polyeuctes, against the tearful pleas and urgent advice of his father-in-law, determined to take his stand for Christ with Nearchus. Both were beheaded on the orders of the father-in-law. Polyeuctes' martyrdom became the subject for several operas and plays.

POST, George Edward (1838–1909) An American Presbyterian medical missionary in Lebanon from 1863 until his death, Post became a renowned teacher, physician, botanist and linguist in the Middle East, serving many years on the faculty of the Syrian Protestant College, now known as the American University of Beirut.

PONTIANUS, Pope ([?]–236) Elected Bishop of Rome in 230, Pontianus called a synod in 232 to confirm decrees against Origen's heretical teachings. Pontianus was condemned as a slave to the mines when Emperor Maximinus issued an edict against Christians. He encountered his rival, antipope Hippolytus, in the slave camp, where the two became reconciled. Before they both died, victims of the rigors of working the mines, Pontianus reconciled Hippolytus the schismatic to the Church.

POTHINUS ([?]–177) Also known as Photinus, Pothinus, a bishop of Lyons, was one of the famous "Forty-eight Martyrs of Lyons," executed after ghastly tortures during the persecution of Emperor Marcus Aurelius. Pothinus, reputed to have been past ninety at the time of his martyrdom, was canonized as a saint in the Roman Catholic Church.

POTTER, Henry Codman (1835–1908) Innovating and industrious American Episcopal Bishop of New York, Potter laid the cornerstone for the massive but yet-unfinished Cathedral of St. John the Divine in New York City. Potter created a sensation in 1889 when he attacked the corruption of New York's infamous Tammany administration during a worship service commemorating the centennial of the U.S. Government. A colorful and popular public figure, Potter was frequently called upon to arbitrate labor disputes, and once shocked the abstemious by opening a saloon "along Christian lines."

PRATT, Orson (1811–1881) One of twelve original Mormon "Apostles," Pratt and his brother, Parley, joined Joseph Smith's new cult in 1830. Pratt and Erastus Snow were the first to enter Salt Lake Valley after the great trek west in 1847.

PRATT, Parley Parker (1807–1857) Like his brother, Orson, Parley Pratt was one of the original twelve "Apostles" in Mormonism and participated in the western migration. He was murdered in the midst of a mission tour in Arkansas by the irate husband of a woman convert who had deserted her family to go with Pratt to Utah.

PRIESTLEY, Joseph (1733–1804) English Presbyterian clergyman who became absorbed with science and entranced with Unitarianism, Priestley pursued both a famous scientific and preaching career. His laboratory experiments led him to discover oxygen in 1774, and make him revered as the father of modern chemistry. Attracted by the Socinian and rationalist ideas of Theophilus Lindsey, Priestley embraced Unitarianism. His sympathies toward Unitarianism and the French Revolution aroused mob action, forcing him to flee to London in 1791, and to the United States in 1794, where he continued his dual career until his death.

PRISCA (2nd c.) A fanatical, Phrygian prophetess of the speedy end of the world and coming of Christ, Prisca and another woman, Maximilla, abandoned their husbands to follow Montanus, a self-styled mouthpiece of the Holy Spirit. Prisca shrilly promoted Montanus' strange doctrines that the heavenly Jerusalem was about to be inaugurated in Phrygia and that intense asceticism was required of the faithful. Prisca, Maximillus and the other Montanists, capitalizing on the deep popular dissatisfaction with the growing wealth and worldliness of the Church's leaders, attracted hundreds of followers.

Montanism, although condemned by a series of synods, thrived for many years.

PRISCILLIAN ([?]–385) A Spanish layman with an ascetic and mystical streak, Priscillian headed a reform movement in the ancient Spanish

Church. His followers, called Priscillianists, showed a marked tendency dualism, stressing the gap between God and the world, spiritual and material, and rejecting the world and material as evil. Although Priscillian served as bishop of Avila, he was suspected of heresy and resented by many self-indulgent clerics. Priscillian and many followers were banished for a time; reinstated briefly, he was arrested, tortured horribly and executed at the instigation of his fellow bishops. Priscillian was the first Christian to be put to death by a state which officially designated itself "Christian."

PROCOP, Andrew (or Procopius), (1380[?]–1434) A Roman priest who joined the early Bohemian reformer John Huss, Procop took an active part in the guerrilla forces waging a civil war to overthrow Emperor Sigismund. Procop's branch of the Hussites, known as Taborites, continued the civil war after the rest of the Hussites agreed to the terms of the Council of Basel. Procop and most of his band were cut down at the Battle of Lipnik in 1434.

PROKOP See **PROCOP.**

PROVOOST, Samuel (1742–1815) One of the first Anglican rectors to be elevated as bishop of the new American Episcopal Church, Provoost headed the diocese of New York from 1787 until his death. Provoost travelled to Canterbury to be consecrated, fulfilling the hopes of American Episcopalians to derive their orders from the parent body in England instead of relying on Bishop Seabury's consecration by non-juror Scottish bishops.

PULCHERIA (399–453) The Empress of the Eastern Empire after many years of nasty family strife which took the form of theological-political battles, Pulcheria finally succeeded her brother Theodosius II in 450. She married a nobody named Marcian, made him Emperor, and ruled firmly but fairly until her death in 453.

Pulcheria sponsored the Council of Chalcedon, the milestone Church Council which denounced the Monophysite heresy and proclaimed the two natures of Christ. Pulcheria and Marcian also built many churches and helped open the University of Constantinople.

PUSEY, Edward Bouverie (1800–1882) High church Anglican theologian and Oxford Hebrew professor, Pusey, joined by other brilliant kindred spirits at Oriel College, Oxford, inaugurated what came to be known as the Oxford Movement. Pusey and his associates, including such notables as Keble, Rose, Newman and Froude, were determined to return the Church to the purity of primitive Christianity. Urging the recovery of such practices as celibacy, oracular confession, prayers for the dead, Pusey assisted Newman in preparing a series of "Tracts for the Times," giving the movement the title "Tractarianism" for a time. Pusey wrote several tracts, including the eighteenth "On the Benefits of Fasting," and the sixty-seventh and sixty-ninth, "On Holy Baptism."

After Newman's defection to Rome, Pusey emerged as the leader of the Anglo-Catholics in the Church of England. He exercised such profound influence that the adherents to the high church party in it were often referred to as Puseyites. His views were frequently resented by other Anglicans; he was once suspended for three years from preaching in his university pulpit for arguing the real presence in the sacrament.

Q

QUADRATUS ([?]–130[?]) The first of the literary defenders of Christianity known as apologists, Quadratus wrote a carefully-reasoned presentation of the Christian faith to the Emperor Hadrian about 125. Although only fragments of Quadratus' writings have been preserved, they show that Quadratus, an intellectual, and many fellow intellectuals were by that time attracted to the Church. Quadratus, who was probably Bishop of Athens, based his appeal primarily on intelligence.

QUESNEL, Pasquier (1634–1719) A French member of the Oratorians, Quesnel found himself in deep trouble with the Vatican when he refused to sign an anti-Jansenist statement circulated by the Jesuits, and insisted that the Biblical ideas of sin and grace must be taken seriously. He fled for a time to Brussels, where he completed his devotional commentary, *Moral Reflections on the New Testament,* but was taken into custody by the Jesuits. Escaping, Quesnel made his way to safety in Amsterdam, where he lived the rest of his life as leader of the Jansenists. Quesnel was opposed by bitter Jesuit hostility and a papal bull by Pope Clement XI in 1713 which condemned one hundred and one of Quesnel's statements, many of which were direct quotations from Augustine.

QUIMBY, Phineas Parkhurst (1802–1866) A New Hampshire clockmaker who dabbled in hypnotism and became absorbed with the power of auto-suggestion, Quimby finally left clockmaking and began lecturing and demonstrating what was then called "mesmerism" (named after the Viennese doctor, Mesmer, who did early experiments in hypnosis) to large crowds.

Quimby, a cool and clever talker and showman, next settled in Portland, Maine, where he began treating illnesses through "mesmerism" or hypnosis and mental suggestion. He "cured" for a time a sickly and unhappy young woman named Mary Baker Patterson who later as Mary Baker Eddy founded Christian Science.

Many students argue that Quimby's notions were actually the basis for many of the ideas in Mrs. Eddy's movement, although she violently denied it. Quimby's theories and terms were also picked up by another disciple, Julius Dresser, who began the New Thought movement.

QUINONES, Fernandez de (1482[?]–1540) A Spanish cardinal active in the court circles of Spain, Quinones' reformed breviary was one of the sources used by Cranmer to prepare the English masterpiece known as the *Book of Common Prayer* in 1549.

R

RABANUS MAURUS See **HRABA-NUS MAURUS.**

RADBERTUS, Paschasius (786[?]–865[?]) A learned monk in the famous monastery of Corbie, France, Radbertus drew upon his wide knowledge of Latin and Greek theology to write *"De corpore et sanguine Domini"* ("Of the Body and Blood of the Lord"), the first comprehensive treatise on the sacrament of the Lord's Supper, in 831. Radbertus maintained with Augustine that only those who partook in faith received the meaning of the sacrament, and agreed with the Greeks that it is the food of immortality. Although Radbertus did not use the term "transubstantiation" (which did not come into use until about the 12th century) he taught that by divine miracle, the elements become the essence of the very body and blood of Christ.

A doctrinal controversy followed, but the Roman Church eventually backed Radbertus' view.

RADEWYN, Florentius (1350–1400) The founder of the Brethren of the Common Life, a lay group of semi-monastic mystics who formed houses in the Netherlands and Germany in the 15th century to promote piety, Radewyn associated for many years with the great Dutch mystic, Gerhard Groote. Radewyn established his first house at Deventer, and gathered a community of those anxious for a warmer, personal religious experience. Radewyn's house at Deventer was followed by others, and the Brethren of the Common Life became well-known and respected for teaching, copying books of edification and pious living. Radewyn, with a down-to-earth practicality, insisted that the Brethren all engage in work. Although a mystic, he abhorred radical excesses, and insisted that his disciples maintain churchly forms.

RAIKES, Robert (1735–1811) Organizer of one of the earliest Sunday Schools, Raikes, scion to the fortune of a wealthy English publisher, brought the ragged urchins from Gloucester streets to a program on Sundays beginning in 1780 to learn catechism and reading. Raikes paid the teacher one shilling sixpence from his own pocket.

In spite of initial opposition by many stodgy churchmen, Raikes' Sunday School idea caught on, so that by 1786, there were an estimated 200,000 children in Sunday Schools in England.

Raikes, a deeply motivated humanitarian, expanded his interests to include prison reform and hospitals.

RAINY, Robert (1826–1906) Free Church of Scotland clergyman and educator, Rainy, Principal of New College, Edinburgh, from 1874 to 1906, led the delicate negotiations leading to the union of the Free Church and the United Presbyterian Church in Scotland in 1900. Rainy later served as the first Moderator of the new united body.

RAPP, Johann Georg (1757–1847) The German linen-weaver who founded the Harmony Society, a communal religious settlement near Pittsburgh, Pennsylvania, Rapp left the Lutheran Church in Germany about 1787 to establish his own sect near Württemberg. Persecution by local authorities led Rapp to emigrate in 1803 to the United States, where Rapp and some followers founded Harmony, a settlement near present day Zelienople, Pa.

Ascetic and autocratic, Rapp (who was given the gratuitous title "Father" by respectful followers) laid down strict rules demanding hard work, celibacy and equality for all members of his Society. In 1815, Rapp moved the community to Indiana to found a new settlement, called New Harmonie. He brought his group to western Pennsylvania, however, in 1824, and sold New Harmonie, Indiana to Robert Owen, the English Utopian, in 1825. Father Rapp and his followers built a new village, called Economy, located near the present city of Ambridge, Pa., along the Ohio River. Rapp continued as absolute ruler of the Order until his death in 1847.

The settlement eventually petered out because of the stricture against marriage; by the time most of Economy was sold off in 1903, only four Harmonyites survived.

RASPUTIN, Grigori Yefimovich (1873[?]–1916) The scandalous and strange Siberian-born evil genius who posed as a "sinless" Russian Orthodox monk (excusing his sensuous sprees on the grounds that his "holy nature" was unaffected by any acts), Rasputin came to exercise a malignant influence over Czarina Alexandra of Russia and to a lesser degree over Czar Nicholas. Rasputin's wild, weird ways hastened the descent into chaos during the closing days of the Russian monarchy in World War I. Rasputin was finally murdered by a band of patriots hoping to rid the royal Romanoff family of his sinister influence.

RATRAMNUS ([?]–868[?]) A monk of the famous monastery of Corbie, France, Ratramnus participated in the doctrinal controversy over the nature of Christ's presence in the sacrament of the Lord's Supper which shook the Church in the 9th century. Ratramnus, writing about 844, answered the argument advanced by a fellow monk at Corbie, Radbertus, that by divine miracle, the elements are made into the very essence of Christ's body and blood. Ratramnus, uneasy with the idea of transubstantiation, wrote that the body and blood of Christ are mysteriously present, yet are not the same as that body which was hanging on the Cross.

RAUSCHENBUSCH, Walter (1861–1918) American Baptist pastor, Rauschenbusch pioneered the "Social Gospel" movement in the United States. Rauschenbusch, serving his first pastorate among the German immigrants living in poverty on the lower East Side of New York City in 1886, quickly became convinced of the need to be concerned with more than mere verbal preaching or "saving souls." Motivated by a profound personal commitment to Christ and grounded in a deep understanding of the Scriptures, Rauschenbusch emerged as the leader of a movement seeking to respond to the Gospel by working to alleviate pressing social problems.

Rauschenbusch was frequently attacked by stand pat churchmen who saw Christianity as an other-worldly matter, and by reactionary public figures who wanted to protect their vested interests. He wrote *Christianity and Social Crisis* in 1907, and *The Social Principles of Jesus* in 1916, both influential volumes in steering the American church into greater involvement in contemporary life.

RAYMUND of Penafort (1175[?]–1275) A Spanish Dominican monk and theologian, Raymund of Penafort joined with Peter Nolasco to found the Order of Our Lady of Mercy for the Redemption of Captives about 1222, which busied itself buying freedom for Christians captured by the Moors. Raymund later came to Rome at the request of Pope Gregory IX to codify canon law. He did such an acceptable job that his work was the authoritative corpus for the Roman Church for nearly seven hundred years. Declining an offer to be an archbishop, Raymund served as the head of the Dominican Order from 1238 until 1240, then retired. He was canonized as a saint in 1601.

RAYMOND du Puy (1120[?]–1160[?]) French-born Grand Master of the Knights of St. John, Raymond du Puy supervised the work of the ancient hospital in Jerusalem during the Crusades of the 12th century and expanded his Hospitallers into a military order. Raymond's Knights of St. John came to have immense influence, growing to become keen rivals to the Knights Templar.

REIMARUS, Hermann Samuel (1694–1768) A German philosopher and professor of Hebrew, Reimarus wrote a series of essays excoriating Jesus as a power-hungry sensationalist and denigrating the Gospel accounts as non-historic fakery. Reimarus' work, kept secret during his lifetime, caused a sensation when it was published posthumously under a pseudonym.

REINKENS, Joseph Hubert (1821–1896) An outspoken German Roman Catholic priest and professor at Breslau, Reinkens so vigorously protested when Pope Pius IX announced the dogma of papal infallibility that he was suspended from the priesthood in 1870 and finally excommunicated in 1872. Reinkens, joining with von Dollinger, helped strengthen the Old Catholic Church, becoming a bishop in that communion. A scholar of note, Reinkens contributed many authoritative works in the field of Church history.

RELLY, James (1722–1778) A rough Welshman who began preaching universalism, Relly was the mentor of John Murray who brought Universalist ideas to America and began the Universalist movement in New England. Relly, who as a young tough came to one of Whitefield's meetings to heckle, was converted. He became one of Whitefield's field preachers but broke with Whitefield by espousing antinomianism. About 1770, Relly veered toward universalism, teaching that everyone would be saved, but attracted little following in England apart from Murray.

RENAN, Joseph Ernst (1823–1892) French historian and philosopher, Renan, who trained for the priesthood but left the seminary before ordination, broke into international prominence with his *Vie de Jesus* ("Life of Jesus") in 1863. Previously, he had achieved a modest reputation as a linguist and historian. His *Vie de Jesus* denuded the Gospel accounts of anything faintly unexplainable or implausible, leaving the figure of Jesus believable to Renan but bland to many. Renan followed his popular but controversial *Vie* with a series of volumes, *History of Christian Origins,* from 1866 to 1883.

RENWICK, James (1662–1688) A Scots Covenanter, Renwick joined Richard Cameron and others protesting King Charles II's attempts to impose episcopacy on Presbyterian-minded Scots.

Renwick signed the Sanquhar Declaration of 1680, denouncing Charles II as a tyrant and usurper of the throne after the Restoration of royalty, and found it unhealthy to remain in Britain.

Returning to preach in southwestern Scotland after a sojourn in the Netherlands, Renwick stubbornly defied the Crown, issuing the *Apologetical Declaration* in 1684 and the *Second Sanquhar Declaration* in 1685. Although offered indulgence by the King in 1687, Renwick rejected the opportunity to acknowledge the Crown and receive amnesty. Outlawed, Renwick and a small fanatic band of guerrillas, the remnants of the Cameronians, were tracked down. Renwick, the last of the Covenanter martyrs, was executed at Edinburgh.

REUCHLIN, Johann (1455–1522) A German humanist and classics scholar, Reuchlin wrote the dictionary and grammar which became the basis for modern study of Biblical Hebrew. Reuchlin, master of Latin, Greek and Hebrew, unintentionally got caught in a bitter fight with a convert from Judaism named Pfefferkorn who wanted to extirpate all traces of the Hebrew origins in Christianity. When Pfefferkorn persuaded civil authorities to enforce his ban against Hebrew, Reuchlin spoke out. Although tried by the Inquisition, Reuchlin spent over ten years trying to defend the cause of studying Hebrew literature.

In spite of persecutions instigated by the Dominicans and suppression of his scholarly works, Reuchlin refused to desert the Roman Catholic cause and join the Lutherans. Most humanists, however, were so repelled by the harsh treatment which Reuchlin received at the hands of the Roman Church that they joined or sympathized with the Reformation.

REYNOLDS, Edward (1599–1667) A stalwart Puritan during Cromwell's Protectorate in England, Reynolds elected to support the Restoration of monarchy in 1660 in the hopes of having Presbyterianism made the state religion. Reynolds, after Charles II's accession to the throne, agreed to serve as Bishop of Norwich. Although Parliament emphatically rejected Presbyterianism and established Anglicanism by passing rigid laws in 1662 against dissenters, Reynolds managed to remain at his post, where he showed great leniency toward nonconformists. Previously, Reynolds had attended the Westminster Assembly in 1643, helping to frame the great Presbyterian Confession.

RICCI, Matteo (1552–1610) An Italian Jesuit missionary to India, Ricci finally won permission to begin mission work in China in 1583. Ricci opened Roman Catholic missions in China, but was opposed by other Roman orders for compromising the Church's position by relaxing the ban against ancestor worship. He lived at Peking many years, where he published the first detailed geography of China for westerners.

RICE, Luther (1783–1836) An American Baptist mission enthusiast, Rice, a co-worker with missionary Adoniram Judson for a brief time, helped form the American Board of Commissioners for Foreign Missions, which pioneered in mission endeavors by American churchmen.

RICHARD I, King of England (the "Lion-hearted") (1157–1199) Contrary to romantic legends, Richard was in real life a calloused, cold-blooded Crusader who once slaughtered 2,700 defenseless Moslem prisoners-of-war. He fomented bitter dissension and intrigues within the Crusader armies, feuding constantly with Philip Augustus of France, one of his co-leaders. Richard the Lion-hearted's senseless slaying of the 2,700 enemy P.O.W.'s aroused the gentlemanly Saladin to renew the hostilities, resulting in a stalemate whereby Jerusalem remained in Moslem hands. Sullenly accepting a truce, war-loving Richard headed home to England.

RICHARD of Chichester (1197–1253) One of the few beacons of culture in the gloomy 13th century, Richard studied at Oxford, Paris and Bologna, served as chancellor of Oxford University and Canterbury Cathedral, then became Bishop of Chichester, England. Richard's unswerving moral standards and strict ideas of church discipline irritated King Henry III. The author of profound prayers sometimes set to music ("Day by day, Dear Lord, of Thee three things I pray: to see Thee more clearly, love Thee more dearly, follow Thee more nearly, day by day"), Richard was canonized by the Church in 1262.

RICHARD of St. Victor ([?]–1173) A Scots-born mystic and theologian, Richard of St. Victor ranked as one of the great teachers in the Medieval Church. He studied at the Abbey of St. Victor at Paris under the noted scholar, Hugh of St. Victor, and later served as head of the Abbey. In 1162, Richard of St. Victor began a writing career. He was highly respected by writers and scholars such as Dante.

RICHELIEU, Armand du Plessis de (1585–1642) *De facto* dictator of France from 1624 until his death in 1642, this politically powerful prelate as Chief Minister of the government manipulated King Louis XIII to bring France to a pinnacle of glory. Richelieu became a bishop when only twenty-two, serving at Lucon in Rome, where his administrative talents quickly brought

him to the attention of his superiors. Appointed a cardinal in 1622, Richelieu rose to prominence in Louis XIII's service until he masterminded the affairs of France.

Richelieu had two basic aims: the absolute supremacy of royal authority in France, and the absolute supremacy of French authority in Europe. To accomplish these aims, he first set out to destroy the nobility, then to crush the Huguenots (French Protestants). After razing all fortified castles and arresting contentious nobles, Richelieu tried to extinguish the Huguenot threat by skillfully playing off the Protestant states against one another, using intrigue and even subsidies to Gustavus Adolphus IV to invade Germany. The Thirty Years War ensued, but Richelieu's France emerged as the prevailing power in Europe.

Richelieu, the Father of the French Monarchy, made the Bourbons the strongest kings. Richelieu, a patron of learning and the arts, rebuilt the Sorbonne and in 1635 founded the French Academy.

RIDDLE, Matthew Brown (1836–1916) American Presbyterian New Testament professor at Pittsburgh's Western Theological Seminary from 1887 to 1913, Riddle helped prepare the American Revised Version of the New Testament and edited several Biblical commentaries.

RIDLEY, NICHOLAS (1500[?]–1555) An outstanding scholar and cleric who supported Henry VIII's Reformation in England, Ridley, who rose to become bishop of Rochester in 1547 and bishop of London in 1550, died a martyr's death when ferociously Catholic Queen Mary ascended to the throne. Ridley, beloved for his concern for the destitute and deprived, persuaded the king and the city of London to build several hospitals. A close associate of Archbishop Cranmer, Ridley helped prepare the liturgy and polity of the Anglican Church.

Ridley was drawn into the plot to put Lady Jane on the throne instead of Mary when young King Edward VI died, and was sent to the tower by the unforgiving Mary. He steadfastly refused to retract his stand for Protestantism, but readily admitted his complicity in the plan to crown Protestant Lady Jane Grey. At Mary's orders, Ridley died in the flames with Hugh Latimer.

RIGDON, Sidney (1783–1876) An American religious figure from western Pennsylvania, Rigdon became a Baptist preacher and later associated himself with Alexander Campbell. After meeting Joseph Smith, Jr., in 1830, he became an enthusiastic follower and preacher in the Mormon movement. After Smith's death in 1844, Sidney Rigdon sought the leadership of the Mormon Church on the basis that he was the only remaining member of the presidency. Due to the fact that he lacked the strength of personality that was required in such a crisis and that his influence was already on the wane within the church, he lost his claim to leadership and was later excommunicated. Students point out that it was through Sidney Rigdon that some of the thinking of the Disciples of Christ was brought into Mormonism. He was also associated with the now discredited theory of the Spaulding Manuscript having been the basis of the Book of Mormon.

RIGGS, Elias (1810–1901) An American Protestant missionary to the Near East and Bible translator, Riggs spent nearly all the years between 1832 and his death in 1901 in Turkey. He prepared excellent translations of the Bible into Armenian, Bulgarian and Turkish, and wrote numerous grammars and aids to language study for missionaries.

RIGGS, Stephen Return (1812–1883) An American Presbyterian missionary to the American Indians, Riggs wrote extensively for and about the Dakota tribe. He organized numerous mission schools in the west for his beloved Dakotas, laboriously preparing textbooks, grammars and dictionaries of their language and translating the Bible into Dakota.

RINKART, Martin (1586–1649) German Lutheran pastor in his home town of Eilenburg in the grim first half of the 17th century when the Thirty Years War, famines and plagues ravished Germany, Rinkart repeatedly rallied his people during his thirty year ministry. In one year, 1637, Rinkart buried over 4,000 plague victims from his town. On another occasion, during the Thirty Years War, Rinkart personally interceded with the Swedish occupations at Eilenberg to have an enormous ransom reduced. A gifted musician and poet, Rinkart wrote the words to the lovely hymn, "Now Thank Thee We All Our God," at the close of the Thirty Years War.

RITSCHL, Albrecht (1822–1889) A well-known and influential German Protestant theologian who taught theology at Bonn from 1846 to 1864, and Gottingen from 1864 until his death, Ritschl broke from the school of his mentor, F. C. Baur, to originate a theology purged of all supernatural aspects. Ritschl even jettisoned such traditional dogmas as Original Sin, the Incarnation, the Resurrection, the Trinity and all miracles. Ritschl's ultra-liberalism, hailed by some and hated by others, left a deep imprint on subsequent theological thought and Biblical scholarship in Germany throughout the 19th century.

ROBERT, Bellarmine See **BELLARMINE, Robert.**

ROBERT of Jumieges ([?]–1052) A French Norman prelate, he left Jumieges Abbey for England when the exiled heir to the English throne, later known as King Edward the Confessor, seized the throne. Robert was rewarded with honors and titles, including the archbishopric of Canterbury, in Edward's England. Later, however, he was forced to flee during civil struggles between Edward and Godwin, Edward's father-in-law. Robert of Jumieges was stripped of his titles, which caused William the Conqueror to invade England in 1066 to redress the insult to Normans.

ROBERT de Molesme (1029[?]–1111) Deeply ascetic and reform-minded, Robert de Molesme founded a monastic community in the forest of Molesme in southern France in 1075. Robert, unable to prevent his monks from growing slack and indolent after the order grew prosperous, moved to another monastery at Citeaux near Châlons in 1098. A few years later, when the Molesme monastery pleaded with him to return and Pope Urban II ordered him to go back, Robert agreed to head the Molesme community once again, making it a dynamic center for monastic reform. He was later canonized.

ROBERT de Sorbon See **SORBON.**

ROBERTS, Benjamin Titus (1823–1893) A dissident Methodist Episcopal clergyman who was thrown out of the Genesee, New York, Conference in 1858 for his strident objections to his denomination's policies, Roberts rallied other discontented pastors and laymen to found his own Free Methodist Church in 1860. Roberts headed the breakaway group until he died, organizing a denominational organ, *The Earnest Christian*, establishing a theological seminary and writing a series of books.

ROBERTS, Brigham Henry (1857–1933) An English-born Mormon brought to Utah by his parents, who were fanatic English converts to Mormonism, Roberts used his considerable oratorical skills as a Mormon missionary and spokesman. He became a member of the First Council of Seventy, and was the most prominent Mormon in the early 20th century. Active in politics, he was denied a seat in the U.S. House of Representatives in 1898 because of his polygamy.

ROBERTS, Issachar Jacob (1802–1871) American Baptist missionary to China and the Far East, Roberts helped open the first Baptist mission program at Hong Kong in 1842, then moved to the mainland where he met the revolutionary Tien Wang. Roberts accompanied Tien Wang during his rebellion at Taipang and became a trusted advisor for the brilliant but unstable young warlord for two years until forced out following a quarrel with Tien's chief assistant.

ROBERTSON, James (1839–1902) A Scottish-born Canadian Presbyterian pastor, Robertson was the real-life model for the character, the "sky pilot," in Ralph Connor's stories, and superintended Presbyterian missions in the vast wilderness of the Canadian northwest with firmness, love and humor.

ROBINSON, Frank Bruce (1886–1948) Founder and driving spirit behind "Psychiana," a mail-order cult peddling "transforming power of God" correspondence courses averaging

$24.00 for twenty-four lessons, Robinson built up a thriving operation at Moscow, Idaho. His movement touched over three million people throughout the U.S.A. at a time when most American churches were begging. Robinson, one of the earliest and boldest exponents of advertising religion, confidently assured Depression-prone Americans that Psychiana could show the way to have God meet all their needs.

After Robinson's death, Psychiana lacked Robinson's sensational but sure touch and quickly withered.

ROBINSON, John (1576[?]–1625) The brave and beloved non-conformist preacher remembered by the Pilgrims who sailed on the *Mayflower*, Robinson remained behind at Leiden, Holland.

Robinson became the leader of a group of Separatists at Norwich, England, in the early 1600's. After several parishioners were excommunicated by the authorities for joining Robinson's Norwich band, Robinson moved his congregation to Scrooby, Nottinghamshire. In 1608, Robinson and many from the Scrooby group emigrated to the Netherlands, settling first at Amsterdam, then at Leiden, where he was ordained as a pastor and William Brewster was elected ruling elder. Robinson tearfully gave his blessing to the band sailing on the *Mayflower*, and corresponded regularly with the Plymouth members of his congregation until his death.

ROCK, Johann Friedrich (1678–1749) A German mystic and preacher who came to head a movement within German Pietism in the 18th century known as "Inspirationists," Rock maintained that the era of direct, divine inspiration had not ended, but that God continued to speak directly to men, particularly through him and his followers. Rock siphoned off a following from among the German Pietists.

The Inspirationists waned after Rock's death, but revived in the early 19th century. Persecuted, his followers emigrated to the United States, settled briefly at Buffalo, New York, in 1842 where they called themselves the Ebenezer Society, then moved west to Iowa in 1855, where they took the name "The Amana Church Society."

RODEHEAVER, Homer Allan (1880–1956) Popular revivalist song leader and hymn writer, Rodeheaver directed from 1909 until 1931 the musical portion of Billy Sunday's meetings where his trombone became his trademark.

RODRIGUEZ, Simon (16th c.) A Spaniard studying at Paris, Rodriguez met the dedicated ex-soldier Ignatius Loyola who founded the Jesuits. He became one of the original members of Loyola's band which grew to become the powerful Society of Jesus in the Roman Catholic Church.

ROGERS, John (1500[?]–1555) The first English Protestant martyred by rabidly Catholic Queen Mary, Rogers wrote the first Bible commentary to be published in English. Rogers, converted by Bible translator William Tyndale, was forced to live on the Continent for safety's sake for many years. He served as a pastor at Wittenberg, where he edited an English version of the Scriptures, incorporating the portions of the Bible already translated by Tyndale and adding marginal notes. In 1537, he published his completed notes and commentary under the pseudonym, "Thomas Matthew."

Returning to England in 1548, Rogers became a Church of England rector. Rogers injudiciously preached a stern sermon against Roman Church threats three days after Queen Mary's accession to the throne. A marked man, he was seized, tried, tortured and subsequently burned.

ROMUALD of Ravenna (950[?]–1027) A leading ascetic and reformer in the 10th and 11th century, Romuald, an Italian monk, promoted reform by organizing groups of hermits into settlements known as "deserts." Romuald demanded discipline and dedication from his monks, dispatching them as missionaries and preachers to all of southern Europe.

Romuald's best known "desert," Camaldoli, located near Arezzo, lent Romuald's movement its name, and continues to exist today.

ROSE, Hugh James (1795-1838) Enthusiastic Anglo-Catholic sympathizer with the views of Keble, Pusey, Newman and Froude, the group of young Church of England clergymen who inaugurated what came to be known as the "Oxford Movement," Rose was a brilliant scholar at Cambridge and Durham. Rose in 1832 founded the *British Magazine* to promote the aims of the group at Oriel College, Oxford, and to restore a purity and spirituality to the English Church. This well-known high church leader later edited an encyclopedia and dictionary.

ROSE of Lima (1586–1617) The first Roman Catholic born in the western hemisphere to be canonized, Rose of Lima was a nun from Peru who was credited with extraordinary miraculous powers during her lifetime in South America. Sister Rose, who became a Dominican tertiary in 1606, gained wide fame as an ascetic and mystic among the masses. She was canonized in 1671.

ROSE of Viterbo (1235–1252) An Italian Franciscan tertiary, Sister Rose of Viterbo responded to a vision during a near-fatal illness when she was twelve and began preaching on the streets of her home town, urging the populace to throw off Ghibelline control and rally behind the papacy. She was driven from the town in 1250 on orders of the angry Emperor Frederick II, but later returned to live in seclusion in her father's peasant home. Too poor to afford the dowry required to enter a convent, Rose remained in lay order, practicing penitence and prayer until her death. She was declared a saint in 1457.

ROTHE, Johann Andreas (1688–1758) A close associate of the great German Pietist Count von Zinzendorf, Rothe was appointed Lutheran pastor of the church on Zinzendorf's estate at Berthelsdorf. Rothe and Zinzendorf, welcoming a colony of Hussites exiled from German-speaking Moravia, tried to incorporate the Moravians into the Saxony Lutheran Church.

ROTHMAN, Bernhard (1495[?]–1535) A German Evangelical preacher who was a friend of Melanchthon, Rothman introduced the Reformation to the city of Munster. Later, however, he fell under the influence of the radical Anabaptist, Jan Mathys from Haarlem, and became part of the fanatic band attempting to bring in the Kingdom on earth by force. He probably died in the seige of Munster in 1535.

ROUS, Francis (1579–1659) An English Puritan composer, Rous in 1643 set many of the Psalms to music and gathered them in a collection for congregational singing. Rous, originally a Presbyterian but later a Congregationalist, was a member of Parliament at the time of the Protectorate and enthusiastically backed Oliver Cromwell.

Many of Rous' Psalm tunes and

words set to English metre became classics, and are in wide use.

ROUSE See ROUS

ROUSSEL, Gerard (1480[?]–1550) One of the very few men in his day who managed to walk the thin line of sympathizing with the Reformers yet remaining within the Roman communion, Roussel was a close friend of John Calvin during their student days, and a companion of the great humanist-reformer, Lefèvre d'Etaples. Roussel even shared exile in 1521 with d'Etaples, and in 1525 was forced to flee to escape heresy charges, yet never broke with Rome. Recalled to Paris in 1526 by King Francis I to become Court Preacher, Roussel later was elevated as Bishop of Oleron. Roussel subsequently found his sermons and writing condemned by the Sorbonne on two occasions. He died from injuries suffered when a mob attacked him in the midst of a sermon urging fewer Church festivals.

RUBEANUS, Crotus (1480[?]– 1539[?]) A German humanist from Dornheim, Rubeanus, together with Ulrich von Hutten, in 1514 and 1517, wrote the satire, *Letters of Obscure Men,* which purported to be an attack on the advocate of Hebrew study, Johann Reuchlin, who had been denounced by the Church. Rubeanus' clever piece, deliberately written in bad Latin and created to give the impression that those opposing Reuchlin were also opposed to learning and progressive thought, helped rally the humanist scholars behind Reuchlin and enlist them for the Reformation.

RUDOLF II, King of Bohemia (1552– 1612) Roman Catholic ruler of a largely Protestant country, Rudolf II was forced to grant a decree known as the *Majestätsbrief* in 1609, granting an unusual degree of freedom to Protestant subjects. Unfortunately, however, Rudolf's inept successors tried to suppress the toleration granted by Rudolf and precipitated a revolt which exploded into the Thirty Years' War in Europe.

RUFINUS, Tyrannius (345[?]–410[?]) An Italian pagan convert to the Gospel, Rufinus, associate of Jerome and most other 4th century Church notables, translated many Greek works into Latin, which saved countless texts from being lost. Rufinus founded a monastery on the Mount of Olives, Jerusalem, where he wrote and translated.

RUSSELL, Charles Taze (1852-1916) The Pittsburgh haberdasher who prowled through Scripture to try to fix the date for the Second Coming, Russell finally settled on 1914. "Pastor" Russell built up a fanatical following calling itself the Watch Tower Bible and Tract Society, now usually known as Jehovah's Witnesses.

The persuasive Russell, who had been by turns a Presbyterian, a Congregationalist, an Adventist and a dabbler in Oriental faiths, forsook belief in hell, then abandoned the Trinity and the divinity of Christ (reducing Jesus to merely the greatest "witness") and began predicting in 1872 that Jesus would re-appear in 1914.

By 1874 Russell had a congregation; by 1879 he had founded the forerunner of his magazine, "Watchtower"; by 1884 he had a large group, popularly called Russellites, but officially known as the Watch Tower Bible and Tract Society.

Russell's lurid extramarital affairs, followed by a messy divorce trial in 1909, and a conviction for fraud for selling "miracle wheat" in 1911 badly shook the Society.

Russell suffered further criticism from the faithful when 1914 produced no Second Coming. He glibly solved this difficulty, however, by explaining that Christ had indeed come in 1914, but had returned invisibly without his body. Russell added that this meant that Christ established His Kingdom in 1914, Satan was cast out of heaven in the same year, and that, following a transition period, Armageddon will come, when Jehovah will select exactly 144,000 Witnesses to reign with Him in heaven.

Russell, never a man to pass up earthly comforts, died in his private Pullman car in 1916.

RUSSELL, Howard Hyde (1855–1946) Attorney-turned-preacher, Congregationalist Russell founded the Anti-Saloon League in Ohio in 1893, promoted his prohibition program into a big-time, nation-wide movement which once stretched into thirty-six states. Russell and the National Anti-Saloon League became a potent force lobbying for the Prohibition Amendment to the United States Constitution, crossing the country on a horse-drawn water wagon and parading through leading cities. In 1919, Russell went international, forming the World League Against Alcoholism. Long after the repeal of the Volstead Act, Russell continued stumping United States towns, holding his colorful "Church vs. Booze" stage trial.

RUTHERFORD, Joseph Franklin (1869–1942) A Missouri lawyer who preferred to be addressed by the title "Judge," Rutherford took over the Watch Tower Bible and Tract Society when its founder, Charles Taze Russell, died in 1916. Rutherford originated the more-manageable title, "Jehovah's Witnesses" for the Society in 1931 and coined the slogan, "Millions Now Living Will Never Die."

Rutherford, authoritarian Society president until his death in 1942, insisted on passing on new revelations as gleaned from his study of Scriptures, such as the teaching that those unable to see the truth as revealed to the Watchtower Society are doomed and entitled to no second chance (and causing a series of internal rifts within the Society which have resulted in the spawning of break-away groups, including The Dawn Bible Students Association). A secretive man who shunned personal contact with the faithful, Rutherford preferred to promote the Society through his tracts and books, of which 337 million were distributed, according to the Witnesses.

RUTHERFORD, Samuel (1600[?]–1661) A kindly, Christ-conscious Calvinist, Rutherford was revered as a leader of the Covenanters in the early 17th century in Scotland. Rutherford, while serving a Scottish country pastorate, wrote an elaborate treatise against Arminianism in 1636, causing the Bishop of Sydserf and the High Commission Court to depose him and clap him into jail. During his two years in the freezing Aberdeen jail, Rutherford wrote over two hundred letters, remarkable both for their clarity and charity. He was released in 1638 in time to witness the signing of the Covenant of 1638, became Professor of Divinity at St. Andrews, and in 1643 went to London to attend the Westminster Assembly as one of the eight Scottish Commissioners.

In 1644, Rutherford wrote the famous *Lex Rex*, a pioneering piece on the limited prerogatives of the crown and the larger powers of subjects. His *Lex Rex* brought him fame and honor until the Restoration of monarchy, at which time he was driven from his post and tried for treason.

RUYSBROECK, Jan van (1293[?]– 1381) A Dutch mystic and literary figure, Ruysbroeck was a friend of Tauler, Groot and many of the members of the band of mystics who called themselves simply "Friends of God." Ruysbroeck (also Ruysbruck) served as a priest for a time then organized the abbey at Groenendael. Opposing the type of mysticism represented by Meister Eckhardt and the pantheism of the popular woman writer, Bloemardinne, Ruysbroeck began a writing career.

His works, including such a classic as *The Adornment of the Spiritual Marriage,* were admired both for their graceful literary style and for their insights into the spiritual life.

RYERSON, Adolphus Egerton (1803– 1882) A Canadian Methodist who packed several careers into his lifetime as a pastor, editor, educator and administrator, Ryerson served as Superintendent of Education for Upper Canada from 1844 to 1876, designing Ontario's school system, and from 1874 until 1878 ably headed the Methodist Episcopal Church of Canada as its first president.

S

SABELLIUS (3rd c.) A North-African-born presbyter and preacher whose views on the nature of God were labelled heretical, Sabellius taught at Ptolemsis in Upper Egypt before coming to Rome about 215. Sabellius' fiercely fanatical band of followers called Sabellians or strict modalists taught that the second and third members of the Trinity were merely various aspects of God, so that Father, Son and Holy Spirit became in effect all one and all the same. This blurring of Creator, Saviour and Comforter into a crypto-Unitarianism was opposed by Dionysius of Alexandria and other outspoken critics. Sabellius, who persisted in expounding his ideas, was finally excommunicated by Pope Callistus.

SACHEVERELL, Henry (1674[?]–1724) A flash-in-the-pan Anglican pulpit idol who incited strong feelings against non-conformist groups by polemical preaching in 1709, Sacheverell was censured by Parliament but became a kind of hero to the high church group. He rode the crest of a wave of adulation for a time, gaining a good-paying parish and peddling 40,000 copies of his famous anti-Dissenter sermons before sinking into well-deserved obscurity.

SADOLETO, Jacopo (1477–1547) A prelate with a desire to introduce reforms in the Church, Sadoleto was one of several able Roman churchmen appointed as cardinals by Pope Paul III who in 1538 brought to the pope a series of recommendations to help heal divisions, improve the administration and better morals within the Roman Catholic Church. The recommendations, however, were politely ignored. The sensitive Sadoleto, anxious for reform without revolution, had helped found the "Oratory of Divine Love" at Rome about 1517, which brought about the spiritual revival in the Roman Church which came to be known as the Counter-Reformation.

Sadoleto's loyal defense of Roman dogma elicited one of Reformer John Calvin's most brilliant treatises, *Reply to Sadoleto*, in which Calvin ably vindicated the Reformed cause.

SALES, Francis de See **FRANCIS de Sales.**

SALMERON, Alfonso (1515–1585) A young Spanish student living at Paris at the same time as the dedicated Ignatius Loyola, Salmeron and Ignatius' other compatriots at the University of Paris became the organizing nucleous of the Society of Jesus, better known as the Jesuits. At the Council of Trent, Salmeron served as theologian for popes Paul III, Julian III and Pius IV.

SAMPSON, Thomas (1517–1589) One of the earliest members of the party in the English Church which wanted to purify the Church, Sampson, Dean of Christ Church, Oxford, and Laurence Humphrey opposed the use of prescribed vestments in the Church in 1564. The acrimonious debate over clerical attire came to be known as the "Vestiarian Controversy," and Sampson's party came to be called "Puritans." '

SANCROFT, William (1617–1693) A quirky, quixotic Archbishop of Canterbury who crowned James II of England in 1685 but then opposed James' Declaration of Indulgence, Sancroft was put on trial for sedition by the despotic James, but finally acquitted. Sancroft surprisingly declined to swear allegiance to his new sovereign, William of Orange, however, after James was deposed in 1690.

SANDEMAN, Robert (1718–1771) Scots-born originator of the Sandemanians, a cult which flourished for a time in Britain and New England, Sandeman married the daughter of John Glass, leader of a sect opposing State control of church bodies. Sandeman served for a time with the Glassites, then founded his own series of congregations, emphasizing communal ownership of property, weekly communion and various unusual practices such as vegetarianism and the "kiss of peace."

SANKEY, Ira David (1840–1908) Musical member of the great evangelistic team of Moody and Sankey, Sankey wrote and edited dozens of hymns which became hits in the English-speaking church. Sankey, an exuberant Methodist choir leader and Sunday School teacher, was introduced to Moody at a YMCA convention at Indianapolis in 1870. Sankey joined Moody on the phenomenal mission tour of the British Isles in 1873, where Sankey's moving vocal renditions and rousing hymn-leading became an indispensable part of Moody's meetings. Sankey, after Moody's death in 1899, pumped out a stream of song books and compositions.

SARAVIA, Adrian (1531–1616) A Belgian Walloon Protestant theologian who moved to England, Saravia became a starchy Anglican defender of the episcopal system. In 1590, Saravia affirmed that episcopacy was ordained by God, and denounced Puritans as insufferable upstarts flaunting divine law. Saravia helped lay the foundations for the high church party in the Church of England.

SARPI, Paolo (1552–1623) Great Venetian patriot who punctured papal pretensions by demonstrating that interdicts and excommunications from Rome had lost their force in the 17th century, Sarpi served for many years as Venice's official state counselor and unofficial scholar-in-residence. Sarpi, denied advancement in the Church through devious plots, took up his studies at Venice, where he published excellent studies in physiology and anatomy. He discovered how the iris of the eye contracts, and anticipated some of Harvey's work on the circulation of the blood.

When the bellicose Pope Paul V strained papal prerogatives in 1606 with unreasonable demands on the Venetian state, Sarpi advised Venice to ignore Paul's bluster and keep cool. Sarpi entered into the controversy by publishing a series of carefully prepared pamphlets disputing the Pope's right to employ censures. Eventually, a face-saving compromise was hammered out, but Sarpi emerged the hero and the papacy realized that its ancient weapons no longer cowed recalcitrants.

Sarpi, a champion of toleration, even longed for a Protestant free church at Venice, in which the Bible would have been an open book and the decrees of the Council of Trent rejected.

SAVONAROLA, Girolamo (1452–1498) A flinty Florentine reformer whose outspoken excoriations made him despot of the city for a time, Savonarola defied the worldly, powerful Italian Establishment including Lorenzo de' Medici and Pope Alexander VI, to turn Florence from a hive of wicked swingers into a haven of somber worshippers. Savonarola upbraided the 15th century Italian Church in sermons before spellbound audiences at St. Marks, Florence. After Lorenzo de' Medici's death, Savonarola incited Florence to throw out the rest of the de' Medicis and set up what became a theocratic dictatorship under Savonarola. He quickly removed the signs of corruption which had made Florence notorious, permitting "burning of the vanities"—bonfires of lewd verses and statuary.

Spurning Pope Alexander VI's conciliatory advances, Savonarola continued to roast the papacy. Although Savonarola was excommunicated in 1497, and Florence was placed under a papal interdict, Savonarola dominated the situation, calling for a General Church Council to depose Alexander.

His hold began to slip, however, as Florence grew tired of Savonarola's tight control and rigid Puritanism. In 1498, Savonarola dramatically tried to counter the restlessness and rising opposition in Florence by agreeing to undergo a trial by fire, offering to prove that he had never acted from wrong motives. Through no fault of Savonarola's, the trial was postponed. Savonarola, suddenly unpopular, was accused of cowardice by the fickle populace. He was seized, put through a hasty trial, brutally tortured for nearly a week, hanged and burned in the public square.

SCHAFF, David Schley (1852–1941) Son of the illustrious Protestant Professor Philip Schaff, David Schaff was also a distinguished Church historian. He taught at Pittsburgh's Western Theological Seminary from 1903 until 1925, and acted as co-editor of the Schaff-Herzog Encyclopedia.

SCHAFF, Philip (1819–1893) A Swiss-born professor of Church history who came to the German Reformed Theological Seminary at Mercersburg, Pennsylvania, Schaff carved out an influential career by teaming with theologian John Williamson Nevin to promulgate the Mercersburg Theology. Schaff wrote prolifically, penning such classics as the five-volume *History of the Christian Church*, 1882–1892, the three-volume *Creeds of Christendom*, 1877, and editing the Schaff-Herzog *Encyclopedia of Religious Knowledge*, 1882–1884.

A broad-visioned churchman, Schaff foresaw trends toward Church unity emerging years before the ecumenical movement was conceived. Schaff attracted both criticism and credit by pointing out evangelical aspects of Catholicism and the catholicity of true evangelicalism.

SCHELL, Hermann (1850–1906) A thoughtful, earnest German Roman Catholic scholar Schell tried to reinterpret Catholicism in modern, intellectual terms. In spite of the reactionary movement in Catholicism in the late 19th and early 20th century known as Ultramontanism which repudiated scientific inquiry and centralized authority in the person of the pope, Schell and a tiny handful valiantly urged modern historical criticism and Biblical investigation. Schell died a year before stubborn, anti-intellectual Pope Pius X issued his encyclical condemning "Modernism" and crushing inquiry by minds such as Schell's.

SCHLEIERMACHER, Friedrich Daniel Ernst (1768–1834) The most influential theologian of the early 19th century, Schleiermacher served as a hospital chaplain at Berlin, where he wrote his epochal *Addresses on Religion* in 1799. He served as a professor at Halle from 1804 to 1807, and was a Berlin pastor and Professor of Theology at newly-founded University of Berlin from 1810 until his death. In 1822, Schleiermacher published the significant *Christian Belief According to the Principles of the Evangelical Church.*

Schleiermacher, reacting against both the chilly rationalism and stifling orthodoxy of the 18th century which reduced Christianity to a system of proofs and rules of behavior, emphasized inward feeling and a personal sense of dependence as the basis for all religion. To Schleiermacher, Christianity is the best religion since it most fully accomplishes what all religions aim to achieve. Strongly Christocentric, Schleiermacher insisted that Christ alone is mediator of God's pardon and reconciliation.

Schleiermacher was denounced by the correctly orthodox as too radical and by the rationalists as too idealistic. Nearly every subsequent thinker has been indebted to Schleiermacher's pointing out the antithesis lying at the basis of all thought and life between ideal and real, between sense and intellect.

SCHMUCKER, Samuel Simon (1799–1873) An American Lutheran clergyman and educator, Schmucker headed the progressive "American" school of thought as opposed to a reactionary, "old-country" wing within U.S. Lutheranism in the 19th century. Schmucker helped found Gettysburg Seminary in 1826, organized what is now called Gettysburg College in 1832 and assisted in forming the Evangelical Alliance in 1846.

SCHWARTZ, Christian Friedrich (1726–1798) Deeply influenced by Francke, the great German pietist,

Schwartz left the University of Halle as one of the earliest Protestant foreign missionaries. Schwartz worked in India from 1750 until his death in 1798, bringing in more converts than any other Protestant worker, yet winning the esteem of both Moslem and Hindu leaders. After Schwartz's death, the Raja of Tanjore, a non-Christian, erected a monument to Schwartz's honor depicting Schwartz placing his hands on the Raja's head, bestowing a benediction.

SCHWARZ, Diebold (1485–1561) An early follower of Martin Luther, one-time Roman priest Schwarz anticipated Reformer Luther by conducting the first Reformed Mass in the German language in 1524. Schwarz translated the old Roman service into simple German but expunged all suggestions to the Roman Catholic doctrine of the sacrifice. At the time of his German Reformed Mass, Schwarz was an assistant pastor at Strassburg Cathedral, and soon after became pastor of Old St. Peter's, Strassburg. Schwarz, a close friend of Calvin, Bucer and other leaders of the Reformation, was associated with Calvin during Calvin's stay at Strassburg, and influenced Calvin's ideas about Reformed worship.

SCHWEITZER, Albert (1875–1965) Brilliant philosopher, theologian, musician and interpreter of Bach, Schweitzer turned his back on acclaim, honors and advancement in Europe to open a jungle hospital on the Lambarene River in steamy French Equatorial Africa in 1913. Schweitzer, a sensitive, studious son of an Alsatian pastor, empathized with all suffering creatures and cultivated what he called a "reverence for life." Deliberately resolving at the age of twenty-one to follow the intellectual pursuits of theology, philosophy and music until he was thirty, then to lead a life of sacrificial service to his fellow man, Schweitzer excelled in all three fields. Schweitzer's *The Quest of the Historical Jesus* in 1911 secured his fame as a thinker and his organ recitals in European capitals won him acclaim as an expert on Bach.

After completing medical studies, Schweitzer applied to the Paris Mission Society, but was turned down because of views expressed in his controversial book. Going deeply into debt, Schweitzer nonetheless sailed for Africa, built his own hospital and rendered heroic service.

During World War I, with war hysteria in France, Schweitzer was arrested in Africa and imprisoned in France. In spite of enormous debts, the collapse of his work and his wife's severe illness, Schweitzer continued his writing career in prison, completing *Civilization and Ethics*.

Schweitzer returned to Lambarene in 1924 and resumed his medical work among the millions "without help or hope of it." A modern-day St. Francis of Assisi in a pith helmet, Albert Schweitzer came to be the best-known and most admired Christian of the mid-twentieth century. The world showered him with honors, including the Nobel Peace Prize.

SCHWENCKFELD, Kaspar von Ossig (1489–1561) Trained as a diplomat but influenced by the writings of Luther and Tauler, Schwenckfeld served the Duke of Liegnitz and spread the Reformation throughout Liegnitz and Silesia. Schwenckfeld gradually adopted the stance of a mystic, veering away from Lutheranism and toward heresies such as deifying the humanity of Christ. Harshly criticized by Luther and other Protestants, the gentle Schwenckfeld and his followers withdrew from the Lutheran Church. Later, Schwenckfeld was condemned and hounded by hostile ecclesiastical and political authorities at Württemberg, where he died.

Although Schwenckfeld had no intention of organizing a denomination, his followers coalesced into a separate body. Many Schwenckfelders fled persecution in Germany by emigrating to the U.S. in 1754, where they settled near Philadelphia. A few Schwenckfelders linger today in Silesia; about 2,500 live in the United States in a handful of congregations.

SCIFFI, Clara See **CLARE OF Assisi.**

SCOTUS, Duns See **DUNS SCOTUS.**

SCUDDER, Ida Sophia (1870–1960) American medical missionary in India, "Dr. Ida," third generation of an outstanding missionary family in India, performed Herculean labors organizing hospitals, clinics, nursing schools and medical education at Vellore. Ida Scudder resolved to study medicine one memorable night in 1894 when three young girls died in childbirth because superstitious Indian families refused to permit a male physician to attend the girls. Returning to India with a medical degree in 1900 at the age of thirty, Dr. Scudder embarked on a campaign against fear and apathy, dispensing expert gynecological care and fighting plagues. She opened the first medical college for women in Asia at Vellore in 1918, founded the Cole dispensary at Thotapalayam, and directed the Schell Hospital at Vellore.

SEABURY, Samuel (1729–1796) The first American Protestant Episcopal Bishop in the United States, Seabury helped shape the liturgy, constitution, tradition and direction of the American

Episcopalianism. Seabury, imprisoned and maligned during the American Revolution for his outspoken Tory views, nonetheless became a staunch upholder of the new Republic after the War. Seabury was elected bishop in 1783 when ten rectors gathered in Connecticut after Revolution to try to rebuild the shattered Anglican communion in America. Seabury sailed to England, but due to the unsettled political situation, was unable to secure consecration at the hands of English bishops. After waiting for more than a year, Seabury finally had to settle for consecration at Aberdeen in 1784 by Scottish bishops, who were not subject to the Church of England.

Although Seabury returned to the United States and was formally recognized in 1789 by the General Convention of American Episcopalians, his claims as bishop were sniffed at by both purists who looked down on his consecration by Scottish bishops and by super-patriots who never forgave him for his Loyalist stand.

SEAGRAVE, Gordon Stifler (1897–1965) Gruff-talking but gentle-hearted American Baptist medical missionary who was known as the "Burma Surgeon," Dr. Seagrave won a chestful of medals and the lifelong gratitude of hundreds of Allied troops for his battle surgery during World War II. Seagrave served forty years in Burma, opening hospitals at Namkham and elsewhere and training Burmese staffs.

SEBASTIAN ([?]–288[?]) One of the hazy figures in early Church history, Sebastian died a martyr's death at Rome during the persecution of the Emperor Diocletian. According to unverifiable legend, Sebastian, believed to be born in Gaul of Italian parents from Milan, served as an officer in the crack Praetorian Guard, where he became a Christian. He is alleged to have worked many miraculous cures and spread the faith before Emperor Diocletian heard about it. Reputedly nursed back to health after he was horribly wounded by arrows in an attempt to execute him, Sebastian resumed his Christian witness before being clubbed to death on the orders of the irate Diocletian. The patron saint of archers, Sebastian was frequently portrayed skewered with arrows by Italian Renaissance artists.

SEIPEL, Ignaz (1876–1932) Austrian Roman Catholic priest and national political leader, Seipel led the Christian Socialist Party in the Austrian Assembly in 1919, and later served twice as Chancellor of Austria. He rebuilt the shaky state finances and instituted numerous reforms, 1922–23 and 1926–29.

SELNECKER, Nickolaus (1530–1592) A Lutheran theologian at Leipzig, Selnecker in 1577 helped prepare the *Formula of Concord,* the last great Lutheran creed. Selnecker, a Lutheran scholastic, assisted in introducing the era of high orthodoxy in Lutheranism.

SEMLER, Johann Salomo (1725–1791) A leading 18th century German church historian and Biblical scholar, Semler, from 1752 until his death, taught at the University of Halle, where he came to be known as the father of German rationalism. Semler fearlessly criticized Biblical materials and ecclesiastical documents. He was the first to insist that there was not equal value in all portions of Scripture. Revelation, he agreed, was in Scripture, but not all Scripture is revelation. Semler pioneered in discovering the origins of the Gospels and the Epistles.

SERGIUS, Patriarch of Constantinople ([?]–641) Syrian-born Patriarch of

Constantinople from 610 to 641 during the reign of Emperor Heracleus, Sergius tried to help his emperor knit together feuding fragments in the empire and the church in the face of threatened invasions by the fanatic Arab Moslems and the Persians. The eastern church was bitterly divided over expressions of Christ's divinity. Anxious to conciliate the Monophysites and unify the empire, Sergius proposed a compromise formula that Christ has "one divine-human energy" and ordered a halt to all discussion. Sergius wrote *Ekthesis*, issued by the emperor, which was supposed to end the matter.

A learned monk, Sophronus, however, protested, and kept the controversy alive. While the Church was dissipating its energies on theological hair-splitting, the Moslem hordes swarmed across the Middle East and North Africa, capturing Damascus in 635, Jerusalem and Antioch in 638, and Alexandria in 641.

SERGIUS I, Pope (630[?]–701) A native of Syria, Sergius I, serving as pope from 687 to 701, angered Emperor Justinian II by opposing several articles of the Council of Constantinople of 692, but was protected by the powerful Exarch of Ravenna.

SERGIUS II, Pope ([?]–847) Pope for three difficult years, 844 to 847, Sergius II served during the raids by the wild Saracen Moslems from North Africa, who poured up the Tiber valley as far as the outskirts of Rome, pillaging and burning.

SERGIUS III, Pope ([?]–911) Sergius III finally established his claims as pope in 904 after a sticky dispute with two rivals known as antipopes Christopher and Leo V. Sergius had Christopher and Leo strangled. He reputedly was the father of an illegitimate son who became Pope John XI.

SERGIUS IV, Pope ([?]–1012) A docile tool in the hands of Roman feudal nobility, Sergius IV blessed the efforts of Italian princes to throw out the Saracens, Moslem invaders from North Africa who had been occupying portions of Italy for several centuries. Sergius IV ruled from 1009 to 1012.

SERRA, Junipero (1713–1784) A Spanish Franciscan missionary to North America, "Father Juniper" arrived at Mexico City in 1750 and labored among the Indians of the Sierra Gorda area for nineteen years before heading northwest to open mission work in what is now California. In 1769 Serra founded a mission post at the location of present-day San Diego, the first in what is now California. He established additional mission outposts in the following years at San Carlos (1770), Monterey (1770), San Antonio, near Los Angeles (1771), San Francisco (1776), and Santa Clara (1777), all of which became the first settlements in California. Supervising a band of only sixteen followers, Serra made his headquarters at Monterey and traveled on foot frequently to oversee each mission until his death in 1784.

SERVETUS, Michael (1511–1553) Although a Spanish medical genius (the first to discover the pulmonary circulation of the blood) Servetus is remembered primarily as a skeptical, Unitarian-leaning gadfly to both the Reformed and Roman Establishment, who aroused the ire of nearly everyone in Europe. Servetus died in Calvin's Geneva, condemned as a heretic.

Servetus first came into prominence in 1531 when he published a rash article in which he questioned the Trinity and renounced belief in Original Sin or infant baptism. Harrassed by the authorities in Germany, Servetus fled to Paris where he first met Calvin and where he studied medicine. Servetus, using the pseudonoym Michel de Villeneuve, disagreed with the medical faculty at Paris, went to Louvain, read theology, then practiced medicine in a succession of leading cities throughout Europe.

At the height of his fame as a physician at Vienna in 1553, Servetus broke into print again when he published his *Christianismi restitutio*, a full-scale denial of all traditional orthodoxy. Convicted of heresy by the Roman Catholic authorities, Servetus escaped the death penalty by a prison break. Heading for Italy, Servetus unaccountably stopped at Geneva, where he had been denounced by Calvin and the Reformers. He was seized the day after his arrival, condemned as a heretic when he refused to recant, and burned in 1553 with the apparent tacit approval of Calvin.

SEVERUS ([?]–538) A patriarch of Antioch from 512 until 518, Severus was forced out of his see because of his Monophysite sympathies and forced to flee to Egypt, where he lived during his last twenty years. Severus, anxious to assert the divinity of Christ, subordinated the humanity of Jesus to the point that the ultimate reality of Jesus' nature is the divine. Severus headed the Monophysites, those who shared his views on the nature of Christ, and regarded the Chalcedonian Council and Creed (which declared that Christ was both God and man, truly and completely both human and divine) with profound suspicion, and helped perpetuate controversy in the Eastern Church.

SHAFTESBURY, Anthony Ashley Cooper, Third Earl of (1671–1713) Although a punctiliously proper Anglican, Shaftesbury wrote treatises in philosophy and ethics which based men's actions not on hope of reward or fear of punishment but on an inward "moral sense." Shaftesbury turned Christian ethics away from obeying the will of God to a humanistic balancing of selfishness and altruism. Shaftesbury's *Characteristics of Men* in 1711 deeply affected subsequent ethicists and natural theologians, and helped smooth the way for the rise of Deism.

SHAFTESBURY, Anthony Ashley Cooper, Seventh Earl of (1801–1885) An English blueblood who took his Christian faith more seriously than his title or standing, Shaftesbury carried his commitment to Christ with him to his seat in Parliament. Shaftesbury fought doggedly for social justice, introducing legislation which was frequently denounced by conservative churchmen. After many defeats, Shaftesbury finally succeeded in having the Ten Hours' Bill passed in 1847, which protected children from working in mines and mills, and later pushed through the Factory Act of 1874. Shaftesbury spent great amounts of money, energy and time on 19th century causes considered controversial or radical by many at the time, including schools for slum children, working men's institutes, foreign missions, and other agencies working with the exploited poor in England's cities.

SHARP, James (1618–1679) Unscrupulously ambitious Scottish Presbyterian cleric who betrayed his colleagues to win appointment as Archbishop of St. Andrews, Sharp helped restore episcopacy to Scotland in 1661. Sharp previously had been sent as an emissary of the Scottish Kirk to London. Although he sold out to Anglican politicians, he pretended for a time to be loyal to his associates and Kirk, successfully stopping all petitions from Scotland to king, parliament and council. When episcopacy was forced on Scotland and

Sharp received appointment as Chief Bishop, Sharp lied further, assuring his erstwhile Presbyterian colleagues that there would be no changes.

Instead, Parliament passed stiff resolutions requiring officeholders to disown the covenants of 1638 and 1643, and levying heavy fines for absence from episcopal services. At Sharp's urging, repression in Scotland increased when in 1664 a High Commission Court was instituted. Sharp was assassinated in 1679, and a revolt, The Pentland Uprising, broke out.

SHELDON, Charles Monroe (1857–1946) American Congregational pastor and journalist, Sheldon wrote the best selling *In His Steps* in 1896, suggesting that all Christian decisions could be resolved simply by asking, "What would Jesus do?" Sheldon served as a pastor in Topeka, Kansas, edited the *Christian Herald* magazine from 1920 to 1925, and churned out thirty-one other books.

SHOEMAKER, Samuel Moor (1893–1963) American Episcopal rector who emphasized one-to-one personal evangelism, "Sam" Shoemaker served at Calvary Episcopal, New York, and Calvary Church, Pittsburgh, where he reached the group which referred to itself as "the golf club crowd." Shoemaker, uniquely gifted to stir laymen, helped the laymen who founded Alcoholics Anonymous to prepare AA's famous "Twelve Steps."

SIGEBERT of Gembloux (1030[?]–1112) A Belgian Benedictine, Sigebert wrote *Chronographia*, a carefully documented history of world events from 381 until 1111, and chose to stand by his Emperor, Henry IV, rather than the pope during the monumental struggles between the papacy and the crown.

SIGISMUND, Emperor (1368–1437) Ruler of Germany, Hungary and Bohemia and Holy Roman Emperor from 1411 to 1437, Sigismund was the slippery statesman who insisted on the Council of Constance in 1414.

The Council of Constance settled the disgraceful squabble which had produced the great Schism and declared Bohemian preachers John Huss and Jerome of Prague heretics.

The wily Sigismund had promised Huss safe conduct, but broke his word on the grounds that it was necessary to kill heretics. Earlier, in 1396, Sigismund had mounted a Crusade against the Moslems which ended in a disastrous defeat by the Turks.

SILVERIUS, Pope ([?]–538[?]) The son of Pope Hormisdas (who had married before taking orders) Silverius served as pope during 536, but was accused of selling out to the Goths attacking Rome. Silverius was driven into exile and supplanted by counter-pope Vigilius. Although Silverius was cleared of all charges and ordered reinstated by Emperor Justinian I, he died in lonely exile. He was later canonized by the Catholic Church.

SILVESTER See **SYLVESTER**.

SIMEON, Charles (1759–1836) An ardent Evangelical or low churchman in the Church of England, Simeon taught for many years at Cambridge University, where he helped Cambridge become a center for Evangelicalism in the early 19th century.

SIMEON Metaphrastes (second half of the 10th c.) The most illustrious of the Byzantine hagiographers, Simeon Metaphrastes compiled a renowned collection of the lives of the saints in the Eastern Church, arranging them in a menology for the twelve months of the year. Much of our knowledge of the biographies of early Eastern churchmen is due to Simeon's careful research and records. He is honored as a saint by the Greek Church.

SIMEON STYLITES (390[?]–459) An eccentric Syrian ascetic with a streak of exhibitionism, Simeon lived on a pillar from 423 until he died in 459. He gradually boosted the height of his column until it towered over sixty feet and spent his entire time on the cramped area on the top, fasting, praying, snatching sleep while hunched over a parapet, and preaching to admiring followers below. His meagre wants were hoisted in a basket. Simeon started a fad among monks in his area, who found their own pillars and imitated his ways, calling themselves Stylites or Pillar Saints.

SIMEON "The New Theologian" ([?]–1040[?]) The most outstanding mystic in the 11th century Greek Church, Simeon asserted that a vision of God is possible for a believer. Simeon's noble-sounding but misty-worded writings were the quintescence of devotional beauty, but added nothing to theological thinking. He is venerated in the Eastern Church.

SIMON of Sudbury ([?]–1381) A dour oligarch who was rewarded for his services to both the papacy and the English crown by being named Archbishop of Canterbury in 1375, Simon ruthlessly suppressed all dissent by restless peasants and reform-minded priests. Simon personally took charge at the second trial of Bible translator John Wycliffe in 1338. In 1381, Simon jailed John Ball, the Wycliffite priest who had supported the peasant uprising in England led by Wat Tyler. Simon of Sudbury's harsh highhandedness aroused Tyler's supporters to loot Simon's Lambeth residence, drag Simon from hiding in the Tower and decapitate him.

SIMON, Richard (1638–1712) A Roman Catholic parish priest-scholar who remained in his hometown of Dieppe, France, during his entire career, Simon relieved his humdrum existence in a provincial location by doing such precise studies of Hebrew and Greek Biblical materials that he is venerated as the father of modern Biblical historical criticism.

Simon stirred both acclaim and anger by publishing *Critical History of the Old Testament, A Critical History of the New Testament, Critical History of the Principal Commentators of the New Testament,* and *New Observations of the Text and Versions of the New Testament,* which together formed a kind of watershed in Biblical studies. Simon was rejected by nearly all his contemporaries, Catholic and Protestant, and was even suspected of heresy by his superiors.

SIMONS, MENNO See **MENNO SIMONS.**

SIMPLICIUS, Pope ([?]–483) Pope from 468 until 483, Simplicius headed the Church at a time when it was growing more wealthy and worldly. Immediately preceding his reign, it had been decreed that it was not permissible for the higher clergy to engage in secular occupation to earn a living. About the same time, the Church became the recipient of vast estates and properties. Simplicius decreed that ecclesiastical income be divided in quarters, one each for the bishop, the other clergy, the upkeep of property and programs, and the poor.

SIMPSON, Albert Benjamin (1844–1919) Founder of the Christian and Missionary Alliance, Simpson was a

Canadian-born American Presbyterian who moved from Toronto, to a Louisville, Kentucky, pastorate in 1873. The same year he experienced a profoundly moving experience which he described as "the fullness of the blessing of Christ." Simpson moved to New York after this consciousness of personal sanctification, but suffered a severe illness. A healing experience saved him from the life of being a complete invalid. Simpson began speaking of the "Four-fold Gospel," stressing Jesus Christ as Saviour, Sanctifier, Healer and Coming King.

In 1881, Simpson left his comfortable pastorate and opened a mission. The following year, he founded a mission training center. His missionary society began in 1887, and was called the "Christian Alliance." In 1889, he founded a second missionary society, "The International Missionary Alliance." The two were combined in 1897, and named the Christian and Missionary Alliance, which became in effect a denomination.

SIMPSON, Matthew (1811–1884) A prominent and influential 19th century American Methodist bishop, Simpson was a licensed physician who left his practice to become a circuit-rider holding thirty-three "meetings" or services on a six-weeks preaching circuit. He quickly gained fame as a spellbinder of an orator. Simpson became first president of what is now DePauw University and edited the "Western Christian Advocate" before his election as bishop in 1852. A fervent abolitionist, Simpson occasionally advised Abraham Lincoln during the Civil War.

SIXTUS I, Pope ([?]–125) Probably of Greek origin, Sixtus I ruled from about 116 to 125 during the early days of Emperor Hadrian's reign. This early bishop of Rome is reported to have been martyred. He has been canonized by the Roman Church.

SIXTUS II, Pope ([?]–258) An adroit diplomat, Sixtus II persuaded the churches in North Africa and Italy to accept the Church of Rome's procedure of re-baptizing heretics, ending a vexing division. Sixtus II, serving only from 257 to 258, was seized and killed during the Emperor Valerian's persecution. He was subsequently declared a saint.

SIXTUS III, Pope ([?]–440) Reigning from 432 to 440, Sixtus III endorsed the infamous "robber" Council of Ephesus and tried to bring some accord among contentious clerics, including John of Antioch and Cyril of Alexandria.

SIXTUS IV, Pope (1414–1484) A Franciscan monk who rose to head his order before his elevation as pope in 1471, Sixtus IV is principally remembered for building the Sistine Chapel and Bridge, levying crushing taxes to finance his series of costly wars with Florence, and practicing nepotism to a degree that even surprised the blasé Italians.

SIXTUS V, Pope (1521–1590) A stern, vigorous pontiff who in 1560 was relieved from his post as Inquisitor in Venice for being too harsh, Sixtus V relentlessly suppressed Church dissent and civil disorder during his reign from 1585 to 1590. Sixtus V is remembered as the pope who set the number of cardinals at seventy.

SLESSOR, Mary (1848–1915) Indomitable Scottish Presbyterian missionary to Africa, Mary Slessor, forced as a girl to work in the Dundee mills to support her drunken father and the impoverished family, sailed to the Dark

Continent in 1876. She pioneered mission programs in many parts of East Africa and won publicity and honors, including a decoration from the King of England.

SMITH, John See Smyth, John.

SMITH, Joseph, Jr. (1805–1844) Like many other New Englanders transplanted to western New York, Joseph Smith sought buried treasures, attended camp meeting revivals with his family and puzzled over the conflicting claims of rival protestant faiths. He had migrated to western New York from Vermont at the age of ten with his parents.

While looking back to his religious conversion, he recorded, "So great were the confusion and strife among the different denominations, that it was impossible for a person as young as I was, and so unacquainted with men and things, to come to any certain conclusion who was right and who was wrong." Joseph Smith built a new religious society. In his history, written by himself, he reported a series of visions in the 1820's which, he said, revealed to him his divine appointment to restore Christ's church. On April 6, 1830, at Fayette, New York, Smith and five other men organized the "Church of Christ" (later named "Church of Jesus Christ of Latter Day Saints").

On March 26, 1830, Smith published *The Book of Mormon,* which was represented as a record of several groups of ancient Hebrew peoples transplanted to ancient America. Smith claimed to have "translated" miraculously this record from golden plates unearthed three years earlier by angelic direction.

From 1830 forward, Smith was acknowledged by his followers ". . . as a prophet, [and] an apostle of Jesus Christ"; the church was admonished to "give heed unto all his words and commandments." With this type of charisma, Smith led his Saints on what was intended to be a pilgrimage to build the New Jerusalem in preparation for the expected imminent return of Christ, and the beginning of the Millennial Reign.

Persecution from without and dissension from within resulted in the continual movement of Smith's community. From New York the migration westward paused at Kirtland, Ohio. A few months later (July, 1831) a sizable contingent of the Saints moved to and established the "New Jerusalem" in Independence, Jackson County, Missouri.

Since Smith remained in Kirtland, the church membership was divided by nearly a thousand miles of rugged, wooded terrain. Persecution at the hands of Jackson County militants forced the Independence, Missouri Mormons to flee across the Missouri River to Liberty, Clay County, Missouri. Others went back to Kirtland. In 1836 the Missouri legislature organized lands in the northern part of the state for a Mormon sanctuary, naming it Caldwell County. The Mormons soon established their headquarters at Far West, and in 1838 Smith and many of his Kirtland followers departed dissension-racked Kirtland in favor of the new settlements of Northern Missouri. Again, the dual forces of persecution and inner turmoil forced the Saints to flee Missouri.

In 1839 they established the city of Nauvoo, Illinois. By 1844, Nauvoo (population: about 15,000) was the largest community in the state, with its own militia and several thousand immigrants from England. In Nauvoo, Smith exercised an almost absolute ecclesiastical and political authority. He was prophet-president of the church, mayor of the city, sole trustee, recorder of deeds for Nauvoo (despite the fact that Carthage was the seat of Hancock County) and editor of the church paper,

Times and Seasons. In 1844 he announced his candidacy for the United States Presidency.

However, Smith's "revelations" sponsoring celestial marriage (a natural precursor to polygamy, or plural marriage) and his destruction of an antichurch press engendered the fury of local citizens who jailed him at Carthage, Illinois, to await trial on the rather dubious charge of treason. But, on June 27, 1844, a mob stormed the Carthage jail, where Smith and his brother Hyrum were shot to death. Two years later many of Smith's followers began their trek westward to the Great Salt Lake Valley under the leadership of Brigham Young, President of the church's Council of the Twelve Apostles. Many others remained in Illinois and neighboring states, splitting into a number of factions. A sizable number of those not part of the Salt Lake migration regrouped and emerged into what eventually was called the Reorganized Church of Jesus Christ of Latter Day Saints, now headquartered in Independence, Missouri.

SMITH, Joseph, III (1832–1914) Son of Joseph Smith, Jr., founder of Latter Day Saintism, Joseph Smith III headed the Reorganized Church of Jesus Christ of Latter Day Saints for fifty-four years. After the death of the founder, the church split into several factions, and in 1852 a group dissatisfied with all LDS bodies formed the New Organization, later called the Reorganized Church. Joseph Smith III, who had been designated by his father to succeed as leader, accepted the presidency of the Reorganization in 1860 and served until his death in 1914. After sojourns in Plano, Illinois, and Lamoni, Iowa, he moved to Independence, Missouri, which had been selected in 1831 as the center place for Latter Day Saints.

SMITH, Rodney ("Gipsy") (1860–1947) A bouncy English revivalist who commanded great attention in the pre-World War I era, "Gipsy" Smith, illiterate son of itinerant gipsy tinkers, conducted evangelistic rallies throughout the English-speaking world for many years. He was converted at a Salvation Army rally while in his teens, and almost immediately began a stunningly successful career as revival preacher. After winning headlines for his revivals for the Salvation Army at Hull and Hanley, England, Smith was asked to resign from the Salvation Army because of a minor infraction of Salvation Army rules. Smith continued his preaching career as an independent, holding revivals in the United States, Australia, South Africa and Britain, then serving from 1897 until 1912 as special missioner for the National Free Church Council in Britain.

SMITH, Samuel Stanhope (1750–1819) An American Presbyterian pastor and educator, Smith in 1775 became the first president of Hampden Sidney College, then served as president of Princeton from 1795 to 1812, rebuilding an institution badly wrecked by the Revolutionary War. Smith also helped draw up the Book of Government of the Presbyterian Church in the U.S.A.

SMITH, Thomas Southwood (1788–1861) An evangelically-minded English churchman who left his pastorate among the poverty-stricken in order to study medicine, Smith devoted his life to improving conditions among slum dwellers. Smith helped expose the evils of child labor, and helped secure passage of the Factory Act prohibiting children to be hired in British mines and mills. His work on epidemics helped prepare the path for other researchers.

SMITH, Uriah (1832–1903) An American Seventh Day Adventist, Uriah Smith was the leading literary producer of the movement for many years at Battle Creek, Michigan, writing Adventist material, editing denominational materials and supervising the Adventist publishing house.

SMITH, William Robertson (1846–1894) Learned Scottish Free Church Semitic scholar, Smith was the subject of a celebrated heresy trial in Scotland in the late 19th century. Smith, professor of Old Testament at the Free Church College, Aberdeen, provoked howls of protest when he published articles in the 1876 *Encyclopedia Britannica* on "Angels" and "Bible." Smith's articles, defending the findings of the then-new Higher Criticism, led to such extreme criticism that he demanded a trial by the Free Church General Assembly. Although acquitted of heresy, Smith was suspended from his professorship after a vote of no-confidence.

He had become a national celebrity, however, and the champion of all progressive thinkers. After serving as the distinguished editor of the Ninth Edition of the *Britannica*, Smith resumed his academic career, acting as librarian and professor at Christ College, Cambridge.

SMYTH, John ([?]–1612) Unsettled enthusiast for Separatist causes, Smyth began his clerical career as a Church of England rector, acquired Puritan ideas, switched to being a Separatist preacher, then later rejected infant baptism to become the spiritual father of the leaders of the English Baptists.

During his days as a peppery Separatist, Smyth organized Separatist groups in the north of England from which many of the *Mayflower* pilgrims originally came. About 1602, Smyth gathered his first congregation at Gainsborough. He quickly attracted adherents throughout the countryside, and collected a second congregation in the home of William Brewster at Scrooby. When the authorities began to take measures against the Gainsborough congregation, Smyth led the group to Amsterdam, where they were soon joined by the Scrooby congregation under William Brewster and John Robinson.

Smyth became enamored with Mennonite ideas and Anabaptist teachings in the Netherlands, re-baptized himself about 1609 and started baptizing others in his congregation by pouring. Smyth broke with the Separatists and established an Arminian Baptist congregation before dying of tuberculosis in Amsterdam in 1612.

Two of his converts, Thomas Helwys and John Murton, led many of Smyth's congregation back to England, where they established the first permanent Baptist church.

SMYTHE See **SMYTH**.

SNOW, Lorenzo (1814–1901) Influential American president of the Church of Jesus Christ of the Latter Day Saints, Mormon Snow made numerous proselytizing journeys abroad and throughout the U.S. Snow coined the untheological and unbiblical epigram, "As man now is, God once was; as God now is, man may be," which found its way into Mormon dogma.

SNOWDEN, James Henry (1852–1936) American Presbyterian scholar, preacher and journalist, Snowden, a progressive yet popular figure in American Protestantism, was acclaimed as the man who helped more than any other to bring the Presbyterian Church to accept and use the results of scientific inquiry and keep the Presbyterian Church, U.S.A., united during the bitter Modernist-Fundamentalist controversy. Snowden, a dazzling dialectician, even bested famed Bible-baiting lawyer Clarence Darrow in debate. An incredibly productive author, Snowden wrote thirty-nine books on a variety of subjects and edited the two leading denominational journals for over thirty-eight years. A theologian with a knack for expressing profundities with simplicity, Snowden taught at Pittsburgh's Western Theological Seminary from 1911 to 1929. Snowden's good sense and balanced judgment were conceded to be the reasons why no Presbyterian congregation in the Pittsburgh area withdrew from the denomination during the nation-wide strife between "Fundamentalists" and "Modernists" in the 1920's and 30's.

SOCINUS, Faustus Paulus (1539–1604) Brainy Italian anti-Trinitarian theologian, Socinus worked among the fledgling Unitarian societies in Poland from 1579. Socinus, who leaned toward Arian views as early as 1559 in Siena, made his first of many flights to avoid persecution and/or prosecution for heresy when he was only twenty. He published anonymously while at Florence and in Poland, until 1598, when he finally signed his name to a tract he had written. When the angry citizens of Cracow discovered his identity, Socinus was driven from the city. Socinus' followers in Poland and Unitarians generally in Europe are frequently called Socinians.

SODERBLOM, Nathan (1866–1931) Lively and influential Swedish pacifist and ecumenist, Soderblom was one of the earliest to envision and promote unity among Christians. This one-time theological professor at Upsala who in 1914 became Archbishop and Chancellor of the University of Upsala labored to bring about the Christian Conference on Life and Work at Stockholm in 1925, one of the great steps leading ultimately to the creation of the World Council of Churches in 1947. Soderblom, an uncompromising pacifist, was awarded the Nobel Peace prize in 1930.

SORBON, Robert de (1201–1274) The French theologian who established the residence hall for poor theological students in Paris' Latin Quarter which ultimately came to be known as the distinguished university, the Sorbonne, Sorbon served as chaplain to pious King Louis IX of France. Sorbon enlisted Louis' help to finance a place where penniless priests-to-be could read theology.

What was intended to be simply a dormitory and reading room grew into one of the world's most illustrious intellectual centers, with faculties, libraries, classes, degrees and a student body of 10,000.

SOTO, Domingo de (1494–1560) Spanish intellectual and Thomistic thinker, Soto served as Emperor Charles V's imperial theologian and his own Dominican Order's official representative at the epochal Council of Trent, beginning in 1545. Soto, a disciple of the Salamancan theologian, Francisco de Vittoria, continued Vittoria's revival of Thomas Aquinas' theology in the Spanish awakening in the 16th century. A powerful apologist who later taught at Salamanca, Soto was one of the ablest spokesmen for the Roman Catholic position during the early confrontations with Protestantism.

SOUTHWELL, Robert (1561[?]–1595) A neat poet and nerveless priest who spent much of his creative life in exile on the continent, Southwell returned to England in 1586 in spite of severe legal strictures against Roman Catholic priests. Southwell survived for a few years by conducting a furtive ministry, but was eventually captured and tortured repeatedly. Refusing to renounce his stand as a Jesuit, he was finally executed. Most of his lovely verses were published posthumously.

SOZZINI See SOCINUS.

SPALDING, Catherine (1793–1858)
A compassionate and capable American nun, Mother Catherine became one of the original Sisters of Charity of Nazareth in 1813. She later headed the order and helped found many Roman Catholic schools, hospitals and orphanages in Kentucky.

SPALDING, John Lancaster (1840–1916)
An American Roman Catholic archbishop, Spalding held a series of important U.S. diocesan posts and helped found the prestigious Catholic University of America.

SPANGENBERG, Augustus Gottlieb (1704–1792)
A quiet, practical, hard-working organizer and administrator, Spangenberg succeeded the enthusiastic and occasionally erratic Count von Zinzendorf as leader of the Moravians. Spangenberg, a Halle professor who was fired from his post for his pietistic leanings in 1735, linked himself to the Moravian Brethren community on the estate of the generous Count von Zinzendorf. From 1735 until 1739, Spangenberg organized Moravian settlements in the American colonies. Spangenberg then served intermittently in Germany and England for several years, founding the Society for the Furtherance of the Gospel in England. He returned to the colony of Pennsylvania, where he acted as bishop, directing Moravian activities, until called back to Germany to succeed Zinzendorf.

Spangenberg strengthened Moravianism, eliminating some of the oddities introduced by Zinzendorf which had brought the movement criticism and ridicule.

SPARKS, Jared (1789–1866)
One of the early leaders of the Unitarian movement in the United States, Sparks, a New Englander, served a Congregational parish in Baltimore. At his installation in 1819, Sparks invited William Ellery Channing to give the sermon, which became a sort of manifesto and creed of the liberals within Congregationalism who in 1825 formed the American Unitarian Association.

SPEER, Robert Elliot (1867–1947)
Much-respected American Presbyterian mission board executive and a principal architect of the modern ecumenical movement, Robert E. Speer served from 1891 to 1937 as Secretary of the Board of Foreign Missions for the Presbyterian Church, U.S.A. Speer, a well-educated theologian who refused ordination as pastor, brought both vision and voice to the cause of Christian missions. He was a pioneer administrator in the Student Volunteer Movement, sending dozens of bright, young, American Christians to minister overseas. In addition to his brilliant career in the Presbyterian Church, Speer found time to be president of the Federal Council of Churches and Moderator of the Presbyterian General Assembly, the first layman ever elected to that office.

SPELLMAN, Francis Joseph (1889–1967)
American Roman Catholic Cardinal and Archbishop of New York from 1939 until his death in 1967, Spellman wielded considerable clout in the U.S.A. political and Church scene. Spellman, a close personal friend of Pope Pius XII from their student days together in Rome, was the first American to be appointed to the Secretariat of State in the Vatican. During his tenure as Archbishop of New York, Spellman

built over one-half billion dollars' worth of new buildings for his Catholic parishes and practiced the custom of celebrating Christmas with American servicemen in lonely posts.

SPENER, Philip Jakob (1635–1705) The warm-hearted founder of the German pietist movement, Spener was a Lutheran pastor who emphasized a deep personal awareness of Christ's presence and careful devotional habits. Spener began holding prayer and Bible study sessions in his home while serving as a pastor at Frankfurt in 1666. The success of his home prayer meetings led him to publish *Earnest Desires for Reform of the True Evangelical Church* in 1675.

Spener's stiff colleagues, however, resisted his stress on personal religion, sniffing that it did not fit in with their precise textbook orthodoxy. In spite of the sneers and sniping Spener received the prestigious appointments of court chaplain at Dresden and later rector of St. Nicholas', Berlin.

Spener, determined to encourage pietism, helped found the University of Halle. The hostility of the hyper-orthodox continued, however; in 1695 Spener was charged by the theological faculty of Wittenburg with 265 theological "errors" in his writings, criticizing Spener for slighting dogma in favor of devotionalism. Spener, nonetheless, continued his campaign for personal morality and pietist methods.

SPOONER, William Archibald (1844–1930) An unintentionally and unconsciously hilarious Anglican cleric-educator at Oxford's New College from 1867 to 1924, Spooner convulsed several several generations of students with his transpositions of sounds and syllables, which came to be known as "Spoonerisms." ("Is the *bean dizzy*?", etc.)

SPOTSWOOD, John (1565–1639) A Scots cleric with little theological integrity but immense personal ambition, Spotswood shucked his Presbyterian ordination to ingratiate himself with Leading People. He went to mass in France with the Catholic Duke of Lennox in 1601, embraced Episcopalianism under Anglican King James VI of Scotland. As the King's toady, Spotswood won the coveted appointment of Archbishop of Glasgow, the Primate of all Scotland. In 1618 the harsh, haughty royal sycophant issued the Perth Articles, ordering tough penalties against non-Episcopalians. Spotswood aroused such intense dislike toward episcopacy and toward himself among fellow-Scots that they finally threw him out in 1638.

SPURGEON, Charles Haddon (1834–1892) Gifted English Baptist pulpiteer and exegete, Spurgeon began his homiletical career at sixteen, becoming known as the "Boy Preacher," and accepted his first pastorate at eighteen. His fame and following propelled him to London when he was only twenty. His congregation at the New Park Street Chapel repeatedly had to enlarge its facilities until it finally erected the 6,000 seat Metropolitan Tabernacle. Spurgeon, however, refused to be a popular pulpit idol. Combining conviction and content in his sermons, he displayed a hardcore Calvinism which rejected both the sentimentalism and the rationalism infecting 19th century church thinking.

STANISLAUS (1030–1071) The patron saint of Poland, Stanislaus as the Bishop of Cracow in 1071 excommunicated King Boleslav II for outrageous conduct, but was brutally murdered by the vengeful monarch. Stanislaus, canonized in 1253, is still deeply revered in Poland.

STANLEY, Arthur Penrhyn (1815–1881) The model for the character, "Arthur," in Hughes' best-selling novel, *Tom Brown's Schooldays,* Stanley was an Anglican priest and Oxford professor who came to stand as unofficial spokesman for the broad church faction within the Church of England. Stanley's liberal ideas provoked numerous controversies in the stuffy 19th century Anglican Establishment.

STAUPITZ, Johann von ([?]–1524) Sensitive, sympathetic spiritual advisor to Martin Luther in 1505 while the Reformer was still a guilt-ridden monastic, von Staupitz headed the Augustinian community at Erfurt, Germany. Staupitz, whose insights into the Gospel meant love and laughter as well as learning, gently led Luther from cringing terror before a punishing Deity. An exemplary preaching-monastic, Staupitz persisted in the Medieval theology and mystical piety of the Middle Ages. However, he was startlingly modern in his counseling technique when he advised the troubled Luther to busy himself by undertaking preaching and assuming the chair of Bible at Wittenberg University—a position Staupitz himself had held.

STEBBINS, George Coles (1846–1945) A cheerful American revival musician, Stebbins helped direct the music and lead the singing for over twenty-four years for the Moody-Sankey evangelistic meetings. He wrote 1,500 Gospel Songs and hymns, including "There Is a Green Hill Far Away," and edited several collections of popular religious songs.

STEPHEN I, King of Hungary (997–1038) Founder of the Hungarian monarchy, King Stephen established the Christian faith in his kingdom after several unsuccessful previous efforts by others. He was later canonized, and is admired in Hungarian history as St. Stephen.

STEPHEN I, Pope ([?]–257) An assertive pontiff who engaged in hot controversy over baptism with Cyprian of Carthage (who wanted to deny the validity of baptism administered by heretical priests) Stephen insisted that the meaning of the sacrament lay not in the purity or orthodoxy of the priest but in the faith of the believer and the formula used. Stephen, pope from 254 to 257, was later canonized.

STEPHEN (II) Pope ([?]–752) Elected in 752, this pontiff-elect died three days before being consecrated. His name, nevertheless, was carried in official Vatican lists until 1960, causing great confusion in the numbering of subsequent popes named Stephen.

STEPHEN II, Pope ([?]–757) Chosen pope after the sudden demise of Stephen (II) in 752, Stephen II had to contend with invading Lombards. He finally persuaded Pepin the Short, King of the Franks, to act as protector to keep the Lombards out of Rome and off Church lands. Under Stephen II, the Papal State was established.

STEPHEN III, Pope ([?]–772) A vicious, vacillating prelate, Stephen III ordered shockingly bloody punishments against his predecessor, a usurper named Constantine II, and Constantine's followers. Stephen worked ineffectively with Charlemagne. During his reign from 768 to 772, a Lateran Synod in 769 laid down procedures for electing popes in which laymen were excluded from balloting.

STEPHEN IV, Pope ([?]–817) Pope from 816 to 817, Stephen IV allied himself closely with his protectors, the Frankish kings.

STEPHEN V, Pope ([?]–891) Forced to find a new papal protector after the collapse of Charlemagne's Empire in 887, Stephen V placed the crown of the Holy Roman Emperor on the head of Guido of Spoleto. Stephen reigned from 885 to 891.

STEPHEN VI, Pope ([?]–897) Completely controlled by Spoleto politicians during his papacy from 896 to 897, this puppet even permitted the macabre mockery in which the corpse of a predecessor, Pope Formosus, was put on trial. Finally thrown out after popular revulsion undermined his authority, Stephen VI was imprisoned and executed by being strangled to death.

STEPHEN VII, Pope ([?]–931) Pope from 929 to 931.

STEPHEN VIII, Pope ([?]–942) Completely dominated by Alberic II who then ruled Rome, this docile pontiff feebly urged monastic reform being promoted by the monks of Cluny Monastery, France. Stephen VIII served from 939 to 942.

STEPHEN IX, Pope ([?]–1058) Stephen IX, a firm, decisive leader, took steps to end interference by secular rulers in the election of bishops and popes. He encouraged necessary improvements of the morals of priests by demanding celibacy among all clergy. Previously, Stephen served as one of the party sent to Constantinople in 1054 which so offensively handled the delicate relations between the Byzantine and Latin churches that a breach opened which has never been closed. He served as pope from 1057–58.

STEPINAC, Aloysius (1898–1960) Heroic Croatian nationalist in Yugoslavia who opposed Tito's Communist regime following World War II, Archbishop Stepinac suffered arrest in 1946 on trumped-up charges of collaborating with the Nazis. Archbishop Stepinac, shut in prison until 1951 when he was released during a serious illness, was then exiled to an obscure village by Tito. The brave Stepinac, however, was awarded a cardinal's hat in 1952, causing the Yugoslav government to sever relations with the Vatican.

STEWART, James (1831–1905) A Scottish missionary in South Africa from 1861 until his death in 1905, Stewart went out as an assistant to David Livingstone, returned to Scotland to get a medical degree, and dedicated the remainder of his life to bringing healing and education to Africans. In 1867 near Capetown, Stewart founded Lovedale Institute, the first great industrial educational mission enterprise in Africa, and the prototype of several programs Stewart established. Stewart of Lovedale, as he came to be called, was the first missionary to train African medical assistants.

STIGAND, William (1002–1064) Archbishop of Canterbury who loyally backed English leaders when the Normans invaded England. Stigand was dismissed by an ecclesiastical investigating committee from Rome sent at the behest of the Norman leader, William the Conqueror. Stigand was sentenced to life imprisonment at Winchester, where he died of starvation.

STODDARD, Solomon (1643–1729) Influential and erudite Congregational minister who dominated the political and ecclesiastical affairs of western Massachusetts for half a century, Stoddard preached at Northampton (Mass.) from 1672 until his death in 1729. Stoddard's writings carried immense weight in the late 17th–early 18th century. His theology and form of

Church discipline was surprisingly broadminded. He endorsed the controversial "Halfway Covenant," permitting non-communicants to have their children baptized and allowing communion to be served to those who were uncertain whether or not they were saved —a practice which came to be called "Stoddardeanism." Stoddard defended Stoddardeanism against such able critics as Increase Mather by a series of carefully reasoned and researched writings, including *The Inexcusableness of Neglecting the Worship of God Under the Pretence of Being in an Unconverted Condition* in 1708. As pastor at Northfield, Stoddard was succeeded by his illustrious grandson, Jonathan Edwards —who roundly criticized Stoddardeanism!

STOECKER, Adolf (1835–1909) German Lutheran theologian and sociopolitical activist, Stoecker tried to lure German working classes back to the Church by founding the Christian Socialist Labor Party in 1878, but received scorn from those he particularly hoped to attract. This determined Junker, serving as Court Preacher at Berlin from 1874 until 1889, finally won election to the national diet of Germany. He resorted, however, to vicious attacks on Jewish capitalists, originating much of the anti-Semitism in 20th century Germany. Seeking to Christianize politics, Stoecker unfortunately ended by politicizing Christianity.

STONE, Barton Warren (1772–1844) American Evangelical frontier preacher who broke with the ultra-conservative Presbyterians during the Great Revival of the early 1800's, Stone organized an independent string of congregations which ultimately merged with Alexander Campbell's followers to create the Disciples of Christ.

Stone, pastor of Presbyterian congregations at Cane Ridge and Concord, Bourbon County (Ky.), hosted America's most famous Camp Meeting in August, 1801, at Cane Ridge. The Cane Ridge Meeting led Stone to reject the rigid, mechanical concept of predestination in favor of the idea that everyone is free to confess his sin, receive Christ's grace and be saved. Stone later came to the idea that creeds, confessions and denominational apparatus were a hindrance to the Christian life.

In 1803, Stone withdrew from his presbytery, formed his own Springfield Presbytery but hoped to remain within the Presbyterian Synod of Kentucky, while stressing personal conversion experience.

Frozen out of the Presbyterian body, Stone and a cluster of congregations in the Kentucky-Tennessee backwoods rejected denominationalism, refused all titles except "Christian" and repudiated all creeds except the Scriptures. Stone and his group joined with the Campbellites in 1832, becoming the Disciples of Christ.

STONE, Ellen Maria (1846–1927) Intrepid American missionary teacher to Turkey who made the headlines in 1901 when she was kidnapped by bandits, Miss Stone was finally released after American church groups raised the $65,000 ransom money. She subsequently wrote and lectured about her experiences, promoting mission work.

STONE, John Timothy (1868–1954) A well-known American Presbyterian church leader, Stone preached at Chicago's Fourth Presbyterian Church for twenty-one years before becoming president of McCormick Seminary in 1928.

STONE, Samuel (1602–1663) An English-born Puritan pastor who emigrated to Massachusetts colony in 1633, Stone and Thomas Hooker a few years later took a group of colonists from Cambridge, Massachusetts, and founded Hartford, Connecticut. After Hooker's death, Stone practically ruled Hartford as his private preserve. He quarrelled with his ruling elder, William Goodwin, in 1659, causing Goodwin and others to leave to found the town of Hadley, Massachusetts.

STORCH, Nikolaus (16th c.) A weaver from Zwickau, Germany, who steeped himself in the Scriptures and became one of the "prophets of Zwickau" claiming direct revelation from God, Storch fanned a powerful movement of radical Protestantism among the peasants for a time, then dropped out of history. In 1521, Storch and his colleague, Stubner, stormed into Wittenberg, where they unsettled Melanchthon by their shrill denunciations of infant baptism and predictions of a speedy end of the world.

STOWE, Harriet Elizabeth Beecher (1811–1896) Daughter of the noted American preacher, Lyman Beecher, and husband of Lane Seminary professor, Calvin Ellis Stowe, Harriet Beecher Stowe expressed her avid abolitionist views in one of the most influential novels of all time, *Uncle Tom's Cabin, or Life Among the Lowly,* in 1852. Mrs. Stowe's novel sold over 500,000 copies and hardened sentiment against slaveholders among American Northerners.

STRAUSS, David Friedrich (1808–1874) While a young University of Tubingen scholar in 1835, Strauss rocked the academic community and the Church by publishing his *Life of Jesus* the epoch-making book in German theological thinking in the first part of the 19th century. Strauss' work created

a sensation and produced an entirely new school of thought in treating the rise of Christianity. Strauss blasted both the traditional orthodox view of the Gospels, the current rationalist interpretations, and the "mediating" or middle-ground theologians, and received broadsides of abuse from all sides in return.

Strauss maintained that the simple, meager facts of Christ's life have been covered over with layers of myths created by Messiah-expecting followers who inflated their human teacher into a superhuman figure. Coolly discarding John's Gospel version as having dubious historical value, Strauss gave prime place to Matthew.

Strauss began a trend which inclined to treat the Gospel strictly as a subject to be analyzed and criticized without any sense of personal commitment or appreciation. He continued to publish during the rest of his life. The storm of protest his writing aroused prevented him from being awarded a chair in any theological faculty and even thwarted a new career in politics in 1848.

STRACHAN, John (1778–1867) The first Anglican Bishop of Toronto, Strachan built dozens of Canadian parishes, pressured the government to open public schools, and founded the great University of Toronto. In 1850, after the university became non-denominational, Strachan helped establish Trinity College, Canada's most distinguished Episcopal institution of learning.

STRONG, August Hopkins (1836–1921) A prominent American Baptist pastor and seminary professor, Strong headed Rochester Theological Seminary from 1872 to 1912 and wrote several widely-used theological textbooks, including the classic *Systematic Theology* in 1886.

STRONG, Josiah (1847–1916) An American Congregational minister with a passion for social concerns, Strong served as secretary of the Evangelical Alliance from 1886 to 1898, then resigned to found and lead the League for Social Service (which in 1902 became the American Institute for Social Service). Strong campaigned for accident prevention, coining the slogan, "Safety First."

STROSSMAYER, Joseph Georg (1815–1905) Esteemed 19th century Croatian patriot and bishop of Djakovo (in present-day Yugoslavia), Strossmayer headed a movement to set up a separate, free Croatian state. He carried his love for independence into his participation in Roman Catholic affairs; in 1870, at the Vatican Council, he led the opposition to Pope Pius IX's plans for pronouncing the dogma of papal infallibility. A loyal Catholic, however, Strossmayer later agreed to accept the new dogma and continued as bishop.

STUBNER, Markus Thoma (16th c.) A bathhouse owner at Zwickau who with Muntzer and Storch led a radical, left-wing reformed movement prophesying an immediate end of the world and claiming direct inspiration from God for every utterance, Stubner gathered a large following for several years, then faded from history. Stubner and Storch upset Melanchthon and some of Luther's followers by going to Wittenberg in 1521, where they opposed infant baptism and forecast a quick apocalyptic conclusion to history.

STURMI of Fulda (710–779) The first German Benedictine, Sturmi founded the great monastery of Fulda in 744, where he developed one of the finest schools in Europe, which trained many of the brightest minds of the Medieval Church.

STURZO, Luigi (1871–1959) Italian anti-fascist priest and political figure, Don Sturzo identified with the Italian peasantry and organized many of the earliest cooperatives, trade unions and political structures in Italy. In 1919, Sturzo founded the party which grew into the powerful Christian Democrat Party, second only to the Italian Socialist Party. Sturzo was exiled by Mussolini in 1924, wrote and taught sociology in the United States until after World War II.

SYLITES, Simeon See **SIMEON Stylites**.

SUAREZ, Francisco (1548–1617) An eminent Spanish Jesuit theologian, Suarez was one of the first to oppose the then-sacred dictum that kings had a divine right to rule. He wrote *De Legibus ac Deo Legistore* in 1612, stating that all men are equal under God, and a five-volume commentary on Aquinas' theology in which he took issue with Dominican Thomistic thinkers.

SUDBURY, Simon of See **SIMON of Sudbury**.

SUNDAY, William Ashley ("Billy") (1862–1935) An Iowa orphan who played major league baseball for several years, Billy Sunday turned from a specialty of stealing bases to saving souls in 1896 when he became a sensational Presbyterian revivalist. Billy pitched dramatic, simplistic addresses against sin in general and liquor in particular, usually smashing a chair or going into a ballplayer's slide to drive home his message. Appearing in enormous, specially-built pine-board "tabernacles" wherever he held a "meeting," Billy was invariably flanked by massed choirs, bands, orchestras and local dignitaries.

Billy Sunday's career peaked during World War I, but he continued his athletic appeals for the Gospel until his death in 1935.

SUSO, Heinrich (also **SEUSE**) (1300[?]–1366) One of the founders of the stream of mystical speculation in Germany, Suso became a disciple of Meister Eckhart at Cologne after experiencing a spiritual crisis as a young, nineteen-year-old Dominican. Suso won a reputation as a Thomistic mystic. He wrote easy-to-read treatises on the devotional life which became bestsellers, including *Little Book of Truth* about 1329, *Horologe of Wisdom* about 1337, and *The Little Book of Eternal Wisdom* about 1348.

SWEDENBORG, Emmanuel (1688–1772) A Swedish scientist, engineer, clairvoyant and thinker, Swedenborg claimed to have received direct revelation of Jesus Christ and instructions to disclose a new spiritual dispensation. His writings, which he intended to supersede all existing religious teachings, attracted a group calling itself the Church of the New Jerusalem. Swedenborg, one of the best-trained and far-reaching minds of the 18th century, wrote algebra textbooks and scientific papers on hydraulics and metallurgy, flying machines, navigation and currency control. From about 1738, he worked almost exclusively in human physiology and psychology, trying to locate the soul by careful investigation of the brain and nervous system. To a great degree, Swedenborg's anatomical studies anticipated many of the studies of anatomist Charles Bell and the research of Sigmund Freud.

From 1743 to 1745, Swedenborg experienced a protracted emotional crisis, during which he asserted he had received three direct disclosures of Christ.

He kept a diary during the next sixteen years, recording his visions, dreams and extra-sensory perception experiences. He also wrote *Heavenly Secrets,* published posthumously in 1783, in which he told of the visitations of the "spiritual world" and gave his own interpretation of various Scriptural material. A series of writings followed, all claiming to take precedence over Christian doctrine and rejecting such traditional orthodoxy as the Atonement and the Trinity, (causing his books to be banned in Sweden).

Swedenborg always maintained that his revelations were given to restore Christianity to its original pristine purity and to bring enlightenment. Against his wishes, a sect known as Swedenborgians or the Church of the New Jerusalem came into existence.

SWIFT, Elisha Pope (1792–1865) The father of the Presbyterians' foreign mission Board, and co-founder with Francis Herron of Western Theological Seminary, Pittsburgh (now Pittsburgh Theological Seminary), Swift was both an educated evangelical and evangelical educator.

Swift graduated from Williams College, where he participated in the famous "Haystack Prayer Meeting" in which Adoniram Judson and others decided to carry the Gospel overseas. Swift, becoming pastor of Pittsburgh's Second Presbyterian Church in 1819, pressed the Synod of Pittsburgh to organize a denominational mission enterprise. In 1831, he finally persuaded the Synod to form the Western Foreign Mission Society, of which Swift became the first secretary.

Swift helped found Western Seminary in 1827. In addition to teaching at the seminary, Swift also served as one of the first five professors at the college which is now the University of Pittsburgh.

SWITHIN ([?]–862) An early bishop of Winchester, England, who allegedly worked many miracles, Swithin asked to be buried in the churchyard where rain could fall on his grave. After his death, on two different occasions, July 15, 971, and July 15, 1093, Swithin's bones were removed as relics to different churches, causing, according to legends, torrential rains for forty days each time, and giving rise to the old English saying that if it rains on July 15, it will continue raining for the next forty days!

SYLVESTER I, Pope ([?]–335) According to legend—which most historians now discredit—Sylvester I baptized Emperor Constantine. Sylvester reportedly called an early Church Council at Rome where he warned against heresies such as Arianism. He was later canonized.

SYLVESTER II, Pope (940[?]–1003) A professorial pontiff who taught math and science at Reims, France, before his elevation, Sylvester became the first Frenchman to be named pope. Sylvester continued his scientific career, inventing one of the first operating mechanical clocks, fabricating an astrolabe and a globe, writing many treatises on mathematics and natural sciences, and earning the reputation of being a magician. He reigned from 999 to 1003.

SYLVESTER III, Antipope (11th c.) Elected in 1045 after Pope Boniface IX was deposed, Sylvester served barely three months before being ousted by the returning Boniface. In 1046, the Council of Sutri stripped Sylvester of both his bishopric and his priesthood, and sent him to a monastery, where he died.

SYLVESTER IV, Antipope (12th c.) A rival to Pope Paschal II from 1105 to 1111, this interloper claimed the papal chair for six years.

SYMMACHUS, Pope ([?]–514) A Sardinian-born, ex-pagan convert who reigned as pontiff from 498 until 514, Symmachus went through a protracted controversy with a counter-pope named Laurentius who aspired to the papal chair. He was later canonized.

SYNESIUS of Cyrene (375[?]–430[?]) Bishop of Cyrene, Synesius lived during the catastrophic upheavals caused by the barbarians, who broke across the frontiers of the Roman Empire and even sacked Rome itself in 410. Synesius studied under Hypatia, but enjoyed sports as much as his studies. Reluctant to accept the bishopric for fear of having to relinquish his hunting, Synesius nonetheless became an efficient administrator. He interceded to the Emperor for aid to Cyrene when the barbarians threatened Cyrene. Synesius, a Neo-Platonist philosopher like his mentor Hypatia, wrote during the political turmoil disparaging the present life and longing for a closer communion with God.

T

TAIT, Archibald Campbell (1811–1882) Scottish-born Archbishop of Canterbury from 1856 until 1882, during the uproar over disestablishing the Anglican Church in Ireland, Tait reluctantly agreed to support disestablishment after a personal appeal from Queen Victoria. Tait later irritated starchy high churchmen by sponsoring the Public Worship Regulation Act of 1874.

TALMAGE, Thomas DeWitt (1832–1902) Popular-press Presbyterian clergyman whose solid, Victorian sermons were printed weekly in an estimated 3,600 newspapers throughout the U.S.A., for years, Talmage served prominent congregations in Brooklyn, New York, and Washington, D.C.

TANCRED (1075[?]–1112) A hero in the bloody First Crusade, Tancred distinguished himself in the struggle to wrest the Holy Land from the Moslems by his conspicuous courage (leading the advance wave of troops and being the first to storm the walls of Jerusalem) and remarkable restraint (refusing to revel in the orgy of bloodletting to which most Crusaders abandoned themselves after the capture of Jerusalem).

TATIAN (2nd c.) One of the earliest Christian apologists (writers who prepared careful, literary defenses of the Christian faith), Tatian, disciple and pupil of the great apologist Justin, wrote extensively in the 2nd century. Tatian combined Matthew, Mark, Luke and John into his widely-read *Diatessaron.*

Later, Tatian went to the East, perhaps as a missionary, and lapsed into the heresy of rejecting all matter and physical acts as evil, forbidding marriage, meat and wine. He was denounced as a heretic in 173.

TAULER, Johannes (1300[?]–1361) Evangelically-minded German Dominican, Tauler combined a mystic's emphasis on personal union with God with an activist's insistence on works during one of the most terrible periods of German history. Tauler, soured by the sordid war between Emperor Louis of Bavaria and Frederick of Austria and the intrusion of Pope John XXII as a combatant, was a disciple of the noted mystic, Meister Eckhart. Tauler became one of the "Friends of God," the loosely-knit fellowship of believers who stressed "God born within" and minimized fussy distinctions between clergy and laity.

Tauler preached in German in the area near Strassburg for many years. During the bubonic plague of 1348–9 which decimated Europe's population, Tauler ignored a papal interdict in order to minister to the ill and forgotten.

Tauler's sermons, popular even today, are a bugle-call for a vital relationship with God and a blunt rejection of salvation-by-ceremonies, leading some to dub him a Protestant before Protestantism.

TAUSEN, Hans (1494–1561) The father of the Danish Reformation, Tausen defied grim persecutions to preach Luther's doctrines at Viborg,

Denmark. Tausen, a Franciscan monk, studied at Wittenberg from 1523 to 1524 under Martin Luther. As Protestant bishop of Ribe from 1542, Tausen was the first to use the Danish tongue in worship and the first Danish cleric to marry. Tausen had considerable skill as a Hebrew scholar and translated the first five books of the Old Testament into Danish.

TAVERNER, Richard (1505[?]–1575) Taverner, Clerk of the Privy Seal in England from 1536 to 1553, issued the first translation of the Bible to be printed in England. A student of Scripture, Taverner wrote commentaries on several New Testament books.

TAYLOR, Edward Thompson (1793–1871) The real-life model for "Father Mapple" in Melville's *Moby Dick*, Taylor was a salty, uneducated ex-seaman who presided for over forty years (1830–1871) as chaplain at Boston's Seaman's Bethel.

TAYLOR, Jeremy (1613–1667) A Church of England theologian and writer of devotional books, Taylor is best remembered as the author of the ironic *Liberty of Prophesying*, a plea for tolerance based on the right of private judgment and the difficulty of knowing the correct interpretation of the Bible. In spite of the broadminded appeal of his book and the gentle spirit of his devotional works, *Holy Living* and *Holy Dying*, Taylor in real life was a cantankerous royalist prelate who while bishop of Down in Ireland once ordered thirty-six ministers out of their pulpit for lack of episcopal ordination.

TAYLOR, John (1808–1887) An English-born convert to Mormonism in 1836, Taylor served as a missionary for the Latter Day Saints for many years, and succeeded Brigham Young in 1877 as leader of the Twelve Mormon Apostles. Taylor, president of the Mormon Church from 1880, was a practicing polygamist who lived in hiding from 1882 until his death to escape legal penalties, but continued to direct Mormonism.

TAYLOR, Nathaniel (1786–1858) A dry-intellectual New England Congregationalist clergyman-educator, Taylor headed the Yale Divinity School during the bitter controversies which racked American Congregationalism during the early 19th century. Taylor's precise, cerebral appeals to logic to the point of ignoring witness and emotion caused a fervent group of Taylor's opponents to found Hartford Seminary in 1834.

TEILHARD de CHARDIN, Pierre (1881–1955) French Jesuit theologian-philosopher-scientist, he has been hailed as the new Galileo and Thomas Aquinas by many thinkers. Forbidden by his Jesuit superiors to publish during his lifetime, Teilhard de Chardin looked at science through the eyes of a theologian and at theology through the eyes of a scientist, and dedicated himself to finding possible evidence of agreement between them.

Teilhard de Chardin, descended from an ancient Auvergne noble family, was ordained in 1911, but plunged into scientific studies. World War I, in which Teilhard was a much-decorated hero as a stretcher bearer at the front, was a shattering spiritual crisis. Teilhard, already renowned for his paradoxical, daring thinking, completed scientific studies at Sorbonne after the War, and was shipped off on a three year expedition to Inner Mongolia. An expert paleontologist and geologist, Teilhard was the co-discoverer of Peking man, one of the earliest hominids. Returning to teach in Paris at the Catholic Institute, Teilhard's quips and innovative thoughts were so embarrassing to his Jesuit superiors that he was quickly exiled again on another scientific expedition. The remainder of his life became a pattern of brief teaching sojourns following long periods of anthropological research, a form of banishment by the Society.

Teilhard, the first theologian to think of Christ other than in terms of a static universe, wrote that as evolution has been an ascent from Point Alpha toward man and reflective consciousness, the pattern converges on an ultimate center or Point Omega. For Teilhard de Chardin, Omega is to be identified with the Christ of revelation. Teilhard suggested that in Christ, the real Omega became man and therefore partner of the evolution current for which he himself is responsible.

Turning to man and his role in the universe, Teilhard enlarged traditional boundaries of science to include the study of human persons in relationship to the material world. Teilhard rethought Christian revelation concerning the person of Christ. To Teilhard, the person of Christ as God incarnate is also the ultimate meaning of man in the evolutionary process.

Chardin found himself not only pushed into long, lonely and anguishing exiles, but was eventually barred from holding ecclesiastical office and teaching positions. In 1947, he was forbidden by his Superior General to publish anything whatsoever on a philosophical or theological nature. His ten books, including *The Phenomenon of Man* (written in 1940) and *The Divine Milieu* (written in 1927) were finally published posthumously. Even so, the Vatican banned his writings from all Catholic bookstores in 1957.

TELEMACHUS (5th c.) Sensitive Syrian monk who ended the grisly sport

of forcing combatants to fight to the death in the Roman arenas, Telemachus leaped into the ring in Rome's *Colosseum* one day to register his protest and stop the carnage. His act infuriated the sports fans, who poured out of the stands to kill him. Telemachus' sacrifice, however, persuaded Emperor Honorius to do away with gladiatorial contests.

TEMPLE, Frederick (1821–1902) A progressive Archbishop of Canterbury from 1896 until his death, Temple distinguished himself by his being one of the first to endorse the findings of the natural sciences in the 19th century and one of few to identify with English working classes.

TEMPLE, William (1881–1944) The gregarious Archbishop of Canterbury from 1942 until his death in 1944, Temple towered as one of the top theologians and statesmen in the 20th century world Church. Temple, following in his famous father Frederick's footsteps, worked tirelessly for educational and social reform and occasionally upset his staid Anglican colleagues by his pro-labor sympathies. In 1924, Temple organized and galvanized the Conference on Christian Politics, Economics and Citizenship at Birmingham. A genial, gaitered mixer who thawed Anglican relationships with other Christian bodies, Temple helped lay the groundwork for the creation of the World Council of Churches.

Temple, a practical, practicing theologian, penned such widely read and well-written books as *Nature, Man and God* (1934), *Christianity and the Social Order* (1942) and *The Church Looks Forward* (1944.)

TENISON, Thomas (1636–1715) One of the first Archbishops of Canterbury to favor missions, Tenison also displayed remarkably tolerant views toward non-Anglicans for his age. In 1701, Tenison helped found the illustrious early mission board, the Society for Propogation of the Gospel.

TENNENT, Gilbert (1703–1764) Son of the distinguished Presbyterian-pastor William Tennent, founder of the first Log College at Neshaminy, Pennsylvania, Gilbert Tennent, trained at his father's crudely equipped seminary, helped spearhead the Great Awakening in the American colonies in the 1740's. Tennent, an eloquent but scholarly Biblical preacher with a flair for imaginative, vivid similes, once compared his starchy, non-evangelical Presbyterian confreres to Scribes and Pharisees. A pleader for a genuine change of heart, Tennent was one of revivalist George Whitefield's most outspoken defenders. When colonial Presbyterianism split into New Light and Old Light factions over the revival question from 1741 to 1750, Tennent emerged as the leading spokesman for the evangelical New Light wing, but worked valiantly to unite the two groups. Tennent served many years as a trustee of the College of New Jersey (now Princeton) and was instrumental in raising the funds to build Nassau Hall.

TENNENT, William (1673–1746) One of the earliest of the wave of Presbyterian Ulstermen (the "Scots-Irish") which poured into the American colonies in the 18th century, Tennent, perturbed by the absence of centers of theological education to train pastors, began taking young students into his own home at Neshaminy, Pennsylvania in 1736. Tennent's rough facilities, sneeringly nicknamed "Log College" by pseudo-sophisticates, produced a stream of well-trained, deeply dedicated frontier pastors and set the pattern for many "log college" centers of education in the American wilderness. Tennent, later aided by his son, Gilbert, operated Log College until his death, at which time it was decided to establish a Presbyterian institution known as the College of New Jersey, today called Princeton University.

TENNYSON, Alfred (1809–1892) Poet-laureate of England from 1850 until his death, Tennyson, a rector's son who was granted a baronetcy for his melodic, meditative verses, won favor, fame and fortune in Victorian England. Tennyson's views were broad church Anglican, and were effectively expressed in his classic *In Memoriam.*

TERESA of Avila (1515–1582) Spanish mystic and founder of the Discalced or Barefooted Carmelites, Teresa, a Carmelite nun from the time she was sixteen, began at the age of forty to go into trances, during which she experienced visions of Christ. Teresa's spiritual-psychic accomplishments, however, were not appreciated by fellow members of her order or her superiors. Dissatisfied with the deterioration of discipline in Spanish monasticism, Teresa resolved to found her own convent, and, in spite of intense opposition by local churchmen, finally won papal permission in 1562 to establish her own house and her own order. Her Barefooted Carmelites, sometimes called Teresians, operating from Teresa's headquarters convent at Avila, Spain, became known for their ascetic poverty and strict devotional habits. Teresa herself frequently scourged herself and perpetually wore a hair-cloth garment. Revered as a mystic and miracle worker, Teresa was canonized in 1622 by Pope Gregory XV. In Spain she is second only after St. James as patron saint.

TERTULLIAN, Quintus Septimus Florens (160[?]–230[?]) Fiery fanatic polemicist and ascetic, Tertullian was the first great writer of Christian literature in Latin. Tertullian, son of a pagan Roman government official in North Africa, studied law and classics, but converted to Christianity about 197 after wondering at the courage of Christian martyrs. Becoming a priest in North Africa, Tertullian became upset with the lax worldliness of many clerics and fell in with the ultra-severe ascetic, premillenarian Montanists. He later broke with Montanism, however, and founded the Tertullianists. Tertullian penned sizzling theological treatises, but is best remembered for his "Apologies"—careful, concise defenses of the Christian faith.

TETZEL, Johann (1465[?]–1519) Peripatetic peddler of papal pardon, Tetzel exasperated Martin Luther to the point of posting ninety-five theses against the commercialism of indulgences, triggering the Protestant Reformation. Tetzel, a plodding, stubborn German Dominican, served as Inquisitor in Poland and Saxony before going into the indulgence business to raise funds to build St. Peter's. Tetzel, who never understood Luther's objections to selling indulgences, testily replied with his own 106 theses, winning himself an honorary doctorate from the Church but the contempt of all theologians. Bewildered, Tetzel retired to a Leipzig monastery in 1518 and died a year later.

THAYER, Joseph Henry (1828–1901) American Congregational pastor and Greek textual critic, Thayer prepared a monumental *Greek-English Lexicon of the New Testament.* He also served on the committee to prepare the *American Standard Version of the New Testament* and helped found the American School of Oriental Research, Jerusalem.

THEOBALD ([?]–1161) An independent-minded Archbishop of Canterbury, Theobald persistently defied King Stephen and twice suffered banishment (once for attending the papal conference at Rheims in 1130 and later for refusing to recognize King Henry's son, Eustace, as successor). Theobald, who took young theologians into his home as students, was mentor for Thomas à Becket.

THEODORA (500[?]–547) Ex-chorus girl who became Queen by marrying Emperor Justinian I, Theodora dominated her husband and, after Justinian's coronation in 527, had a hand in all the affairs of the Eastern Church and Empire. Theodora, beautiful, brainy and brutal, possessed a Byzantine delight in intrigue, which sometimes shaped the course of the Church in the East. She professed a zealous, at times misguided commitment to the Church, leaning toward the Monophysite position.

THEODORE of Canterbury See THEODORE of Tarsus.

THEODORE, Pope I ([?]–649) A stiff Greek pope who sternly opposed the Monothelite heresy during his pontificate from 642 to 649, Theodore did not hesitate to excommunicate Paul, Patriarch of Constantinople, in 649 for refusing to acquiesce to Roman standards.

THEODORE, Pope II ([?]–897) This pope's reign lasted only twenty days.

THEODORE of Mopsuestia (350[?]–428) Leader of the Church wing at Antioch and Bishop of Mopsuestia from 392, Theodore championed orthodox Christianity against the Arians during the controversies over the nature of Christ which wracked the Church during the 4th and 5th centuries. Theodore, a close friend of John Chrysostom, followed Chrysostom into a career in the monastery. Theodore was a theologian, preacher and writer of considerable renown. He attended the great Council of Constantinople in 394, preached before Byzantine Emperor Theodosius, and wrote a number of Biblical commentaries and treatises.

His writings, however, betray Pelagianist touches in his thinking, causing Theodore of Mopsuestia to be condemned posthumously in 553 as a heretic. His pupil, Nestorius, picking up many of Theodore's ideas, veered into heresy.

THEODORE STUDITES (759–826) The oft-banished but outspoken head of the great monastery of the Studios at Constantinople, Theodore Studites triggered a monastic revival spreading throughout the East as far as Russia, Bulgaria, Greece and Serbia. Theodore Studites was exiled repeatedly: for denouncing Emperor Constantine's adulterous marriage, for objecting to the appointment of a layman-politician as Patriarch in 809, and criticizing Emperor Leo V the Armenian's dislike of icons.

THEODORE of Tarsus (602[?]–690) Born in Tarsus, this outstanding monastic, scholar and ecclesiastical administrator became Archbishop of Canterbury in England in 668. Theodore upgraded the morals and worship of the slumping Church in ancient Britain, tying it firmly to Rome. Theodore was the first Archbishop of Canterbury whom all Christians in Britain agreed to obey. He succeeded in convening the Synod of Hertford in 673, and divided his see into dioceses, placing capable bishops over each.

THEODORET ([?]–457) The ablest theologian of the school of Antioch and the Bishop of Cyrus (near Antioch in Syria) during the fierce heresy struggles in the 5th century, Theodoret did not agree with his friend and ex-classmate Nestorius but opposed efforts by the vindictive Cyril of Alexandria to persecute Nestorius after Nestorius' condemnation at the Council of Ephesus in 431. Theodoret, the subject of abuse and acrimony for befriending Nestorius, was falsely accused by Cyril of being a secret Nestorian. Theodoret, anathematized and deposed at the infamous "robber" Council of Ephesus in 449, was finally acquitted and restored at the Council of Chalcedon in 451. A scholar with a passion for history, Theodoret wrote *Ecclesiastical History,* continuing the study begun by Eusebius.

THEODORIC ("the Great"), **King of the Ostrogoths** (455[?]–526) Imaginative invader who successfully conquered Italy, Theodoric ruled his Ostrogoth kingdom from Ravenna, where he tried to blend the best of Roman and Germanic institutions.

THEODOSIUS I ("the Great"), **Flavius, Emperor** (346–395) Baptized in 380, the year after his coronation as emperor, Theodosius harshly but effectively supported the orthodox viewpoint in the Eastern Church. He issued an edict after his baptism threatening heretics with punishment, put down the Arians, pacified the Goths, and in 381 called the Second Council of Constantinople, which promulgated Chalcedonian Christianity once and for all.

Theodosius, in spite of his pious professions, had occasional outbursts of Byzantine brutality. He once ordered the massacre of all the inhabitants of Thessalonica, forcing his erstwhile friend, Bishop Ambrose of Milan, to demand penance.

THEODOSIUS II, Emperor (401–450) Emperor in the East during one of the most disgusting episodes in Church history, the bitter theological-political battle between the sees of Alexandria and Constantinople over wording in defining Jesus' nature and the role of Mary, Jesus' Mother, Theodosius II tried in a bumbling way to halt the dispute. Theodosius II and Valentinian III, Emperor in the West, called the Council of Ephesus in 431, remembered as the "robber" synod in which the unscrupulous Cyril of Alexandria took charge. His greatest contribution was the Theodosian Code from which the later Justinian Code was taken.

THEODOTUS, "the Tanner" or **"the Currier"** (2nd c.) A tanner from Byzantium, Theodotus was the earliest eloquent Dynamic Monarchian. He repudiated Christ during a persecution by glibly explaining that he merely denied a man but not God, since Christ, he claimed, was but the adopted form of the one God. Theodotus was excommunicated by Pope Victor about 192, but a heretical group of followers persisted in holding Theodotus' views.

THEODOTUS ("the Money-changer") (2nd c.) A money-changer from the East who became entranced by Theodotus "the Tanner's" heretical views, Theodotus "the Money-changer" assumed leadership of a schismatic group of Dynamic Monarchians. His sect deviated from traditional Christology so far that it ended by putting Melchizedek above Christ, causing what came to be known as the Melchizedekian heresy.

THEODULF of Orleans (760[?]–821) A Spanish-born prelate in charge of several abbeys near Orleans, France, Theodulf introduced reform to French monasticism and served on a diplomatic mission for Charlemagne. Theodulf wrote excellent poetry, several pieces of which have been set to music, including the Palm Sunday hymn, "Glory, Laud and Honor."

THEOPHANES (758[?]–817) A saintly Greek monk who founded and headed a monastery at Sigriano in Asia Minor, Theophanes, a pious partisan of icon and image veneration, became deeply involved in the controversy over the use of images and suffered imprisonment and banishment in 815 by Emperor Leo V. He was later pronounced a saint.

THEOPHILUS, of Alexandria ([?]–412) A devious, disputatious churchman who contrived to become Patriarch of Alexandria in 385, Theophilus enraged the citizens of Alexandria by razing most pagan shrines, including the ancient temple of Serapis. He got into a furious altercation with the supporters of Origen, and after having Origenism condemned at the Synod of Alexandria in 401, vengefully hunted down Isidore and others who had supported Origenism. In 403, Theophilus brought trumped-up charges against John Chrysostom and engineered the banishment of that illustrious leader of the Church.

THEOPHILUS of Antioch ([?]–181[?]) An Eastern philosopher who was converted from paganism, Theophilus in 169 became Bishop of Antioch in Syria, where he won fame as an apologist or writer defending the Christian faith. Theophilus' three-volume masterpiece was addressed to an unnamed learned pagan friend, and painstakingly pointed out the errors of idolatry and the superiority of Christian Scripture to pagan writings.

THEOPHORUS See IGNATIUS, Bishop of Antioch.

THERESA of Avila See TERESA of Avila.

275

THERESA of Lisieux (1873–1897) Meditative French Carmelite nun who became the center of the cult of the "Little Flower" in pietistic French Catholicism, Sister Theresa wrote her autobiography, published under the title *The Story of a Soul* in 1896–1897 before her early death from tuberculosis in 1897. The autobiography made Sister Theresa immensely popular. She was canonized in 1925. In 1944 she was named co-patron of France with Joan of Arc.

THIRLWALL, Connop (1797–1875) A progressive, enlightened Anglican bishop at St. David's, Wales, in the Victorian era, Thirlwall upset his stodgy peers in Parliament by voting to admit Jews to Parliament and to disestablish the Anglican Church in Ireland (the only bishop so to vote). Thirlwall, a competent Biblical student, helped revise the English translation of the Old Testament.

THOBURN, Isabella (1840–1901) Sister of the distinguished James Thoburn, Isabella Thoburn in 1869 became the first missionary of the newly-organized Women's Foreign Missionary Society of the Methodist Episcopal Church. Miss Thoburn, serving in India for thirty-two years, founded the school for Indian girls at Lucknow which, renamed the Isabella Thoburn College, is now connected with the famous Lucknow University.

THOBURN, James Mills (1836–1922) Brother of Isabella Thoburn, the noted woman missionary-educator in India, James Thoburn served as the Methodist bishop for much of Southeast Asia. Thoburn, a forward-looking, long time (1859–1908) missionary, pioneered much of the Protestant work in India.

THOLUCK, Friedrich August Gottrue (1799–1877) A greatly beloved German Protestant Evangelical professor at Halle from 1826 until his death in 1877, Tholuck combined sanctity and scholarship in his preaching and teaching. Tholuck, who accepted the critical studies of Biblical material yet retained sympathies with the best points of Pietism, steered Halle away from becoming the center of the rationalism to a cordial yet cerebral Evangelism.

THOMAS AQUINAS See **AQUINAS, Thomas.**

THOMAS, John (1805–1871) Founder of the sect known as the "Christadelphians," ("brothers of Christ"), Thomas emigrated to the U.S.A. after studying medicine in London, and settled in Brooklyn, New York. Thomas joined the Campbellites for a time, but left to strike out on his own, founding an independent group and preaching a message loaded with luridly literalist interpretations of the apocalyptic passages of the Bible, especially Daniel and Revelation. Thomas, shrilly certain that the age was about to come to a close, predicted the formation of a world-wide theocracy with headquarters in Jerusalem in which only members of his group would be saved. Preaching what he called a "conditional immortality" for his Christadelphians, who alone had the truth in the Scriptures, Thomas dismissed the Christian faith as "fables predicted by Paul." Thomas and his Christadelphians remained unstructured, meeting weekly to break bread and study Thomas' interpretations of Scripture.

THOMAS, Norman Mattoon (1884–1968) Activist Presbyterian minister who championed pacificism and socialism, Thomas won grudging respect for his consistent opposition to military conscription (he was a conscientious objector in World War I), Fascism, Communism and injustice (he helped found the American Civil Liberties Union). Thomas, who believed in taking his convictions into politics, was a perennial candidate for years in the United States, running six times for the presidency on the Socialist ticket.

THOMAS à BECKET See BECKET, Thomas à.

THOMAS à KEMPIS See KEMPIS, Thomas à.

THOMAS of Stitny (1331–1401) A powerful, pre-Reformation preacher of reform in Bohemia, Thomas of Stitny denounced corruption rampant among the clergy, stressed the centrality of the Bible and urged regular observance of the Lord's Supper. Thomas, who aroused Bohemia by his oratory, helped prepare the way for the great John Huss.

THOMASIUS, Christian (1655–1728) Progressive, enlightened German legal scholar, Thomasius founded the University of Halle in 1691 after being driven from the University of Leipzig by reactionary theologians. Thomasius, although no Pietist partisan, opposed persecuting the Pietists. Exceptionally forward-looking and fair-minded, he scorned popular belief in witchcraft and the use of torture in courts. Thomasius introduced the use of German in place of Latin in the German universities and helped frame the foundations of modern German jurisprudence. Thomasius' University of Halle became the headquarters for German Pietism.

THOMSON, James ([?]–1826) Intrepid Scottish pioneer Baptist colporteur and evangelist to South America from 1818 to 1826, Thomson roamed the cities and villages of Chile, Peru, Ecuador, Colombia and Argentina, valiantly singlehandedly distributing Scriptures and trying to establish Bible-study schools. His work, at first seemingly successful, was eventually obliterated by the apathy of the peasants and the opposition of the priests. Permanent Protestant work did not begin in South America until 1845.

THOMSON, William McClure (1806–1894) American Presbyterian missionary to the Middle East from 1831–1874, Thomson opened the first boarding school for boys in the old Turkish Empire at Beirut in 1835 and wrote popular works on Biblical archaeology and geography, including the best-selling *The Land and the Book.*

THORLAKSSON, Gudbrandur (1542–1627) The great Lutheran bishop of Iceland, Thorlaksson with tact and firmness brought the Protestant Reformation to Iceland. Reformer Thorlaksson translated many hymns from German and Danish into Icelandic and printed an excellent translation of the Bible at Hólar in 1584.

THROCKMORTON, Job (1545–1601) A controversialist English Puritan layman, Throckmorton is believed to have been the author of tracts published in 1588–1589 carrying the pseudonymous signature "Martin Marprelate." The "Marprelate Tracts," stinging satire against Anglican bishops, particularly Archbishop Whitgift, infuriated the Anglican establishment and delighted the Puritans. Indicted in 1591, Throckmorton denied authorship or complicity in producing the tracts. Most scholars, however, think that Throckmorton and an associate, John Penry, were the writers. Throckmorton also served for a time in Parliament.

THURSTAN (also **TURSTIN**) ([?]–1140) Named Bishop of York, Thurstan, determined to keep his see independent, refused to give submission to the Archbishop of Canterbury and was therefore denied consecration for a long time. Thurstan is best remembered in history as the north country patriot who raised an army which staved off the attacking Scots in 1138.

TIBURTIUS ([?]–232) Converted to the Christian faith by his brother Valerian, Tiburtius steadfastly refused to burn the pinch of incense to Roman deities. He and his brother were both beheaded at Rome, and were both canonized.

TIBURTIUS ([?]–286) The son of Chromatius, a prefect of Rome, this man named Tiburtius was also decapitated for his allegiance to Christ. Tiburtius, martyred on the Via Labicana, was also named one of the early saints.

TILLICH, Paul Johannes Oskar (1886–1965) The influential philosophical theologian who had the knack of listening and conversing to modern man caught up in the meaninglessness of existence, Tillich spun out a productive career of teaching and writing in Germany and the United States. Tillich, a Prussian-born Lutheran pastor's son, served on the faculties of some of Germany's most illustrious universities, including Berlin, Marburg, Dresden, Leipzig and Frankfurt. Blacklisted by the Nazis in 1933, Tillich accepted an invitation from his American friend, Reinhold Niebuhr, to take refuge in the United States, where he settled permanently and took out citizenship.

Perceptively noting that modern man's problem is the apparent purposelessness of life, Tillich boldly tried to communicate the meaning of the Gospel to his contemporaries. He wrote a three-volume *Systematic Theology* from 1950 to 1963 in which he tried to translate traditional Christian ideas into meaningful terms for those both inside and outside the faith. Tillich, deeply immersed in the arts and sciences, occasionally drew the criticism from some theologians that he psychologized the meaning of the Gospel. He avoided jargon; he frequently coined his own terms, some of which have become permanent parts of modern religious vocabulary, such as "the ground of all being."

Tillich's works, including the *Religious Situation* (1948), *The Shaking of the Foundations* (1948), *The Courage to Be* (1952), *Love, Power and Justice* (1954), *The Eternal Now* (1963) and others appealed to moderns because Tillich insisted on a concern for faith ("ultimate concern") without abandoning reason, for the Church without ignoring the community outside, for the "ground of all being" without forgetting the dilemmas of modern existence.

In his last years, Tillich was a popular preacher and lecturer at Harvard.

TILLOTSON, John (1630–1694) A staunch Calvinist who took orders in the Church of England and rose to prominence as the Archbishop of Canterbury in 1691, Tillotson opposed King Charles II's favoritism toward Roman Catholics, especially by the Declaration of 1672. Tillotson, with an eye on his Calvinist colleagues in other communions, unsuccessfully presented a scheme to include English Presbyterians within the Church of England. He was subjected to vehement attacks by many ultra-strict Anglicans for his warmth toward the Presbyterians, but esteemed by most English Protestants for his evangelical sermons.

TINDAL, Matthew (1657–1753) A rationalistic opportunist who found it helpful to his career to join the Roman fold during ardent Catholic King James II's reign, but flipped back to the Church of England after James was deposed, Tindal ended by becoming a leading Deist. Tindal, saturated with the rationalistic viewpoint of his age, attempted to prove that natural law as operating in the hearts of men is the only revelation. He penned *Letter to the Clergymen of the Two Universities on the Subject of the Trinity and the Athanasian Creed* in 1694, and *The Rights of the Christian Church Asserted* in 1706, which set off a minor furor in England. At the instigation of the high church Anglicans, Parliament ordered his works publicly burned in 1710. Pushed more deeply into Deistic opinions and farther from traditional orthodoxy, Tindal in 1730 wrote *Christianity as Old as the Creation, or The Gospel a Republication of the Religion of Nature,* a sort of manifesto for English Deism.

TINDAL, William See TYNDALE.

TINDALE, William See TYNDALE.

TINGLEY, Katherine Augusta Westcott (1847–1929) An American cultist who rose to prominence in the American Theosophical Society, in 1898 Mrs. Tingley melded theosophy with a new organization known as the Universal Brotherhood, a cult with headquarters at Point Loma, California. The thrice-married Mrs. Tingley's religious career did not bloom until she was past forty, when she claimed gifts as a spiritualist medium and began a meteoric rise.

TIRIDATES, King of Armenia (238[?]–314) The first ruler of a country to be converted, Tiridates was won to the Christian faith and baptized by Gregory the Illuminator. Armenia, therefore, has the distinction of becoming the first nation to have a Christian ruler. Tiridates fostered the growth of a strong Armenian Church which had a powerful impact on the spread of the Gospel.

TISCHENDORF, Lobegott Friedrich Konstantin von (1815–1874) A competent and persistent paleographer and Biblical scholar, von Tischendorf discovered the ancient manuscript known as *Codex Sinaiticus* moldering in archives of remote St. Catherine's Monastery in the fastnesses of the Sinai peninsula in 1844. Von Tischendorf recognized the value of his find, the oldest and most complete text of the Old and New Testaments (plus the Shepherd of Hermas and the Epistle of Barnabas) written in Greek and dating back to the 4th century. Von Tischendorf tried unsuccessfully to persuade the monks to donate the manuscript to the Russian Czar, and made three trips to St. Catherine's before he was able to purchase all of his discovery. (Bought by the Czarist government, the *Codex Sinaiticus* was sold after the Revolution to the British for $500,000 and now is in the British Museum.) Von Tischendorf published ten carefully researched papers on his find, and prepared critical editions of the Roman text of the Septuagint.

TOLAND, John (1670–1722) An Irish-born Deist, Toland abandoned Roman Catholicism for Protestantism at sixteen while a Dublin student. He wrote *Christianity Not Mysterious* at twenty-six, and spent most of his career trying to extrude all supernatural elements from Biblical material to reduce the Gospel to mere religion, and then explained all religion as part of a rational system. Toland, while an Oxford scholar, provoked a furious controversy by his notions. He left Oxford and lived abroad most of the rest of his life. In

1705, Toland originated the word "pantheism."

TOLSTOY, Leo Nikolayvich (1828–1910) Russian romantic who tried to attain a sinless simplicity by pacifism, vegetarianism and poverty, Tolstoy was a novelist, essayist and moral philosopher who achieved such a following that it took on the appearance of a religious sect. Tolstoy emphasized the themes of sympathy, sincerity and stern justice, penning such masterpieces as *War and Peace, Anna Karenina, The Death of Ivan Ilyich* and *The Power of Darkness.* He was passionately concerned for social justice. Tolstoy freed his own serfs long before the Emancipation Act of 1861, opened a school for peasant children, who were never subjected to the usual rough Russian disciplining in his classroom. Tolstoy rebelled against the Orthodox Church as a decadent, reactionary drag in society. His personal credo was expressed in *A Confession, My Religion, What I Believe* and *A Short Exposition of the Gospels.*

In 1880, he gave up his life of ease and tried to identify with suffering humanity by adopting the life of a peasant, working in the fields and going without meat and tobacco. Eight years later, Tolstoy abruptly announced to his family that he planned to divide his considerable wealth among the poor and live in complete poverty. His family finally persuaded him to turn his estate over to his wife, but Tolstoy insisted on never having a penny of his own from then on, refusing money for his writing and associating only with peasants and attempting to recover an idyllic agrarian way of life, even to making his own shoes.

Tolstoy's moral and religious teachings attracted a devoted coterie. Declaring that God is not personal but is supreme Good and Reason, Tolstoy reduced Jesus to a great man, but not the only teacher of truth, and stated that God and the Kingdom are "inside." Tolstoy, espousing a limp, impossible idealism whereby social conditions would improve when all men learned to understand and love each other, opposed all forms of violence and militarism, causing many followers to be jailed or sent to Siberia.

In 1901, he was excommunicated by the Orthodox Church, and when he died in 1910, he was denied a Church funeral and burial in an Orthodox cemetery.

TOMLINSON, Ambrose Jessup (1865–1943) Forceful one-time Indiana Quaker who founded the Appalachian-white branch of the Church of God movement in the United States, A. J. Tomlinson went through an emotion-packed conversion experience at a Pentecostal revival in 1892 and worked for a time with William Rich Spurling and the Pentecostals in Tennessee before striking out on his own. Tomlinson organized his own Church of God among the Appalachian poor whites, stressing a shattering personal emotional "conversion," a Biblical literalism and charismatic gifts. Tomlinson himself assumed the title of General Overseer of his sect, and ruled somewhat despotically at Cleveland, Tennesee. After his death in 1943, the movement split into warring factions, two of which were headed by Tomlinson's sons.

TOMLINSON, Homer Alvin (1892–1968) Self-anointed "king of the world," Homer Tomlinson, son of the Church of God Founder, A. J. Tomlinson, was the fractious, flamboyant founder of his own break-away sect, also named the "Church of God" (one of at least 200 U.S. religious bodies that carry that name or some variant). Tomlinson, regarded as a crackpot by many of his rivals, sought the U.S. presidency on a platform pledging a new Garden of Eden. A sometime Madison Avenue advertising man, Tomlinson operated his sect for a time from Queens Village, New York. He once was jailed for trying to sledgehammer to pieces the shrine of the rival Church of God Prophecy, operated by his brother Milton on Burger Mountain (N.C.).

TOPLADY, Augustus Montague (1740–1778) A crusty Calvinist Church of England priest, Toplady is remembered today primarily for his deeply devotional hymns, including "Rock of Ages." During his lifetime, however, Toplady was better known as the rigid predestinarian protagonist of the Wesleyan movement. Toplady vehemently denounced John Wesley as an Arminian in a series of treatises, and penned several other now-ignored doctrinal pieces.

TORQUEMADA, Jean de (1388–1468) Not to be confused with the grim Inquisitor, this Spaniard named Torquemada was a distinguished cardinal and astute theologian who served at the Councils of Constance, Basel and Florence, where he helped draft a plan to try to reunite the Roman and Greek Churches.

TORQUEMADA, Tomás de (1420–1498) The dispicable Dominican fanatic who made the Inquisition in Spain an instrument of torture and terror, it is said Torquemada directed the incineration of 10,220 persons for the "glory of God" during his eighteen years as Grand Inquisitor. This efficient sadist, appointed Inquisitor-General in 1483 by Pope Sixtus IX, set up four, smoothly-operating tribunals at Seville, Cordova,

Jaen and Villa Reál, where he extracted immense fortunes from his victims. When Torquemada turned his attention against Spanish Jewry, he caused a wholesale exodus of over one million Jews, including many of Spain's cultural, intellectual and scientific leaders. Torquemada became so widely loathed and feared that he was forced to surround himself with bodyguards constantly.

TORREY, Charles Turner (1813–1846) American Abolitionist hero, Torrey served a Congregational pastorate in Maryland, where he led efforts to spirit black slaves north via the Underground Railroad. He was arrested and jailed for aiding runaway slaves in 1843. The severe treatment and long sentence in prison brought on tuberculosis which killed him when he was only thirty-three. Torrey was revered as a martyr by the Abolitionists, who coined the slogan, "Tórrey's blood crieth out."

TORREY, Reuben Archer (1865–1928) An American Congregationalist, Torrey became associated with Dwight L. Moody in 1889, headed the Moody Bible Institute until 1908, and promoted many evangelistic efforts throughout the world. Torrey wrote a number of books on Biblical material.

TRAVERS, Walter (1548[?]–1635) An intelligent, articulate English Puritan with firm non-conformist convictions, Travers quit Cambridge after a row with authoritarian Anglican (later Archbishop) Whitgift, and wrote the inflammatory *Declaration of Ecclesiastical Discipline*. Travers severely criticized English universities and the established church, and was forced to live abroad in Geneva (where he became a close friend of Reformer Beza) and Antwerp on occasion. Travers' *Declaration* summed up the radical Puritan position, and gave Travers a reputation of being Puritan standard-bearer for a time.

TREGELLES, Samuel Prideaux (1813–1875) An outstanding New Testament Greek Scholar, Tregelles, born a Quaker and an adherent of the Darbyite Plymouth Brethren for a time before joining the Presbyterian Church in England, wrote numerous publications dealing with his excellent critical edition of the New Testament from 1857 to 1872. Previously, in 1854, Tregelles published *An Account of the Printed Text of the Greek New Testament* which helped advance Biblical scholarship.

TRENCH, Richard Chenevix (1807–1886) A studious Irish-born Anglican prelate, Trench wrote the still-popular *Notes on the Parables of Our Lord* in 1840 and *Notes on the Miracles of Our Lord* in 1846. Trench served as a professor for a time at Kings College, London, then in 1864 was consecrated Archbishop of Dublin, where he presided during the disestablishment of the Church of England in Ireland.

TROELTSCH, Ernst (1865–1923) German Protestant theologian who served as professor at Heidelberg before becoming Pfleiderer's successor at Berlin in 1908, Troeltsch applied Ritschl's ideas examining the development of the Church's doctrine. He added a dose of Schleiermacher, concluding that all religion, including Christianity, grew not out of revelation but out of inner feelings. Troeltsch was one of the first to note the close connection between faith and culture. After World War I, he became active in politics, serving in 1921 on the German Federal Cabinet as Minister of Education. In 1923, he wrote *The Social Teachings of the Christian Churches*.

TRUMBULL, David (1817–1889) Pioneer missionary who established the first permanent Protestant witness in South America, Trumbull arrived in Chile in 1845, where he worked for forty-five years. Trumbull, under the auspices of the Presbyterian Foreign Mission Board during his last years, ministered among the seamen and the ill in the foreign colony primarily, but also founded a girls' school, a union church and a Bible-distribution center.

TULLOCH, John (1823–1886) A Scots-Kirk preacher and Professor of Theology at St. Mary's College, St. Andrews, Tulloch wrote the once-much-discussed *Rational Theology and Christian Philosophy in England in the Seventeenth* Century in 1872, and headed the nearest thing to a "liberal" group within the Church of Scotland in the Victorian era.

TUTTLE, Daniel Sylvester (1837–1923) A Protestant Episcopal priest who rode west with the early "sod-busters," Tuttle in 1867 became bishop of a huge chunk of the American frontier, including all of what is now Montana, Utah and Idaho. In 1903, Tuttle was elected Presiding Bishop of the Episcopal Church.

TYLER, Wat or Walter ([?]–1381) Hot-eyed, reform-minded rebel leader, Tyler headed the angry mob which poured from the countryside into London in 1381 in what is known as the Peasants' Revolt. Tyler, a follower of preacher John Ball (who in turn had been influenced by pre-Reformation reformer John Wycliffe), was an illiterate serf with a passion for justice and a penchant for oratory. Protesting the insufferably high taxes and harsh restrictions on serfs, Tyler made blunt demands: end serfdom, the poll-tax, and the Statute of Labourers of 1351;

put a ceiling on rents on non-monastic and non-crown lands; permit everyone the right to buy and sell throughout England. Tyler and his angry, armed throng invaded London to take their case to King Richard II. Tyler, stabbed by the Lord Mayor of London during a disturbance which broke out when the peasants tried to present their grievances, died of wounds.

TYNDALE, William (1494[?]–1536) Concerned that every ploughboy might read the New Testament in English, Tyndale devoted his life to translating Scriptures, finally suffering martyrdom for his efforts. Tyndale, a Church of England scholar, found his dream of an English Bible thwarted by the Bishop of London, but discovered a group of well-to-do London cloth merchants to support him. In 1524, Tyndale began working on his translation at Wittenberg, Germany, where he visited Martin Luther.

Tyndale's New Testament translation was published in 1534 at Worms, in spite of violent efforts to stop publication and arrest Tyndale. Copies of Tyndale's New Testament which were smuggled into England, however, were seized on orders of Archbishop Warham and Bishop Tonstall.

Tyndale was harassed and threatened and finally forced to seek refuge at Marburg to save his life. He valiantly began work on the Old Testament, completing the first five books. Seeking greater quiet and safety to continue his translating, Tyndale moved in secret to Antwerp. He was turned in by an English informer, however, and condemned for heresy, then brutally strangled to death in 1535. His last prayer was "Lord, open the King of England's eyes!"

Much of the Tyndale translation's hearty vocabulary and majestic sentence structure were carried over to the King James translation of 1611, where sixty percent of the New Testament is based on wording from Tyndale's great translation.

TYRELL, George (1861–1909) A sensitive, early scientific-age Irish Jesuit who tried to interpret traditional Catholic doctrine in the light of the findings of modern science, Tyrell fell into disfavor with his superiors and suffered expulsion from the Society of Jesus. Tyrell, influenced by the Modernist movement in the Catholic Church (a group of progressive priest-thinkers trying to express the faith meaningfully for the 20th century), wrote a series of letters to the London *Times* in 1901 taking issue with the papal encyclical *Pascendi* which denounced scientific inquiry. Tyrell also carried on a wide correspondence with a wide circle of the leading minds of his day. Without his permission in 1906, portions of a private letter to friends were published in which he criticized the Church's stand toward Modernism. Tyrell was expelled by the Jesuits and virtually cut off from the Roman communion. Tyrell, however, refused to abandon the position that he was faithful to genuine Catholicism which he felt the Church had forsaken in his day.

U

UGOLINO See **GREGORY IX,** Pope.

ULFILA (310[?]–383) An ancient Germanic tribesman, Ulfila evangelized among the Visigoths. Ulfila, born into a Christian family which had received the Gospel when some of its warrior members had been taken prisoner by the Romans and converted, became a "reader" in the worship services of the informally-organized Gothic Christian community. In 341, he was ordained bishop by the Arian bishop of Constantinople, Eusebius of Nicomedia. Ulfila sided with the Arian party, but worked tirelessly and fearlessly preaching and organizing for the faith among his tribesmen. He was forced finally to flee about 348 after a sharp persecution. Settling in Roman territory in the area of modern Plevna, Bulgaria, Ulfila continued his labors. Ulfila's monument was the translation of the entire New Testament and a portion of the Old into the Gothic language.

UNAMUNO, Miguel de (1864–1936) Spanish thinker and literary figure with a Quixotic element of tragedy in his life, Unamuno taught and served as rector of Salamanca University until ousted for criticizing the corruption in the government. Later, in 1924, he was banished to the Canary Islands for denouncing Primo de Rivera's dictatorship. Although the ban was eventually lifted, Unamuno lived most of the rest of his life in Paris, where he wrote many of his moving, mystical, meditative pieces. Unamuno's works include *The Christ of Valazquez* (1920), *Essays and Soliloquies* (1925) and *The Agony of Christianity* (1928).

UNNI ([?]–936) Archbishop of Hamburg, Germany, from 918 until his death, Unni tried valiantly to extend the Church into the unchurched areas of Scandinavia, but did not meet with notable success.

URBAN I, Pope ([?]–230) One of the early bishops of Rome, Urban I was a son of a Roman noble named Pontianus and ruled from 222 to 230. He was reckoned officially a saint in ancient times.

URBAN II, Pope (1042[?]–1099) The pope who proclaimed the First Crusade in 1095 at the Council of Clermont, Urban achieved instant popularity among the masses and a position of leadership among rulers who had opposed him. Previously, Urban II had struggled with Emperor Henry IV. Urban, in fact, had not been able to oust Henry's appointee, Antipope Clement III, until 1093. Urban had both convictions and the courage to do something about them. In addition to summoning churchmen everywhere to his Crusade, at the same Council of Clermont he excommunicated French King Philip I for an adulterous second marriage. Urban in 1098 tried to reunite the Roman and Greek branches of the Church. He was more successful in arranging to have popes elected without the approval of any emperor. A stern puritan, Urban II upgraded the moral tone of the Church by demanding strict celibacy among all clergy and forbidding his clergy to be assigned Church offices by laymen. His pontificate lasted from 1088 to 1099.

URBAN III, Pope ([?]–1187) Urban III stoutly insisted that the papacy be free from the Roman Senate. His term as pope was cut short when he was shoved into exile by the determined Senate. He died after serving only a little more than a year.

URBAN IV, Pope ([?]–1264) A somewhat chauvinistic French pontiff who stacked the College of Cardinals with Frenchmen, Urban unwittingly created a French bloc in the Church which dominated papal politics for a century and a half. Urban, however, possessed some remarkable skills: he brought the unruly Manfred to heel by an excommunication; he straightened out the tangled finances of the Church; he adroitly strengthened the Church's position in the international political maneuvering. He ruled for 1261 to 1264.

URBAN V, Pope (1310–1370) A onetime Benedictine abbot, French-born Urban V held the chair from 1362 to 1370, during which time he issued the famous bull against heretics, *In Coena Domini*, and founded the now-famous universities of Cracow and Vienna.

URBAN VI, Pope (1318–1389) A tactless tyrant, Urban VI provoked the disgusting thirty-nine year long schism in which two rival papacies, one at Rome and the other at Avignon, rent the Church. Urban was popularly acclaimed in Rome when he was elected in 1378 as the first Italian Pontiff after a long time of French popes. He soon chilled even his most enthusiastic Italian supporters by his ruthless tactics, crushing all opposition even to the point of ordering the deaths of five cardinals who proved uncooperative. Urban managed to extirpate vestiges of French influence in the papal court but so angered the Cardinals that fifteen of them held a conclave at Fondi only four months after Urban's elevation, declared his election invalid, and installed Robert of Geneva as pope (who took the name Clement VII). Urban VI forced Clement VII to race to safety to Avignon, France, where Clement set up rival papacy which endured until 1417. Urban VI and Clement VII consumed most of their energies hurling condemnations at one another and trying to line up backers. Urban managed to retain the allegiance of England, Scandinavia, most of Germany and north and central Italy, or roughly half of Europe. His dismal reign extended from 1378 to 1389.

URBAN VII, Pope (1521–1590) Urban VII, chosen by a Spanish faction, died only twelve days after his election in 1590.

URBAN VIII, Pope (1568–1644) Effete and erudite, yet vain and vacillating, this long-term (1623–1644) pope was the last to practice nepotism on a grand scale, but enriched his relatives to an extent that astonished even the Romans. Urban, at the urging of the Jesuits, effectively quashed the predestinarian Jansenists within the Roman Catholic Church. In 1616, Urban took part in the disciplining of the great scientist Galileo. Although revising the breviary and penning some verses, including some which were set to music and put into some hymnals, he is also remembered as the vandal who melted priceless bronze from the Pantheon to make cannons to fortify Castel Sant' Angelo.

URSINUS, Zacharias (1534–1583) A lesser-known German Protestant theologian, Ursinus was one of the authors of the Heidelberg Catechism in 1562. Ursinus became a disciple of gentle Philip Melanchthon at Wittenberg and later studied under John Calvin at Geneva. In 1561, Ursinus was appointed professor at Heidelberg, where electorpalatine Frederick III asked him and Kaspar Olevianus to prepare a catechism. Their effort is still admired as a model of charity and Christ-centered personal expression of Calvinism. Ursinus, forced to leave Heidelberg in 1576 when his patron, the Elector, died, served as a professor at Neustadt-ander-Haardt for the rest of his days.

URSULA ([?]) A shadowy figure in history, Ursula was apparently a British Christian princess who made a pilgrimage to Rome, allegedly accompanied by 11,000 attendants. Ursula and her party were massacred by wild pagan tribesmen near Cologne, either in the 3rd or 5th century. She was later declared a saint.

USSHER, James (1581–1656) A learned Irish Anglican Archbishop of Ireland, Ussher confidently prepared a chronology of Biblical events based on his studies and reckoned that the creation of the universe occurred in 4004 B.C. Ussher's dates were almost universally accepted until the mid-nineteenth century, when scientific investigations punctured Ussher's pretensions, particularly the 4004 B.C. creation story. Ussher, stoutly Calvinist, had strong sympathies toward the Calvinist Puritans in spite of his Anglicanism. He was one of the few respected by all parties as a would-be reconciler. Ussher's *Reduction of Episcopalianism*, published posthumously in 1656, spelled out a plan to include Presbyterians within the established church.

V

VAIL, Thomas Hubbard (1812–1889) An American Protestant Episcopal cleric, Vail founded Bethany College, Topeka, Kansas, where he became the first president, and was consecrated the first Bishop of Kansas.

VALDES See **WALDO, Peter.**

VALDEZ See **WALDO, Peter.**

VALENS, Emperor of the East ([?]–378) Brother of Valentinian I who divided the Roman Empire, giving Valens the Eastern half, Valens was a Christian who unfortunately came to be swayed by the appeal of the Arian clergy of Constantinople. In 365, Valens exiled the venerable theologian and upholder of Orthodoxy, Athanasius, for the fifth time.

VALENTINE ([?]–269) Although legends and customs abound about February 14, the feast day of this popular saint, few facts are actually known about him. Valentine, apparently a Christian priest at Rome, died for the faith during the horrible persecutions under Roman Emperor Claudius II on February 14, 269.

VALLA, Lorenzo (1405–1457) A perceptive Italian humanist scholar and priest, Valla advanced historical criticism by examining many records and documents with a cold, historian's eye.

VANDERKEMP, Johannes Theodorus (1747–1811) A Dutch-born missionary to South Africa, Vanderkemp, although a pastor's son, came to the Christian faith tardily after sixteen misspent years in the army, medical studies at Scotland and several years in a comfortable medical practice at Rotterdam. Vanderkemp, shaken after the tragic drowning of his wife and daughter, volunteered to the London Missionary Society and left for South Africa in 1799. Before leaving, however, Vanderkemp organized the first missionary society in the Netherlands. In South Africa, Vanderkemp penetrated into areas previously untouched by the Church, founding the Mission Institute at Bethelsdorp, and organizing the South African Society for Promoting the Spread of Christ's Kingdom.

VAN DYKE, Cornelius Van Allen (1818–1895) Well-known American medical missionary to the Near East and Arabic scholar, Van Dyke ministered in Syria from 1840 until his death. He completed the Arabic translation of the Bible begun by Eli Smith, publishing it in 1865. Van Dyke is credited for helping revive Arabic literature by writing Arabic in a clear, simple, yet lovely style.

VAN DYKE, Henry (1852–1933) A versatile Presbyterian with eclectic tastes, Van Dyke ably served as pastor of prestigious congregations (including New York City's Brick Presbyterian from 1883–1899), U.S. Minister to the Netherlands and Luxembourg under President Woodrow Wilson from 1913 to 1916, a navy chaplain during World War I, and a Princeton University professor from 1919 to 1923. Van Dyke gained a large following as a popular lecturer and writer. He wrote a string of books, including the widely translated and perennial-favorite Christmas fantasy, *The Other Wise Man* in 1896.

VAN RAALTE, Albertus C. (1811–1876) Patriarchal leader of the Dutch Reformed colony of immigrants in Michigan and Wisconsin during the mid-nineteenth century, Van Raalte had a hand in helping the transplanted Frieslanders to organize colleges, educational institutions and industrial efforts such as the woodworking shops which developed into furniture industries. As a young pastor in the Netherlands, Van Raalte had opposed efforts by autocratic Dutch King William I to bring the democratic Reformed Church under royal control. Van Raalte finally led a large group of Frieslander Separatists to Michigan in 1846, the start of a great influx of Dutch to the upper Great Lakes area.

VASCONCELLOS, Simão (1599–1670[?]) An early Portuguese Jesuit missionary, Vasconcellos arrived at Brazil about 1630. In 1663, he published *Cronica da Companhia de Jesus no Brazil*, a record of Jesuit efforts in Brazil, and later wrote other valuable historical reminiscences of early colonial Brazil.

VASEY, Thomas (1731–1826) One of the early followers of John Wesley, English-born Vasey was ordained as a presbyter in 1784 by Wesley and Thomas Coke and sent to the American colonies. Vasey worked diligently as a Methodist circuit rider on the frontier, organizing congregations, visiting isolated farms, and helping to plant the roots of American Methodism.

VENN, John (1759–1813) An Anglican with an urgent sense of missionary zeal, Venn agitated for the organization of a mission board and finally, helped by Thomas Scott, formed the Church Missionary Society in 1799. Venn served as rector at Clapham for many years, where he attracted a group of likeminded Evangelicals who came to be known as "the Clapham sect."

VERBECK, Guido Herman Fridolin (1830–1898) A Dutch-born American Presbyterian sent to Japan by the Dutch Reformed Church in the U.S.A., Verbeck arrived in Japan at the time when Christianity was outlawed but patiently and painfully won recognition and respect from the Japanese authorities. In 1868, Verbeck was asked to set up a Japanese educational system and supervise foreign teachers at the Imperial University at Tokyo.

VERGIL See **VIRGILIUS**.

VERMIGLI See **PETER, Martire Vermigli**.

VICTOR I, Pope ([?]–199) An early Bishop of Rome, Victor vigorously promoted the claim of Rome to have jurisdiction over all other bishops and congregations, although many resisted. Victor opposed the Adoptionist or Monarchian heresy which taught that Jesus, a mere man, was "adopted" by God and raised to divine status. Ruling from 189 to 199, Victor is thought by some to have died a martyr. He was later canonized.

VICTOR II, Pope ([?]–1057) Pontiff from 1055 to 1057, Victor II was the pawn of his relative, Emperor Henry III, and faithfully blessed all Henry's policies. At the Council of Florence in 1055, Victor II surprised everyone by throwing out several bishops for immorality and simony.

VICTOR III, Pope (1027[?]–1087) A faltering administrator who disliked decision making, Victor was elected after an involved, undignified hassle. His main concern as pope seemed to be to advance the interests of his home monastery, Monte Cassino, where he finally retired after less than two years in office.

VICTOR IV, Antipope ([?]–1164) A tool to advance the political ambitions of Emperor Frederick Barbarossa, Victor allowed himself to be elected "pope" by a group of five dissident Cardinals in 1159 in opposition to Pope Alexander III and confirmed as "pontiff" at a Emperor-called Council at Pavia in 1160. Crusty Pope Alexander III promptly retaliated by excommunicating Emperor Frederick, precipitating a mighty European diplomatic crisis and undercutting Victor IV's claims.

VIDALIN, Jon Thorkelsson (1666–1720) A learned, eloquent Lutheran bishop of Iceland, Vidalin had gifts as a poet and preacher. He wrote a popular postil which became a classic in Icelandic Church literature and was set to music.

VIEIRA, Antonio (1608–1697) A forceful Portuguese Jesuit preacher and writer, Vieira molded public opinion against slavery by lucid writings and powerful sermons. Vieira served as a missionary in Brazil from 1623 to 1641, returned to Portugal where he received an appointment as King John IV's court preacher and carried out numerous delicate diplomatic chores in various European capitals for the Portuguese royal house. Back in Brazil in 1652, Vieira showed such a passion for the welfare and rights of the Indians that he enraged the slaveholding aristocracy. He was forced to leave Brazil in disgrace, tried by the Inquisition and imprisoned for two years, 1665 to 1667. Released finally, Vieira worked from 1669 to 1675 at Rome for the relief of persecuted Jews. Vieira persuaded his superiors to permit him to resume his labors in Brazil in 1681, and energetically continued to work to eliminate slavery. Vieira is revered in Portuguese literature as one of the top prose writers, and was esteemed as one of the most articulate orators in his day.

VIGILANTIUS (370[?]–406[?]) An outspoken presbyter from western Gaul (now France) who was theologically consistent and courageous, Vigilantius denounced the veneration of relics and saints and opposed the double set of standards in vogue in the Church, one for laity, and another for clergy. Critic Vigilantius even attacked traditionalist Jerome for advocating worship of relics. Vigilantius, peculiarly modern in many respects, also denounced priestly celibacy and poverty.

VIGILIUS, Pope ([?]–555) A wavering weakling who was dominated by Emperor Justinian I, Vigilius acquiesced to Justinian's pressures to downgrade Chalcedonian or orthodox Christianity and in 548 issued *Judicatium* which favored the Monophysites and criticized the Christology of the Council of Chalcedon. In 553, Vigilius meekly agreed to Justinian's condemnation of portions of writings of Theodore of Mopsuestia, Theodoret of Cyrus and Ibas of Edessa (the famous "Three Chapters") at the Fifth General Council at Constantinople. Vigilius occupied the papal throne from 537 to 555, ending his career in disgrace for vacillating.

VILATTE, Joseph René (1848–1925) Apostate Roman priest who founded the Old Catholic Church in America, Vilatte was a French-Canadian who joined the Old Catholics in Europe and received the assignment to oversee the handful of Old Catholic parishes in

North America. Vilatte styled himself "Archbishop," stirred up some discord in Roman Catholic circles for a time, named and consecrated his own successor, then returned to the Roman Catholic Church in time to retire to a monastery in France, where he died.

VILLEGAIGNON, Nicolas Durand de (1510–1571) The distinguished but dictatorial French Huguenot who helped establish the Protestant colony in 1555 in Brazil which had the backing of such notables as Calvin and Beza, Villegaignon later fell into a series of acrimonious disagreements with the colonists over doctrine and discipline. Villegaignon reversed himself and odiously suppressed Protestant worship, even executing as heretics those who crossed him. The colony finally fell apart. Villegaignon, despised by the Protestants and doubted by the Catholics, retired to France.

VINCENT, Ferrer (1350[?]–1419) The greatest preacher of his time, Vincent was a Spanish Dominican friar who held huge, open-air Church rallies throughout southern and central Europe. Vincent also served as confessor to Antipope Benedict XIII until Benedict's deposition in 1417. In 1399, Vincent embarked on his first preaching mission, holding outdoor meetings which attracted enormous crowds in France, Switzerland and Northern Italy. A loyal Spaniard, Vincent worked from 1408 to 1416 to revitalize the spiritual life of Spain. He was canonized in 1455.

VINCENT, John Heyl (1832–1920) The originator of the idea of uniform Sunday School lessons for U.S. Protestantism and the creator of the Chautauqua lectures, Vincent was an imaginative American Methodist cleric. In 1865, Vincent produced the first standard Sunday School curriculum, writing a monthly manual with lesson ideas based on Biblical material for teachers. Noting the need to educate adults, in 1878, Vincent founded the Chautauqua Literary and Scientific Circle, which grew into an immensely popular cultural and educational agency among U.S. Protestants. Vincent, a fount of ideas, was elected a Methodist bishop in 1888.

VINCENT de Lérins ([?]–434[?]) A French monk at Lérins, France, Vincent in 435 wrote two *Commonitorium* under the pen-name Peregrinus in which he attempted to reply to some of the heresies then in vogue. Vincent's writings were a somewhat clumsy attempt to state clear-cut guidelines for orthodoxy, presenting the theory and norm for each doctrine. Vincent de Lérins claimed to define "what has been believed everywhere, always, by all," and later was declared a saint in the Roman Church.

VINCENT de Paul (1580–1660) An organizational genius who could mobilize resources to meet every need of his day from ransoming Christian captives in North Africa to organizing a relief program for war-stricken Lorraine, Vincent de Paul focused the attention of 17th century France on the plight of the oppressed and gathered money and manpower to meet the needs. Vincent's career as a young priest was colored permanently when he was captured by Barbary pirates and forced into slavery for two years before escaping. Returning to France, he was astonished to note the gap between the affluent nobility and the poor peasant. Vincent de Paul, at home both in fashionable drawing rooms (he was chaplain to Queen Margaret of Valois for a time) and in the squalor of the poverty class (he was also head of a parish in bone-poor Brittany in 1625) founded a band of missionaries to look after the forgotten and suffering. Vincent de Paul's Congregation of the Missionary Preachers also came to be called Lazarists after they shifted in 1632 to the priory of St. Lazare in Paris, and received official recognition by Pope Urban VIII in 1632.

Father Vincent's Order grew to twenty-five houses during his lifetime. Vincent also set up confraternities of charity to tend the indigents, destitute and ill, particularly in the burgeoning slums of Paris. Enlisting the services of the famous Louise de Marillac and organizing a group of women into an order known as the Daughters of Charity, Vincent alleviated much of the distress among the poor in Paris. Vincent also had a flair for tapping the interest and commitment of those not desiring to enter religious orders. He organized secular orders such as the Ladies of Charity, groups of well-to-do women volunteers, who donated money and services on a part-time basis. Vincent, beloved by the poor and respected by the rich, was canonized in 1737.

VINCENT of Saragossa ([?]–304) An early Spanish cleric, Vincent of Saragossa suffered martyrdom following a series of excruciating tortures during the persecutions of Emperor Diocletian. The account of Vincent's sufferings, known as "Acts," was widely circulated, especially in the Mediterranean countries, where he was deeply venerated. In Burgundy, Vincent became the patron saint of the vinedressers.

VIRET, Pierre (1511–1571) Able and eloquent member of the great trio of Protestant Reformers in Switzerland of Calvin, Farel and Viret, Viret became an early active adherent of the Reformed cause and was ordained by Farel in 1531. Viret returned immediately to his home town of Orbe, Vaud

Canton, Switzerland, where he served as pastor and promoted Reformed views. Bitterly opposed by the local Roman Catholic leaders, Viret narrowly escaped being poisoned by a priest-inspired plot at Orbe. Viret, moved to Lausanne, where he led the Reformation from 1537 to 1559 in that center. Viret, a close associate of John Calvin, helped pave the way at Geneva for Calvin to return in 1541 after the defeat of the Libertine party which had ousted Calvin earlier.

VIRGILIUS ([?]–784) One of the great monastics produced during the flowering of the Irish Church in the 8th century, Virgilius emigrated to the Continent where he had an eminent career as an abbot, evangelist, administrator and scholar. Virgilius served as Bishop of Salzburg, Austria for a time. One of the greatest teachers of his age, he taught that the earth is a sphere and spoke of the existence of antipodes.

VITALIAN, Pope ([?]–672) Ambitious but inept, Vitalian tried to bring the Byzantine Church under Roman jurisdiction by ingratiating himself with Constans II, the Emperor, but succeeded only in losing many of Rome's priceless bronze art treasures to the unmoved, greedy Emperor. Vitalian did manage, however, to get the entire English Church to recognize Rome's authority, thanks to the efforts of Theodore of Tarsus, Vitalian's appointee as Archbishop of Canterbury. Vitalian was later canonized.

VITTORIA, Francisco de ([?]–1546) A learned Spanish Dominican scholar, de Vittoria served as a distinguished professor at Salamanca, Spain, where he participated in the great intellectual reawakening in Spain begun by the famous Ximines. Vittoria aroused a profound new interest in the theology of the great Medieval scholastic, Thomas Aquinas.

VITUS ([?]–286[?]) The facts of Vitus' career are lost in the mists of legend. It is generally thought that he was tortured and put to death as a young boy (seven years old, according to some reports, twelve, according to others) with his tutor, Modestus, and his nurse, Crescentia. Vitus became the patron saint of the sufferers from many illnesses, especially chorea (popularly known as St. Vitus' Dance).

VLADIMIR I, Emperor of Russia (956[?]–1015) The undisputed monarch of Russia after a bold series of conquests, Vladimir, following a radical change after his conversion to Christianity, imposed the Greek Orthodox Church on his sometimes-unwilling subjects. Vladimir incorporated a captive Byzantine princess named Anna into his harem, and probably received the news of the Gospel from her. He was baptized and abruptly abandoned his bloody, brutish ways. Vladimir, determined to make the Greek Orthodox Church the state religion, began the forced mass conversion of the Russian people, occasionally lapsing into reliance on harsh measures to get his people to accept the faith. He is revered as a saint by the Eastern Church.

VOETIUS, Gisbert (1588–1676) An unbending Dutch Calvinist who carried the doctrine of predestination farther than his mentor ever intended, Voetius took a leading role at the Synod of Dort in 1618 where the Arminian-leaning Remonstrants were excoriated. Voetius particularly opposed the milder, more liberal Calvinist theologian Coccejus and the philosopher Descartes. Beginning in 1634, Voetius served forty years as a professor of theology at Utrecht.

VOLIVA, Wilbur Glenn (1870–1942) Superintendent of the sect known as the Christian Catholic Church in Zion from 1907 until his death, the Ohio-born Voliva was associated for four years with the Christian Church (Campbellites) before involving himself with the Christian Catholic Church in Zion in 1899.

W

WALAFRID STRABO (809[?]–849) An esteemed 9th century abbot and author, Walafrid Strabo headed the monastery at Reichenau, wrote much of *Glossa Ordinaria*, and penned liturgical material and biographies of the saints. Walafrid Strabo, once a monk at Fulda under the distinguished Hrabanus, combined his skills as a Latin scholar and poet with statecraft, serving as advisor to King Louis the Pious.

WALDENSTROM, Paul Peter (1838–1917) Founder of the reform movement in Sweden known as the Swedish Mission Covenant, Waldenstrom was a maverick Swedish Lutheran who resigned from the State Church, disgusted from bucking its ecclesiasticism. Waldenstrom insisted on emphasizing Scripture, sometimes denigrating the place of creeds and the place of the institutional church. Following his leaving the established church, Pastor Waldenstrom developed the Evangelical National Institute, which later took the name of the Swedish Mission Covenant, or sometimes simply "Waldenstromians." Followers who emigrated to the United States in the late 19th century carried Waldenstrom's ideas with them, and founded the body known as the Evangelical Covenant Church in America.

WALDO, Peter (1140[?]–1218[?]) Resolute pre-Reformation reformer who anticipated most of the 16th century Protestant leaders' doctrines and practices and even stole a march on St. Francis of Assisi's discipline and poverty, Peter Waldo was the first to insist upon the Scriptures in the local language of the common people. Waldo began as a wealthy merchant or money-lender at Lyon, France. Following a startling conversion, he became absorbed in the Bible, even hiring two priests to translate large chunks of Scripture into the Lyon dialect. Waldo, determined to take the Gospel directly to the people, handed over his house to his wife, installed his daughters in a convent, gave away the residue of his property to the poor, and embarked on a preaching career. He attracted others, and they organized themselves into pairs of itinerant preachers, reciting long selections of Scripture in French which they had memorized. Waldo and his Bible-by-rote-group dubbed themselves simply the "Poor Men of Lyon," becoming an informally-structured lay order practicing celibacy and poverty.

Waldo and his "Poor Men of Lyon," however, soon ran afoul of the intractable traditionalist archbishop of Lyon, Guichard. Ignoring Guichard's protests and threats, Waldo serenely continued his preaching and Bible recitations. When Waldo finally found himself blocked by Guichard, the doughty preacher went over the head of the archbishop and appealed directly to the third Lateran Council in 1179. Waldo and his unlettered, barefooted laymen, regarded with a mixture of amusement and contempt by the sophisticated theologians and leaders at the Council, were prohibited from preaching anywhere except when permitted by local clergy.

Waldo, realizing that he had to choose between obeying God or the Church hierarchy, continued carrying Scripture and sermons in French to the countryside. At the same time, he began questioning the ceremonial structure and the sacramental system of Roman Catholicism. Waldo eventually jettisoned many non-Biblical beliefs, including Purgatory, veneration of saints and relics, absolution and oath-taking.

In 1182, the inevitable break occurred. Waldo and his pairs of preachers were thrown out of the see of Lyon by Guichard's successor, Archbishop John of the Fair Hands. The following year, Waldo and his followers were formally declared heretics by the Council of Verona. Waldo and the Poor Men of Lyon, forced to flee, went underground. For the next thirty-five years, Waldo reportedly turned up in various locations, including Metz, Lombardy and Bohemia.

His followers, absorbing a cluster of several other 12th century lay sects, came to be known as Waldensians or Waldenses. They rejected masses for the dead, Purgatory, invocation of the saints, adoration of Mary, indulgences and images. Continuing Waldo's emphasis, they translated the Latin Vulgate into French and Italian dialects. Waldo's followers even devised their own catechetical materials based on the Lord's Prayer, the Ten Commandments and Scripture passages. Ferociously suppressed by a succession of popes and emperors throughout the 13th, 14th, 15th and 16th centuries, Waldo's followers were forced to retreat to remote mountain fastnesses of the Piedmont and isolated areas of Provence.

WALLIN, Johan Olof (1779–1839) A renowned Swedish Lutheran hymnwriter, churchman and poet, Wallin compiled the popular Psalm Book in Sweden which came to be known as *Wallin's Psalm Book* and included 130 of his hymns. In 1837, Wallin was consecrated Archbishop of Sweden.

WALTER ("the Penniless") ([?]–1097) Also known as "Gauthier sans avoir," Walter, a French knight, assumed charge of a ragtag collection of peasants which swelled to some 40,000 as it set out to liberate the Holy Land at the start of the First Crusade. Walter's untrained, unequipped, unprepared horde was hacked to pieces in an ill-conceived assault on Belgrade, and most of the survivors were lost in the forests or perished from disease or exposure. The undaunted Walter led his wraith-like handful of diehards across the Bosphorus as the advance-wave of the Crusade. Walter died in a skirmish at Nicaea and his pathetic crew was either butchered by the Turks or sold as slaves.

WALTHER, Carl Ferdinand Wilhelm (1811–1887) American Lutheranism's outstanding 19th century personality, Walther left as his monument the Missouri Synod Lutheran Church but left his imprint on all of American Lutheran thinking and programming. Walther, born in Germany and educated at Leipzig, found his pietism and conservative theology under fire from the rationalism-infected State Church power structure. Seeking more congenial surroundings, Walther accompanied a party of 750 German emigrants headed by Dresden pastor Martin Stephan and settled in Missouri. Walther, displaying remarkable organizing and intellectual abilities, helped found Concordia Seminary, St. Louis, in 1839. In 1847, he headed the group founding the Evangelical Lutheran Synod of Missouri. The versatile German-American also possessed exceptional gifts as a musician and a journalist. For many years, Walther edited two church periodicals.

WARBURTON, William (1698–1799) A blustery Anglican prelate who relished acerbic polemical exchanges, Warburton authored *The Alliance Between Church and State* in 1736, stoutly defending the primacy of episcopacy but conceding that non-conformists should be tolerated, and the two-volume *The Doctrine of Grace* in 1762, fiercely attacking Methodism.

WARD, Nathaniel (1578–1652) An early colonial writer, Ward was an English Puritan whose career unfolded on both sides of the Atlantic. Ward served in England as an Anglican rector until thrown out for his Puritan views by the ferocious Archbishop Laud in 1633. Emigrating to New England, Ward became pastor at Ipswich, Massachusetts, in 1641, where he helped prepare the first set of laws for the colony, the *Body of Liberties.* Ward returned to England in 1647, took a parish at Sheffield, and continued his writing career by producing a series of sprightly-worded pamphlets.

WARD, William George (1812–1882) A passionate defender of the high church movement in Anglicanism in the early 19th century who finally embraced Roman Catholicism in 1845, Ward, although somewhat eclipsed by the more distinguished convert, John Henry Newman, graced Rome's collection of scholarly ex-Anglicans. Ward, writing an intemperate outburst against the Church of England, *The Ideal of a Christian Church* in 1844, was demoted from his Oxford position. He followed Newman and others from the Oxford Group into the Roman Catholic communion, taught at St. Edmund's at Ware, and edited the *Dublin Review.*

WARE, Henry (1764–1845) An American Congregationalist who helped foment the Unitarian party within the Congregational Church in early 19th century New England, Ware was the focal point of a furious controversy over his appointment as Professor of Divinity at Harvard in 1805. Ware edged Harvard closer to Unitarianism, and helped promote the organization of Harvard Divinity School in 1816, where he later served as a faculty member.

WARFIELD, Benjamin Breckenridge (1851–1921) Presbyterian theologian and educator, Warfield taught a granite-like inflexible theological system at Pittsburgh's Western Theological Seminary from 1878 to 1887 before moving to Princeton Theological Seminary, where he served as professor for years and president from 1902 to 1903 and 1913 to 1914. The conservative Warfield took his stand on the plenary inspiration of Scripture, Calvin's *Institutes* and the *Westminster Confession,* and wrote a series of carefully written textbooks which were "standards" for theological education in conservative circles for many years.

WARHAM, William (1450–1532) A dogged Archbishop of Canterbury (from 1504 until his death), Warham frequently found himself at cross purposes with the determined King Henry VIII and the arbitrary Cardinal Wolsey. Warham, although Counselor for the Queen, acquiesced to Henry's demands for a divorce in 1530 and reluctantly agreed to write Pope Clement VII on Henry's behalf. In 1530, however, Warham refused to acknowledge Henry as Supreme Head of the Church without adding the conditional clause, "so far as the law of Christ allows." Warham's last two years were spent protesting Acts of Parliament which infringed on prerogatives of the pope or Church.

WARNER, Daniel Sidney (1842–1925) Founder of the Church of God (Anderson, Indiana), the Ohio-born Warner, following a soul-wrenching conversion experience at a schoolhouse revival, became active in John Winebrenner's Church of God in North America. He was expelled, however, in 1877 for urging what he called "entire sanctification," a perfectionism which Warner claimed was dispensed by God's grace. Warner began publishing *Gospel Trumpet*, a periodical promoting his views, about 1880. After a series of seven moves, he finally settled in Anderson, Indiana. He insisted that he was only trying to foster a reform movement for those in all denominations, but soon found that he had developed a separate denomination. Warner's Church of God (Anderson, Indiana), not to be confused with over two hundred other bodies bearing the title "Church of God," emphasizes Warner's ideas of sanctification, foot-washing, communion and baptism by immersion.

WATSON, John (1850–1907) An English-born, Scottish-educated Presbyterian minister at Liverpool from 1880 until 1905, Watson wrote under the pen name "Ian Maclaren," publishing a series of popular "kailyard" fictional pieces sentimentalizing Scottish country life, including *Beside the Bonnie Briar Bush* and *Days of Auld Lang Syne*. Watson under his own name wrote several less-popular theological tomes and enjoyed success on the American lecture circuit.

WATTS, Isaac (1674–1748) Lyrical English Independent pastor and theologian who created the modern Protestant hymn, Watts wrote over 600 hymns, including such cherished classics as "O God, Our Help in Ages Past," "Joy to the World," "When I Survey the Wondrous Cross," "This Is the Day the Lord Hath Made," "Come Holy Spirit

Heavenly Dove," and "Jesus Shall Reign Where'er the Sun." Watts broke the tradition of using only metrical paraphrases of the Psalms or selections from the Medieval office for congregational singing and introduced the use of verses set to music. Many of Watts' greatest hymns were written when he was in his first pastorate, a young man under twenty-two. In 1706, he finally published many of his selections in *Horae Lyricae*, followed in 1707 by *Hymns and Spiritual Songs*, and in 1715 by *Divine and Moral Songs for Children*. The prolific Watts also had a considerable reputation as a lucid writer and forceful speaker. He wrote theological works which were used as textbooks at such places as Cambridge, Oxford, Harvard and Yale until the beginning of the last century.

WEBB, Thomas (1724–1796) One of the first Methodist circuit-riding preachers in the American colonies, Webb had been a captain in the British army, badly wounded in North America before his conversion at Bristol, England. This early Wesleyan was renowned for his vigorous preaching along the Eastern Seaboard from 1766 until his death.

WEEMS, Mason Locke (1759–1825) Remembered as "Parson" Weems in American history, Weems, an ordained Church of England priest, served a series of Maryland parishes from 1784 to 1794, at which time he embarked on his career as an itinerant bookseller and pamphleteer. Weems' twenty-six titles, including the widely-read biography of George Washington, extolled Puritan virtues and idealized American heroes.

WEIDNER, Revere Franklin (1851–1915) Confessional and conservative Lutheran in the United States, Weidner became the first president of Evangelical Lutheran Seminary in Chicago in 1891, following a teaching career at Augustana College and Seminary in Rock Island, Illinois, and a series of pastorates.

WELLHAUSEN, Julius (1844–1918) Master researcher of Old Testament texts and literature, Wellhausen was the first to discover that the "P" (for "Priestly") document within the pentateuch was the most recent rather than the most ancient part of the first five books of the Old Testament. Wellhausen's theories were not received with universal acclaim in all circles, however, in Germany. He was asked to leave his professor's post at Griefswald in 1882 for his liberal interpretations of the Bible, moved briefly to the University of Halle, taught for seven years at Marburg, finally settled down at Gottingen in 1892. Wellhausen theorized that the first five books of the Bible were not written by Moses but by various authors at different periods after the Exile. He stimulated Old Testament research and the study of Aramaisms in the New Testament.

WENCESLAUS, Duke of Bohemia (907[?]–929[?]) Deeply influenced by his saintly grandmother, Luduila (who was murdered by Wenceslaus' resentful widowed pagan mother), Wenceslaus grew up in turmoil-filled Bohemia and was placed on the throne when he was only fifteen. He ruled only seven years, dying at the hands of his brother, Boleslav, but unified the Slavs in Bohemia and promoted Christianity in the nation. Wenceslaus later came to symbolize Czech nationalism. He became the subject of a welter of popular legends, including the one in the *English Christmas Carol* by John Mason Neale. Later canonized by the Church, Wenceslaus is a favorite of the Czechs. His statue towers over Wenceslaus Square in the heart of Prague.

WESEL, John Ruchrath von ([?]–1479) An incautiously-outspoken pre-Reformation German preacher, von Wesel in many ways was a prototype of Martin Luther. He daringly opposed the sale of indulgences, publishing a tract in 1450 criticizing the practice and standing up to the pope's hucksters, including the formidable Cardinal Cuso at Erfurt. Later, after interludes at Basel, Switzerland, and Mainz, von Wesel preached seventeen years at Worms. His excoriations of Roman practices were eventually too much for the hierarchy. He was seized and imprisoned in 1479, dying from the effects of torture and maltreatment.

WESLEY, Charles (1707–1788) Younger, more somber brother of the exuberant John Wesley who founded the Methodist Church, Charles Wesley accompanied brother John on most of his travels for the first twenty years of Methodism, but made his mark on the Church primarily through writing hymns.

Charles Wesley, eighteenth child of Samuel and Susanna Wesley, rescued from his father's flaming rectory at Epworth in 1709, followed his brother to Oxford in 1726. In the spring of 1729 Charles Wesley and two other undergraduates, Robert Kirkham and William Morgan, began their own "Oxford group," emphasizing high church Anglicanism. Wesley and the others, ridiculed by the others at Oxford, were dubbed "Methodists" or the "Holy Club." Charles' "Holy Club" came to be dominated by John when the latter returned to Oxford in 1729, and concerned itself with being morbidly preoccupied with stringent, joyless rule-keeping to save their own souls.

Following ordination as an Anglican priest, Charles accompanied John to Georgia, where they encountered the warm, intensely personal piety of the Moravians. The Georgia interlude, however, was a fiasco for the stiff, legalistic Wesley brothers. Charles, always the more delicate of the pair, returned to England in 1736, leaving John to two more years of strenuous but senseless effort in the colony. Charles, groping for a more meaningful personal faith, turned to the Moravians. When John returned from Georgia, both brothers received instructions from Moravian Peter Bohler and joined the Fetter Lane Society. Charles, critically ill in May, 1738, experienced a profoundly joyous, personal conversion experience—preceding John Wesley's rebirth by three days.

Joined by the dynamic orator and friend from Oxford days, George Whitefield, Charles and John preached wherever they found a pulpit, then took to the open fields to carry their exultant news to the English lower classes. Charles, always overshadowed by his aggressive, robust brother, traveled nearly everywhere with John during the years in which the Methodist movement burgeoned in England. Anglican to the core and conservative by temperament, Charles frequently found himself at loggerheads with John over some of the innovations of the Methodists, such as non-episcopal ordination. Lacking John's ruggedness, Charles was forced to stop itinerating after 1756.

Charles Wesley's greatest contribution was his hymn-writing. He penned over 6,000 pieces, including "Ye Servants of God, Your Master Proclaim!," "Hark, the Herald Angels Sing!," "Christ the Lord Is Risen Today!," "O for a Thousand Tongues to Sing," "Jesus, Lover of My Soul," "Love Divine, All Loves Excelling," "Soldiers of Christ, Arise," and "Christ, Whose Glory Fills the Skies."

WESLEY, John (1703–1791) The launcher and captain of the great 18th century Evangelical movement which affected the course of the English-speaking world and gave rise to the Methodists, John Wesley was a high church Anglican who revolutionized the character and condition of lower class Englishmen.

Wesley, fifteenth child of Samuel and Susanna Wesley, was raised in the rectory at Epworth, Lincolnshire, England. When only six, he and his younger brother Charles were rescued from the flames which destroyed the rectory—an event which left a deep impression on John and led him to describe himself as "a brand snatched from the burning."

After schooling at Charterhouse, London, and Christ Church College, Oxford, John Wesley was ordained an Anglican deacon in 1725, and served as his father's assistant from 1726 to 1729. At this time, John Wesley led an active, gay social life, although he was inwardly experiencing the spiritual struggles which persisted until his conversion at the Aldersgate Street meeting in 1738. In 1729 John Wesley returned to Oxford, where his pious serious-minded younger brother Charles and a handful of undergraduates had organized a Bible-study and prayer circle, nicknamed the "Holy Club," the "Godly Club," "Bible Moths" and "Methodists" from the regularity and strict method of their lives and studies by derisive fellow students. John Wesley, a fellow at Lincoln College, quickly assumed leadership of the "Holy Club."

Wesley and the circle of Oxford students, painfully obsessed about their own salvation, set out to discipline themselves to live intensely strict lives. They examined their own motives, made rules for themselves, assigned precise chores such as visiting the Oxford jail, fasted, prayed by schedule, met regularly, and did everything humanly possible to achieve a sense of personal salvation. They were, however, a joke to others at Oxford and restless, dissatisfied searchers to themselves.

John and Charles Wesley accepted an invitation from Governor Oglethorp of Georgia in 1735 to come as missionaries to the colony. John Wesley's motive in going to Georgia, as he frankly wrote, was "the hope of saving my own soul." The experience, however, only brought him a deeper sense of self-disdain. He found himself terrified at the prospect of death during a severe storm during the Atlantic crossing, and envious of the cheerful confidence of the twenty-six Moravians on board. In Georgia, John Wesley proved to be a joyless prig. He worked strenuously to be the punctiliously proper parson, but was tactless and unpopular with the colonists, and silly and indecisive about marrying a Georgia girl, Sophy Hopkey.

Disgusted with himself, Wesley returned to London in early 1738. He fortunately fell in with Peter Bohler and the Moravians, who showed the agitated young Anglican that it was impossible to save his soul by legalistic righteousness and precise self-discipline. On May 24, 1738, John Wesley reluctantly attended an Anglican "society" in Aldersgate Street, London. Wesley dated his rebirth from that evening. Listening to a reading of Luther's preface to the *Commentary on the Epistle to the Romans,* Wesley felt his "heart strangely warmed." He exultantly described the experience: "While he was describing the change which God works in the heart through faith in Christ, I felt . . . I did trust in Christ, Christ alone for my salvation; and an assurance was given me that he had taken away my sins, even mine and saved me from the law of sin and death." The basic Reformation doctrine of justification by faith had gripped Wesley.

John Wesley, joined by his brother Charles and the eloquent George Whitefield, hurled himself into preaching his intensely personal experience of joyous liberation through Christ. The Wesley-Whitefield emotional enthusiasm was too much, however, for the chilly, crusty Church of England. Finding nearly all pulpits closed to them, John and Charles Wesley spoke tirelessly in "societies" in the vicinity of London. Noting Whitefield's unparalleled success in preaching in the open fields to rough Bristol miners, John Wesley hesitantly decided to try the same. He was astounded at the response of the crowds. "My heart was so enlarged I knew not how to give over, so we continued three hours," he wrote.

Wesley, while lacking Whitefield's dramatic punch, spoke persuasively and earnestly, preaching over 40,000 sermons and traveling over 225,000 miles before he "first began to feel old at eighty-five." His services sometimes produced strong emotional outbursts among worshippers, such as fainting, shrieks and hysteria, which caused him to be denounced by proprieties-conscious clergy. Frequently attacked by rowdies and interrupted by hecklers, especially in the early days of his open-air meetings, Wesley fearlessly and cheerfully talked them down, usually converting his opposition in the process.

Wesley always thought of himself as a loyal Anglican and never left the Church of England. He organized his converts into groups which he called "classes," which he intended to be an order within the established church. In Bristol, in 1739, he founded the first "society" and erected a chapel; later in 1739, he took over an old London foundry and turned it into a chapel for those from the Moravian Fetter Lane

Society who desired a Wesley-type "society." In spite of Wesley's intentions to keep his societies within the Church of England, an independent organization developed, with its own network of chapels or congregations and separate institutional apparatus.

Wesley, an ingenuous organizer, began using lay preachers and lay leadership throughout the movement. In 1744, he brought together his preachers in London for the first of the "Annual Conferences." Wesley, refusing to permit the sacraments to be administered by unordained men, finally yielded to pressures of circumstances where few episcopally-ordained were available and began ordaining his own ministers.

Wesley's lower and middle-class lay preachers carried Methodism into northern England as far as Newcastle by 1743. By 1750, Wesley was making the first of several triumphal tours into northern England and Scotland. Beginning in 1747, Wesley made twenty visits to Ireland, where he was enthusiastically received. Methodism took hold in the American colonies so deeply that by 1771, Wesley dispatched the tireless Francis Asbury, and in 1784, ordained Asbury and Thomas Coke as "superintendents" for the American Methodists.

Wesley inevitably attracted controversy. He and his colleague George Whitefield, a convinced Calvinist, wrangled over predestination. Wesley's dispute with others over perfectionism was more serious. Wesley took the line that it was possible to achieve proper motives—love of God and neighbor—and that such an attainment would mean a freedom from sin. Wesley was also criticized for preaching an intensely personal gospel.

No one, however, could deny the social effects of Wesley's message. The Evangelicals, influenced by Wesley, created a new social conscience in England. William Wilberforce, encouraged by Wesley, carried out his campaign to end slavery; John Howard worked to effect prison reform. Evangelicalism, spawned by Wesley, strained to end many of the brutal and decadent practices of British and American life.

Although arbitrary and autocratic in his leadership, John Wesley in 1784 had the grace and good sense to turn over decision-making powers to his Methodist "conferences," issuing a *Deed of Declaration* providing for Methodist self-government. He continued his long horseback tours, which had been partly a result (or perhaps a cause) of an unhappy marriage with a peculiarly unsympathetic widow named Mary Vazeille. He died in 1791, active almost to the end, "leaving behind nothing but a good library of books, a well-worn clergyman's gown, a much-abused reputation, and—the Methodist Church."

WESLEY, Samuel (1662–1735) The father of the remarkable brothers, Charles and John Wesley, founders of Methodism, Samuel Wesley served as Anglican rector at the country parish of Epworth in Lincolnshire, England from 1695 until his death. Wesley's father and father-in-law had both been Non-Conformist clergymen who had been thrown out of their parishes when Anglicanism was re-established in 1662, but Samuel Wesley chose to serve as a clergyman of the Church of England. He was a conscientious, if impractical, rector, writing a *Life of Christ in Verse* and commentary on the book of Job. From 1726 to 1729, he took his son John Wesley on as his assistant at Epworth.

WESLEY, Susanna Annesley (1669–1742) One of the most influential mothers of history, this iron-willed woman raised eleven children (eight others died as babies) and looked after the household on a parson-poor budget in a provincial parish. She left her stamp, however, on history through two of her illustrious sons, John and Charles Wesley, founders of Methodism, whom she schooled in her kitchen. Daughter of a Non-Conformist clergyman ejected from his parish when Anglicanism was made the established church in 1662, Susanna Wesley, nonetheless, was an ardent Anglican all her life. Married to the Rev. Samuel Wesley in 1689, rector of Epworth parish in rural Lincolnshire during his entire ministry, Susanna made a home through devout faith, severe economies and near-constant toil. Susanna Wesley helped save the lives of infant Charles (then only two) and young John (six years old) when fire destroyed the rectory one night, and implanted the notion in John's mind that he was a "brand snatched from the burning." The genuine Godliness and practical piety of this forceful woman were passed on to her distinguished sons.

WESTCOTT, Brooke Foss (1825–1901) Noteworthy Anglican New Testament scholar and Church historian, Westcott with F. J. A. Hort toiled twenty-eight years to produce the authorative *New Testament in the Original Greek*, published in 1881. Westcott, a divinity professor at Cambridge from 1870 until 1890, helped publish the revised edition of the New Testament in English. He was elevated as Bishop of Durham in 1890, where he showed astonishing skills in identifying with coal miners, helping resolve a bitter strike in 1892. Westcott wrote numerous scholarly articles and books on textual study of the New Testament.

WETTSTEIN, Johann Jakob (1693–1754) Precise pioneer in New Testa-

ment manuscript studies, Wettstein was a Swiss Protestant scholar who worked at Basel and later at Amsterdam. His monumental *Greek New Testament with Various Reading*, published in 1751–1752, represented a lifetime of careful research and advanced textual studies and exegesis.

WHATCOAT, Richard (1736–1806) An energetic early Methodist, Whatcoat was dispatched by John Wesley in 1784 to the young United States to bolster the fledgling Methodist movement. Whatcoat, previously a lay preacher, ordained a presbyter by Wesley and Thomas Coke, was empowered to ordain other clergymen—a break with Anglican procedures but a necessity for Methodist growth. Whatcoat worked faithfully building up Methodism along the Eastern Seaboard, and participated in the first American Methodist Conference at Baltimore, December, 1784. In 1800 he was elected a bishop.

WHATLEY, Richard (1787–1863) Liberal, literate logician who took orders in the Church of England, Whatley brilliantly deflated the pretentious efforts of several critics of the faith during the 19th century, including Scottish skeptic David Hume. Whatley, consummately skilled in logic and rhetoric, published what were accepted as the definitive works in those fields for years. In 1831, he was elevated as Archbishop of Dublin, where he supported progressive causes and helped found the broad church movement, opposing the high church tractarianism of Newman and the Anglo-Catholic Oxford Movement.

WHEELOCK, Eleazer (1711–1779) A New England Congregational preacher driven by a concern to offer Indians an education, Wheelock ran a series of Indian schools before opening the last and most successful, known today as Dartmouth College. Wheelock tutored youths in his home in Massachusetts, opened a private academy, then converted it into Moors Indian Charity School in 1743. Determined to found a flourishing educational center for Indians, Wheelock obtained an enormous tract in the New Hampshire wilderness in 1769, established Dartmouth, and served as first president.

WHITE, Ellen Gould Harmon (1827–1915) Chief Prophetess of the Seventh Day Adventists, Maine-born Mrs. White was attracted as a girl to premillenarian William Miller's predictions of the end of the world, and helped create the body known as Seventh Day Adventists. Ellen White, subject to vivid dreams and visions as a child, interpreted these as fresh divine revelation. Adding selected Old Testament injunctions such as sabbath observance and tithing to Miller's adventism, Ellen White provided the major emphases to Miller's movement as early as 1844. In 1846, she married "Elder" James White, who embarked on a career publishing Adventist periodicals, "Present Truth" and "Review and Herald." The Whites moved the operation to Battle Creek, Michigan, in 1855, where in 1863 they officially organized the denomination known as Seventh Day Adventists. Ellen White, officiating as head of the movement, traveled widely. After a split in the ranks in 1901, when cereal-inventor Dr. J. H. Kellogg and his famous sanitorium pulled out, Ellen White shifted the home office of the sect to Tacoma Park, Washington.

WHITE, Wilbert Webster (1863–1944) Founder and first president of New York's Biblical Seminary, Ohio-born Presbyterian pastor and educator, White served at Biblical Seminary from 1900 to 1944. He wrote extensively on Biblical subjects and before founding Biblical Seminary taught Old Testament at Xenia Seminary and Moody Bible Institute.

WHITE, William (1748–1836) Philadelphia-born Protestant Episcopal bishop, White was an architect of the American Episcopal Church. He was ordained in London in 1772, but returned to Pennsylvania in 1776 to accept the post of rector of Philadelphia's Christ Church, where he served for the following sixty years.

White, an unswerving patriot, served as Chaplain for the Continental Congress and altered the wording of the Anglican service to fit the circumstances in the new Republic. During and after the American Revolution when relationships with Britain were extremely delicate and the Anglican Church in the colonies was disorganized and demoralized, White supervised the reorganization of the Protestant Episcopal Church in the U.S.A.

White drafted the first American Episcopal constitution, inserting the democratic idea of laymen participating in Church government. With William Smith, White prepared an American version of the *Book of Common Prayer*. In 1786, White was elected Bishop of Pennsylvania. White, in spite of some antagonism initially toward Bishop Seabury, who represented a different line of consecration, eventually accepted Seabury and the Connecticut representatives as colleagues, and worked amicably with them to bring about the General Convention of 1789, formally establishing the American Episcopal Church. White was elected Presiding Bishop in 1796.

WHITEFIELD, George (1714–1770) Spectacularly effective pulpiteer, Whitefield helped kindle the Great Awakening and the Wesleyan movement throughout the English-speaking world. Whitefield, son of an impoverished Gloucestershire innkeeper, entered Oxford in 1733, where he encountered John and Charles Wesley and their Bible-studying "Holy Club." Whitefield, however, escaped the introspective period of doubt over personal salvation which plagued the Wesleys until 1738. During a near-fatal illness in 1735, Whitefield experienced a spiritual crisis which left him with a serene sense of God's forgiving grace through accepting Christ by trust. Bursting with zeal to preach, Whitefield, although only twenty-two, was ordained in the Church of England in 1736 and embarked on his meteoric preaching career on both sides of the Atlantic.

In 1738, Whitefield made his first of seven exhausting but productive preaching tours in the American colonies. His dynamic preaching in New England in 1740 detonated the spiritual revival known as the "Great Awakening." Free from denominational bias (unusual for a time when sectarian loyalties ran deep), Whitefield cheerfully preached in all pulpits. His remarkable voice and compelling presence affected vast audiences and boosted membership in all Protestant groups.

Whitefield was the first in the Wesleyan movement to experiment with open-air services. After his success in reaching tough Bristol miners in outdoors preaching, Whitefield convinced the dubious John Wesley to take up field-preaching when regular pulpits were closed to the Methodists.

Whitefield held stiff Calvinistic views. He and Wesley, a strenuous Arminian, disputed over predestination, exchanging a series of polemical letters from 1740 to 1741, but managed to remain friends to the end. A group of Calvinistic Methodists, however, formed a rival group to Wesley's Methodists in 1743.

Whitefield served as chaplain to the Countess of Huntingdon, founder and superintendent of a string of Methodist chapels, but positive in her predestinarianism.

Never an organizer, Whitefield was preeminently an awakener. He died in 1770 during his seventh preaching tour in America.

WHITFIELD, Henry (1597[?]–1657[?]) A Puritan-sympathizing Church of England rector, Whitfield brought down the wrath of dispeptic Archbishop Laud by protecting several Puritan preachers and fled to New England about 1639. He helped found Guilford, Connecticut, but in 1650, went back to England, settling in Winchester.

WHITGIFT, John (1530–1604) Imperious, iron-handed Anglican Archbishop of Canterbury to whom Puritans were an anathema, Whitgift tried to impose a rigid conformity to his stringent State religion upon all Englishmen. Whitgift, an uncompromising advocate of episcopacy, hounded Presbyterian Cartwright from Cambridge in 1570, and in 1583 prepared articles forcing all clergymen to subscribe to royal supremacy, the Prayer Book and the Thirty-Nine Articles. Determined to quash all opposition, this martinet in 1586 had a decree passed imposing censorship of the press, making it illegal to print anything without the approval of Archbishop of Canterbury or the bishop of London. Whitgift, lampooned in the "Marprelate Tracts," became infuriated and got tougher powers granted to the Court of High Commission so that stiffer punishments could be meted out for offenses against the established church.

In 1595, Whitgift finally arranged to have a law passed declaring Puritanism a statutory offense. An unswerving Calvinist in his theology, Whitgift injected Calvinism into Anglicanism when he prepared the *Lambeth Articles* in 1595. Whitgift, who crowned James I of England, helped open the Hampton Court conference before his death.

WHITMAN, Marcus (1802–1847) Founder of the first Protestant church on the Pacific coast, this American Presbyterian medical missionary to the Indians in the American Northwest was martyred when he and his eleven associates were suddenly attacked by the Cayuse tribe. Whitman, his wife Narcissa (who with Mrs. Spalding were the first white women to cross the Rockies and reach Oregon overland) and the Rev. and Mrs. Henry H. Spalding and a small party opened a chain of mission stations in the Walla Walla Valley under the auspices of the American Board of Commissioners for Foreign Missions in 1837. During the fall and winter of 1842–43, Whitman made an astonishing 3,000 mile ride to the East, successfully petitioning the Board to rescind its action to close two of Whitman's stations ("Lupivai," near present-day Lewiston, Idaho, and "Wai-ilatpu," near Walla Walla, Washington).

WHYTE, Alexander (1836–1921) Pulpit orator at Edinburgh's prestigious Free St. George's Church from 1870 until 1909, Whyte served as principal of New College, Edinburgh, from 1909 until his death. He produced a shelf full of sermonic writings which were widely read at the turn of the century.

WIBERT of Ravenna ([?]–1100) A pliable Archbishop of Ravenna who allowed himself to be duped by Emperor Henry IV into being elevated as a counter-pope to oppose headstrong Hildebrand as pontiff, Wibert assumed the name "Clement III" from 1080 to 1100. Wibert actually resided in Rome from 1084 until 1093, until driven out by legitimate Pope Urban II. When disasters struck the German Emperor, Wibert's significance sank. After Pope Urban issued the ringing call for the First Crusade in 1095, Wibert's popularity completely evaporated.

WICLIF See **WYCLIFFE**.

WIGGLESWORTH, Michael (1631–1705) The English-born funereal New England Puritan clergyman who wrote gloomy verses about his grim God, Wigglesworth, minister at Malden, Massachusetts, nearly fifty years (1656–1705) is remembered for his best-selling, oft-quoted *The Day of Doom*. Published in 1662, *The Day of Doom* is a rambling ballad depicting the Last Judgment in horrifyingly lurid details.

WIGHTMAN, Edward ([?]–1612) With Bartholomew Legate, Wightman was one of the pair of Englishmen who were the last to be put to death in England for holding dissenting views in religion. Wightman, who was labelled an "Arian Baptist," espoused anti-Trinitarian ideas which had been carried to England by some radical Dutch Anabaptists and Continental Socinians.

WILBERFORCE, William (1759–1833) A well-to-do English Evangelical, Wilberforce led the abolitionist movement in Britain, agitating and pressuring as a Member of Parliament to secure the passage of bills to end the pernicious practice of slavery. Wilberforce, experiencing a conversion-rebirth at the age of twenty-five in 1784, became a ringleader in the Clapham Sect, a group of Evangelicals who met informally in London to caucus and discuss means of effecting social reforms. In spite of intense opposition and vilification, Wilberforce succeeded in 1807 in pushing through the bill which ended the slave trade in the British colonies. He continued, laboring to end slavery throughout the Empire, but died just before legislation was finally passed in Commons.

WILCOX, Thomas (1549[?]–1608) An outspoken Presbyterian Puritan who served as a pastor in London during the intense struggles between the advocates. of Episcopacy and Presbyterianism as the State religion, Wilcox and John Field published a pamphlet, *An Admonition to Parliament,* arguing that Presbyterianism was divinely ordained. Wilcox's and Field's immoderate appeal outraged the intemperate Archbishop Whitgift, who took drastic steps to try to suppress Puritanism.

WILDER, Robert Parmalee (1863–1938) Intense, aggressive founder of the Student Volunteer Movement, the missionary crusade which captivated campus leaders during the late 1800's and early 1900's, Wilder supervised several generations of great international conventions of college-age Christians.

Wilder, son of pioneer missionary Royal G. Wilder, was born in India, educated at Princeton, where he organized daily prayer groups and the Princeton Foreign Mission Society. At Princeton, Wilder coined the slogan, "The Evangelization of the World in This Generation," which fired the imagination and enthusiasm of hundreds of youths. The Student Volunteer Movement sprang into life in 1886 at a student conference at Mount Hermon under Dwight L. Moody, where Wilder fanned the evangelistic message into missionary commitment. Wilder carried the missionary challenge to colleges through the Student Volunteer Movement, the British Student Christian Movement and the Y.M.C.A.

WILFRID (634–709) A monastic churchman in the ancient British Church, Wilfrid, although born in Northumbria and educated at Lindisfarne, the great monastery of the Celtic Church, was won to Roman usages while on a pilgrimage to Rome. At the Synod of Whitby in 664, Wilfrid pushed King Oswy to repudiate the practices of the Celtic Church and to favor Roman customs, particularly the Roman method of fixing the date for Easter and the Roman tonsure. Wilfrid's efforts ended the hegemony of Columba's great Celtic Church in Britain and effectively subjected British Christianity to Rome for nine centuries.

Wilfrid, later Bishop of York, quarrelled with Theodore, Bishop of Canterbury, over the boundaries for their jurisdictions, but got the pope to rule in his favor. Wilfrid, who made several trips to Rome, was once blown by unfavorable winds to Friesland on the Dutch coast; undaunted, Wilfrid immediately set to work preaching to the natives, and earning the distinction of being the first British missionary to the Continent. Wilfrid was later honored by canonization.

WILFRITH See **WILFRID**.

WILKINSON, Jemima (1752–1819) Quirkish Quaker lady who convinced hundreds of her impossible claims, Jemima Wilkinson developed one of America's wackiest cults. Miss Wilkinson's rise to fame began after a serious illness when she dramatically announced that she had been raised from the dead, revivified by the spirit of Christ and empowered to produce miracles. She attracted a coterie of gullible followers, whom she settled in a community near Seneca Lake, New York, in 1788. Her outlandish creed, besides her resurrection, included Shaker-like celibacy and total submission to her whims. The Wilkinson sect, growing restless during Jemima's advancing years, dissolved after her death.

WILLARD, Frances Elizabeth Caroline (1839–1898) Gracious, gumptious lady extolled by Congress after her death as "first woman of the 19th century, the most beloved character of her times," Frances Willard assumed secretaryship of the Women's Christian Temperance Union in 1874 and boldly built the W.C.T.U. into the most influential women's organization in the United States in the late 1800's.

WILLIAM de Champeaux (1070[?]–1121) Eminent Medieval Schoolman and educator, William (or Guillaume) of Champeaux headed the noted school of St. Victor near Paris, making it a mecca for Europe's brightest students and teaching such distinguished churchmen as Abélard. William later served as bishop of Chalons.

WILLIAM of Occam See OCCAM.

WILLIAM of Orange, Prince of Nassau (1533–1584) Hero of Dutch independence, William courageously rallied the Dutch against rabidly anti-Protestant King Philip II of Spain, who tried to stamp out Protestantism in his Netherlands provinces. William, who had switched from Lutheran to Catholic to placate Philip's predecessor, Charles V, returned to Protestantism, and in 1568 led a revolt against Spain. Although defeated several times, William persisted tenaciously, and in 1576 persuaded the northern and southern provinces to join him and break away from Spain. In 1579, the seven northern provinces formed a league which later became the Dutch Republic. William, however, was murdered by the relentless Philip's agents in 1584. Nick-named "the Silent" because of his cautious, taciturn nature, William is respected as the father of the Dutch Republic and the saviour of Protestantism in the Netherlands.

WILLIAM ("the Pious") (886–918) The Count of Auvergne and Duke of Aquitaine, William I, nicknamed "the Pious," was perturbed about the laxity in Medieval monasticism. He founded the great monastery at Cluny as a reform measure, placing it directly under the pope.

WILLIAM of Saint Carilef ([?]–1096) A nimble-witted opportunist, this Norman-French Bishop of Durham, England, won his see by appointment by William the Conqueror after the Norman invasion, double-crossed William in a plot but agilely escaped charges, and prudently thereafter took the King's side against all troublesome churchmen. William of Saint Carilef began construction on stately Durham Cathedral.

WILLIAM of Tyre (1130[?]–1184[?] or 1190[?]) Archbishop of Tyre from 1175, William of Tyre wrote a twenty-three volume history of the Latin Kingdom of Jerusalem. In addition to telling the story of the Crusaders, William attended the Lateran Council in 1179.

WILLIAM of Wickham (or Wykeham) (1324–1404) *De facto* ruler of England during doddering Edward III's last days, William of Wickham, Bishop of Winchester and Lord Chancellor of England, encountered the enmity of the calculating John of Gaunt, triggering a long, bitter power struggle in England. William, impeached and punished, won a pardon when King Richard II took the throne, served again as Lord Chancellor. He founded New College, Oxford, in 1380 and established England's first public school, Winchester College.

William of Wickham also rebuilt ancient Winchester Cathedral, making it into a Gothic masterpiece.

WILLIAMS, Eleazar (1789[?]–1858) Unstable half-breed Indian Episcopal lay reader, Williams served for a time as missionary among the Oneidas in up-state New York and translated the Prayer Book into Iroquois before heading a party of Oneida chiefs which trekked to Wisconsin to found an Indian nation. Williams, beginning in 1839, undermined his mission efforts with some bizarre pretensions, including the claim that he was the "lost dauphin" who was the rightful successor to the French crown.

WILLIAMS, George (1821–1905) Founder of the Young Men's Christian Association, Williams was a twenty-three year old London drapery clerk who met with a cluster of fellow-clerks to study the Bible and pray in his tiny room overlooking St. Paul's Churchyard. Williams and his ten friends, determined to establish a group to spread Christianity, founded the Young Men's Christian Association on June 6, 1844. The Association caught on immediately, spanning the Atlantic in 1851, when Y.M.C.A.'s were opened in Montreal and Boston. Williams, earnest and industrious, rose to become a partner in the drapery firm, but devoted most of his wealth to the Y.M.C.A., mission work and Bible Societies. He was knighted by Queen Victoria in 1894, by which time the Y.M.C.A. had spread to 5,000 branches throughout the world.

WILLIAMS, John (1796–1839) Enterprising English Non-Conformist missionary, Williams, a onetime ironmonger, was sent by the London Missionary Society to the Society Islands in the South Pacific in 1816, where he performed outstanding service spreading the Gospel and improving the lots of the islanders. Williams, unusually progressive for his time, learned the local dialects, built a sixty-foot boat, voyaged to other island groups, including the Herveys, Samoa and the New Hebrides, to evangelize and plant churches. His career ended when he was murdered and eaten by cannibals while visiting Erromanga in the New Hebrides.

WILLIAMS, Roger (1604[?]–1684) Tolerance-preaching Baptist clergyman and colonial statesman, Roger Williams founded Rhode Island colony, the first democratic state of modern times. Williams, London-born and Cambridge-educated, was ordained a Puritan minister in 1629, but displeased his intolerant congregations with his sermons on religious liberty. Fleeing to Boston in 1631 to avoid arrest in England, Williams quickly found himself labelled as a troublemaker. He offended the Boston leaders by declining the position of teacher in the Boston Church because it was connected with the Church of England, and accused the Boston congregation of controlling civil affairs in the town.

After a sojourn at Salem, which ended when the civil authorities complained about his preaching, Williams moved to Plymouth, where he fraternized with the Indians and learned their language. Returning to Salem in 1633, Williams irritated the community leaders by denouncing them for not paying the Indians for lands they had appropriated. Williams, tried as a heretic, was sentenced to be deported to England. He escaped, however, and survived the rigorous winters by living with the Indians.

In 1636, Williams and a group of others banished from Massachusetts founded Providence, on land donated by the Narragansett Indians. Williams' colony became the first to grant freedom of worship, separation of Church and State and equality to all citizens. Williams journeyed to England in 1644, and secured a charter for his Rhode Island colony. Under Williams, Rhode Island became a haven for the persecuted and the prototype of a working democracy. Williams, a prolific writer, produced a stream of pamphlets which influenced the thinkers of the founders of the American Republic.

WILLIBALD (700[?]–786) An English churchman, Willibald made a pilgrimage to Rome and the Holy Land in 721, the first recorded trip by an English pilgrim, and wrote the first travel book in English. Willibald stayed ten years at Monte Cassino abbey, served in Germany under his cousin, Boniface, built a monastery, and became Bishop of Eichstatt.

WILLIBRORD (657[?]–739) One of the earliest British missionaries to the Continent, Willibrord tried to organize congregations and hold services in Frisia on the Dutch coast with the encouragement of Pippin of Heristal. The Northumbrian-born evangelist was consecrated a missionary bishop by Pope Sergius I in 695, and installed as the first Bishop of Utrecht. Willibrord's efforts, however, produced few permanent results.

WILSON, Robert Dick (1856–1930) Learned conservative American Old Testament professor and co-founder (with J. Graham Machen) in 1929 of Westminster Seminary, Presbyterian Wilson taught at Pittsburgh's Western (now Pittsburgh) Theological Seminary from 1880 to 1900, Princeton Seminary from 1900 to 1929, and wrote numerous treatises on philology and Semitic studies.

WIMPINA, Konrad ([?]–1531) The first rector of the University at Frankfurt-on-Oder, and a distinguished German Catholic theologian, Wimpina participated in the sizzling polemics resulting from Luther's nailing his ninety-five theses criticizing the sale of indulgences. Wimpina tried to reinforce the arguments of papal-pardon peddler Tetzel. Wimpina later was appointed as the Elector's theologian at the Diet of Augsburg, where he was one of three Roman Catholics designated to dispute the Lutherans.

WINCHESTER, Elhanan (1751–1797) A onetime Baptist minister from Philadelphia, Winchester took up an Arminian and Universalist position about 1780, teaching that all men would eventually receive the blessings of salvation when even the most reluctant would choose to surrender to God. Winchester, persuasive and loquacious, remained Trinitarian in theology but strengthened the cause of Universalism in America.

WINEBRENNER, John (1797–1860) Founder of the Church of God (Harrisburg, Pa.) Winebrenner was a deeply evangelical Pennsylvanian who began his ministry as a pastor in the German Reformed Church in America. Winebrenner accepted a congregation at Harrisburg, after his ordination in 1820, but upset the staid burghers of his denomination by his revivalist tactics and noisy protests against slavery and liquor. He was finally ordered out of the German Reformed Church in 1828, and two years later organized the denomination known today as the General Eldership of the Churches of God in North America. True to founder Winebrenner's tradition, the Harrisburg Church of God (not to be confused with the more than 200 other groups bearing the title "Church of God") stresses personal conversion and emphasis on the Bible.

WINER, Johann Georg Benedikt (1789–1858) A German Protestant theological professor at his alma mater of Leipzig University in his home town of Leipzig, Winer advanced the cause of Biblical studies by preparing *Grammar of the Idioms of the New Testament*, a grammar of the language of the Chaldees, and a thesaurus-like collection of background material for understanding the Scriptures.

WINFRID See **BONIFACE.**

WINIFRED ([?]–650[?]) Welsh heroine and saint, Winifred was allegedly beheaded by an infuriated rejected suitor, Prince Carodoc of Hawarden, but reportedly miraculously revivified by her uncle, St. Beuno. A spring gushed forth from the place where her head had landed, and became a well-known Roman Catholic shrine called St. Winifred's Well, Holywell, Flintshire. Winifred spent her last fifteen years as a nun, becoming abbess of the convent at Gwytherin, Wales, and exercising great influence.

WISHART, George (1513[?]–1546) Respected Scottish schoolmaster-turned Reformed preacher, Wishart stirred Scotland with his sermons until martyred by the brutal Beaton, Archbishop of St. Andrews. Wishart introduced the use of the Greek New Testament to his classes at Montrose, but was labelled a heretic and forced to flee in 1538. The same thing occurred the following year at Bristol, England, and Wishart took refuge on the Continent. After extensive travels and studies in Switzerland and Germany with the Reformers, Wishart returned to Britain to teach at Corpus Christi College, Cambridge. Wishart, remembering his fellow countrymen, crossed the border to Scotland in 1544 and quickly attracted a wide following by his persuasive preaching. He kindled an enthusiastic evangelistic fervor in John Knox, then a young cleric, eventually the founder of the Kirk of Scotland. Wishart inevitably aroused the ire of Beaton, Scotland's leading prelate. In 1545, Wishart was convicted of heresy; the following year, he was burned at the stake on orders by Beaton.

WITHERSPOON, John (1723–1794) Peppery, pious but practical Presbyterian pastor from Paisley, Scotland, who became president of the College of New Jersey (now Princeton University) in 1768, Witherspoon bolstered the cause of education, Presbyterianism and American independence during the touch-and-go days of the birth of the Republic. Edinburgh-trained Witherspoon brought 300 books to beef up the college library and a mastery of five languages to add scholarship to the faculty. With twenty years pastoral experience behind him, Witherspoon was a capable, fiscal-conscious administrator. He served in the Continental Congress from 1776 to 1782, rendering strong leadership in such key areas as foreign affairs, finance and supplies for Washington's army. Witherspoon, who as a young man had seen redcoats routed at Prestonpans during the Jacobite uprising, knew that English armies were not invincible; he repeatedly steeled the resolve of timid patriots through pulpit and pamphlets (only Thomas Paine excelled him with a pen). Witherspoon has the added distinction of being the only clergyman to have signed the Declaration of Independence. After the Revolutionary War, Witherspoon helped rebuild the shattered American Presbyterian Church and his college, remaining as president until his death in 1794. He continued to serve in

New Jersey governmental bodies until 1789. At the first Presbyterian General Assembly in the new United States, Witherspoon presided as Moderator.

WOLFF, Christian (1679–1754) German mathematician and philosopher at the University of Halle, Wolff developed a rationalistic philosophy based on reason and a world view of the universe as a huge machine driven by unchanging mechanical laws, ending the sway of Pietism at Halle. Wolff's ideas of natural religion, originally-implanted morality and God as Prime Force came to dominate German theological thought for over two generations. Removed from his teaching post at Halle in 1723 at the instigation of the Pietists, Wolff moved to the University of Marburg until permitted to return to Halle in 1740 by Frederick the Great.

WOLSEY, Thomas (1475–1530) The Machiavellian but humane cardinal who rose from the obscurity of his father's Ipswich butcher shop to become King Henry VIII's chief administrator and statesman, Wolsey provided England with sensitive, skilled diplomacy until he was abruptly discarded by the impatient Henry for being too slow in arranging Henry's divorce from Catharine of Aragon. The delicate, dexterous, determined Wolsey perfectly counterbalanced bluff, boisterous, bellicose Henry.

Ordained a priest in 1498, Wolsey through influential Oxford friends and his own driving ambition rapidly rose to prominence and power. In 1507, he was appointed Chaplain to King Henry VII; in 1509, Dean of Lincoln. When Henry VIII was crowned, Wolsey's fortunes soared. He received the title of Chaplain of Windsor and appointment to the Privy Council in 1511, became Bishop of Lincoln and Archbishop of York in 1514, and Cardinal in 1515.

Wolsey's deft diplomatic finesse pitted England against the prevailing strong nation as he worked, usually successfully and always skillfully, to preserve a balance of power in Europe. The humanist cleric earnestly tried to end the carnage of war on the Continent where rulers prized military glory above peace. Wolsey, personally vain and greedy, amassed a fortune, revelling in luxury—and gaining countless enemies. He was, however, unswervingly loyal to Henry. Although personally opposed to Henry's divorce, Wolsey, a flawless ecclesiastical lawyer, patiently undertook to arrange the divorce. He was suddenly ousted from office, stripped of titles and perquisites by the temperamental Henry and a group of nobles for not hurrying the divorce through papal courts. He died enroute to London to face treason charges.

WOODRUFF, Wilford (1807–1898) The Mormon leader who ended polygamy within the Salt Lake branch of Mormonism in 1891 (after practicing plural marriage himself for many years), Woodruff, a convert to Joseph Smith's doctrines in 1833, was one of the first to push into Utah in 1847. Woodruff became president of the twelve apostles in 1880, president of Mormon Church in 1889.

WOOLEY, Celia Parker (1848–1918) Founder in 1904 of the Frederick Douglass Center, Chicago, one of the earliest and most imaginatively-run settlement houses at the turn of the century, Mrs. Wooley, wife of a Chicago dentist, was one of the first women ministers in the U.S.A. She secured ordination by the Unitarians in 1893 and served pastorates for five years before taking up social work.

WOOLMAN, John (1720–1772) New Jersey Quaker preacher, sometime store clerk, teacher and tailor, Woolman sensitized his fellow Friends against the iniquity of slavery at a time when most accepted the practice as an established institution of society. Woolman inveighed against the evils of trafficking in human lives, refusing to obey orders by his employer to draw up wills transferring slaves, and induced many Quakers to free their slaves. He even petitioned the Rhode Island legislature to outlaw the slave trade.

Beginning in 1743, Woolman devoted most of his time as a traveling preacher, visiting Quakers throughout the colonies and England. He wrote several pamphlets and from 1756 until his death kept a fascinating diary which was later published as *The Journal of John Woolman's Life and Travels in the Service of the Gospel.* Woolman, always a partisan of the exploited and deprived, also preached to the Indians and pleaded with whites to reimburse tribesmen for their lands.

WOOLSTON, Thomas (1670–1733) A disputatious Deist who interpreted all Scripture as allegory, Woolston published a series of sometimes-ingenious attempts to explain the Bible in an allegorical way which aroused the Establishment of England. The first time he was brought to trial, he managed to get the case dropped in 1725. Outraging everyone with later books which intemperately attacked everything in the Bible, Woolston was arrested and convicted for blasphemy in 1729. He died in prison.

WORCESTER, Elwood (1862–1940) One of the first to recognize the tie between personal faith and emotional disorders, Worcester served as an Episcopal rector in Philadelphia and Boston at the Emmanuel Church from 1904 to 1929. Worcester's program, engaging the atten-

tion of many psychiatrists, came to be known as the Emmanuel Movement and pioneered in relating religion to the care of the emotionally disturbed.

WORCESTER, Noah (1758–1837) One of the earliest American pacifists and first leaders of the international peace movement, Worcester served as a Congregational pastor in New Hampshire before becoming editor of the influential Unitarian magazine, *Christian Disciple,* in Boston. In 1814, while still as pastor, Worcester published *A Solemn Review of the Custom of War,* which roused such a storm of indignation over Worcester's anti-war views that he was driven to resign.

WORCESTER, Samuel Austin (1798–1859) Heroic dedicated American Congregational missionary to the Cherokee Indians, Worcester shared the vicissitudes of the unfortunate Cherokees, printing the only newspaper in Indian language for many years and becoming the target for anti-Indian hate programs in the South. Worcester, imprisoned by Georgia from 1831 to 1833 during that State's repressive legal actions against the Cherokees after gold was discovered on Cherokee lands, became the center of a famous Supreme Court decision (Worcester v. Georgia) which declared his sentence illegal. Worcester after his release joined his Cherokees in 1835 in Oklahoma, where they had been forcibly relocated, and patiently took up his missionary endeavors. Using Sequoia's Indian alphabet, Worcester printed the first Cherokee literature, publishing numerous tracts, a hymn book and parts of Scripture.

WULFSTAN (or Wullstan) (1012[?]–1095) Consecrated bishop of Worcester in 1062 over his objections, the last English bishop to be selected by a

Saxon king, Wulfstan gave allegiance to William the Conqueror after the Norman invasion and helped compile the Domesday census. Wulfstan, venerated for his piety and faithful leadership in the Church, was canonized in 1203.

WTENBOGAERT, Johan (1557–1644) Dutch Reformed preacher, Wtenbogaert sided with his friend Jacobus Arminius, who brought about a furious controversy within Dutch Protestantism by doubting the extreme Calvinist doctrine of unconditional predestination. Wtenbogaert became spokesman for Arminianism after Arminius' death in 1609. For many years, Wtenbogaert held the influential post of Court Preacher in the Netherlands.

WYCLIFFE, John (or **Wyclif**) (1302[?]–1384) Often referred to as "The Morningstar of the Reformation," Wycliffe was the earliest to raise the issues which resulted in the Reformation and the first to begin a systematic translation of the entire Bible into English.

Wycliffe, Yorkshire-born and Oxford-trained (Balliol College), disapproved publicly of the wealth and worldliness of the Church hierarchy after accepting his first teaching position at Balliol in 1361. After seeing first-hand examples of papal interference in civil affairs while representing King Edward III at Bruges in 1374 in an attempt to solve a dispute between the Crown and the Pope over authority, Wycliffe stepped up the tempo of his criticisms of the Church. In 1376, he delivered a series of lectures at Oxford "On Civil Lordship." The lectures, presenting the notion that God gives man trusteeship, not ownership, of all power and wealth, caused Wycliffe to be called on the carpet by the outraged Bishop of London. Wycliffe, backed by the powerful Eng-

lish nobility, particularly John of Gaunt, plus the long-suffering commoners and mendicant orders within the Church, refused to retract. In 1377, protected by the English government, he resisted arrest orders and five bulls from Pope Gregory XI. The following year, he frustrated proceedings against him by the Archbishop of Canterbury.

These attacks against Wycliffe intensified the reformer's criticism of the clergy-dominated, pope-centered 14th century Church. Insisting that since the Church consists of all of God's elect, all the elect should read the Bible, Wycliffe worked from 1382 to 1384 preparing a translation of the Scriptures into English. Wycliffe did all of the New Testament and most of the Old Testament himself, and set the standard for English prose.

Although Wycliffe never rejected the papacy, he proclaimed that Christ alone is Head of the Church, the company of the elect, and that the pope may not necessarily be among the elect. Wycliffe, determined to bring the Gospel to the common people, began training and dispatching pairs of "poor preachers," barefooted laymen who lived in poverty and walked through the countryside to preach to the peasants. Wycliffe's "poor preachers," called Lollards, were immensely successful.

About 1381, Wycliffe denied the doctrine of transubstantiation by professing a view similar to consubstantiation and by refusing to acknowledge priestly powers in the Mass. Wycliffe found the opposition intensified. Later that year, the Peasant Revolt brought on a backlash of conservatism in England. Wycliffe was expelled from Oxford, and his Lollards were seized. Although Wycliffe managed to hold on to his parish at Lutterworth, dying of a paralytic stroke in 1384, his remains were exhumed in 1428 on orders from

Pope Martin V, burned and scattered on the waters of the River Swift. Wycliffe's Lollards were cruelly repressed. The spark for the Reformation was blown to Bohemia, where Wycliffe's writings such as *De Dominio Divino* and *De Civili Dominio* were eagerly read by John Huss.

WYNFRYTH See BONIFACE.

WYTTENBACH, Thomas (1472–1526) Half Humanist and part Reformer, who taught at Basel, where one of his pupils was Reformer Huldreich Zwingli. Wyttenbach, a onetime priest from Biel, was one of the earliest to advocate the sole authority of the Bible, the uselessness of indulgences and the sufficiency of Christ's sacrifice on the Cross for forgiveness of sins.

X

XAVIER See **FRANCIS XAVIER.**

XIMENES, Francisco de Cisneros (or
Jimenez) (1436–1517) Firm, reform-
minded prelate who headed the Church
in Spain during Ferdinand and Isabella's reign, Ximenes with royal encouragement effectively rid the Spanish
Church of unworthy and undisciplined
clergy and monks and unleashed a remarkable upsurge of piety and learning.
Ximenes, elevated in 1495 as Archbishop of Toledo at Isabella's insistence
in spite of his personal reluctance, imposed such stern rules on the easygoing
monasteries that over a thousand monks
decided to leave Spain rather than accept Ximenes' asceticism.

The icy Ximenes is also remembered
for unleashing reprisals against Moslems
in Spain in an attempt to force their
conversion. Although no profound
scholar, Ximenes fanned the sparks of
the Renaissance in Spain, producing an
interest in intellectual affairs. Ximenes
personally founded and funded the University of Alcala de Henares in 1498,
and fostered Bible study by publishing
a polyglot Bible from 1502 to 1517,
printing the Old Testament in Hebrew,
Greek and Latin and the New Testament in Greek and Latin (the first printing of the New Testament in Greek).

Y

YATES, William (1792–1845) Earnest English Baptist missionary and able linguist, Yates prepared materials in Sanskrit, Bengali, Arabic and Hindustani, translating all of the Bible into Bengali and much of it into Sanskrit.

YOUNG, Andrew (1869–1922) Dedicated Scottish missionary, Young went first as a layman to the Congo in 1890, then, following medical training at Glasgow, went in 1905 to China under the Baptist Mission Society.

YOUNG, Brigham (1801–1877) Determined, sometimes dictatorial leader of the mainstream of Mormonism after founder Joseph Smith's death in 1844, Young led the trek west in 1847 to Great Salt Lake and presided over Utah's affairs as head of a theocratic state until his death. Young, originally a Methodist, embraced Smith's doctrines in 1832, and rose rapidly in prominence in the Mormon group. In spite of bitter opposition by Sidney Rigdon and other disaffected parties, Young firmly assumed leadership of the Latter Day Saints after Smith died at the hands of a lynch mob. He capably organized the spread of Mormon settlements throughout Utah, repressing dissent and fending off interference by the Federal government. Young, accepting Joseph Smith's revelation permitting plural marriages, took twenty-seven wives.

YVES (also **Ives, Ivo**) (1253–1303) The patron saint of lawyers, Yves of Brittany was such a whiz at canon and civil law at Rennes, France, that his bishop insisted on ordaining him as a priest in 1284. This saintly and able defender of the indigent and deprived was canonized in 1347.

Z

ZACHARIAS, Pope ([?]–752) Pontiff from 741 to 752, Zacharias effectively influenced or controlled Europe's rulers, entering into a mutually advantageous alliance with Frankish King Pippin ("the Short"), and rebuked Eastern Emperor Constantine V for tolerating the destruction of icons. Pope Zacharias called two synods at Rome in 746 and 751.

ZBYNEK ([?]–1411) Archbishop of Prague during the career of early Reformer Jan Huss, Zbynek at first supported Huss, but rapidly became disenchanted as Huss excoriated the clergy and promulgated Wycliffe's ideas. Zbynek, with a papal commission to extirpate any signs of Wycliffitism, promptly excommunicated Huss in 1410, unintentionally making Huss more of a hero in Bohemia than before.

ZEISBERGER, David (1721–1808) Devout, dedicated Moravian missionary to the American Indians, Zeisberger founded a mission village in Ohio in 1772 when he established Schoenbrunn, a settlement of Indian converts along the Tuscarawas River. Zeisberger, born in Moravia and trained at Herrnhut on Zinzendorf's estate in Germany, emigrated to the American colonies in 1738, worked among the Creek Indians of Georgia, helped establish the Moravian-settled towns of Bethlehem and Nazareth, Pennsylvania, in 1740 and 1741 respectively, and began preaching to the Iroquois in 1743. Zeisberger's Indian settlements in Ohio, Schoenbrunn and Gnadenhutten, were regarded with suspicion by both sides during the American Revolution. In 1781, Zeisberger was imprisoned by the British; the following year the entire settlement at Gnadenhutten was barbarically massacred. Following his release, Zeisberger patiently began new mission work among the Indians at Goshen, Ohio, translating hymns and other writings into Indian dialects.

ZELL, Matthew (1477–1548) Early zealous Reformer, Zell preached a Zwinglian Evangelical Protestantism. Zell, serving in Strassburg from 1521 to 1523 as minister in the Cathedral, firmly planted the Reformation in that key city.

ZEPHYRINUS, Pope ([?]–217) An indecisive early Bishop of Rome who ruled from 198 to 217, Zephyrinus tried ineffectively to damp down the hot disputes over Christology between Hippolytus and the Monarchians which were hurting the Church.

ZIEGENBALG, Bartholomaus (1683–1719) Self-sacrificing German Pietist missionary to India, Ziegenbalg left the University of Halle in 1706 to respond to Danish King Frederick's appeal for a Christian witness in India. Ziegenbalg drove himself relentlessly, translating the New Testament into Tamil by 1711, founding a seminary and writing catechetical materials. Burned out by India's climate by 1719, Ziegenbalg died when only thirty-six.

ZINZENDORF, Nikolaus Ludwig von (1700–1760) Although by title and training a member of the German aristocracy, Count von Zinzendorf forsook a career in the Saxony Court to promote pietism through the Moravian Church. In 1722, Zinzendorf permitted a group of exiled Moravian Brethren to settle on his large family estate at Berthelsdorf, seventy miles from Dresden. The Moravian refugees, naming their community "Herrnhut" ("Lord's Watch"), soon came to absorb his interest.

By 1727, Zinzendorf relinquished his court responsibilities to serve as spiritual leader of the Herrnhut community. He tried at first to keep his Moravians tied to the State Lutheran Church, but encountered opposition among the independent-minded exiles and antipathy from Lutheran leaders toward the newcomers. Herrnhut elected its own elders and Zinzendorf drew up a mild monastic discipline (without vows or celibacy) for the community. Accused of fostering an independent sect on his estate, Zinzendorf tried to soften criticism by having himself ordained as a Lutheran pastor in 1734. Two years later, however, he was expelled from Saxony by the authorities for creating a separate Church.

Fired with missionary zeal, Zinzendorf and the Moravians coalesced into a distinct body and traveled tirelessly to proclaim a vital personal relationship to Jesus Christ. Zinzendorf, consecrated a bishop of the Moravian Church in 1737, toured the West Indies in 1738–1739, visited England in 1741, spent two years superintending Moravian efforts in the American colonies, from late 1741 to early 1743.

He returned to Germany in 1743. At the same time, some Moravians displayed certain excesses and peculiarities in behavior and beliefs, causing Moravianism to experience a "sifting period." From 1749 to 1755, Zinzendorf, lived in England, penniless from donating his resources to the Moravian cause. His last five years, in spite of grief over losing his wife and only son, were spent in pastoral oversight of Moravian congregations.

ZOSIMUS, Pope ([?]–418) Tactless, tricky and tyrannical, Zosimus so ineptly handled the North African clergy during the Pelagian controversy that Emperor Honorius finally had to step in. Zosimus had previously earned the enmity of the French clergy by agreeing to a deal with Patroclus, Bishop of Arles, to grant Patroclus exceptional powers in return for Patroclus' help in getting Zosimus elected pope.

ZUMARRAGA (1468–1548) The first Bishop of Mexico, Spanish-born Zumarraga emigrated to the New World in 1528 and energetically directed the development of the Roman Catholic Church in Mexico. Although he upheld the rights of the Indians against exploitive Spanish overlords, Zumarraga with misguided piety stupidly destroyed many priceless Aztec artifacts and writings. He was consecrated bishop in 1533 and appointed archbishop in 1548, but died before word reached Mexico.

ZWEMER, Samuel (1867–1952) Ebullient Michigan-born Dutch Reformed missionary to the Moslem world, Zwemer, responding as a college student to the Student Volunteer Movement appeal in 1886, resolved to carry the Gospel where it had not previously been presented. Zwemer and James Cantine, without backing of any mission board, began Christian work in the Arabian peninsula in 1889. Zwemer, who put in twenty-five years in Arabia, seventeen years in Cairo in the Seminary, and at his Nile Mission Press, and ten on the Princeton Seminary faculty, became a world authority in Islamic studies.

ZWILLING, Gabriel (1487[?]–1558) Fiery fellow monk in the Augustinian monastery with Martin Luther, Zwilling followed Luther out of the monastery but adopted a more radical stance. Zwilling by October, 1521 denounced the mass, attacked images and urged abandonment of monasticism. Although he collected a quick following among his colleagues from the monastery who acclaimed him as a second Luther, Zwilling played a secondary role during the rest of the German Reformation. Luther, incensed at the civil disorder instigated at Wittenberg by Zwilling's and Carlstadt's rabble-rousing, remained cool.

ZWINGLI, Ulrich or Huldreich (1484–1531) The guiding genius of the Reformation in the German-speaking cantons of Switzerland, Zwingli sparked the Reformation in Switzerland at the same time Luther ignited the Protestant movement in Germany.

Although there are many parallels between Zwingli and Luther (both born in 1484; both from common-people stock; both well-educated; both ordained to the Roman Catholic priesthood; both loved music and poetry; both eloquent preachers), the differences between the two giants in training and temperament were greater. Zwingli, unlike Luther, never experienced a violent spiritual crisis or prolonged crisis of the soul, but went through a gradual intellectual conversion.

Ordained in 1506, Zwingli became parish priest at Glarus, Switzerland, where he taught himself Greek and immersed himself in Scripture study. By the time Zwingli transferred to Einsiedeln ten years later, he was an advanced liberal Catholic. He preached boldly against the sale of indulgences and the veneration of the Virgin in 1516. Although some historians date this as the start of the Swiss Reformation, Zwingli at this point still had no idea of separating from the Roman Church.

Zwingli moved to Zurich in 1519 at the age of thirty-six, becoming a popular preacher and pastor. Unlike Luther who broke with Rome painfully, slowly, reluctantly and in gradual stages, Zwingli separated from Rome rapidly and easily. The rupture in Zurich came during Lent, 1522 when Zwingli preached that forbidding meat during Lent was unscriptural. Zwingli, in spite of pressures from the heirarchy and threats from the bishop of Constance, stood fast. In July of the same year, Zwingli and ten other priests publicly protested clerical celibacy and petitioned for permission to marry. When their request was denied, most of the ten, including Zwingli, married anyway.

With Zurich in a state of commotion over Zwingli's preaching and reports of Luther's activities in Germany, Zwingli prepared *Sixty-seven Articles or Conclusions* to be discussed publicly in Zurich. The Sixty-seven Articles, emphasizing Christ as sole Saviour and Mediator, stressing the supremacy of the Word of God, and rejecting the papal system, was the first public statement of the Reformed Faith.

After prolonged, intensive public debates during 1523–1524, Zwingli convinced the Zurich magistrates officially to adopt reformed practices in the canton. The Zurich Reformation was decided by the will of the people, unlike the German, which was decided by the will of princes. With public opinion supporting him, Zwingli abolished Roman worship, substituting his own liturgy, including a "memorial-type" Lord's Supper four times a year. Lamentably, Zwingli apparently condoned the destruction of priceless art treasures in various churches in the zeal of many followers to root out Romanism.

Zwingli's other great battle was with the Anabaptists, radical Protestants who opposed infant baptism and demanded a Church of super-pure separatists. After private conferences and public disputations between Zwingli and the Anabaptists failed to bring accord but exacerbated the antipathy, the Zurich government tried to repress the Anabaptists with sickening cruelty, drowning many of the leaders.

From 1524 to 1529, Zwingli engaged in a controversy with Martin Luther over the Eucharist, engaging in a heated correspondence and finally in 1529 meeting face to face at Marburg. The Colloquy of Marburg brought the Zwinglian and Lutheran viewpoints into closer contact at any time before or since. The two Reformers managed to agree on fourteen out of fifteen points, differing only on the mode of Christ's presence in the Lord's Supper. Zwingli showed greater courtesy than the sometimes-rude Luther, who refused Zwingli's hand of fellowship offered with tears. Zwingli's party, unable to patch up the differences with the Lutherans, drifted away from Lutheranism, eventually becoming part of the Calvinist Reformed Church.

Zwingli, an activist, believed as a Christian in plunging into public affairs. A militant patriot who three times had accompanied Swiss troops to Italy, Zwingli leaped into the fray when conflict broke out between Zurich and the five Catholic cantons of Switzerland in 1531. Zwingli, hoping to conquer the opposing cantons and incorporate them into a Protestant confederation, took part in the fighting, but was killed in the battle of Kappel.